"Anyone who's eager to contemplate man's capacity for excellence, even someone who knows zip about philosophy, will find in Mr. Comte-Sponville a charming, sophisticated and lucid guide to the way we ought to be." —Adam Begley, *New York Observer*

"An essential book, which gives virtue back its true meaning—something which the hypocrites and those self-appointed moral guardians who worry about our happiness have always kept from us." —*Elle*

"Innovative . . . Comte-Sponville's menu of bite-sized essays is varied, spicy, and has something for everyone."
  —Frederic Raphael, *Los Angeles Times*

"Remarkable . . . Comte-Sponville rehabilitates the notion of virtue."
  —*The Times Literary Supplement* (London) "Books of the Year"

"*A Small Treatise on the Great Virtues* is any anti-deconstructionist's cause to celebrate—a lucid, heartfelt, ethical treatise meant for the common man. . . . Sponville writes with passionate intensity and easy erudition. Feel this book, don't learn it. Experience it, don't memorize it."
  —Norah Vincent, *The Village Voice*

(continued next page)

A SMALL TREATISE

on the

GREAT VIRTUES

André Comte-Sponville

TRANSLATED BY CATHERINE TEMERSON

A SMALL TREATISE

on the

GREAT VIRTUES

The Uses of Philosophy in Everyday Life

A HOLT PAPERBACK

metropolitan books/henry holt and company new york

Holt Paperbacks
Henry Holt and Company, LLC
Publishers since 1866
175 Fifth Avenue
New York, New York 10010
www.henryholt.com

Originally published in France in 1996 by Presses Universitaires de France, Paris,
under the title *Petit Traité des Grandes Vertus*

LIBRARY OF CONGRESS CATALOGING-IN-PUBLICATION DATA
Comte-Sponville, André.
   [Petit traité des grandes vertus. English]
   A small treatise on the great virtues: the uses of philosophy in everyday life /
André Comte-Sponville; translated by Catherine Temerson.—1st American ed.
      p. cm.
   Includes bibliographical references and index.
   ISBN-13: 978-0-8050-4556-7
   ISBN-10: 0-8050-4556-2
   1. Virtues.   I. Title.
BJ1521 .C6613 2001
179'.9—dc21   2001030299

Originally published in hardcover in 2001 by Metropolitan Books

First Holt Paperbacks Edition 2002

Designed by Kathryn Parise
Printed in the United States of America

7   9   10   8

To Vivien, Fabien, and Louis

Contents

CONTENTS

A SMALL TREATISE

on the

GREAT VIRTUES

PROLOGUE

If virtue can be taught, as I believe it can be, it is not through books so much as by example. In that case what would be the point of a treatise on virtues? Perhaps this: to try to understand what we should do, what we should be, and how we should live, and thereby gauge, at least intellectually, the distance that separates us from these ideals. A modest enterprise, but a necessary one nonetheless. Philosophers are like schoolboys (it is only the wise who are masters), and schoolboys need their books: that's why they sometimes write them when the books they have in their hands no longer satisfy them, or crush them. Now, what book could we need more urgently than a treatise on ethics? And what aspect of ethics could be more deserving of our interest than the virtues? I don't believe any more than Spinoza did in the utility of denouncing vice, evil, and sin. Why always accuse, why always condemn? That's a sad ethics indeed, for sad people. As for the good, it exists only in the irreducible multiplicity of good deeds—too numerous for all the books in the world—and in the good inclinations—multiple, too, though less numerous—to which tradition has given the name

1

"virtues," which is to say, "excellences" (for that is the meaning of the Greek word *aretē*, translated by the Romans as *virtus*).

What is a virtue? It is a force that has or can have an effect. Hence the virtue of a plant or a medication, which is to cure, or of a knife, which is to cut, or of a human being, which is to will and to act in a human way. These examples, which come from the Greeks, say more or less what is essential: virtue is a capacity or power, and always a specific one. The virtue of hellebore is not that of hemlock; a knife's virtue is not that of the hoe; man's virtue is not that of the tiger or the snake. The virtue of a thing or being is what constitutes its value, in other words, its distinctive excellence: the good knife is the one that excels at cutting, the good medicine at curing, the good poison at killing . . .

Note that in this first and most general sense, virtues are independent of the uses to which they are put, of the ends to which they are directed or that they actually serve. The knife has no less virtue in the hands of a murderer than in the hands of a cook, nor does a healing plant have more virtue than a poisonous one. It's not that this first meaning is devoid of normative intent: no matter whose hand it is in, the best knife—for most purposes, in any case—will be the one that cuts the best. Its specific capacity also determines its excellence. But this normative value remains objective or morally immaterial. The knife need only accomplish its function; it need not judge that function. In that respect, of course, its virtue is not like ours. An excellent knife is no less excellent for being in the hands of a wicked man. Virtue is capacity, and as far as virtue is concerned, capacity is sufficient.

But where man is concerned and where morals are concerned, that answer is not enough. If every being or thing has its specific capacity in which it excels or can excel (the excellent knife, the excellent medicine), we might well ask what man's distinctive excellence resides in. For Aristotle, the answer is the rational life, which sets man apart from the animals.[1] But a rational life requires not only reason but many other things as well: desire, education, habit, memory, and so on. A man's desires are not the same as a horse's; nor does an educated person desire what a savage or an ignoramus does. All virtues are historical, as are all

the qualities that make up what we call our "humanity"; and in the virtuous man, humanity and virtue inevitably converge. It is a man's
virtue that makes him human, or rather it is this specific capacity he has
to affirm his own excellence, which is to say, his humanity, in the normative sense. Human, never too human. Virtue is a way of being,
Aristotle explained, but an acquired and lasting way of being: it is what
we are (and therefore what we can do), and what we are is what we have
become. And how could we have become what we are without other
human beings? Virtue thus represents an encounter between biological
evolution and cultural development; it is our way of being and acting
humanly, in other words (since humanity, in this sense, is a value), our
power to act *well*. "Nothing is so fine and so justifiable," wrote
Montaigne, "as to play the man well and duly."[2] To do so is virtue itself.

What the Greeks taught us in this regard, what Montaigne taught us
too, we may also read in Spinoza: "By virtue and power I understand
the same thing; that is, virtue, with respect to man, is his very essence or
nature insofar as he has the power of bringing about certain things,
which can be understood through the laws of his nature alone" (and
also, I would say, through the laws of history, but for Spinoza human
nature is part and parcel of human history).[3] In the general sense, virtue
is capacity; in the particular sense, it is human capacity, the power to be
human. It is what we also call the moral virtues, those qualities that
make one man seem more human—or, as Montaigne would put it,
more excellent—than another man, and without which, as Spinoza
says, we could legitimately be described as inhuman.[4] Such a definition
assumes that there lies within us a desire for humanity, a historical
desire, obviously (there is no such thing as natural virtue), without
which moral life would be impossible. To aspire to virtue means to try
not to be unworthy of what humanity has made us, individually and
collectively.

Virtue, it has been said ever since Aristotle, is an acquired disposition to do what is good. But that is saying too little: virtue is good itself,
both in spirit and in actuality. But there is no Absolute Good or good-
in-itself that can simply be known and then applied. Good is not

something to contemplate; it is something to be done. And so with virtue, too: it is the effort to act well and in that very effort itself virtue defines the good. This particular formulation poses a number of theoretical problems that I have discussed elsewhere.[5] The present book is entirely about practical morals, in other words, about morals. The virtues (I speak in the plural, for they cannot be reduced to a single one, nor would one of them alone suffice) are our moral values, but not in any abstract sense. They are values we embody, live, and enact—always singular, as each of us is, and always plural, as are the weaknesses in us that they combat or rectify. It is these virtues that I have chosen as the subject of the present book. I do not describe all of them or discuss any one of them exhaustively. My aim is simply to indicate, for those virtues that seem the most important, what they are, or ought to be, and what it is that makes them always necessary and always difficult.

How did I set about my task? I asked myself what the dispositions of heart, mind, or character are whose presence in an individual tends to increase my moral regard for him and whose absence tends to diminish it. The answers to that question resulted in a list of thirty or so virtues. Of these, I eliminated ones that seemed to be covered by some other virtue (kindness by generosity, for example, or honesty by justice) and those that it did not seem absolutely necessary to treat. Eighteen virtues remained—many more than I had initially envisioned—without my being able to reduce their number any further. My treatment of each of them, I realized, would thus have to be even more succinct than I had planned, and that constraint, part of my project from the very beginning, has never ceased to govern its outcome.

That this book begins with politeness, which precedes morality, and ends with love, which exceeds it, is of course deliberate. As for the other virtues treated here, their order, though not absolutely fortuitous, owes more to something like intuition, to the demands of pedagogy, ethics, or aesthetics, as the case may be, than to any deductive or hierarchical scheme. A treatise on virtues, especially a small one like this, is not a system of morals; it is applied morals, not theoretical morals, and (to the extent possible) living morals rather than speculative morals. But with regard to morals, what could be more important than how they are lived and applied?

I have relied heavily on the writings of others, whom I cite. No one need read the notes; indeed it is best not to concern oneself at all with them at first. They are meant not to be read but to be used; they are there not for the reader but for the student—whatever his or her age or profession. As for the book's content, I have tried to avoid the pretense that I was inventing what in fact the tradition offered me, and which I have merely taken up anew. Not that I have put nothing of my own into this work—quite the contrary. But we can make our own only what we have received or transformed or become, thanks to others or in opposition to them. It would be ridiculous for a treatise on virtues to strive for originality or novelty. Besides, it is braver and more honorable to confront the masters on their own ground than to avoid any comparison with them by somehow insisting on being original. For the last 2,500 years, if not more, the greatest minds have thought about the virtues; my desire was to continue their efforts, in my own way and with the means available to me, using their ideas to formulate my own.

Some will regard this enterprise as presumptuous or naive. The latter reproach I take as a compliment; as for the first, I'm afraid it is nonsense. To venture to write about the virtues is to subject one's self-esteem to constant bruising, to be made acutely aware, again and again, of one's own mediocrity. Every virtue is a summit between two vices, a crest between two chasms: hence courage stands between cowardice and temerity, dignity between servility and selfishness, gentleness between anger and apathy, and so on.[6] But who can dwell on the high summits all the time? To think about the virtues is to take measure of the distance separating us from them. To think about their excellence is to think about our own inadequacies or wretchedness. It's a first step—possibly all we can ask of a book. The rest we must live, and how can a book do that for us? I do not mean to say that thinking about the virtues is useless or of no moral consequence. Thinking about the virtues will not make us virtuous, or, in any case, is not enough in itself to make us so. But there is one virtue it does develop, and that virtue is humility—intellectual humility in the face of the richness of the material and the tradition, and a properly moral humility as well, before the obvious fact that we are almost always deficient in nearly all the virtues and yet cannot resign ourselves to their absence or exonerate ourselves for their weakness, which is our own.

This treatise on the virtues will be useful only to those lacking in them. Its potential readership thus being so large, the author may perhaps be excused for having—not in spite of his unworthiness but because of it—dared undertake this venture. Moreover, the pleasure I took in it, which was intense, seemed ample justification to me. As for any pleasure readers should happen to find in these pages, that would be a bonus: no longer a question of work for me but a matter of grace. To them, therefore, my gratitude.

POLITENESS

Politeness is the first virtue, and the origin perhaps of all the others. It is also the poorest, the most superficial, and the most debatable of the virtues, and possibly something other than a virtue as well. In any case, as virtues go it's a small one, an easy virtue, one might say, as used to be said in reference to certain women. Politeness doesn't care about morality, and vice versa. If a Nazi is polite, does that change anything about Nazism or the horrors of Nazism? No. It changes nothing, and this *nothing* is the very hallmark of politeness. A virtue of pure form, of etiquette and ceremony! A show of virtue, its appearance and nothing more.

Politeness is certainly a value, but it is an ambiguous one, insufficient in itself. It can clothe both the best and the worst, which makes it suspect. Such attention to form must be hiding something, but what? Politeness is artifice and we tend to be wary of artifice; it is an adornment and we tend to be wary of adornments. Diderot speaks somewhere of the "insulting politeness" of those on high; one might also mention the obsequious or servile politeness of those below. Unadorned contempt and crass obedience seem preferable.

But that's not the worst of it. A polite bastard is no less vile than any other bastard and in fact may be more vile. Is it because he is also a hypocrite? Probably not: politeness makes no moral claims for itself. A polite bastard, moreover, could just as easily be cynical without being any less polite or any less wicked for it. So what is it about him that shocks us? It's the contrast, undoubtedly, but not the contrast between an appearance of virtue and virtue's absence (which would be hypocrisy): our hypothetical bastard really *is* polite—besides, there's no difference between seeming to be polite and actually being so. The contrast is rather between the appearance of one virtue (in the case of politeness, appearance is reality: what you see is all there is) and the absence of all others; or, better yet, between the appearance of virtue and the presence of vice—in this case meanness, arguably the only true vice. Yet, taken in isolation, the contrast is more aesthetic than moral, which would explain why we respond to polite villainy with surprise rather than horror, astonishment rather than disapproval. There is, of course, an ethical dimension to the contrast: politeness makes the wicked person even more hateful because it implies a good upbringing, in the absence of which the wickedness might have been somehow excusable. The polite bastard is no wild animal, quite the opposite, and wild animals we generally do not resent; he is anything but unsocialized, and those who are we tend to find excuses for. He is the very antithesis of the crude, coarse, ignorant brute, who may frighten us, to be sure, but whose native and shortsighted violence can at least be explained by his lack of education. The polite bastard is not an animal, or a savage, or a brute. On the contrary, he is civilized, educated, well bred; there is no excuse for him, you could say. With the boor, who can tell whether he's ill-intentioned or simply ill-mannered? Genteel torturers, however, never leave us in doubt. Just as blood is more visible on white gloves, so horror is more apparent when it is also civilized. Nazis, at least some of them, are said to have excelled in this role. And, indeed, part of the ignominy we associate with the Nazis has to do precisely with this mixture of barbarism and civilization, of violence and courtesy; with this cruelty that was sometimes polite, sometimes bestial, but always cruel, and more blameworthy perhaps for its politeness, more inhuman for its human forms, more barbaric for its gestures of civility.

I have digressed, perhaps, but not so much by accident as out of vigilance: the important thing about politeness is, first of all, not to be taken in by it. Politeness is not virtue and cannot take the place of virtue.

In that case, why call it the first of the virtues, the origin of all the others? The contradiction is not as great as it may appear to be. The origin of the virtues cannot be a virtue (for if it were, it would itself require an origin, but then it could not be the origin it requires); it may be of the very essence of the virtues that the first one is not virtuous.

But why is politeness the *first*? The priority I have in mind is not cardinal but temporal: politeness comes before the other virtues in the sense that it serves as a foundation for the moral development of the individual. A newborn baby doesn't have and can't have moral standards. Nor does an infant or, for quite some time, a small child. What the small child does discover, however, and discovers quite early on, is prohibition. "Don't do that: it's nasty; it's bad; it's not nice; it's naughty . . ." Or else, "It's dangerous." Very soon he comes to learn the difference between what's simply bad (a misdeed) and what is also bad *for* him (a danger), between the hateful and the harmful. A misdeed is a strictly human evil, an evil that does no harm (at least not to the person who commits it), an evil without immediate or intrinsic danger. But then why is it prohibited, why must it not be done? Because. Because that's the way it is; because it's nasty, it's not nice, it's naughty, and so forth. For children, fact precedes right; or rather, right and wrong are simply facts themselves, like any others. Some things are allowed, some are forbidden; some things are done, some are not done. Good or bad? The rule suffices; it precedes judgment and is the basis for it. But then does the rule have no foundation other than convention, no justification other than usage and the respect for usage? Yes, it is a de facto rule, a rule of pure form, a rule of politeness! Don't say bad words; don't interrupt people; don't shove; don't steal; don't lie. To the child, all these prohibitions appear identical ("It's not nice"). The distinction between the ethical and the aesthetic will come only later, and gradually. Politeness thus precedes morality, or rather, morality at first is nothing more than politeness: a compliance with usage and its established rules, with the normative play of appearances—a compliance with the world and the ways of the world.

Now, a principle of Kantian ethics is that one cannot deduce what one should do from what is done. Yet the child in his early years is obliged to do just that, and it is only in this way that he becomes human. Kant himself concedes as much. "Man can only become man by education," he writes. "He is merely what education makes him," and the process begins with discipline, which "changes animal nature into human nature."[1] What better way to say it? Custom precedes value; obedience, respect; and imitation, duty. Hence politeness ("one doesn't do that") precedes morality ("one *shouldn't* do that"); morality only comes into being little by little, as an internalized politeness that has freed itself from considerations of appearance and interest and focuses entirely on intentions (which politeness doesn't concern itself with). But how could this morality ever come into being if politeness were not there to begin with? Good manners precede and prepare the way for good deeds. Morality is like a politeness of the soul, an etiquette of the inner life, a code of duties, a ceremonial of the essential. Conversely, politeness can be likened to a morality of the body, an ethics of comportment, a code for life in society, a ceremonial of the inessential. "Paper money," Kant says, but it's better than nothing and it would be as crazy to do away with it as to mistake it for real gold.[2] "Small change," he also says, merely the appearance of virtue, yet that which renders it "comely."[3] And what child would ever become virtuous without this appearance and comeliness?

So morality starts at the bottom—with politeness. But it has to start somewhere. There are no natural virtues; hence we must *become* virtuous. How? "For the things we have to learn before we can do them,"

Aristotle explains, "we learn by doing them."[4] Yet how can we do them if we haven't learned them? There are two ways out of this circular causality: apriority is one way, politeness is the other. But apriority is beyond our reach; politeness is not. "We become just," Aristotle continues, "by doing just acts, temperate by doing temperate acts, brave by doing brave acts."[5] But can we act justly without being just? Temperately without being temperate? Bravely without being brave? And if we cannot, then how do we become just, temperate, brave? Through habit, Aristotle seems to say, but that answer is obviously inadequate: a habit presupposes the prior existence of what we would be making a habit of and therefore cannot account for it. Kant provides a more helpful answer. For him, these first semblances of virtue can be explained in terms of discipline, in other words, as a product of external constraint: what the child cannot do on his own because he has no instinct for it "others have to do . . . for him," and in this way "one generation educates the next."[6] No doubt. And in the family, what is this discipline if not, first of all, a respect for usages and good manners? A discipline that is more normative than restrictive, it wants not order so much as a certain amiable sociability—not police discipline but polite discipline. It is by mimicking the ways of virtue, that is, through politeness, that we stand a chance of becoming virtuous. "Politeness," La Bruyère notes, "does not always produce kindness of heart, justice, complacency, or gratitude; but it gives to man at least the appearance of it, and makes him seem externally what he really should be."[7] Which is why it is insufficient in an adult and necessary in a child. Politeness is only a beginning but at least it is that. To say "please" or "excuse me" is to pretend to be respectful; to say "thank you" is to pretend to be grateful. And it is with this show of respect and this show of gratitude that both respect and gratitude begin. Just as nature imitates art, morality imitates politeness, which imitates morality. "It is in vain to point out to children the meritorious side of actions," Kant says, and obviously he is right.[8] But who for that reason would forgo teaching them to be polite? And what would we know about duty without having learned those lessons ourselves? If we can become moral (and for morality even to be possible—and immorality, too, for that matter—it must be the case that we can), it is not through virtue but through education, not for goodness' sake but for form's sake, not for moral reasons but for reasons of politeness. Morality is first artifice, then artifact. By imitating virtue we become virtuous. "For when men play these roles," writes Kant, "virtues are gradually established, whose appearance had up until now only been affected. These virtues ultimately will become part of the actor's disposition."[9] Politeness precedes morality and makes it possible. If politeness is the "disposition to represent ourselves as better than we are," as Kant maintains, it is one that tends to make us moral.[10] We must first acquire "the appearance and manner of good," not because they are sufficient in themselves but because they can help us attain the thing that they imitate—virtue—and that is acquired only by such imitation.[11] "Even the appearance of the good in others must have value for us," Kant also writes, "because in the long run something serious can come from such a play with pretenses which gain respect even if they do not deserve to."[12] Without this play of pretenses, this make-believe, the transmission of morals and the development of a moral sense within each of us would not be possible. "States of character arise out of like activities," says Aristotle.[13] Politeness is that pretense, or semblance, of virtue from which the virtues arise.

Politeness thus rescues morality from circular causality (without politeness, we would have to *be* virtuous in order to *become* virtuous) by creating the conditions necessary for its emergence and even, to some extent, its flourishing. The differences between someone who is perfectly polite and someone who is simply respectful, kindly, and modest are infinitesimal; we end up resembling what we imitate, and politeness imperceptibly leads—or can lead—to morality. Every parent knows this; it's called bringing up one's children. I am well aware that politeness isn't everything, nor even the essential thing. Yet the fact remains that, in everyday language, being *well brought up* means first of all being polite, which is highly revealing. Were it a matter of courtesy alone, who among us, apart from obsessives or utter snobs, would correct our children a thousand times (A thousand times? What am I saying? Much more than that ...) so that they might learn to say "please," "thank you," and "excuse me." But that's how children learn respect, through this training. The word *training* rubs us the wrong way, I know; but who could do without the thing? Love is not enough when it comes to bringing up children; it's not even enough to make them lovable and loving. Politeness isn't enough either, and that is why both politeness and love are needed. Family upbringing is located, it seems to me, between these two poles, between the smallest virtue, which is not yet morality, and the greatest, which is already something more. Of course, education means more than moral education: children need to acquire language, too. But if politeness is the art of signs, as Alain claims, then learning to speak falls within that domain as well.[14] The issue is still usage and respect for usage, usage being proper only to the extent that it continues to be respected. *Le bon usage* (in English, "proper usage") is the title of Maurice Grevisse's beautiful French grammar, and it could also be the title of a manual of social skills. To do as is done, to say as is said. It is revealing that in both cases we speak of correctness, which is nothing more than minimal and, as it were, obligatory politeness. Virtue and style come only later.

Politeness, then, is not a virtue but a simulacrum that imitates virtue (in adults) and paves the way for it (in children). Politeness in the child may not be different in nature from politeness in the adult, but it is different in its significance. In the child, it is essential; in the adult it is inessential. What could be worse than an ill-mannered child, except perhaps a wicked adult? We aren't children anymore. We know how to love, how to will, and how to judge. And so we are capable of virtue, and of love, for which politeness is no substitute. Better a generous oaf than a polite egoist, an honorable lout than a refined scoundrel. Politeness, Alain says, is merely a calisthenics of self-expression; in other words, it is of the body, while the important things are of the heart and of the soul.[15] There are even some people whose politeness disturbs us in its perfection. Indeed, consummate politeness smacks of insincerity, for honesty sometimes demands that we displease, shock, or offend those around us. We all know people like this, people who, for all their honesty, will remain prisoners of good manners all their lives, not revealing themselves to others except from behind a glazed screen of politeness, as though having once and for all confused truth and decorum. If taken too seriously, politeness is the opposite of authenticity. People preoccupied with decorum can be like grown-up children, too well-behaved, too rule-conscious, the dupes of custom and propriety. What they seem to have missed out on is that process by which we become men and women, namely adolescence—beautiful, marvelous, uncivil adolescence that relegates politeness to its proper insignificance, that has no use for usages and loves only love, truth, and virtue! Today's adolescent will be tomorrow's adult, more indulgent, wiser perhaps, and better behaved. Yet if one absolutely has to choose one kind of immaturity over another, better an overgrown adolescent—from a moral standpoint—than a child who is too obedient to grow up. It is better to be too honest to be polite than to be too polite to be honest!

There is more to life than good manners; and politeness is not morality. Yet it is not nothing. Politeness is a small thing that paves the way for great things. It is ritual without God; ceremonial without religion; protocol without monarchy. An empty form whose sole value lies in that very emptiness. A self-satisfied politeness, one that takes itself too seriously and believes in itself, is one that, taken in by its own manners, falls short of the very rules it prescribes. Self-satisfaction, always impolite, is particularly amiss in something as insufficient as politeness.

Politeness is not a virtue but a quality, and a purely formal one at that. Taken on its own, it is secondary, negligible, nearly insignificant; next to virtue or intelligence it is nothing, and that is what politeness, with its exquisite reticence, must know how to express as well. It is quite clear, however, that intelligent, virtuous persons are not exempt from its obligations. Even love cannot dispense with form entirely, and that it cannot is something children must learn from their parents, their parents who love them—even if too much, even if badly—and who nonetheless are forever correcting them with regard to form. Philosophers will argue over whether form isn't really everything, whether the distinction between morality and politeness isn't merely an illusion. It could be that usage and respect for usage is all there is—that politeness *is* everything. Yet I believe nothing of the sort. Love holds its own, and so does gentleness and so does compassion. Politeness is not everything; indeed it is almost nothing. *Almost*, but not quite: for man, too, is *almost* an animal.

2

FIDELITY

The past is no more; the future is still to come. Oblivion and improvisation are facts of nature. Is there anything more improvised, time after time, than spring? Is there anything more quickly forgotten? Its very repetition, striking as it is, is only an illusion: the seasons seem to repeat only because we forget them. This same forgetfulness makes nature appear always new to us, whereas in fact it rarely innovates. True invention, or true creation, presupposes memory. Bergson understood as much and therefore had to invent duration, which is for the world what memory is for man; memory of this sort, however, could only be God, which is why there is no such thing. If the universe has a history—and it does—then that history consists of a series of chaotic or chance improvisations, without a plan (not even the plan to improvise) and without memory. The opposite of a fashioned work, the universe appears as such only by chance. An improbable, never-ending jam session. For whatever endures or repeats inevitably changes; and nothing begins that does not come to an end. Inconstancy is the rule, oblivion the order of things. Reality, from moment to moment, is always new; and this complete, this perennial newness, is the world.

Nature forgets, and it is in forgetting that its materiality resides. Matter is forgetfulness itself; only where there is mind is there memory. Oblivion, therefore, will have the last word, just as it had and always will have the first word. A child's kingdom, the material world, a realm of inconstancy, forgetfulness, innocence! To become is to become unfaithful; the seasons themselves are fickle in their flight.

Yet in the face of oblivion there is mind and there is memory, volatile and short-lived though the latter may be. This fragility is the essence of mind, which, no less mortal than we are, is yet alive within us, as mind, in remembering its mortality. The mind is memory and may be only that. To think is to remember our thoughts; to will is to remember what we want. Not that we can think only the same thoughts or want only what we have wanted before. But without memory, what would an invention be? What would a decision be? Just as the body is the present of the present, the mind, to use Augustine's phrase, is the present of the past, in both senses of the word *present:* that which the past bequeaths to us and that which remains within us. It is also memory.[1] With memory, the mind begins. The concerned mind, the faithful mind.

Concern, the memory of the future, reminds us of itself often enough. Such is its nature, or rather such is ours. Who, other than the wise or the mad, would forget they have a future? And who, other than the wicked, would think only of their own? Of course human beings are selfish, but not as thoroughly selfish as we might sometimes think: look how people without children worry about future generations. Or how people who smoke with abandon fret over holes in the ozone layer. Giving no thought to themselves, they lose sleep over others. Who would hold this against them? The fact of the matter is that we scarcely ever forget the future (we are more likely to forget the present), and our ignorance of it makes it all the more difficult for us to put it out of our minds.

The future worries us, it haunts us; its strength lies in its nonexistence. The past has less power over us; it would seem we have nothing more to fear—or hope—from it. And there is some truth to this view. Epicurus sees it as a form of wisdom: in the tempest of time we find the deep haven of memory. But forgetting offers even safer haven. If neurotics suffer from remembering, as Freud says, then forgetfulness must in some way nurture psychological well-being. "God save man from forgetting to forget," Aragon writes. Nietzsche, too, understands on which side life and happiness lie: "It is possible to live almost without memory, indeed to live happily, as the animals show us, but without forgetting it is utterly impossible to *live* at all."[2] A point well taken. But is life the goal? Is happiness the goal? At least this kind of life and this kind of happiness? Should we envy animals, plants, and stones? And suppose we do, should we then give ourselves over to this envy? What would be left of the mind? What would be left of humanity? Should we strive only for health and hygiene? François George, writing on Nietzsche, uses the term *healthy thinking;* its strength and its limitations are one and the same.[3] Even if the mind is a disease, even if humanity is a misfortune, this illness and this misfortune are ours—for they are us, and we exist only through them. Let's not make a clean sweep of the past. All the dignity of man resides in thinking; all the dignity of thinking resides in memory. Forgetful thought is perhaps still thought, but it is unmindful thought. Forgetful desire is certainly desire, but it is desire devoid of volition, it has neither heart nor soul. Science, which tends not to look back as it moves forward, offers a rough idea of what I mean by forgetful thought, and the animal world can help us understand what I mean by forgetful desire. Not all science, of course, and certainly not all animals (some are said to be faithful). No matter. Man is mind only through memory and he is human only through fidelity. Beware, O Man, of forgetting to remember!

The mind, by definition, is the faithful mind.

If I approach fidelity from so distant a perspective, it is because the problem is so vast. Fidelity is not one value or one virtue among others; it is the how and wherefore of all values and virtues. What would justice be if the just were not also faithful? What would peace be without the fidelity of the peaceable? What would freedom be if free minds were not also true? And what would truth itself be worth without the fidelity of the truthful? It would still be true, but it would have no value and thus could not give rise to virtue. There may be no health without forgetfulness, but there is no virtue without fidelity. Health or virtue? Health *and* virtue. For virtue does not ask that we forget nothing or be faithful indiscriminately. We must be more than healthy, but we don't have to be saints. "We need not be sublime," Vladimir Jankélévitch points out, "only faithful and serious."[4] Fidelity is the virtue of memory; it is memory itself as a virtue.

But what kind of memory? And of what? Under what conditions? And within what limits? Again, it is not a question of being faithful indiscriminately; this would no longer be fidelity but simply traditionalism, dogged small-mindedness, stubbornness, routine, fanaticism . . . Every virtue can be set against two excesses, an Aristotelian would remind us: fickleness is one, obstinacy is another, and fidelity rejects both equally. The golden mean? If you wish, but not as the halfhearted or frivolous might understand the term (we're not talking about being a little bit fickle and a little bit stubborn). It's more like hitting the bull's-eye on a target than it is like staking out a middle-of-the-road political compromise. A summit, as I have said, between two chasms. Fidelity is neither fickle nor stubborn, and it is in being neither fickle nor stubborn that it is what it is.

Is fidelity intrinsically valuable? Valuable for itself? By itself? No, or not solely. What gives it value is, above all, its object. One doesn't change one's friends the way one changes one's shirt, to loosely paraphrase Aristotle, and, similarly, it would be as ridiculous to be loyal to one's garments as it would be reprehensible not to be to one's friends— except, as the philosopher says elsewhere, when there is "excess of wickedness" on their part.[5] Fidelity does not excuse everything; being loyal to the worst is worse than repudiating it. The SS swore allegiance to Hitler, and their fidelity in crime was criminal. Fidelity to evil is evil fidelity. And "fidelity to one's foolishness," as Jankélévitch observes, "is an added foolishness."[6] And here, out of fidelity—the stubborn loyalty, perhaps, of the pupil to his master—I cite Jankélévitch at greater length:

> Is fidelity praiseworthy or not? "It all depends," in other words: everything hinges on the values to which one is being faithful. Faithful *to what?* . . . No one calls resentment a virtue, though it's a kind of faithfulness—to hatreds or angers. To have a good memory for the affronts one has suffered is bad fidelity. No one calls pettiness a virtue either, though it, too, is a kind of fidelity—to little things—a tenacious memory for the trivial. . . . Hence the virtue we seek is not fidelity of any kind whatsoever, but only good fidelity, noble fidelity.[7]

So be it: loving fidelity, virtuous fidelity, intentional fidelity.[8] It is not enough to remember. One can forget without being disloyal and be disloyal without forgetting. As a matter of fact, infidelity *presupposes* memory; you can only betray something you remember (an amnesiac can neither keep his word nor fail to keep it), which is why fidelity and infidelity are two opposing forms of remembrance, one virtuous, the other not. Jankélévitch speaks of fidelity as "the virtue of Sameness," but in a world where everything changes, and such is our world, sameness exists solely through memory and will.[9] No one bathes twice in the same river or loves the same woman twice. Pascal: "He no longer loves the person whom he loved ten years ago. I quite believe it. She is no longer the same, nor is he. He was young and she also; she is quite different. He would perhaps love her yet, if she were what she was then."[10] Fidelity is the virtue of sameness, thanks to which sameness exists or persists.

Why would I keep yesterday's promise since I am no longer the same today? Why indeed? Out of fidelity. According to Montaigne, in fidelity lies the true basis of personal identity: "The foundation of my being and identity is purely moral; it consists in the fidelity to the faith I swore to myself. I am not really the same as yesterday; I am the same only because I *admit* to being the same, because I take the responsibility of a certain past as *my own*, and because I intend to recognize my present commitment as still my own in the future."[11] There is no moral subject without fidelity of oneself to oneself, which is why fidelity is an obligation: without it there could be no such thing as duty. It is also what makes infidelity possible: just as fidelity is memory as virtue, so infidelity is memory as vice (rather than a mere lapse of memory). Recollection is not everything: having a good memory is not always good, accurate recollections are not always loving or respectful. Memory the virtue entails more than just memory; fidelity entails more than accuracy. Indeed, fidelity is the opposite not of forgetfulness but of frivolous and self-serving fickleness, of disavowal, treachery, and inconstancy. It is true that fidelity struggles against forgetfulness, against the forgetfulness that infidelity ultimately entails: first you betray what you remember, then you forget what you betrayed. Infidelity thus self-destructs as it triumphs, while fidelity can triumph only—and always only provisionally—by refusing to be annihilated, that is, by repeatedly and endlessly struggling against forgetfulness and denial. *Desperate* fidelity, writes Jankélévitch, and I certainly would not take issue with his view of an "unequal struggle between the irresistible tide of oblivion that eventually engulfs all things, and the desperate but intermittent protests of memory."[12] In advising us to forget, Jankélévitch continues, "the exponents of pardon are recommending something that needs no recommendation; the forgetful need no reminders to forget, there is nothing they want more. The past, on the other hand, is in need of our compassion and gratitude; for the past cannot stand up for itself as can the present and the future."[13] Such is the duty of memory: compassion and gratitude for the past. The difficult, demanding, imprescriptible duty of fidelity!

This duty obviously admits of degree. In the text I just cited,

Jankélévitch is thinking of the Nazi concentration camps and the martyrdom of the Jewish people. Absolute martyrdom calls for absolute duty. We need not be faithful in the same way and to the same extent to our first loves or to the champion cyclists who filled our childhood with excitement. Our fidelity ought to be directed only toward worthy objects and in proportion to their worth (I realize I am using the word *proportion* in connection with magnitudes that are by nature nonquantifiable). First of all, then, we owe fidelity to suffering, to selfless courage, to love. But that said, I wonder: is suffering a value? Taken in itself, certainly not, or if so, then strictly a negative value: suffering is an evil and we would be mistaken to see it as redemptive. Yet though suffering may not be a value, every suffering life is one, through the love it demands or deserves. To love the sufferer (Christian charity, Buddhist compassion, or Spinozist *commiseratio*) is more important than to love beauty or greatness, and a value is simply that which is worthy of love. Hence all fidelity—whether to a value or to a person—is fidelity to love and through love. Fidelity is faithful love—here common usage makes no mistake, or rather errs only in limiting love to the couple. Not that all loves are faithful (which is why fidelity cannot be reduced to love); but all fidelity is loving, always, and for that reason good and lovable (fidelity in hatred is not fidelity but rancor or relentlessness). Fidelity, then, in all its different degrees, is also an object worthy of itself!

As for its specific spheres, they are too many to enumerate. I will discuss only three, and all too briefly: thought, morality, and the couple.

That there is such a thing as fidelity of thought is clear enough. Thought cannot be illogical or haphazard; if it were, it would no longer be thought. Dialectics, so useful to the sophist, can be called thought only because it is faithful to the laws and strictures it imposes on itself, faithful even to the contradictions it accepts and overcomes. "The dialectic should not be confused with a fluttering of ideas," says Sartre. Faithfulness is what distinguishes one from the other, as can be seen in Hegel's great *Science of Logic*, which is absolutely faithful in its entirety to the task it sets for itself and to its improbable rigor. More generally, it can be said that thought manages to avoid being vacuousness or idle prattle only thanks to the effort it makes—and this effort is constitutive of thought—to resist forgetfulness, changing fashions and interests, the charms of the moment, the seductions of power. All thought, notes Marcel Conche, "is in constant danger of being lost if we make no effort to preserve it. There can be no thought without memory, without a struggle against forgetfulness and the danger of forgetfulness."[14] This is another way of saying that there can be no thought without faithfulness: in order to think, we must not only *be able* to remember (memory by itself would allow only for consciousness, which is not the equivalent of thought) but also *want* to remember. Faithfulness is this will to remember; or rather, it is the act that carries out this will, and thus a virtue.

Does fidelity also presuppose the will to continue to think what one remembers having once thought? And hence the will not just to remember but also not to change? Yes and no. Yes, since there would be no point in trying to remember a thought if it had value only as a remembrance, as a mental or conceptual trinket. Being faithful to our ideas means not just remembering that we once had them, but also wanting to keep them alive (remembering not just that we had them once but that we *have them still*). But at the same time, no, for wanting to hold to the same ideas at all costs would mean refusing to put them to the test of discussion, experience, or reflection. Being faithful to one's thoughts more than to truth would mean being unfaithful to thought and condemning oneself to sophistry, albeit with the best intentions. We must be faithful to truth first! This is where faithfulness distinguishes itself from faith and a fortiori from fanaticism. Being faithful, in the sphere of thinking, does not mean refusing to change one's ideas (dogmatism), or subordinating them to something other than themselves (faith), or taking them for absolutes (fanaticism); it means refusing to change one's ideas in the absence of strong, valid reasons, and—because one cannot always be examining—it means holding as true, until subsequent reexamination, ideas whose truth has been clearly and solidly established. In other words, neither dogmatism nor inconstancy. One has the right to change one's ideas, but only when it is one's duty to do so. We must be faithful to the truth first, then to its recollection (to truth *upheld*); that is what faithful thought—which is to say, thought itself—is about.

When I say that science has no use for fidelity, let me be clear: I am not speaking of scientists themselves or of the practice of science but of the results that science produces, which must stand on their own merits and not on their filiations. Science lives in the present and is always forgetting its first steps. Philosophy, to the contrary, is always trying to retrace its first steps and has been from the very beginning. What physicist rereads Newton? What philosopher does not reread Aristotle? Science progresses and forgets; philosophy ponders and recalls. Indeed, what is philosophy, if not an extreme faithfulness to thought?

But let us turn to morality. Fidelity is essential to it. Kant would have disagreed, however; fidelity is a duty, he would have said (between friends or spouses, for example), but duty cannot be reduced to fidelity. Moral law, being timeless, is always present before us; the issue is not faithfulness but obedience. Besides, faithfulness to what? If to prescribed duty, then faithfulness is superfluous (since duty carries its own prescriptive force); if to something else, it is secondary (since the only thing that matters absolutely is duty). As for the fidelity that duty demands (for example, being true to one's word, or to one's spouse), Kant regards it as a specific case of duty that can itself be reduced to duty. Fidelity is subordinate to moral law, not the other way around.

Or it is, at any rate, if moral law in the Kantian sense—universal, absolute, timeless, and unconditional—exists; if practical reason—requiring unqualified obedience, regardless of time and place—thus also exists. But what do we know of such reason? Have we ever experienced it? And who could believe in it today? If there were such a thing as universal and absolute moral law, and hence an objective foundation for morality, then Kant would be right. But I am unaware of one. Indeed, this is the fate that our time imposes on us: we must be moral though we no longer believe in the (absolute) truth of morality. In the name of what should we be virtuous, then? In the name of fidelity, out of loyalty to faithfulness! Bergson objects to the naïveté of Kant's claim to have founded morality on the cult of reason, in other words, on a respect for the principle of noncontradiction.[15] Jean Cavaillès, great logician that he was, says the same thing. Certainly morality should be reasonable, since it should be universal (or in any case, universalizable), but reason never suffices on its own: "Before any moderately strong tendency, the principle of noncontradiction is powerless, and the most dazzlingly obvious facts pale. Geometry never saved anyone."[16] There is no virtue *more geometrico*. Is barbarism any less coherent than civilization? Avarice any less logical than generosity? And suppose they were, would this constitute an argument against barbarism or avarice? I am certainly not recommending that we relinquish reason; the human spirit would not survive the loss. We should simply not confuse reason, which is fidelity to truth, with morality, which is fidelity to law and to love. The two can go together, of course, and it is their conjunction that I call spirit or mind. But reason and morality are nonetheless distinct from and irreducible to one another. Morality, in other words, is not true but valid (in the root sense of the word); it is an object not of knowledge but of will (or to the extent that it is an object of knowledge, our knowledge of it is incapable of demonstrating its value). It is not timeless but historical. Not before us but behind us. If morality has no ultimate basis, if it can have none, then fidelity must stand in its stead. In the absence of a timeless and universal moral law to which we might subject our actions, fidelity allows us to adhere instead to the historicity of a value, to an always particular presence within us of the past, whether it be the collective past of humanity (culture and civilization, the things that separate us from barbarism) or a more individual past, our own or that of our parents (the Freudian superego, or our personal upbringing—whatever it is that makes one's own moral code different from that of others). Fidelity to the law is keeping faith with a law that is not divine but human, not universal but particular (even if it is universalizable and should be), not timeless but historical; it is fidelity to history, to civilization, and to Enlightenment values; it is fidelity to the humanity of man! The point is not to betray what humanity has made of itself and, in the process, of us.

Morality begins with politeness; it continues on—changing in nature—with fidelity. We begin by doing what is done; then we take it on ourselves to do what *ought* to be done. We respect good manners first, then good deeds. Good conduct, then goodness itself. And so we learn to be faithful to love received, to the admired example, to a show of trust, to a certain standard, to the patience of our mothers and the impatience of our fathers, to the law, and so forth. The love of the mother and the law of the father. There is nothing new in all this, and of course I'm simplifying greatly. We've all gone through the process. Duty, prohibition, remorse, the satisfaction of having done the right thing, the will to do it, respect for others—all of these, as Spinoza says, "depend chiefly on education," which is certainly no reason for thinking we can do without them![17] True, what's taught is only morality, and morality isn't everything or even the essential thing (love and truth matter more). But who, other than a sage or a saint, could manage without it? And how could morality dispense with fidelity? Fidelity is at the source of all morality; it is the opposite of the "transvaluation of all values," which would also have to do away with fidelity, and cannot, and must be judged accordingly. "We wish to be the *heirs* to all previous morality," Nietzsche writes, "*we do not intend* to start anew. Our whole protest is solely one of morality in rebellion against its previous form."[18] A heritage and rebellion and still fidelity. And why bother to rebel? And against whom? Against Socrates? Epictetus? The Christ of the Gospels? Montaigne? Spinoza? Who could, and who would want to? Isn't it obvious that all of them are essentially faithful to the same values, which can be forsaken only at the expense of humanity itself? "I am not come to destroy but to fulfill . . ." The words of a man of faith—and they are even more beautiful in the absence of faith. Fidelity not to God but to man, and to the human spirit (not to the biological fact of humanity but to humanity as a cultural value). All the barbarities of this century were unleashed in the name of the future, from Hitler's thousand-year Reich to Stalinism's promise of brighter and better tomorrows. No one will ever dissuade me from thinking that it was only a fidelity to the past, to a certain kind of past, that made moral resistance to them possible. The barbarian is indeed the infidel, in this sense: barbarity is infidelity. Even brighter and better futures are morally desirable only when pursued in the name of values that are very old; Marx knew this and Marxists are beginning to understand it as well. There is no future morality. All morality, like all culture, derives from the past. There can be no morality other than a faithful one.

For the couple, fidelity is another story. That some couples are faithful and others are not is a factual truth, which doesn't help us understand much about fidelity, especially if what we take marital or conjugal fidelity to mean is the exclusive, in fact mutually exclusive, use of the other person's body. After all, why would one love only one person? Why would one desire only one person? Being faithful to one's ideas doesn't mean having just one idea (fortunately!); being faithful in friendship doesn't mean having just one friend. Fidelity in these spheres doesn't entail exclusiveness. Why should it be different where love is concerned? In the name of what might one claim exclusive rights to another person? It may be that exclusivity brings convenience and security to a conjugal relationship, that it makes life easier and even happier. In fact, I'm willing to believe that it does, on the condition that the relationship continues to be a loving one. But exclusiveness does not necessarily involve morality or love. Each of us must choose for ourselves, according to our strengths and weaknesses, how we want to live with another. Or rather, each couple must choose for itself: truth is a higher value than exclusiveness, and it seems to me that love is betrayed less by love (the *other* love) than by lying. Others might think differently, and so might I at another moment in my life. But that's not the essential thing, it seems to me. There are couples in "free" relationships who are faithful in their own way (to their love, to their word, to their common freedom). And other couples who are strictly, unhappily faithful, though each partner would rather not be faithful. The problem in both cases is not fidelity so much as jealousy, not love so much as suffering, and that is not my topic. Fidelity and compassion are not one and the same. Both are virtues, to be sure. But that's just it: they are two different virtues. Not causing suffering is one thing; not betraying is another, and the latter is what's called fidelity.

If we want to grasp the essence of marital or conjugal fidelity, we need to understand what makes a couple a couple. Mere sexual commerce, even if repeated, is obviously not sufficient. Nor is mere cohabitation, even if lasting. A couple, as I understand the term, presupposes both love and duration, and therefore fidelity, since love can last only if passion—usually too short-lived to make a couple but just long-lasting enough to unmake one—is made to last, too, by dint of memory and will. That's what marriage means, and what divorce interrupts. Though not necessarily. A friend of mine, a remarried divorcée, told me that in a certain sense she was still faithful to her first husband. "I mean to our life together, to our history, our love. I don't want to disown all that," she explained. No couple, clearly, could ever last without this kind of faithfulness of each of the partners to their shared history, without that mixture of trust and gratitude that renders happy couples—there are a few—so moving as they grow older, more moving than new lovers, whose love is still something of a dream. To me, this kind of fidelity seems more precious than the other kind, and more essential to the couple. That love will subside or decline is always the likelier course of events, and it is useless to grieve over it. But whether a couple separates or continues to live together, they will remain a couple only through this fidelity to love received and given, to love shared, to the deliberate and grateful memory of that love. Fidelity is faithful love, I have said, and that attribute defines the couple, too, even the "modern" and "liberated" one. Fidelity means preserving love for the sake of what once took place, love for love in this case, love in the present, willing and willingly maintained, for love in the past. Fidelity is faithful love, and faithful first to love.

How can I swear to you to love you forever and to love no one else? Who can take an oath to his feelings? And once love dies, what's the point of maintaining the fiction and the responsibilities and demands it gives rise to? But there's also no reason for disowning or denying what once was. Must we betray the past in order to love the present? I swear to you, not that I will love you forever, but that I will remain forever faithful to the love we know now.

Unfaithful love is not the same as *free* love; unfaithful love is forgetful love, turncoat love, a love that forgets or detests what it has loved and therefore forgets or hates itself. But is this kind of love still love?

Love me for as long as you want to, my love, but *do not forget us.*

3

PRUDENCE

Politeness is the origin of the virtues; fidelity, their principle; prudence, their precondition. Is prudence itself a virtue? According to tradition it is, and so we must begin by explaining that tradition.

Prudence is one of the four cardinal virtues of antiquity and the Middle Ages.[1] It is the one perhaps most often overlooked. For modern-day thinkers, prudence falls more within the domain of psychology and calculation than within that of morality and duty. Even Kant doesn't regard it as a virtue; it is nothing more than enlightened or shrewd self-love, he explains, certainly not reprehensible but without absolute moral or prescriptive value.[2] Prudence dictates one should look after one's health, but can anyone honestly say it is meritorious to do so? Prudence is too advantageous to be moral, just as duty is too absolute to be called prudent. Yet Kant's position on this issue is not necessarily the most modern or the most sound. It was Kant, after all, who drew the conclusion that veracity is an absolute duty under all conditions and whatever the consequences, even if, to cite the example Kant himself uses, murderers who are chasing your friend ask you whether he hasn't taken refuge in your house. It is better, Kant says, to be imprudent than to be derelict in one's duty, even if an innocent person's life, or one's own life, is at stake.[3]

To my mind, this kind of reasoning is just the sort that has become unacceptable to us, since we no longer believe sufficiently in this absolute to be willing to sacrifice our lives, our friends, or our fellowmen to it. Indeed, I suspect we would find such an ethic of conviction (*Gesinnungsethik*), as Max Weber calls it, rather frightening. What is the value of having absolute principles, if it is to the detriment of simple humanity, good sense, gentleness, and compassion? We have learned to be wary even of morality, and the more absolute it claims to be, the more suspicious we are of it. Preferable, for us, to an ethic of conviction is what Max Weber calls an ethic of responsibility (*Verantwortungsethik*), which, without disregarding principles (how could it?), concerns itself as well with foreseeable consequences of action.[4] Good intentions can lead to catastrophe, and purity of motivation has never been able by itself to prevent the worst. Good motives aren't enough, and it would be wrong to act as though they were: hence an ethic of responsibility requires that we answer not just for our intentions or principles but also for the consequences of our acts, to the extent that they can be foreseen. It is an ethic of prudence, and the only valid ethic. Better to lie to the Gestapo than to turn in a Jew or a Resistance fighter. But in the name of what? In the name of prudence, which is the apt determination (for man and by man) of what *better* means. This is applied morality, but then what should one make of a morality that cannot be applied? Without prudence, the other virtues are merely good intentions that pave the way to hell.

I began by speaking of prudence as one of the ancient virtues. The fact is that the word *prudence* is so burdened with history that it is inevitably subject to misunderstanding; moreover, it has all but disappeared from the contemporary moral vocabulary. This does not mean, however, that we are no longer in need of it.

Let us look at the matter more closely. We know that the Romans translated the Greek *phronēsis* as *prudentia*, particularly in their translations of Aristotle and the Stoics. What does the term describe? An *intellectual* virtue, Aristotle explains, inasmuch as it is bound up with truth, knowledge, and reason; prudence is the disposition that makes it possible to deliberate correctly on what is good or bad for man (not in itself but in the world as it is, and not in general but in specific situations) and through such deliberation to act appropriately.[5] It could be called good sense, but in the service of goodwill. Or intelligence, but of the virtuous kind. It is in this respect that prudence is the precondition for all the other virtues; without it, we cannot know what use to make of the other virtues or how to attain the goal (the good) they put before us. Aquinas demonstrates that of the four cardinal virtues prudence is the one that must govern the others.[6] Without prudence, he says, temperance, courage, and justice could tell us neither what should be done nor how to do it; they would be blind or indeterminate virtues (the just person would love justice without knowing how to achieve it in practice, the courageous person would not know what to do with his courage, and so forth), just as prudence alone, without the other virtues, would be either utterly empty or else merely shrewd. Prudence has something modest or instrumental to it: it is enlisted to serve ends that are not its own and is concerned, for its own part, with the choice of means.[7] But this is what makes it irreplaceable: no action, no virtue—no virtue *in action*, at any rate—can do without it.[8] Prudence does not reign over the other virtues (justice and love each have more merit); it governs them. And indeed, what would a kingdom be without a government? Merely loving justice does not make us just, nor does loving peace make us peaceable by itself: deliberation, decision, and action are also required. Prudence determines which of them are apt, as courage provides for their being carried out.

The Stoics considered prudence a science ("the science of what to do and what not to do," they said).[9] Aristotle legitimately rejected their opinion since science has to do with certainties whereas prudence deals strictly with contingencies.[10] Prudence presupposes uncertainty, risk, chance, and the unknown. A god would have no need of it, but how could a man do without it? Prudence is not a science; rather, it replaces science where science is lacking. One deliberates only when one has a choice to make, in other words, when no proof is possible or adequate—that's when one must want not just good ends but also good means, in order to achieve them. To be a good father, it is not enough to love one's children, nor is it enough to wish them well for that wish to come true. Love does not excuse a lack of intelligence. The Greeks knew this, perhaps better than we. *Phronēsis* is like practical wisdom: wisdom of action, for action, in action. Yet it doesn't take the place of wisdom (real wisdom, *sophia*), for it is also not enough to act well in order to live well, or to be virtuous in order to be happy. In this Aristotle was right, and almost all the other ancients were wrong: virtue is not the only prerequisite for happiness any more than happiness is the only prerequisite for virtue.[11] Prudence, however, is a prerequisite for both, and even wisdom cannot do without it. For wisdom without prudence would be unsound wisdom, and therefore wouldn't be wisdom at all.

Epicurus may have made the essential point: prudence, because it chooses (by "measuring . . . and by looking at the conveniences and inconveniences") which desires should be satisfied and by what means, "is a more precious thing even than philosophy"; from it "spring all the other virtues."[12] What good is the truth if we don't know how to live? What good is justice, and why would we want it, if we're incapable of acting justly? Prudence, one might say, is a true *savoir-vivre* (unlike politeness, which is merely an apparent one) central to the art of enjoyment. We "oft times pass over many pleasures," Epicurus explains, "when a greater annoyance ensues from them," or seek out pains that allow us to avoid worse ones or that bring us a greater or more durable pleasure.[13] Hence it is always for pleasure that we go to the dentist or to work, but for a pleasure that is most often deferred or indirect (to avoid or eliminate pain). This pleasure prudence foresees or calculates. A temporal virtue, always, and sometimes temporizing. For prudence takes the future into account, recognizing all the while that how we confront it depends on us (in which regard prudence relates not to expectation but to will). A virtue of the present, like all virtues, but essentially forward-looking or anticipatory. The prudent man is attentive not just to what is happening but also to what can happen; he is both attentive and careful. *Prudentia*, Cicero notes, comes from *providere*, which means *to foresee* as well as *to provide*.[14] A virtue of duration, of the uncertain future, of the propitious moment (the *kairos* of the Greeks), a virtue of patience and anticipation. One cannot live in the moment. One cannot always take the shortest route to pleasure. Reality imposes its laws, its obstacles, its detours. Prudence is the art of taking them into account; it is lucid and reasonable desire. Romantics, who prefer their dreams, will sniff at it. Men of action, on the other hand, know that there is no other path, even when the goal is improbable or exceptional. Prudence is what differentiates action from impulse and heroes from hotheads. Basically it's what Freud calls the reality principle, or at least it's the virtue that corresponds to it. It's about enjoying as much and suffering as little as possible, while still taking into account the constraints and uncertainties of reality; in other words, to come back to Aristotle's intellectual virtue, it is about enjoying and suffering *intelligently*. Hence prudence is for human beings what instinct is for animals—and, as Cicero says, what providence is for the gods.[15]

The ancient concept of *prudence* (*phronēsis, prudentia*) goes far beyond the mere avoidance of danger, which is more or less what it has come to mean for us. The two are nevertheless linked, and, in the eyes of Aristotle or Epicurus, the former includes the latter. Prudence determines what to choose and what to avoid, and danger comes under this last category, giving us our modern meaning of prudence as precaution. Nevertheless, there are some risks we must know how to take and dangers we must know how to confront—whence prudence in the ancient sense of the word, as the "virtue of risk and decisions."[16] The modern concept, far from superseding the ancient, depends on it. Prudence is not the same as fear or cowardice—as the modern meaning would suggest. It assumes courage: without courage prudence amounts to pusillanimity, just as without prudence courage amounts to recklessness or folly.

It is worth noting that even in its narrow and modern sense, prudence is still a precondition to virtue. Only the living are, or are able to be, virtuous (the dead, at best, only can have been so); only the prudent are alive and can remain alive. Absolute imprudence would necessarily be fatal in very short order. And what of virtue then? What would be left of it? How could it continue to come into being? I noted, with regard to politeness, that a child at first cannot differentiate between what is simply bad (a misdeed) and what is also bad *for* him (pain and danger). He also cannot distinguish between morality and prudence, since both are subject for the most part, and for a long time, to parental dictates. But we have grown up (thanks to our parents' prudence, and, later, our own), and so now that distinction, which is constitutive of both morality and prudence, is for us to respect. But just as it would be wrong to mistake one for the other, it would also be an error to be perpetually setting one against the other. As Kant observes, prudence advises and morality commands.[17] We therefore need the one and the other, and both together. Prudence is a virtue only when it is in the service of honorable ends (otherwise it amounts to shrewdness) and, by the same token, ends are entirely virtuous only when served by adequate means (otherwise they would amount to worthy sentiments). This is why "it is not possible," as Aristotle puts it, "to be good in the strict sense without practical wisdom, nor practically wise without moral virtue."[18] Prudence doesn't satisfy the requirements of virtue (since prudence confines itself to deliberating over the means, while virtue insists on considering the ends as well), but no virtue can dispense with it. The reckless driver is not just dangerous; he's also morally reprehensible for taking so little account of other people's lives. Conversely, safe sex, which boils down to prudent sexuality, clearly represents a moral attitude (because in practicing safe sex one shows concern not just for one's own health but for the health of the other person, should one happen already to be a carrier of disease). Free and unrestricted sex between consenting adults is not wrong, but carelessness is. In these times of HIV and AIDS, behaviors that in themselves wouldn't be at all reprehensible can become so, not because of the pleasures they provide, which are innocent, but because of the risks they entail or might expose a partner to. Sexuality without prudence is sexuality without virtue, or in any case, it is sexuality whose virtue is deficient. It's the same with every other area of human conduct. The imprudent father may well love his children and want their happiness. Something is lacking in his fatherly virtue, however, and probably also in his love. Should something tragically wrong happen that he might have averted, he will realize that though he might not be entirely responsible, he isn't entirely innocent. First of all, do no harm; first of all, protect. Such is the essence of prudence, and without it the virtues themselves would be powerless or even harmful.

I have already stated that prudence doesn't preclude risk taking, nor does it always mean avoiding danger. Take the mountain climber or the sailor: for them, prudence is part of the job. What risks to take? What dangers to face? How far can I push my limits and toward what goal? The pleasure principle determines these choices, and this we call desire or love. But how? By what means? With what precautions? These things the reality principle decides, and when the decision is made *for the best*, we call it prudence.

"Prudence," says Augustine, "is love that chooses with sagacity."[19] But what does it choose? Not the object of love, of course—desire takes care of that—but the means for attaining or safeguarding it. The sagacity of mothers, of lovers. To protect or win the love of those they love, they do what they have to do or (since intellectual virtues always entail the risk of error) at least what they think they must do, and out of their concern humanity—theirs and ours—originates. Love guides them; prudence enlightens them. May it also enlighten humanity itself! If prudence, as I have said, takes the future into account, it is because it would be dangerous and immoral to forget that future. Prudence is that paradoxical *memory of the future*, or better yet (since memory as such is not a virtue), that paradoxical and necessary *fidelity to the future*. Parents wanting to safeguard the future of their children know this— not because they wish to determine that future for them but because they wish to give them the right and, if possible, the means to determine it for themselves. Humanity needs to understand this as well if it wants to safeguard the rights and promise of a future humanity.[20] More power means more responsibilities. Ours have never been so heavy, implicating as they do not just our own and our children's existence but also (because of advances in technology and their awesome consequences) the existence of humanity as a whole for centuries to come. Ecology, for example, is a matter of prudence and is in this respect a moral concern. We deceive ourselves if we think that prudence is a thing of the past; it is the most modern of our virtues, or rather the virtue that modern times has made the most necessary.

Prudence is applied morality, in both senses of the word *applied:* it is the opposite of abstract or theoretical morality, but also the opposite of casual morality. The fact that this last notion is a contradiction in terms shows just how necessary prudence is for protecting morality both from fanaticism (always imprudent in its enthusiasm) and from itself. How many horrors have been committed in the name of the Good? How many crimes in the name of virtue? Almost always violations of tolerance, they have most often been sins against prudence as well. We must be wary of our Savonarolas, who are blinded by the Good. They are too attached to their principles to consider individuals, too sure of their intentions to bother with the consequences.

Morality without prudence is either futile or dangerous. "*Caute,*" says Spinoza: "Take care."[21] That is the maxim of prudence. We must watch out for morality as well, when it disregards its limits or uncertainties. Good will is no guarantee, nor is good faith a valid excuse. In short, morality is not sufficient for virtue; virtue also requires intelligence and lucidity. It is something that humor reminds us of and that prudence prescribes.

It is imprudent to heed morality alone, and it is immoral to be imprudent.

4

TEMPERANCE

Temperance is not a matter of refusing to enjoy ourselves or of enjoying ourselves as little as possible. That would not be virtue but sadness, not moderation but impotence, not temperance but asceticism. Spinoza summarily counters such a grim perspective in what is probably his most Epicurean scholium, which can never be quoted often enough:

Nothing forbids our pleasure except a savage and sad superstition. For why is it more proper to relieve our hunger and thirst than to rid ourselves of melancholy?

My account of the matter, the view I have arrived at, is this: no deity, nor anyone else, unless he is envious, takes pleasure in my lack of power and my misfortune; nor does he ascribe to virtue our tears, sighs, fear, and other things of that kind, which are signs of a weak mind. On the contrary, the greater the joy with which we are affected, the greater the perfection to which we pass, that is, the more we must participate in the divine nature. To use things, therefore, and take pleasure in them as far as possible—not, of course, to

the point where we are disgusted with them, for there is no pleasure in that—this is the part of a wise man.[1]

Nearly the entire concept of temperance turns on the point
expressed within those two dashes. Temperance is the opposite of disgust or of the path to disgust; it is not about enjoying less but about
enjoying better. Temperance, which is moderation in sensual desires,
also promises purer or more fulfilling pleasures. It is enlightened, mastered, cultivated taste. Spinoza, in the same scholium, continues: "It is
the part of a wise man, I say, to refresh and restore himself in moderation with pleasant food and drink, with scents, with the beauty of green
plants, with decoration, music, sports, the theater, and other things
of this kind, which anyone can use without injury to another."[2]
Temperance is that moderation which allows us to be masters of our
pleasure instead of becoming its slaves. It is free enjoyment and hence
better enjoyment, for it enjoys its own freedom as well. What a pleasure smoking is when you can do without it! Or drinking when you're
not hooked on alcohol! Or making love when you aren't a slave to
desire! These pleasures are purer for being freer, more joyful for being
better mastered, more serene for being less needy. Is this easy to
achieve? Certainly not. Is it possible? Not always, at least in my experience, and not for everyone. That is why temperance is a virtue, in other
words, an excellence; Aristotle would see it as the summit between two
chasms, intemperance and insensibility, the sadness of the debauchee
and that of the person who can't experience pleasure, the disgust of the
glutton and that of the anorexic.[3] What a misfortune to have to endure
one's body! What happiness to take pleasure in it and exert it!

The intemperate person is like a slave, all the more subjugated
in that his master—the monkey on his back—is with him wherever
he goes. He is the prisoner of his body, of his desires or habits, of
their strength or weakness. Epicurus is right in preferring the term
autarkeia—independence—to the term *sōphrosynē*—temperance or
moderation—used by Aristotle and Plato. But the one can't exist without the other: "We regard independence of outward things as a great

good, not so as in all cases to use little, but so as to be contented with little if we have not much, being honestly persuaded that they have the sweetest enjoyment of luxury who stand least in need of it, and that whatever is natural is easily procured and only the vain and worthless hard to win."[4] In a society that is not too badly off, one almost never lacks in bread and water; but even in the wealthiest society, one almost always lacks in gold or luxury. How should we be happy since we're dissatisfied? And how should we be satisfied since our desires are limitless? Epicurus, by contrast, made a feast of a little cheese or dried fish. What a joy it is to eat when one is hungry! What happiness to be no longer hungry after eating! And what freedom to have nature as one's only master! Temperance is a means to independence, and independence a means to happiness. Being temperate is being able to content oneself with little; the *little* is not what is important: what matters is the ability and the contentment.

Temperance, then—like prudence and perhaps all the other virtues—pertains to the art of enjoyment. It is the work of desire on itself, of life on itself. Its aim is not to surpass human limits but to respect them. It is one instance, among others, of what Foucault calls *the care of the self*, an ethical rather than a moral virtue, and one that has less to do with duty than with common sense.[5] Temperance is prudence applied to pleasure, the point being to enjoy as much as possible as well as is possible, by intensifying sensation or our consciousness of it and not by multiplying the objects of pleasure ad infinitum. Pity Don Juan, who needs so many women. Or the alcoholic, who needs so much to drink. Or the glutton, who needs so much to eat. Epicurus learned to take his pleasures as they came: when they are natural, satisfying them is as easy as attending to the body's needs. What is simpler than quenching a thirst? What is easier—except in cases of extreme poverty—than satisfying the hunger for food or sex? What is more limited—and fortunately so—than our natural, necessary desires?[6]

It is not the body that is insatiable. The limitlessness of desire, which condemns us to neediness, dissatisfaction, or unhappiness, is a disease of the imagination. We have dreams that are greater than our stomachs, and foolishly we reproach our stomachs for being small! The wise man, on the other hand, as Lucretius says of Epicurus, puts "a limit to desire and fear"—and the limits he puts on them are those of the body and of temperance.[7] The intemperate scorn these limits or else try to cast them off like so many shackles. They are no longer hungry? They make themselves vomit. No longer thirsty? Salted peanuts, or liquor, will revive their thirst. They have no desire to make love? A pornographic magazine will get the machine started again . . . But to what end? And at what price? Shackled by pleasure instead of being freed from it (by pleasure itself), they are prisoners of lack, so much so that they miss it in their satiation! How sad, they say, to be not in the least bit hungry or thirsty. It's because they want more, always more, and don't even know how to be content with *excess*. That's why the debauched are sad, that's why alcoholics are unhappy. Indeed, what could be more depressing than a glutton who has had his fill? "I ate too much," he says as he slumps down into his chair, heavy, bloated, and exhausted. "Excess," writes Montaigne, "is the pest of pleasure, and self-restraint is not its scourge, it is its spice."[8]

The gourmet is already aware of this; unlike the glutton, he prefers quality to quantity. It's a step in the right direction. But the wise man aims even higher, closer to what is essential; the quality of his *pleasure* means more to him than the dish that occasions it. He is a gourmet, if you wish, but of a second order, which should in fact be the first: he is a gourmet of the self, or rather (since the self is only one dish among others), of life, of the anonymous and impersonal pleasure of eating, drinking, feeling, loving . . . He isn't an aesthete but a connoisseur. He knows that there is pleasure only where there is taste, and taste only where there is desire: "Plain fare gives as much pleasure as a costly diet, when once the pain of want has been removed, while bread and water confer the highest possible pleasure when they are brought to hungry lips. To habituate one's self, therefore, to simple and inexpensive diet supplies all that is needful for health, and enables a man to meet the necessary requirements of life without shrinking, and it places us in a better condition when we approach at intervals a costly fare and renders us fearless of fortune."[9] In a developed society, as Epicurus's was and as ours is, what's necessary is easy to secure; what isn't necessary is harder to obtain or retain serenely. But who is content with the necessary? Or able to love the superfluous only when it happens to come our way? The wise man, and perhaps no one else. Temperance intensifies his pleasure when there is pleasure to feel, and takes its place when it's not there. And so it's always there, or almost always. What a pleasure to be alive! What a pleasure to be lacking in nothing! What a pleasure to have mastery over one's pleasures! The wise Epicurean cultivates his sensual delights intensively rather than extensively. It is the best that attracts him, not the most, and that suffices to make him happy. He lives "on a little with contented mind," as Lucretius puts it, all the more secure in his well-being for knowing that "a little is never lacking" or, should it ever be, that absolute penury would be its own cure.[10]

What could the person for whom life is sufficient possibly lack? Perhaps this happy poverty was the secret that Saint Francis of Assisi rediscovered. But the lesson is especially valid for our affluent societies, where people suffer and die more often from intemperance than from famine or self-deprivation. Temperance is a virtue for all times but is all the more necessary when times are good. It is not a virtue meant for extraordinary circumstances, like courage (which is most necessary when times are hardest), but an ordinary, humble virtue, to be practiced on a regular rather than an exceptional basis, a virtue of moderation, not heroism. It is the opposite of Rimbaud's beloved "*déréglement de tous les sens.*"[11] This may be why our age, which prefers poets to philosophers and children to wise men, tends to forget that temperance is a virtue and sees it only as a form of hygiene. "I have to be careful," they say. Pity the age that ranks only physicians higher than poets!

Thomas Aquinas saw quite clearly that this cardinal virtue, though not as lofty as the other three (prudence is more necessary, courage and justice more admirable), often surpasses them in difficulty.[12] For temperance bears on the desires that are the most necessary to the life of both the individual (drinking and eating) and the species (making love) and on those that are the strongest and the most difficult to master.[13] There can be no question of suppressing these desires—apathy is a defect.[14] The most we can do is control them as much as possible (which is to say, exercise self-control), organize them, keep them in balance, harmony, and peace. Temperance is the voluntary regulation of life force, a healthy affirmation of our power to exist, as Spinoza would say, an affirmation especially of the power of the mind over the irrational impulses of our affects or appetites.[15] Temperance is not an emotional state; it is an ability, which is to say, a virtue.[16] It is "the virtue that overcomes all types of intoxications," as Alain says.[17] Thus it must also overcome—and this is where it touches on humility—"the intoxications of virtue," temperance included.[18]

5

COURAGE

Of all the virtues, courage is no doubt the most universally admired. What is unusual is that the prestige it enjoys seems not to depend on the society, the period, or even, for the most part, the individual. Cowardice is everywhere despised and bravery everywhere esteemed. The forms can vary, of course, as can the contents; each civilization has its fears and its corresponding forms of courage. But what doesn't vary, or varies hardly, is that courage, the capacity to overcome fear, is always more valued than cowardice or faintheartedness, which succumb to it. Courage is the virtue of heroes, and who doesn't admire heroes?

This universality proves nothing, however, and might even be suspect. Something admired by all is therefore also admired by the wicked and by fools—and what kind of judges could they be? Beauty is also admired, though it isn't a virtue, while many people scorn gentleness, which is one. That morals are "universalizable" in principle does not prove that they meet with universal acclaim. Virtue isn't entertainment and has no use for applause.

The most suspect thing about courage is its indiscrimination: it can serve good or evil ends without changing their nature. Courageous wickedness is still wickedness. Courageous fanaticism is still fanaticism. Is that kind of courage—courage to do evil, courage in doing evil—still courage? It seems hard to believe. Are the murderer and the SS officer virtuous because they display a courage we might somehow admire? Had they been a bit more cowardly they might have caused less harm. What is this virtue that can serve the worst purposes, this value that seems indifferent to values?

"Courage is not a virtue," says Voltaire, "but a quality shared by blackguards and great men alike."[1] An excellence, then, that is neither moral nor immoral in itself. Intelligence and strength, too, are admired, ambiguous (they can serve good as well as evil), and thereby morally neutral. Yet I tend to think that courage is a more telling excellence. Take your average bastard: whether he is intelligent or stupid, sturdy or frail changes nothing of his value, morally. To some extent, stupidity might even excuse him, as could perhaps some physical handicap that might have affected his character. Extenuating circumstances, one might say: if he hadn't been stupid or had that limp, would he have been as wicked? Intelligence or strength, on the other hand, far from mitigating an individual's ignominy, compounds it, making it both more harmful and more blameworthy. It's not the same with courage. If cowardice can sometimes serve as an excuse, courage in and of itself retains its ethical aura even, it would seem, in a bastard. (The fact that it does, however, doesn't prove it is always a virtue, as we shall see.) Given two SS officers who are similar in every way, except that one is cowardly and the other courageous, the latter might be more dangerous, but can he be considered more culpable? More contemptible? More hateful? If I say of someone, "He is cruel and cowardly," the two adjectives add up. If I say, "He is cruel and courageous," they subtract from each other.

But let us leave aside warfare, a subject that would take us too far afield. Let us imagine, instead, two terrorists in times of peace who each blow up a commercial airplane filled with holiday travelers. How can we not despise the one who carries out his attack from the ground, at no personal risk, more than the one who remains inside the aircraft and, with full knowledge of what he is doing, dies along with the other passengers? Let us consider this example at greater length. We can suppose that the two individuals have similar motivations—ideological, for example—and that their acts have identical consequences for the victims. We can also assume that the consequences are too grave and the motivations too questionable for the former to be justified by the latter—in other words, that both attacks are morally reprehensible. But one of our two terrorists is also a coward, since he knows he runs no risk, while the other is courageous, since he knows he is going to die. Does it make any difference? Again, not as far as the victims are concerned. But what about as far as the two bombers are concerned? Courage versus cowardice? No doubt, but are we dealing with morality or psychology? With virtue or character? That psychology and character can—in fact necessarily do—play a part is undeniable. But there is an added factor that touches on morality: the heroic terrorist, by reason of his self-sacrifice, at least gives evidence of his sincerity and, perhaps, of the selflessness of his motives. I take as proof the fact that whatever sort of respect (certainly mixed) we might have for him would diminish, indeed might vanish, if we learned, in reading his diary, for example, that his infamous act had been performed in the conviction that he would stand to gain—as is the case with a religious fanatic—much more than he would lose, namely, eternal happiness in the afterlife. In this latter scenario, selfishness would again or still be the motivating factor, and the moral value of the act would dwindle accordingly. What we would be dealing with is merely someone who is prepared to sacrifice innocent lives for his own happiness—in other words, your garden-variety bastard, someone courageous perhaps when it comes to this life but someone whose courage is nonetheless self-motivated, at least postmortem, and therefore devoid of any moral value. Selfish courage is still selfishness. In contrast, let us imagine an atheistic terrorist; if he sacrifices his life, how can we impute base motives to him? Selfless courage is heroism, and though this proves nothing about the value of the act, it does reveal something about the value of the individual.

That which we respect about courage, then, and which has its culmination in self-sacrifice is first of all the acceptance or incurring of risk without selfish motivation; in other words, a form, if not always of altruism, then at least of disinterestedness, detachment, or a distancing from the self. That, in any case, is what we find in courage that is *morally* worthy of respect. Let's say someone attacks you in the street in such a way as to prevent any possible escape. Will you defend yourself tooth and nail or plead for mercy? What we have here is a question of strategy or, shall we say, temperament. It goes without saying that the first attitude might be deemed more glorious or virile, but as we shall see, glory is not morality nor is virility virtue. On the other hand, if in the street you hear a woman calling for help because a thug is trying to rape her, the courage you may or may not evince, though obviously owing something to your character, will also bring into play your sense of moral responsibility—in other words, your virtue or lack thereof. In short, whereas courage is always respected from a psychological or sociological standpoint, it is only really *morally* estimable when at least partially in the service of others and more or less free of immediate self-interest. This is probably why the supreme form of courage, particularly for an atheist, is courage in the face of death, for the self can derive no concrete or positive gratification from it.[2] I say "immediate," "concrete," and "positive" because we all know that the ego is not so easily put aside: even the hero can be suspected of pursuing glory or fleeing remorse—of seeking his own happiness and well-being, albeit indirectly and posthumously, through virtue. There is no escaping the ego, or the pleasure principle. But finding pleasure in serving others, and well-being in acting generously, far from calling altruism into question, is its very definition and the principle of virtue.

Self-love, says Kant, though not always blameworthy, is the source of all evil.[3] And love of others, I would hasten to add, is the source of all good. But let's not make too much of the distance between them. We can love others, of course, only if we can love ourselves (which is precisely why the Scriptures enjoin us to love our neighbor "as thy-self"), and perhaps we only love ourselves in proportion to the love we have already received and internalized. Nonetheless, there is a differ-ence of emphasis or orientation between someone who loves only him-self and someone who also loves another person, sometimes even selflessly; between someone who only likes to receive or take and someone who also enjoys giving—in short, between basely selfish behavior and sublimated, purified, and liberated egoism (yes, selfish-ness free of the self) that goes by the name of altruism or generosity.

But let us return to courage. What I draw from my examples—and we could find a great many others—is that courage, a psychological trait to begin with, becomes a virtue only when it serves others, either directly or else indirectly by serving a general cause that itself serves other people. As a character trait, courage is primarily a low sensitivity to fear, either because it is minimally felt or because it is easily or even pleasurably withstood. This is the courage of daredevils, of the cool-headed, of those who love a fight—the courage of "tough guys"—and we all know that such courage may have nothing virtuous about it. Does this mean that it is entirely neutral from a moral standpoint? The matter is not so simple. Even in a situation in which I would be acting out of pure self-interest, my courage (in fighting off an attacker instead of pleading with him for my life) would testify to greater self-possession, dignity, and freedom, qualities that are themselves morally significant and impart to courage something of their own value, retrospectively, as it were: though not always moral in essence, courage is that without which morality would be impossible or ineffectual. What room is there for duty in the life of someone who capitulates entirely to his fears? Hence the respect—I would be tempted to call it a premoral respect—that courage, even purely physical or strictly self-serving courage, invariably meets with. Courage commands respect. The fascination with courage is dangerous, to be sure (since, morally, courage proves nothing), but can be explained perhaps by the fact that the courageous person at least manifests an inclination to wrench himself away from the sway of instincts and fears. Call it mastering oneself or one's fears, it's a disposition or a mastery that, though not always moral, is the necessary—though not sufficient—condition of all morality. Fear is egoistic, and so is cowardice. But it doesn't follow that this first kind of courage—physical or psychological courage—is a virtue or, if it is a virtue (that is, an excellence), that it is moral. The ancients saw courage as a mark of virility (the word *andreia*, which means courage in Greek, and the word *virtus* in Latin come from *anêr* and *vir*, respectively, root words that denote man, not in the general sense but man as opposed to woman) and many people would still agree today. It is sometimes said of a daring act that "it took balls," which tends to show that physiology, at least in a figurative sense, counts for more here than morality. We shouldn't let ourselves be overly impressed, however, by this kind of physical or martial courage. Obviously, women can demonstrate this kind of courage as well, but from a moral standpoint such demonstrations prove nothing. A bastard can demonstrate physical courage just as easily as a decent person can. It amounts merely to a felicitous or efficient control of one's aggressiveness: this pathological courage, as Kant would call it, or passionate courage, to use Descartes's term, is certainly useful but primarily to the person who feels it, which is why it is devoid of any properly moral value of its own.[4] Holding up a bank is dangerous and therefore requires courage. But it is not for that reason moral or at any rate would require very special circumstances (having to do with the motives for the act) to become so. By contrast, *courage as a virtue* always presupposes some form of selflessness, altruism, or generosity. Virtuous courage certainly does not rule out a certain insensibility to fear or even a certain relish for it. But it does not presuppose them. This kind of courage is not absence of fear but the capacity to overcome it by a stronger and more generous will. It is no longer (or no longer just) physiology: it is fortitude, moral strength in the face of danger. It is no longer a passion: it is a virtue, one that is the precondition of all the others. It is no longer the courage of the tough: it is the courage of the gentle, and of heroes.

It might be recalled that I said of prudence, too, that it was the precondition of all the other virtues. Well, why not? Why should the virtues have only one other as their precondition? Without prudence, the other virtues would be blind or mad; without courage, they would be futile or pusillanimous. Without prudence, the just person would lack the means to combat injustice; without courage, he wouldn't dare take on the fight. In the former instance, he wouldn't know what steps to take to attain his goal; in the latter, he would retreat before the risks involved. Hence the imprudent and the cowardly can't really be just (they cannot *act* justly, which is true justice). All virtue is a form of courage and all virtue is a form of prudence.

Thomas Aquinas explains this very well: *fortitudo* (moral strength, courage), like prudence but in a different way, is "a condition of every virtue" and also, in the face of danger, simply one virtue among many.[5] A general as well as a strictly cardinal virtue, it supports the others like a pivot or hinge (*cardo*). As Aristotle says, "It is requisite for every virtue to act firmly and immovably," in other words, with what we call firmness of mind. But it is also that special virtue (*courage*, strictly speaking) that permits, as Cicero says, the "deliberate facing of dangers and bearing of toils."[6] Courage, then, is the opposite not only of cowardice but also of laziness and spinelessness. Are these two kinds of courage identical? Obviously not. Danger isn't work and fear isn't lassitude. But in both instances, the basic animal impulse that prefers rest, pleasure, or flight must be overcome. Inasmuch as every virtue requires effort—and, except for the virtues of grace and love, every virtue always does—every virtue requires fortitude as well, which is why the word *coward*, as Alain notes, "is the gravest of insults": not that cowardice is the worst fault in man but because, without courage, we cannot hold out against the worst in ourselves or in others.[7]

We must now ask ourselves what the connection is between courage and truth. Plato, who pondered this point at length, tried without ever really succeeding to reduce courage to knowledge (in the *Laches* and the *Protagoras*) or to opinion (in the *Republic*): courage, he explains, is the "science of things that are or are not to be feared" or, more modestly, the "constant safeguard of an upright and legitimately accredited opinion on the things that are or are not to be feared."[8] What both these formulations ignore is that courage presupposes fear and that the burden of courage is simply to stand up to it. But one can courageously face an illusory danger or shrink in cowardice before a real one. Fear is both a necessary and a sufficient element in courage, and it doesn't matter whether fear is justified or illegitimate, reasonable or unreasonable. Don Quixote shows courage in tilting at windmills, whereas science, for all the reassurance it offers, has never made anyone courageous. No other virtue is more resistant to intellectualism. Think of how many ignorant heroes and cowardly scientists the world has known. And the wise? If they were utterly wise, like Epicurus or Spinoza, they would no longer fear anything and courage for them would be superfluous. Philosophers, of course, need the courage to think, but thinking alone has never supplied it. Science or philosophy can sometimes drive away fears by dispelling their objects, but courage, I repeat, is not the absence of fear; it is the ability to confront, master, and overcome fear, which assumes that fear either exists or might reasonably exist. For example, eclipses no longer frighten us, because we know what they are, but that does not mean we face them with courage; what it means, at most, is that we have lost an opportunity we might have had to demonstrate our courage—or lack thereof. Similarly, if we could be convinced, like Epicurus, that death meant nothing to us (or, like Plato, that it is desirable), we would no longer require courage to bear the thought of it. Scientific knowledge suffices in one instance, wisdom and faith in the other. But we need courage only in those instances when in fact they do not suffice—either because we simply lack them or because they are irrelevant to or ineffective against our distress. Knowledge, wisdom, and opinion can provide fear with its objects or deprive it of them. They do not impart courage but rather offer an opportunity to exercise it or do without it.

Jankélévitch saw this quite clearly: courage is not knowledge but a decision, not an opinion but an act.[9] This is why courage needs more than reason alone: "Reasoning tells us *what* to do and if it must be done, but it doesn't tell us *that* it must done; much less does it do what it says."[10] If there is any kind of courage in reason, it consists solely in this: reason is never afraid; in other words, it is never our reason that is frightened or that panics. The heroic philosopher Jean Cavaillès, arrested, imprisoned, tortured, and executed by the Nazis for his Resistance activities, knew this, just as he knew that acting and willing require more than reason: there is no courage *more geometrico;* there is no courageous science.[11] Try proving, under torture, that one *must not* talk! Even if it were possible to do so, do we really believe it would suffice? Reason is reason: it's the same for Cavaillès—who didn't talk under torture—as for anyone else. But not so with will or with courage, which is simply will at its most determined and, in the face of danger or suffering, at its most necessary.

Reason is in every instance universal and anonymous, whereas courage is always singular and personal. And if we sometimes need courage to think, just as we need it to suffer or fight, it is because no one can think for us—or suffer or fight for us—and because reason, or truth, is insufficient and cannot spare us the task of overcoming whatever it is within us that wavers and resists, that would prefer a comforting illusion or a convenient lie. Whence what we call intellectual courage, the refusal to let fear govern the life of the mind, the refusal to submit to anything but the truth, which fears nothing even if it is itself frightening.

Such courage is called lucidity. It is the courage of truth, though there is no truth that by itself can make us lucid. All truth is eternal, while courage has meaning only in finite, temporal terms, in duration. A god would have no need for it. Nor would a sage, perhaps, if he lived exclusively in the realm of eternal or immortal blessings of which Epicurus and Spinoza speak.[12] But he cannot and neither can we, which is another reason why we need courage. The courage to persist and endure, to live and to die, to hold out, fight, resist, persevere. Spinoza calls tenacity (*animositas*) the "desire by which each one strives, solely from the dictate of reason, to preserve his being."[13] But courage resides in the desire, not in reason; in the striving, not in the dictate. To be courageous is to persevere in our being (Eluard speaks of this as "*le dur désir de durer*"—"the difficult desire to endure") and all courage is the courage of willing.[14]

I am not quite as certain as Jankélévitch that courage is the virtue of beginnings or that it is exclusively or essentially that: continuing or persevering takes as much courage, sometimes even more.[15] But it is true that continuing means repeatedly starting anew and that, since courage can be "neither hoarded nor amassed," it can continue only if it is taken up again and again in a ceaseless perpetuation of effort, in a beginning forever rebegun in spite of fatigue and fear.[16] That is why courage remains always necessary and always difficult. "Courage must take us out of fear," says Alain, "and this movement, which is at the start of each of our actions, is also, if restrained, at the birth of each of our thoughts."[17] Fear paralyzes, and any act, even that of flight, must to some extent wrench itself from fear. Courage triumphs over fear, or at least attempts to, and any such attempt is already an act of courage. Were it not, what would virtue be? Or life? Or happiness? A man strong in character, says Spinoza, strives "to act well and rejoice"; this striving in the face of countless obstacles is courage itself.[18]

Like any other virtue, courage exists only in the present. The fact that we once had courage does not prove that we will have it again or even that we have it now. Yet past action is a positive indication, quite literally, an encouraging sign. The past is an object of knowledge and as such has greater significance, morally, than the future, which is merely an object of faith or hope—an object of our imagination. Wanting to give something tomorrow or some other day is not generosity. Wanting to be courageous next week or in ten years is not courage. These are merely projected intentions, daydream decisions, imaginary virtues. Aristotle (or the disciple speaking in his name) refers amusingly, in the *Magna Moralia*, to those who are "void of fear with regard to a danger that is ten years off . . . but, if they come near it, are ready to die with fear."[19] Imaginary heroes but cowards in reality. Jankélévitch, who cites these remarks, rightly adds that "courage is the intention of the moment pending," that the moment of courage thus marks "our point of convergence with the imminent future"; it is a matter of being courageous not tomorrow or later today but *"this very minute."*[20] Very well. But what else is this moment *pending*, this point of contact with the imminent or immediate future, but an enduring present? We certainly don't need courage to face something that no longer is or to overcome something that is yet to be. Neither Nazism nor the end of the world, neither my birth nor my death are objects of courage for me (the thought of death, in my mind right now, can be, as can to some extent the thought of Nazism or of the end of the world; but a thought requires infinitely less courage, as far as these things are concerned, than does the thing itself). What could be more ridiculous than these armchair heroes who confront only abstract dangers, and only in their imaginations? As Jankélévitch goes on to say, "There is no air left for courage to breathe if the threat is already completely played out and if, having broken the spell of possibility and lifted us from the anguish of uncertainty, the danger now become misfortune has ceased being a danger."[21] Can we be so sure? If it were really so, then we would have no need for courage to withstand physical or mental pain, or in times of infirmity or bereavement; it would even be useless.

Yet it is at such times that we need courage most. Can anyone imagine that for those who stood up under torture, like Jean Cavaillès or Jean Moulin, it was the future or merely danger and not the excruciating present reality of suffering that first mobilized their courage? (What future could be worse than their present? What danger graver than torture?) One might argue that under such circumstances the choice, if there is one, is between having the horror cease or having it continue, which only makes sense in relation to the future. No doubt— the present is much more than a moment; it is a duration, what Augustine called a *distension*, always arising out of the past and extending toward the future. Courage is needed, I said before, to persist and endure, to withstand the tension within us, the agonizing struggle between past and future, between memory and will, that is life itself and the effort of living (Spinoza's *conatus*), a struggle that is always necessary and usually difficult. Though we may fear the future, what we must endure is the present (including our present fear of the future); and the immediate and present reality of misfortune, suffering, or anguish requires just as much courage in this enduring present as the threat of danger or what Jankélévitch calls the anguish of uncertainty. Torture in all its forms reveals this truth. Does a terminal cancer patient need courage only with regard to the future, to death? What about a mother who has lost her child? "Be brave," she is told. This counsel may bear on the future, like all advice, but not in the sense that there is danger, risk, or threat awaiting her some time hence; she needs courage, alas, to bear up against a horribly immediate and present misfortune that extends indefinitely hereafter only because it is now everlastingly present and always will be—since death and the past are irrevocable. Courage is also needed to live with a grave disability or to cope with failure or past mistakes, and here, too, courage bears in the first instance on the enduring present; if it bears on the future it is solely because that future is—and can only be—a continuation of this present. The blind person needs more courage than a person who has sight, and not just because life is more dangerous for him. I would go even further and say that to the extent that suffering is worse than fear, or at least in those cases when it is, we need more courage to bear it. Of course, everything depends on the sufferings and fears involved. Let us take an extreme form of suffering—torture—and an extreme fear—the fear of imminent death or imminent torture. Doesn't it seem obvious that more courage is needed to hold out against torture than against the threat of torture, even if the threat is absolutely inevitable and utterly credible? And who, despite his fear of death, wouldn't choose suicide so as not to have submit to such extreme suffering? Indeed, many people made precisely that choice, and many regretted not having had the means to do so. Committing suicide may require courage—it probably always does—yet less than holding up under torture. While courage in the face of death may be the supreme form of courage, by which I mean the model or archetype for all other forms, it is not always or necessarily the greatest form of courage. It is the simplest, because death is the simplest. It is the most absolute, as it were, because death is absolute. But it is not the greatest form of courage, because death is not the worst thing there is. Worse than death is unending suffering, prolonged horror, both immediate and terribly present. And even with respect to fear itself, can anyone doubt that as much courage, and sometimes more, is needed to overcome a present terror as is needed to confront a danger that may await us?

In short, courage doesn't have to do only with the future, with fear, with imminent harm; it also has to do with the present and is always much more a matter of will than of hope. The Stoics knew this and made a philosophy out of it. We hope only for that which does not depend on us; we want only that which does. This is why hope is a virtue for believers only, while courage is a virtue for every man. And what does being courageous require? Wanting to be so, which is to say, being so.[22] Hoping to be so is not enough; only cowards content themselves with that.

Which brings us to the well-known connection between courage and despair.

"Thus it is the most dangerous and desperate affairs in which we exercise the most boldness and courage," writes Descartes, and if this formulation does not altogether exclude the possibility that in such situations one can also hope, Descartes nevertheless suggests that hope and courage cannot have the same object or be one and the same thing.[23] In the face of death the hero can hope for glory or the posthumous triumph of his ideas. But that hope is not the object of his courage and cannot take its place. Cowards hope for victory just as much as heroes do, and probably no one ever flees except in the hope of saving himself. Yet these hopes do not amount to courage, nor, unfortunately, are they enough to provide it.

Not that hope is always a paltry thing. Clearly, it can buttress courage or sustain it, a point emphasized by Aristotle: it is easier to be brave in combat when you hope to win.[24] But is it more courageous? There is reason to think otherwise: that, if hope gives strength to courage, it is particularly necessary to be courageous when there is no hope and that the true hero is the person who is able to face not just risks, which are ever-present, but also the certainty of death and even—this can happen—final and permanent defeat. This is the courage of the vanquished, a courage no less great, in those who possess it, or less praiseworthy than the courage of victors. What could the insurgents of the Warsaw ghetto uprising have hoped for? Nothing for themselves, at any rate, and their courage was all the more patent and heroic for it. Why fight in such cases? Because we must. Because it would be unworthy of us not to. For the beauty of the gesture, as they say, it being understood that this beauty is of an ethical, not aesthetic, nature. "Brave men act," writes Aristotle, "for honor's sake," which can also be translated as: "for the beauty of the courageous action" or "for the love of good."[25] Passions, whether anger, hatred, or hope, can also play a part in the courageous deed and lend their support to it.[26] But without them courage is still possible and also more necessary and more virtuous.

One can even read in Aristotle that courage in its highest form is "without hope."[27] Some commentators take this statement further, calling courage "the antinomy of hope: because he no longer nourishes any hope, the man who is courageous in facing his fatal illness is more courageous than a sailor in a storm; this is why 'those who harbor hopes are not truly brave,' nor are those who are convinced of being the strongest, of being able to triumph in battle."[28] I find that argument a bit extreme; at the very least, it uses a somewhat one-sided interpretation of Aristotle to take him down a path where I, personally, might be willing to venture, at least in the abstract, but where I suspect he had no intention of going and wouldn't agree to follow us.[29] But these distinctions are academic and concern only the history of philosophy. Life teaches us that we need courage to withstand despair and also that despair can sometimes give us courage. When there is nothing more to hope for, when there is nothing more to fear, then, against all hope, courage is at hand to face the present fight, the present suffering, the present action. This is why, Rabelais explains, "according to true military discipline one must never reduce his enemy to the point of despair; for such necessity multiplies his strength and increases his courage."[30]

We have everything to fear from those who fear nothing. For what should they fear if they have nothing more to hope for? Soldiers know this and guard against it; so do diplomats and statesmen. Hope always gives others a hold over us; despair gives us a hold over ourselves. So that we might commit suicide? Often we can do better: death is merely a hope like any other. Alain, who had been a soldier, and a brave one at that, met several true heroes in the war. This was his comment on the subject: "To be totally brave one must lose all hope; I saw infantry lieutenants and second lieutenants who seemed to have written off their lives; their cheerfulness scared me. In that respect I was bringing up the rear; one always lags behind someone."[31] Yes, one always does, and not just in war. Elsewhere, Alain speaks of the courage shown by his teacher Jules Lagneau, not on the battlefield but in a classroom, and recalls the "absolute despair" that enabled him to think "with joy, with no fear and no hope whatsoever."[32] These kinds of courage are all similar and they fill us with fear. But what does our fear prove, except that we need courage? Remember what William of Orange said: "Hope is not necessary for our undertaking, nor success for our persevering." He was reputed to be of a sober temperament; this did not prevent him from acting and daring. Why assume that only optimists are experts in courage? It is certainly easier to undertake or persevere when there is hope or when success is at hand. But when it is easier, we need courage less.

At any rate, what Aristotle clearly shows—and with this we must conclude—is that courage requires moderation. This does not mean that one can be too courageous or that there are perils too extreme to be faced. It means that the risks we incur must be in proportion to the ends we seek; it is admirable to risk your life for a noble cause but unreasonable to do so for trifles or out of sheer fascination with danger. This is what distinguishes the courageous from the reckless and why courage—like every other virtue, according to Aristotle—is a summit between two abysses (or the happy medium between two excesses), in this case, cowardliness and temerity. The coward is too subject to his fears, the daredevil too unconcerned for his life, too heedless of danger, for either of them to be truly (which is to say, virtuously) courageous.[33] Boldness, even if extreme, is therefore virtuous only if tempered with prudence: "The virtue of a free man," writes Spinoza, "is seen to be as great in avoiding dangers as in overcoming them. . . . A free man chooses flight with the same tenacity, or presence of mind, as he chooses a contest."[34]

It remains to be said that courage is not the strongest force, but fate is—or chance, which is the same thing. Courage itself owes much to fate and remains subordinate to it. For every man there are things he can and things he cannot endure; whether or not he will encounter before he dies the thing that will break him depends as much on chance as on merit. Heroes know this, when they are lucid; it makes them humble with regard to themselves and merciful toward others. All the virtues are interdependent, and they all depend on courage.

6

JUSTICE

With justice we embark on the last of the four cardinal virtues. In discussing it, we will have to call on the other three, for the subject is so very vast—and we will need to be just ourselves, for the subject is vulnerable to interests and conflicts of every sort.

In fact, we need justice no matter what virtue we mean to discuss. To speak injudiciously of any virtue is to betray it; this may be why justice encompasses all the other virtues, even though it substitutes for none. All the more necessary, then, to proceed with justice when the subject is justice itself. But who could be so complacent as to think that he knows exactly what it is or that he himself is completely just?

"Justice doesn't exist," Alain writes. "Justice belongs to the realm of things that must be done precisely because they do not exist." He adds, however, that "justice will exist if we act with justice."[1] Fine—but we still need to know what justice is or ought to be. How can we act with justice otherwise?

Of the four cardinal virtues, justice is probably the only one that is an absolute good in itself. Prudence, temperance, and courage are virtues only when they serve good ends, either directly or else by furthering other virtues—justice for example—that transcend them or motivate them. Prudence, temperance, and courage in the service of evil or injustice would not be virtues, merely talents or qualities of mind or temperament, to use Kant's expression. It may be useful to recall this famous text:

> It is impossible to conceive anything at all in the world, or even out of it, which can be taken as good without qualification, except a *good will*. Intelligence, wit, judgment, and any other *talents* of the mind we may care to name, or courage, resolution, and constancy of purpose, as qualities of *temperament*, are without doubt good and desirable in many respects; but they can also be extremely bad and hurtful when the will is not good which has to make use of these gifts of nature, and which for this reason has the term "*character*" applied to its peculiar quality.[2]

Obviously, what Kant says of courage here we could say of prudence or temperance. A murderer or tyrant can act both prudently and with self-restraint and still not in any way be virtuous; we know of hundreds of such cases. If he were just, however, then his act would take on a different value and significance. But of course a just murder or a just tyranny is a contradiction in terms, which is a way of recognizing the singularity of justice. For no one has ever been surprised to hear of a prudent murderer or a sober tyrant.

In short, justice is a good in itself, like Kant's goodwill; indeed it is an essential part of it.[3] We must do our duty, of course, but never at the expense of justice or in opposition to it. In fact, how could we ever simultaneously be dutiful and unjust, since duty presupposes justice—indeed duty is justice itself, in the form of requirement and obligation.[4] Justice, then, is not a virtue like the others. Rather, it is the boundary that defines them, the principle that allows them to coexist. A "complete virtue," as Aristotle calls it, it is the precondition of all value, the requirement for any kind of humanity.[5] It cannot replace happiness (how could it?) but there can be no happiness without it.

The problem, found in Kant and in Dostoevsky, Bergson, Camus, and Jankélévitch, among others, is this: if in order to save humanity it is necessary to condemn an innocent person (or to torture a child, in Dostoevsky's version of the dilemma), should we go along with the sacrifice? The answer is no. For one thing, the price is too high; moreover, to do so would be ignominy. "If legal justice perishes," Kant writes, "then it is no longer worthwhile for men to remain alive on this earth."[6] Utilitarianism, here, reaches its limit. If justice were only a "pledge guaranteeing mutual advantage," as Epicurus envisions it,[7] or a maximizing of collective well-being, as it is for Bentham and Mill, there might be justice in sacrificing a few perfectly innocent and defenseless people for the sake of everyone else's happiness.[8] But this possibility is precisely what justice excludes, or should exclude. John Rawls, who follows Kant on this question, is right: justice is superior to and more valuable than well-being or efficiency; it cannot be sacrificed to them— not even for the happiness of the greatest number.[9] To what could justice legitimately be sacrificed, since without justice there would be no legitimacy or illegitimacy? And in the name of what, since without justice even humanity, happiness, and love could have no absolute value? If we are unjust out of love, we are no less unjust, and what we call love is simply favoritism or partiality. If we are unjust for the sake of our own happiness or that of humanity, we are still unjust, and what we call happiness is merely selfishness or comfort. Without justice, values would be nothing more than interests or motives; they would cease to be values or would become values without worth. But what is justice, and what is it worth?

When we use the term *justice*, we usually mean one of two things: conformity to the law (*jus* in Latin) or equality or proportionality. "It's not fair," says the child who has less than the others or less than he feels entitled to; he might say the same thing to a companion who has cheated at a game they are playing by not respecting its written or unwritten rules, even if the point of the cheating were merely to reestablish an equality between them. Similarly, adults will deem unjust both too glaring a disparity of wealth (we speak of the need for social justice in this case) and an infringement of the law (the detection and prosecution of which it is the responsibility of the justice system to carry out). Conversely, we call someone just who neither violates the law nor infringes on the legitimate interests of others, someone who, as Aristotle explains it, takes only his share of good things and his entire share of evil things.[10] Justice hinges entirely on this twofold respect, a respect for *legality* in the polis and for *equality* among individuals: "The just, then, is the lawful and the fair, the unjust the unlawful and the unfair."[11]

These two meanings, though interconnected (justice requires that individuals be equal before the law), are nonetheless distinct. Whether something is legally just or not is a factual question, and arguments for the value of justice as legality tend to be characterized by their circularity: "All lawful acts are in a sense just acts," Aristotle notes.[12] But what does that prove if the law itself isn't just? And as Pascal observes, more cynically: "Justice is what is established; and thus all our established laws will necessarily be regarded as just without examination, since they are established."[13] How could there be a polis otherwise? How could there be justice if judges were not obligated to place the law—and the letter of the law—above their own moral or political convictions? The law as fact (*legality*) is more important than law as value (*legitimacy*); or rather, the former serves in place of the latter. Without legality, there can be no state, no legal system—no rule of law: "*Auctoritas, non veritas, facit legem.*" Authority, not truth, makes the law.[14] Hobbes wrote those words, and they also hold true for the democracies we live in. Laws are made by the greatest number, not the most just or the most intelligent. Judicial positivism, the doctrine is called today, and it is as insuperable from the standpoint of law as it is insufficient from the standpoint of value. And where does justice fit in? The sovereign decides, and what the sovereign decides is law, by definition.[15] But the sovereign—even when it is the people—is not always just. Pascal again: "No doubt equality of goods is just; but . . ."[16] But the sovereign has decided otherwise: the law protects private property, in modern democracies no differently than in Pascal's day, and when it does so it guarantees inequality in wealth. When equality and legality are at odds, where is justice?

We read in Plato that justice is what keeps each person in his place, with his share, and in the function he is fitted for, thereby preserving the hierarchical harmony of the whole.[17] Would it be just to give everyone the same things, when people have neither the same needs nor the same merits? To require the same things of everyone, when they neither enjoy the same abilities nor bear the same burdens and responsibilities? But then how can equality be maintained among unequal human beings? Or freedom among equals? These issues were discussed among the ancient Greeks, and the debate has hardly changed. Might makes right; this principle, put into practice, is called politics. As Pascal says: "Justice is subject to dispute, might is easily recognized and is not disputed. So we cannot give might to justice, because might has gainsaid justice, and has declared that it is she herself who is just. And thus being unable to make what is just strong, we have made what is strong just."[18] Even democracy cannot bridge this gulf: "The majority is the best way, because it is visible, and has strength to make itself obeyed. Yet it is the opinion of the least able."[19] And sometimes of the least just. Rousseau's concept of the general will is certainly useful in this instance but of dubious value. There is nothing to guarantee that the general will is always just, so its validity cannot depend on its being just (unless one defines justice as the general will, but in that case, the circularity of the definition would obviously make the guarantee worthless, if not simply meaningless). All democrats know this. All republicans know this. The law is the law, whether just or not. But it is therefore not the same as justice, which brings us back to the second meaning—justice not as fact (legality) but as value (equality, equity) or, finally, as virtue.

This second point touches on morality more than on law. When the law is unjust, it is just to fight it—indeed sometimes it may be just to violate it. Antigone's justice versus Creon's. The justice of the Resistance fighters versus the justice of Vichy. The justice of the just versus that of the jurists. Socrates, unjustly condemned, refused to save himself and turned down offers to help him escape; he preferred to die abiding by the laws, he said, than live in violation of them.[20] To my mind, this was a case of taking the love of justice a bit far, or rather of confusing justice with legality. Is it just to sacrifice an innocent life to iniquitous laws or to laws iniquitously applied? What is clear at all events is that such a position, even if sincere, is acceptable only when the life at stake is one's own: Socrates' heroism, based on a debatable principle to begin with, becomes purely and simply criminal if the innocent person he sacrificed to the laws were anyone other than himself. Yes, one should respect the laws, or at least obey and defend them, but not at the expense of justice, not at the expense of an innocent life. For whoever could save Socrates, even illegally, it was just to make the attempt—and only Socrates had the right to reject it. Morality and justice come before legality, at least where the essentials are concerned, which may be a way of recognizing what is essential. And what is essential? Freedom for all, the dignity of the individual, and the rights of others.

Just or not, the law is still the law: no democracy, no republic would be possible if people obeyed only the laws they approved of. True, but no democracy or republic would be acceptable if obedience required us to abjure justice or tolerate the intolerable. Of course, not every unjust law must be disobeyed: the question is one of degree and cannot be resolved once and for all. Matters like these are the province of casuistry, in the good sense of the word. Sometimes the right thing to do is to go underground and fight; sometimes it is better to obey or to disobey quietly. Of course it would be preferable if law and justice went hand in hand, and the moral obligation of every citizen is to strive toward that goal. Justice belongs to no one, to no camp or party; each one of us is morally obliged to defend it. Let me express myself more clearly. Parties do not have morals. Looking after the interests of justice is the responsibility not of parties but of the individuals who belong to them or who oppose them. Justice does not exist, not even as a value, except insofar as there are just people to defend it.

But what is a just person? This question may be the hardest to answer. Is he the law-abiding individual? No, since the law can be unjust. Someone who abides by moral law? That is Kant's answer, but it merely begs the question, for what is moral law? I've known a number of just persons who didn't pretend to know what it is, and even some who denied its existence altogether. Think of Montaigne. In fact, if moral law did exist and if we knew what it was, we would have less need of just people; justice would suffice. Kant, for instance, thought he had deduced from justice—or at least from his idea of it—the absolute necessity of the death penalty for all murderers, a position that other just people have rejected and continue to reject, as we all know.[21] These disagreements among just people are essential to justice for they reveal its absence. Justice does not exist in this world or in any other. On this point, it is Aristotle, and not Plato or Kant, who is right, at least in my reading: justice does not make just people; just people make justice. But how can they, without knowing what justice is? By abiding by the law, as we have seen, and by respecting the principle of equality. But law isn't justice; nor is equality, taken alone. We keep hearing about the judgment of Solomon, but to the extent that equality does figure in that judgment, it is as psychology, not justice; strictly speaking, only his second judgment—to dispense with equality and return the child to his true mother—is just. The first judgment, which would mean dividing the child in two, would be not justice but barbarity. Equality isn't everything. Is it just for a judge to impose the same punishment on every defendant? Is it just for a teacher to give the same grade to every student? Obviously not; punishments or grades should be proportionate to the offense or merit. But who is to judge whether they are? And what scale should be used? How severe should the punishment be for theft? For rape? For murder? And what about special circumstances? The law answers these questions, more or less, and so do juries and judges. But justice does not. The same is true of teaching. Who and what should be rewarded? The hardworking student or the gifted one? Achievement or ability? What to do in the case of competitive examinations in which the success of some depends on the failure of others? What criteria should be applied? What standards used? And wouldn't they have to be evaluated as well? Teachers answer as best they can, for they must. But justice does not; it never does. This is why we need judges to preside in our courtrooms and teachers to correct exams. For those who have no qualms about rendering judgments because they *know* what justice is, it's easy. But just people are those who do not know what justice is and who recognize that they do not know it; they render justice as best they can, not exactly blindly—that would be overstating the case—but with an understanding of the risks (more for others than for themselves) and the uncertainties. To quote Pascal yet again: "There are only two kinds of men: the righteous, who think they are sinners; and the sinners, who think they are righteous."[22] But we never know in which of these categories we belong; if we did know, we would already be in the other!

Yet we do need a criterion, however approximate, and a principle, however uncertain. The principle should favor equality, reciprocity, or equivalence between individuals. This is the origin of the word *equity* (from *aequus*, equal), which would be synonymous with justice if it did not also and above all designate justice in its perfection, a point to which we shall return. The idea of equity is reflected in the symbol of the scale with its two trays in balance, as they should be. Justice is the virtue of order and exchange—equitable order and honest exchange. A mutually advantageous exchange? Yes, in the best of cases, and perhaps in most cases (when I buy bread from my baker, each of us benefits). But how can we guarantee that things will always be this way? We can't; all we can say is that the order and exchange wouldn't be *just* otherwise. For me to carry out an exchange to my own disadvantage (for example, were I to exchange my house for a loaf of bread), I would have to be insane, misinformed, or acting under duress; while the exchange might not necessarily be void juridically in all three cases (this the sovereign power would have to decide), it would clearly be devoid of all justice. For an exchange to be just, it must take place between equals, or at least there can be no difference between the parties to the exchange (in terms of their wealth, power, or knowledge, and so forth) that might make them accept an exchange contrary to their interests or contrary to their free and enlightened will as it would be expressed in a situation of parity. This is a universally recognized principle—which does not mean that everyone abides by it. To take advantage of a child's naïveté, a madman's confusion, an ignorant person's error, or a needy person's poverty, in order to extract from them something that is contrary to their interests or intentions, without their knowledge or through coercion, is always and everywhere unjust, even if in some places and under certain circumstances it is not illegal. Fraud, racketeering, and usury are as unjust as theft is. And ordinary commerce is just only so long as it respects a certain parity between buyer and seller, in rights and duties as well as in the amount of information available to them concerning the object of exchange. We might even go further: theft itself can become just, perhaps, when property is unjust. But when it is unjust, isn't it because a certain relative equality among human beings has been flouted? Proudhon's claim that "property is theft" is surely an exaggeration, indeed a contradiction in terms (for it denies the legitimacy of property while the concept of theft presupposes it). Nevertheless, who can justly enjoy superfluity while others are dying because they lack bare necessities? "Equality of goods is just," says Pascal. And inequality of goods can never be absolutely just, for it dooms some to poverty or death, while others accumulate riches upon riches and pleasures to the point of disgust.

Still, the equality essential to justice is an equality not so much between the *objects* exchanged, which is always open to debate and nearly always possible to come to agreement on (otherwise there would be no exchange), as between the *subjects* involved in the exchange—not their de facto equality but their equality in rights, which presupposes that they are equally informed and free, at least as far as their interests and the conditions of the exchange are concerned. Someone might object that this kind of equality is never fully attained. True, but the just strive toward it; the unjust stand in its way. Let us suppose that you are selling a house that you have lived in for years; you obviously know the property better than any potential buyer. Justice would require you to inform the prospective buyer of any apparent or hidden flaw it might have and even of any inconvenience in the surrounding area, though the law does not require that you do so. Certainly we don't all carry out this obligation, not always and not completely. But we can all see that it would be just to do so and that we are unjust if we do not do so. A buyer appears and you show him your house. Should you tell him that the neighbor is a drunkard who yells after midnight? That the walls are damp in winter? That termites have eaten away the structure? The law might or might not require that you do, depending on the case, but justice always demands it.

One might object that such a requirement would make selling houses very difficult or barely profitable. Perhaps, but who ever said that justice is easy or profitable? It is, but only for the person who is treated justly or who benefits from the just action, and so much the better for him; justice is a virtue, however, only for the person who practices it or does it.

Should we therefore forgo our self-interest? Of course not. But it must be subordinate to justice, not the other way around. And what if it isn't? If it isn't, then be satisfied with being wealthy, Alain would answer, but don't try to be just on top of it.[23]

The principle of justice, therefore, is equality, as Aristotle observes, and first and foremost the equality of men with respect to one another, an equality that the law prescribes or that morality presupposes, at least as a right, even in the face of de facto inequalities of the most obvious, established (legally in some cases), and indeed respectable sort. Wealth confers no special rights (it confers a special power, but power, as it happens, is not justice). Genius and saintliness confer no special rights. Mozart has to pay for his bread like any other person, and before a truly just tribunal, Saint Francis of Assisi would have neither more nor fewer rights than anyone else. Justice is equality, but it is an equality in *rights*, whether established juridically or required morally. Alain, following Aristotle, concurs on this point and amplifies: "Justice is equality. By this I don't mean a chimera, some far-off goal; I mean the relationship that any fair exchange immediately establishes between the stronger and the weaker, between the informed and the ignorant, which consists in this: through a deeper and entirely generous exchange, the strong or knowledgeable person proceeds as though the other person possessed a strength and knowledge equal to his own, thereby becoming an adviser, judge, and instrument of redress."[24] Someone who sells his used car understands this principle very well, and so does the buyer; it is for this reason that they can almost always agree on what constitutes a just deal, even though they may not do all they can to ensure that it actually is entirely just. How can someone be unjust without knowing what justice means? What they both know, if they think about it, is that their transaction is just if and only if equals—in power, knowledge, and rights—*might have* agreed to it. The conditional tense is most appropriate, for justice assumes a condition of equality, which our exchanges must submit to.

From that principle we can derive this criterion, or what Alain calls the golden rule, of justice: "In any contract and exchange, put yourself in the other person's place, but knowing everything you know and supposing yourself to be as free from need as it is possible for someone to be, and see if, in his place, you would approve of this exchange or contract."[25] A golden rule or an iron rule: what constraint could be more rigorous or exacting? It requires that exchanges take place solely between free and equal subjects, and it is here that justice, even as a value, touches on politics as much as on morality. Kant says, "Every action is just that in itself or in its maxim is such that the freedom of the will of each can coexist together with the freedom of everyone in accordance with a universal law."[26] This coexistence of each individual's freedom under the same law presupposes their rightful if not actual equality—or rather, it is this legally ordained coexistence that brings about this equality: This is what justice is. A never-ending task, a constantly threatened achievement.[27]

These issues touch on politics, as I said. The postulation of free and (therefore) equal subjects is the principle behind any true democracy and a litmus test of human rights, and it is for this reason that social contract theory is essential to our modern societies, more essential than the theory of natural law. Both are fictions, of course, but the latter presupposes a reality that makes the theory rather pointless (if natural law existed, one would not need to *achieve* justice; one could simply render it), while the former asserts a principle or a volition: the idea of an original contract, whether in Spinoza, Locke, Rousseau, or Kant, hinges less on the actual *existence* of a freely-arrived-at agreement between equals (these writers know such a contract never existed) than on the postulation for all the members of the body politic of the right to equal freedom, one that makes possible and necessary the kind of agreements that unite—and here we come back to Aristotle—*equality* (since freedom is postulated as equal for all) and *legality* (since under specified conditions, these agreements can have the force of law). Kant, perhaps more clearly than Rousseau or Spinoza, shows not only that such an original agreement was merely hypothetical but also that this hypothesis was necessary to any nontheological construction of law and justice:

Here we have an original contract on which alone a civil and thus consistently legal constitution among men can be based and a community established. Yet this contract . . . need by no means be presupposed as a fact. . . . It is rather a *mere idea* of reason, albeit one with indubitable practical reality, obligating every lawmaker to frame his laws so that they *might* have come from the united will of an entire people, and to regard any subject who would be a citizen as if he had joined in voting for such a will. For this is the touchstone of the legitimacy of all public law. If a law is so framed that all the people *could not possibly* give their consent—as, for example, a law granting the hereditary *privilege* of *master status* to a certain class of *subjects*—the law is unjust; but if it is *at all possible* that a people might agree on it, then the people's duty is to look upon the law as just, even assuming that their present situation or the tenor of their present way of thinking were such that, if consulted, they would probably refuse to agree.[28]

In other words, the social contract "is the rule and not the origin of the state's constitution, not the principle of its foundation but the principle of its administration"; it doesn't explain how states become what they are, it clarifies an ideal—in this case, "the ideal of legislation, government, and public justice."[29] A purely regulatory hypothesis, therefore, but a necessary one; the original contract does not allow us to know the "origin of the state" or what the state is, but it does allow us to know "what it should be."[30] The idea of justice as the coexistence of individual freedoms under an at least possible law is a function not of knowledge but of will (of purely practical reason, Kant would say). It is not a theoretical or explanatory concept for a given society but a guide for passing judgment and an ideal for action.

This is basically what Rawls says. We have to imagine human beings in an "original position" in which no one knows his place in society (what Rawls calls the "veil of ignorance") in order to give ourselves a way to think about justice as fairness (and not as mere legality or utility), which we can do only by bracketing individual differences and each individual's attachment to his selfish or contingent interests, even those that are justified.[31] Here again we have an entirely hypothetical, indeed fictitious, position; yet it serves as a working hypothesis in the sense that it allows us to separate the obligation of justice at least partially from the overly specific interests that require resolution by justice and with which we are almost irresistibly tempted to confuse it.

The original position can be likened to a supposed gathering of *equals without egos* (since everyone is supposed to be ignorant not just of "his class position or social status" but even of his intelligence, strength, or "the special features of his psychology") and therein lies the lucidity of Rawls's formulation.[32] The self is always unjust.[33] Therefore, thinking about justice requires taking the self out of the picture or at least rendering it incapable of influencing the judgment. What the original position achieves is precisely this abstraction or neutralizing of the self. No one has ever occupied that position and no one ever will, but we can try to occupy it, at least temporarily and fictitiously, in order to think and judge. Such a model amounts to a short-circuiting of self-interest (in the original position, "no one knows his situation in society nor his natural assets, and therefore no one is in a position to tailor principles to his advantage"),[34] but without postulating an unlikely altruism (since the parties are unwilling to have their interests, even if indeterminate, sacrificed to those of others).[35] This model has much to tell us about what justice is: neither selfishness nor altruism but a pure equivalence of rights as attested or manifested by the interchangeability of individuals. The point is for each person to count, as they say, but—since in reality all individuals are different and attached to self-interests that put them in conflict—this is only possible if each person can imagine himself in the place of every other person; the *veil of ignorance*, which in Rawls's view characterizes the original position, achieves this state of affairs. Each person, ignorant of what he will be, can ensure his own interest only by ensuring the interest of each and all; this undifferentiated self-interest (an interest that is both mutually disinterested and, through the device of the veil of ignorance, individually disinterested!) is what we can call justice or, at any rate, allows an approximation of it. It is worth considering whether, in Rousseau, the complete alienation of each person (in the original contract) and the double universality of the law (in the republic) doesn't already achieve a comparable result or at least tend in that direction.[36] But before we venture too far into the realm of political thought, we must return to our subject: morality, or rather, justice not as a social requirement but as a virtue.

The two are obviously bound up with each other, and the connection, when unraveled, turns out to be the self. Here, too, justice remains linked both to legality and to equality: to be just, in the moral sense, is to refuse to place oneself above the law or above one's fellowman. In other words, justice is the virtue that leads each person to try to overcome the temptation to place himself above everything and consequently to sacrifice everything to his own desires and interests. The self is "unjust in itself," writes Pascal, "since it makes itself the center of everything; it is inconvenient to others since it would enslave them; for each Self is the enemy, and would like to be the tyrant of all others."[37] Justice is the opposite of this tyranny, and hence (like all other virtues) the opposite of, or the refusal to give in to, selfishness and self-centeredness. It is also the virtue closest to altruism—or to love, the only true altruism. Justice, however, is not love: love is too difficult, particularly love of fellowman (only those near and dear to us do we stand a chance of being able to love) or of people just as they are or as they appear to be (Dostoevsky, crueler than Emmanuel Lévinas, notes that many human beings would be easier to love if they had no faces).[38] Love is too demanding, too dangerous—in a word, it asks too much of us! In contrast to the immoderation of charity, in which the other person is everything, and the immoderation of selfishness, where the self is everything, justice resides in the moderation symbolized by its pair of scales—in other words, in equilibrium or proportion. To each his share, neither more nor less, as Aristotle puts it, and to myself—here is where justice, in spite of its moderation or because of it, remains an almost inaccessible goal for each of us—*as though I were any other person.*[39]

And indeed I am like any other person: this is the truth of justice, a truth that other people, whether just or unjust, will not fail to remind me of should I happen to forget it.

■

"Justice," writes Spinoza, "consists in the habitual rendering to every man his lawful due."[40] In other words, "he is called just who has a constant will to render to every man his own."[41] This is the traditional definition that we can find already in Simonides or Augustine.[42] But what *is* my own? Nothing, by nature, which is why justice presupposes a politically and juridically organized social life. "In the state of nature," writes Spinoza, "there is no one who by common consent is Master of anything, nor is there anything in Nature which can be said to be this man's and not that man's. Instead, all things belong to all. So in the state of nature, there cannot be conceived any will to give to each his own, or to take away from someone what is his. That is, in the state of nature nothing is done which can be called just or unjust."[43] For Spinoza, as for Hobbes, just and unjust are "extrinsic ideas,"[44] or "Qualities, that relate to men in Society, not in Solitude."[45] The "extrinsic" nature of justice does not prevent it from also being a virtue, but this virtue is possible only where law and property are established.[46] And how can they be established except through the consent, whether free or constrained, of individuals? Justice exists only to the extent that human beings want it, of a common accord, and bring it into being. There is no justice, therefore, in the state of nature, nor is there any natural justice. All justice is human; all justice is historical; there is no justice (in the legal sense of the term) without laws or (in the moral sense) without culture—there is no justice without society.

Is it possible, conversely, to imagine a society without justice? Hobbes or Spinoza would answer in the negative, and I tend to agree. What kind of society can there be without laws and a modicum of equality or proportion? Even thieves, it is often remarked, can't form a community, not even a criminal community, without practicing among themselves a certain kind of justice—distributive justice, to use a term that couldn't be more appropriate.[47] How could things not be the same on the scale of a whole society? Hume, however, offers a different answer, which should give us pause. It is based on five hypotheses, of unequal validity, it seems to me, but all suggestive and worthy of consideration.

Of course, Hume in no way challenges the utility or even the necessity of justice for any actually existing society. Indeed, in his theory of justice Hume shows himself to be a utilitarian (well in advance of utilitarianism). "The necessity of justice to the support of society is the sole foundation of that virtue," he writes.[48] Whether the necessity of justice is its *sole* foundation is open to debate; that justice is necessary, however, is beyond dispute. What society could survive without laws, juridical as well as moral? No actual human society, of this we can be sure. But our societies are so complex; how can we know that the necessity of justice is really, as Hume believes, its *sole* foundation? By trying, says Hume, to imagine possible societies in which justice would not be necessary: if justice subsists, at least as a demand, then necessity is not the sole explanation for its existence; if it disappears, we have a strong argument for concluding that, in a given society, necessity alone is sufficient to account for its appearance and constitute the basis of its value. With this in mind, Hume puts forward five successive suppositions, each of which would do away with the *necessity* of justice. If these hypotheses are admissible and the inference justified, one would have to conclude that public utility and necessity are indeed "the *sole* origin of justice" and "the *sole* basis for its merit."[49]

These, in short, are the five hypotheses: extreme abundance, universal love, extreme and generalized poverty or violence (like war or Hobbes's state of nature), a radical inequality of strength and power, and finally the complete separation of individuals, leading to their total isolation from one another.[50] Hume wants to show that in these five instances, justice, in ceasing to be necessary or useful, also ceases to have any value. Is this really the case?

The fifth supposition is undoubtedly the strongest. Since justice regulates our relations with others, in solitude it would be pointless, irrelevant, and meaningless. What value could it have, and what sense would there be in regarding as a virtue a predisposition that would never find any opportunity to be exercised? One can, of course, be just or unjust toward oneself, but only in reference to others, at least implicitly. Judging always involves comparisons of one sort or another, which is why all justice, even self-reflexive justice, is social. There is no justice without society, as we have seen, and hence Hume is right: there is no justice in absolute solitude.

One might perhaps also concede the force of the second hypothesis. If all of us were overflowing with feelings of friendship, generosity, and benevolence for our fellowman, we would no longer need laws or have to abide by the duty of treating others as equals: love would transcend a mere respect for rights, as happens in close-knit families, and would replace justice. I say "perhaps," for the question arises as to whether love would obviate the need for justice, as Hume believes, or whether it would make us just by making us more than just, as I am inclined to think. Aristotle says it beautifully: "When men are friends they have no need of justice, while when they are just they need friends as well."[51] This is to say not that we are unjust toward our friends but that among friends justice goes without saying, included and transcended as it is in the gentle demands of friendship. Whether love does away with justice or makes it a given, however, the fact remains that love, especially if it were universal and boundless, would hardly need to concern itself with obligations that it fulfills in passing, without dwelling on them and without even feeling their weight (since love feels no temptation to lay them aside). And so far as love and solitude are concerned, we can go along with Hume.

The three other hypotheses are far more problematic.

First, abundance. Let us imagine that all possible goods are offered, in an infinite number, to whoever desires them. In such a situation, Hume explains, "the cautious, jealous virtue of justice would never once have been dreamed of. For what purpose make a partition of goods, where everyone has already more than enough? Why give rise to property, where there cannot possibly be any injury? Why call this object *mine*, when upon the seizing of it by another, I need but stretch out my hand to possess myself of what is equally valuable? Justice, in that case, being totally useless, would be an idle ceremonial, and could never possibly have place in the catalogue of virtues."[52]

Yet can we be so sure? There would certainly be no reason to forbid theft or guarantee property. But is property the sole object of justice, as Hume seems to believe?[53] Is it the only human right that can be threatened, the only one that must be protected? In a society of abundance—I'm thinking here of the golden age of Roman and Greek myth or of Marx's communist utopia—it would still be possible to slander one's fellowman or convict an innocent person (there might be no motive for theft, but what about murder?), and these actions would be no less unjust than they are in our societies of limited resources or of "moderate scarcity" (in the words of Rawls, who concurs with Hume on this point).[54] If we agree that justice is the virtue that respects equal rights and gives each person his due, how can we believe that it applies only to property . . . or property owners? Is ownership my only right? Is owning property my only source of dignity? And have we paid our debt to justice merely because we have never stolen anything?

I have the same comment to make, or a similar one, as far as extreme poverty or generalized violence is concerned. "Suppose," writes Hume, "a society to fall into such want of all common necessaries, that the utmost frugality and industry cannot preserve the greater number from perishing, and the whole from extreme misery; it will readily, I believe, be admitted, that the strict laws of justice are suspended, in such a pressing emergency, and give place to the stronger motives of necessity and self-preservation."[55] Yet it seems to me that this contention is refuted by the experience of the Nazi and Stalin-era camps. Drawing on the testimony of survivors, Tzvetan Todorov shows that "even inside the camps, in that most extreme situation, it was still possible to choose between good and evil" and that though the just were "few in number" we must not forget them—lest we finish the work of their executioners.[56] In the camps, as elsewhere, individual differences included ethical differences.[57] Some prisoners stole their fellow prisoners' rations, informed on troublemakers, oppressed the weak, and courted the strong . . . injustice. Others organized resistance and solidarity, shared common resources, protected the weak—in short, despite the generalized horror, tried to reestablish a semblance of law and equity . . . justice. That it took on a different guise is not hard to imagine, but it didn't disappear, either as a demand, a value, or a possibility; in the camps, too, there were just persons and bastards, or rather (let us beware of gross generalizations and oversimplifications), it was possible to be *more or less just*, and some were more just, often heroically and at the expense of their lives. Sacha Petcherski, Milena Jesenska, Etty Hillesum, Rudi Massarek, Maxymilien Kolbe, Else Krug, Mala Zimetbaum, Hiasl Neumeier . . . Should we pretend they never existed? And how many others, though less heroic, were nevertheless more just than they might have been or than it was in their interest to be if their only concern was their own survival? By telling ourselves over and over again that all morality disappeared in the camps, we make good the efforts of those who indeed sought to make it disappear and we forget those who resisted this form of annihilation as they carried on their struggle day by day, minute by minute against the guards, against the other prisoners, and against themselves. How many of these heroes remain unknown? How many just souls have already been forgotten? Without Robert Antelme's account to bear witness, who would remember Jacques, the medical student?

> Were we to go and find an SS and show Jacques to him, to him we could say: "Have a look, you have turned him into this rotten, yellowish creature. You have succeeded in making him what you think he is by nature: waste, offal. Well, we can tell you this, which by all rights would flatten you for good if 'error' could kill: you have enabled him to make of himself the strongest, the most complete of men, the surest of his powers, of the resources of his conscience, of the scope of his actions." . . . With Jacques, you never won. You wanted him to steal. He didn't steal. You wanted him to kiss the kapos' asses in order to eat. He wouldn't do it. You wanted him to laugh in order to look good when a *Meister* was beating some guy up. He didn't laugh.[58]

Jacques, Robert Antelme writes a few paragraphs earlier, "is what in religion they call a saint."[59] Or what everywhere they call one of the just.

Why would it be different in war? Obviously war disrupts the conditions for the exercise of justice and makes it infinitely more difficult and dangerous to practice this virtue: there is no just war, if we mean a war in which the ordinary laws and rights of humanity continue to be complied with. This fact does not, however, prevent a particular soldier or officer from being more just or less just than another in a given situation, which proves sufficiently that war does not purely and simply do away with justice either as a need or as a value. In fact, Hume recognizes the persistence of justice in another passage; the reason, he suggests, is that wars still allow even enemies to maintain common interests or a shared utility.[60] But common interests and shared utility hardly exhaust the need for justice, since the demands of justice can run counter to them! Suppose, for example, that the torture or execution of prisoners were advantageous to both sides (nothing prevents us, at least hypothetically, from holding that opinion). Would it therefore be just? Common interests may indeed reinforce our demand for justice and be the strongest motive urging us to honor it. But if this were the whole of justice, there would no longer be justice or injustice. There would only be the useful and the harmful, self-interest and calculation. Intelligence would be sufficient to justice, or rather, intelligence would simply take the place of justice. But such is not the case, and that it is not is something just people, even when faced with the worst, remind us of.

As for Hume's remaining hypothesis, the fourth one, it is chilling and painful to see so great and engaging a genius write what he writes:

Were there a species of creatures intermingled with men, which, though rational, were possessed of such inferior strength, both of body and mind, that they were incapable of resistance, and could never, upon the highest provocation make us feel the effects of their resentment; the necessary consequence, I think, is that we should be bound by the laws of humanity to give gentle usage to these creatures, but should not, properly speaking, lie under any restraint of justice with regard to them, nor could they possess any right or property, exclusive of such arbitrary lords. Our intercourse with them could not be called society, which supposes a degree of equality; but absolute command on the one side, and servile obedience on the other. Whatever we covet, they must instantly resign: Our permission is the only tenure, by which they hold their possessions: Our compassion and kindness the only check, by which they curb our lawless will: And as no inconvenience ever results from the exercise of a power, so firmly established in nature, the restraints of justice and property, being totally *useless*, would never have a place in so unequal a confederacy."[61]

I quote this paragraph in full in order to avoid misrepresenting it. We can see that Hume's personal qualities, particularly his humanity, are not in question. But in substance, as well as philosophically, such thinking is unacceptable. I agree, of course, that the weak are owed gentleness and compassion; indeed, these virtues are given their proper place in Hume's treatise. But how can we accept the proposition that they can replace justice or absolve us from it? There can be no justice, writes Hume, or even any society, without "a degree of equality." Fine, but only if we understand that the equality in question is not an equality in fact or in power but *in rights*. And to have rights, it is enough to have consciousness and reason, even if only potentially, even without the strength to defend or attack. Were this not the case, children would have no rights, nor would the infirm, nor would anyone in the end (since no individual is so strong as to be able always to defend himself effectively).

Let us briefly imagine those rational and defenseless individuals Hume describes. For example, would I have the *right* (gentleness and compassion are not the issue here) to exploit them or steal from them as I please? "This is plainly the situation of men, with regard to animals," writes Hume.[62] But precisely not, since animals aren't "rational" in the usual meaning of the term.[63] Hume senses as much and therefore offers two other examples, and what examples! "The great superiority of civilized Europeans above barbarous Indians, tempted us to imagine ourselves on the same footing with regard to them [as with the animals], and made us throw off all restraints of justice, and even of humanity, in our treatment of them."[64] Indeed, but was this just? That the Indians were weaker than the Europeans was nonetheless undeniable and, as events made all too clear, justice toward them ceased to be socially necessary. Does this mean that no justice was owed to them? Can we accept that gentleness and compassion were all we owed them—or rather, *didn't owe* them (since, because of their weakness, they are supposed not to have any rights at all)? This proposition is hard to accept, it seems to me, unless we discard the very idea of justice.

Montaigne, so close to Hume on so many other points, is of a different mind altogether on this question. The American Indians' weakness, far from absolving us of justice, rather bids us be just (and not merely compassionate), and we are guilty, deeply guilty, of having overstepped our rights in violating theirs.[65] "Justice which allots to each one what belongs to him," as Montaigne says, does not authorize slaughter and plundering.[66] And of course, although justice was "created for the fellowship and community of men," we have no reason to believe that it was founded solely for their exclusive benefit.[67] The following hypothesis is not in Montaigne, but we can readily assume he would have gone along with it: let us imagine the discovery of a new America on another planet, inhabited by rational but gentle and defenseless beings; would we be prepared to play the conquistadors again, and slaughter and plunder anew? Possibly, if we were sufficiently motivated by self-interest and personal benefit. But it could never be considered just for us to do so.

The second example Hume offers, though apparently more jocular, is just as debatable. "In many nations," he continues, "the female sex are reduced to like slavery, and are rendered incapable of all property, in opposition to their lordly masters. But though the males, when united, have in all countries bodily force sufficient to maintain this severe tyranny, yet such are the insinuation, address, and charms of their fair companions, that women are commonly able to break the confederacy, and share with the other sex in all the rights and privileges of society."[68] I do not question the reality of this slavery, or the address, or the charms. But is this slavery just? And would it be just in a country where it isn't forbidden by law—where it might even be prescribed— to inflict it upon a woman who is completely devoid of insinuation, address, or charms? One could hardly think so, or that if laws did not exist protecting the rights of all women, an unattractive and clumsy woman would have claims only on our gentleness and compassion.

We find exactly the opposite idea in Lucretius (though he too, like Epicurus, is rather utilitarian when it comes to justice). The weakness of women and children in prehistoric times, he argues, far from excluding them from justice, is what makes justice necessary (*morally* necessary) and desirable:

Next, when they had got themselves huts and skins and fire, and woman mated with man moved into one [home, and the laws of wedlock] became known, and they saw offspring born of them, then first the human race began to grow soft.... Venus sapped their strength, and children easily broke their parents' proud spirit by coaxings. Then also neighbours began to join in friendship amongst themselves in their eagerness to do no hurt and suffer no violence, and asked protection for their children and womankind, signifying by voice and gesture with stammering tongue that it was right for all to pity the weak.[69]

Gentleness and compassion cannot substitute for justice, nor are they meant to take over where justice ends: they are more liable to be the origin of justice, which is why justice, whose primary consideration is the weak, can never under any circumstances exclude the weak from its sphere of influence or release us from the duty of honoring justice in our treatment of them. That justice is socially useful and even socially indispensable is obvious, but its scope is not entirely defined by this social usefulness and necessity. Justice that applies only to the strong would be unjust, which brings to light the essential aspect of justice as a virtue: the respect not for relative might but for equal rights, not for power but for the individual.

Pascal is often cynical, even more so than Hume. But when it comes down to the essentials, he makes no concessions: "Justice without might is helpless; might without justice is tyrannical."[70] One wins not for being the more just but for being the stronger; it is always this way. That may keep us from dreaming, but it doesn't prevent us from fighting. For justice? Why not, if we love it? Powerlessness is fatal; tyranny is odious. "We must then combine justice and might": this is the purpose of politics and what makes it necessary.[71]

It is desirable, as I have said, for law and justice to coincide, of course—a heavy responsibility for the sovereign power and particularly, in our democracies, for the legislative branch! Yet we can't unload all the responsibility on our legislators: they have power because we have given it to them—or haven't taken it away. No one obeys innocently. But the dream of an absolutely just law that need merely be applied is also misconceived. Aristotle shows that justice cannot be entirely contained in legislative measures that are inevitably general. This is why, at its best, justice is equity, which aims for or institutes an equality of rights in spite of de facto inequalities and often in spite of even those inequalities that can result from an overly mechanical or uncompromising application of the law. "The equitable is just," Aristotle explains, not legally just, "but a correction of legal justice" allowing the universality of the law to be adapted to the changing complexity of circumstances and to the irreducible singularity of concrete situations.[72] So it is that someone who is fair is therefore just, even eminently so, but in the sense that justice is not mere conformity to law but a value and a moral requirement. Equity, Aristotle also says, "is the sort of justice which goes beyond the written law."[73] For an equitable person, legality is less important than equality, or rather the equitable person is able to correct for the rigors and abstractions of the former by applying the far more flexible, complex demands of the latter (complex because the question is one of treating as equal individuals who are each different from one another). The demands of fairness can take him very far, often at the expense of his own interests: "The man who chooses and does such [equitable] acts, and is no stickler for his rights . . . but tends to take less than his share though he has the law on his side, is equitable"—this disposition, Aristotle says, is equity, which is not different from justice but a form of it.[74] Let us say that equity is applied justice, living justice, concrete justice—true justice.

There is no equity without mercy (to be equitable, says Aristotle, "is to forgive the human race").[75] Not that we should never punish; but for judgment to be equitable, anger and hatred must be overcome. There is also no equity without intelligence, prudence, courage, fidelity, generosity, tolerance—I could go on. Here is where equity becomes one and the same as justice in its largest sense: the complete and comprehensive virtue that contains and presupposes all the others, the one Aristotle suggests we consider "the greatest of virtues," adding, delightfully, that "'*neither evening nor morning star*' is so wonderful."[76]

What is a just person? Someone who places his strength in the service of both law and rights and, decreeing for himself the equality of all men, regardless of the countless inequalities in what they are or can do, thereby institutes an order that doesn't exist but without which no order could ever satisfy us. The world resists that order and so does man. We must therefore resist them, the world and man, and begin by resisting the injustice that each of us carries within himself, which is the self. This is why the fight for justice is an unending fight. That Kingdom is barred to us, or rather we inhabit it only to the extent that we strive to reach it. Fortunate are those who hunger for justice, for they will never be sated!

7

GENEROSITY

Generosity is the virtue of giving. But unlike justice, which requires
that we give "to every man his own," to use Spinoza's definition, generosity entails giving the other person what is not his but yours, which
he lacks. Of course, an act of generosity can also be an act of justice
(when one gives someone something that is owed him in some sense
but that he hasn't yet been granted and may not even be entitled to by
law: for example, when one gives food to someone who is hungry). The
fact that it need not be may account for why we sometimes feel justice
to be a more important, more urgent, and more necessary virtue than
generosity, which, by comparison, can seem something of a luxury, a
supplemental quality of the spirit. "One must be just before one can be
generous," writes Chamfort, "as one must have shirts before one can
have lace."[1] No doubt. But as these two virtues are of different registers, I am not sure the problem always, or even often, presents itself in
those terms. Certainly, both justice and generosity concern our relations with others (at least, for the most part: we sometimes need to be

just or generous toward ourselves), but generosity is more subjective, more individual, more affective, and more spontaneous, while justice, even in its specific applications, is always somewhat more objective, more universal, more intellectual, and more considered. Generosity seems to owe more to the heart or temperament, justice to the mind or reason. A declaration of human rights makes sense, whereas a declaration of generosity sounds fairly nonsensical: generosity does not mean acting in accordance with this or that document or law; it means doing more than what the law requires—at least what the laws of man require—and acting in conformity with the sole requirements of love, morality, or solidarity.

The word *solidarity* gives me pause. I had initially thought to include solidarity as one of the virtues I would discuss in this treatise, and it may not be irrelevant to explain why, when I had to choose (I wanted this to be a *small* treatise), I opted not to include solidarity among them and why I felt that justice and generosity represent better choices.

What is solidarity? It is first a fact, then a duty; a state of mind or a feeling (that we may or may not feel) and only later a virtue, or rather a value. The etymology of the word speaks to the first sense, that of solidarity as fact: to be in solidarity is to be part of a group that is *in solido*, in Latin, "for the whole."[2] Hence, in the French legal code, debtors are said to be *solidaire* when they are jointly responsible for the debt—that is, when each one is individually answerable for the entirety of a sum that they have borrowed collectively. That meaning is not unconnected to *solidity*, from which the word derives: a solid body is one in which all the parts hold together (in which the molecules, one could say, have greater *solidarity* than in liquid or gaseous states); everything that happens to one part also happens to the others or has an effect on them. In short, solidarity is first of all the fact of cohesion, interdependence, a community of interests or a collective destiny. To be in solidarity, in this sense, means to be part of the same whole and consequently to share—whether one likes it or not, whether one knows it or not—a common history. An objective solidarity, one might say: the difference between a pebble and a little pile of sand, between a society and a multitude.

Solidarity as state of mind—subjective solidarity—is simply the feeling or affirmation of this interdependence. "Workers and students, one struggle!" we chanted in May 1968; another slogan from those days: "We are all German Jews." In other words, one group's victory is also the other's, or an action taken against any one of us, different from us though he or she may be—the action in this instance being the decision of the French government to revoke the student visa of Rudi Dutschke, a Jew of German nationality—is an attack against us all. Naturally I am all in favor of such noble feelings. But are they virtues? And if there is virtue here, is it solidarity? In May 1968, there was just as much solidarity between employers and police as there was between workers and students (and perhaps even more), and while that fact is damning of neither side, it does tend to complicate the picture, making any moral claim for solidarity in this instance fairly dubious. Virtues are rarely so nicely shared. Moreover, if solidarity is both community of interests (objective solidarity) and a recognition of these shared interests (subjective solidarity), it has value morally only to the extent that the interests also do, and it is rare that they do to any great extent. One can't have it both ways: either the community is a genuine community that actually exists, such that in defending others, I am merely defending myself (there is certainly nothing blameworthy here, but such actions are too self-interested to be morally motivated), or else the community is illusory, abstract, or ideal, so that my fighting for others is no longer a question of solidarity (since my personal interests aren't at stake) but one of justice or generosity (justice if others are being oppressed, wronged, or despoiled; generosity if they aren't but are simply weak or unhappy). In other words, solidarity is either too selfish or too illusory to be a virtue. It is either self-interest well understood or generosity misconstrued. That solidarity is not a virtue does not mean it has no moral value; it does have value, but only insofar as it avoids the pettiness of self, shortsighted or narrow-minded egoism—in other words, ethical solipsism. Solidarity is more the absence of a fault than a positive quality. Notice how, despite the overuse of the word by politicians, the language resists all attempts to make solidarity a moral or absolute value. Witness in English the absence of an adjectival form. In French, the adjective *solidaire* does exist, but whereas I can describe someone as just, generous, courageous, tolerant, sincere, gentle, and so forth, and everyone will understand that I am enumerating virtues that make for a morally respectable, indeed admirable, person, if I add to my description and say of this person, *"Il est solidaire,"* people will be puzzled at the vagueness of the statement and probably ask, *"De qui?"*—with whom?

Solidarity is an overused, indeed misused, word, an example of our unwillingness to call things by their name. Lexicographers have noted that "in the sociopolitical vocabulary, *solidarity* has become a cautious substitute for *equality*" and, I might add, for *justice* and *generosity*.[3] But why this caution, which only amounts to timidity and bad faith? Do we believe that eliminating those words will make it more acceptable to lack the virtues they designate? Do we imagine that a community of interests can take their place? What sad times, when we do away with big words in order not to be reminded of how small we have become!

This being a treatise on virtues and not a dictionary of *idées reçues*, I set solidarity aside, leaving it in its own world, the world of interests, corporatisms, and pressure groups, whether convergent or competing, global or parochial, legitimate or spurious. I do not in any way subscribe to the belief that we are all "in it together," that is, interdependent. In what way does your death make me less alive? How does your poverty make me less wealthy? Not only does the poverty of the Third World not diminish the prosperity of the West, Western prosperity depends, directly or indirectly, on Third World poverty, which the West in some cases merely takes advantage of and in others actually causes. To be sure, we all inhabit the same earth and thus are ecologically interdependent; that does not mean that we are not also, and more important, in economic competition. Let us not delude ourselves. Africa and Latin America do not need our solidarity; they need justice and generosity. And in our own countries, should we happen to think that the employed might have solidarity with the unemployed, we need only look at what trade unions actually do: we will see that interests are protected only if they are *common* interests and that the problem of unemployment will never be solved or even ameliorated to any significant degree by objective solidarity alone (or, therefore, by subjective solidarity, which differs from generosity only insofar as it involves objective solidarity). Again, the issue is not solidarity (the employed and unemployed may have divergent, indeed conflicting, interests) but justice and generosity—at least if we are considering the problem in its moral or ethical aspects. It would be an understatement to say that these aspects aren't everything: neither politics nor economics can be reduced to ethics and morality, or even submit to them entirely. But to say that they aren't everything doesn't mean they are nothing. Morality counts only as much as we want it to. This is why it counts so little and yet counts.

But let us return to the subject of generosity. Generosity can no doubt be motivated, incited, or reinforced by solidarity. But solidarity can truly be generous only if it goes beyond self-interest, even acknowledged self-interest, mutual self-interest—in other words, only if it goes beyond solidarity. For instance, if it were in my interest to help children in the Third World, I would not need to be generous in order to do so. I would merely need to be lucid and prudent. "Fight hunger to preserve the peace," was the slogan of a Catholic movement in the 1960s, and, generous-spirited youth that we were, we found the slogan shocking, a sordid bargaining. Were we wrong? I don't know. The fact is, if it were in our interest to buy peace with bread, we would do so, unless we were idiots: we would not need to be generous, we would just do it. The fact that we don't do so, or do so in such small measure, proves that we don't really regard such actions as being in our interest and are hypocrites in pretending otherwise; it's not that we have bad eyesight or lack lucidity. We have bad hearts, for our hearts are selfish; it's generosity, much more than lucidity, that we lack.

I don't mean to reduce everything to a question of money, since one can be generous in other ways. Still, money does have the merit of being quantifiable; indeed it serves that very purpose. And so it makes it possible for me to ask questions like the following one: what percentage of your income do you devote to helping those who are poorer or less fortunate than you? Don't count taxes, since they are mandatory, and leave out what you give to family and very close friends, since love alone, much more than generosity, accounts for what we do for them (which at the same time we do for ourselves, their happiness being our happiness). Obviously I am simplifying, in fact, oversimplifying. Take the matter of taxes, for example. If you are middle class or well-to-do, it can be an act of generosity on your part to vote for a political party that has announced its determination to raise taxes. But there are few opportunities to express one's generosity in this way: political parties, it seems, only know how to vaunt their efforts to reduce taxes, which shows what they think of our generosity! Call me pessimistic, but isn't it clear that politicians, whatever they may say, are even more so, and for very sound reasons? Likewise with regard to giving to family or intimate friends: it may be oversimplifying to deny the possibility or the necessity of generosity where our loved ones are concerned. For while it is true that my children's happiness makes me happy, indeed is essential to my happiness, nevertheless there are times when their desires conflict with mine, just as their games may be at odds with my work, their enthusiasm with my fatigue. Occasions like these are just so many opportunities for demonstrating or failing to demonstrate generosity! But this is not what I intended to discuss here. I wanted to raise the issue of money in the plainest terms and, in order to do so, I think it is useful to take a broad look at the family budget. And so I come back to my question: what percentage of your household income goes to expenditures that qualify as acts of generosity, in other words, that contribute to the happiness of persons other than yourself or those close to you? Let each of us answer for himself. My guess is that nearly all of us contribute less than 10 percent and, more often, less than 1 percent. Again, I understand that money isn't everything. But why would we be more generous in nonfinancial or nonquantifiable areas? Why would our hearts be more open than our wallets? The opposite is more likely. And can we really know whether the little we do give comes from generosity and or whether it merely represents the small price we pay for our moral comfort, our pathetic good conscience? In short, I suspect generosity is so great and vaunted a virtue simply because we are so lacking in it, because our selfishness always wins out, because generosity is usually conspicuous only by its absence. "How hollow and full of filth is the heart of man!" says Pascal.[4] That is because it is almost always filled only with self.

But do I have to draw a line between love and generosity, and even cast them as opposites? "Certainly, generosity might not involve love," Jankélévitch admits, "but love is almost inevitably generous, at least toward the loved one and for the time that love lasts."[5] Though the two are not the same, love and generosity, "at its most exalted," are hard to separate one from the other: "For though we can give without loving, it is almost impossible to love without giving."[6] True. But is it love, then, or generosity? It depends on how you define generosity and I'm not going to quibble over words. Yet the idea that I might feel generous toward my children—that I have an obligation to be generous toward them—has never occurred to me. We love our children too much, we worry about them too much: it would be deluding ourselves to see virtue here. Whatever we do for them we do for ourselves as well. Why would we need virtue? Love is sufficient, and what love! Why do I love my own children so much and other people's children so little? Because my children are *mine*, and in loving them I love myself . . . Is this generosity? Hardly. It is merely expansive, transitive, familial egoism. As for the other kind of love, the kind that is free from the self, the love of saints or the blessed, I am not certain that generosity can tell us much about it or that it can tell us much about generosity. Isn't what is true of justice also true of generosity? Doesn't love go beyond both of them, rather than being subordinate to either? Is giving, when we love, a sign of generosity or of love? Even lovers know the difference. A kept woman might speak of the generosity of her clients or protectors. But would a woman who is loved? Or a woman who loves? As for saints, was Christ generous? Is that the word we would use? I very much doubt it, and in fact I have noted that this virtue is hardly mentioned in the Christian tradition, for example, in Augustine or Aquinas; nor, I might add, do we often encounter the word in the Greek or Roman authors. Might it simply be a question of vocabulary? The word *generositas* exists in Latin but usually to refer to the excellence of a lineage (*gens*) or of a temperament. Occasionally, however, as in Cicero, it is used as the simpler translation of the Greek word *megalopsuchia* (greatness of spirit) in preference to the more imposing *magnanimitas*, which is the erudite calque. The same holds true for French: *magnanimité* is rarely heard outside the classroom, and it is *générosité* that best conveys what there might be in greatness that can legitimately be called moral, and therefore in what way it is a virtue. That is how the term *générosité* is used by Corneille and also, as we shall see, by Descartes. In contemporary usage, however, greatness or grandeur counts for less in generosity than does giving, or is generous only because of its ease in giving. Generosity, then, appears to be at the crossroads of two Greek virtues, *magnanimity* and *liberality;* the magnanimous person is neither vain nor low, the liberal person is neither miserly nor prodigal, and a person combining both qualities is always generous.[7]

But this is still not love, nor is it a substitute for love.

Generosity, as I said, is the virtue of giving—giving money (whereby it touches on liberality) or giving of oneself (whereby it touches on magnanimity or even sacrifice). But we can give only what we possess and only on condition of not being possessed by what we own. In this respect generosity is indissociable from a form of freedom or self-possession that for Descartes is its defining attribute. For Descartes, generosity is a passion and, at the same time, a virtue. It is worth quoting in full the definition he gives of it in his famous article in the *Traité des passions:*

> Thus I believe that true generosity, which causes a person's self-esteem to be as great as it may legitimately be, has only two components. The first consists in his knowing that nothing truly belongs to him but this freedom to dispose his volitions, and that he ought to be praised or blamed for no other reason than his using this freedom well or badly. The second consists in his feeling within himself a firm and constant resolution to use it well—that is, never to lack the will to undertake and carry out whatever he judges to be best. To do that is to pursue virtue in a perfect manner.[8]

The writing is labored, but the meaning is clear. Generosity is both the awareness of one's own freedom (or of oneself as free and responsible) and the firm resolution to make good use of that freedom. Consciousness and confidence, therefore: consciousness of being free and confidence in making use of this freedom. This is why generosity is productive of self-esteem, why self-esteem is its consequence and not its source (and here we find the distinction between Cartesian generosity and Aristotelian magnanimity). The principle of generosity, its source, is the will and nothing more: being generous means knowing one is free to act well and willing this freedom for oneself. The generous man is not a prisoner of his emotions or of himself; on the contrary, he is master of himself and for this reason neither makes nor seeks excuses. For him, will suffices. Virtue suffices. And here, as Descartes goes on to explain, is where generosity in this particular sense and the ordinary meaning of the term come together:

> Those who are generous in this way are naturally led to do great deeds, and at the same time not to undertake anything of which they do not feel themselves capable. And because they esteem nothing more highly than doing good to others and disregarding

their own self-interest, they are always perfectly courteous, gracious and obliging to everyone. Moreover they have complete command over their passions. In particular, they have mastery over their desires, and over jealousy and envy. . . .[9]

Generosity, then, is the opposite of selfishness, just as magnanimity is the opposite of pettiness. The two virtues are one, and so are the two faults.[10] What could be less giving than the self? What could be more squalid than selfishness? To be generous is to be free of self, of one's petty little deeds and possessions, one's little resentments and jealousies. Descartes sees in generosity not only the source of all virtue but also "the supreme good, for each individual," which consists, he says, "in a firm will to do well and the contentment which this produces."[11] A generous happiness that, as he further points out, reconciles "the two most opposed and most famous opinions of the Ancients"—that of the Epicureans (who thought the supreme good was pleasure) and that of the Stoics (who thought it was virtue).[12] At last, thanks to generosity, garden and stoa come together. What more pleasant virtue, what more virtuous pleasure, than to enjoy one's own excellent will. And here we also find magnanimity or greatness of spirit; to be generous is to be free, the only true grandeur.

As for knowing what this freedom means in practical terms, that is another question, more metaphysical than moral, which does not necessarily have any bearing on generosity. How many misers have believed in free will? How many heroes have not? To be generous is to be able to will, explains Descartes, and hence to give, when so many others seem to know only how to desire, to demand, to take. Free will? Undoubtedly, since it wills what it wants to! As for knowing whether the will could have wanted something else and even whether such a question means anything (how can one want something other than what one wants?), that is a problem I have discussed elsewhere, and it really lies outside the scope of a treatise on the virtues.[13] Whether determined or not, whether necessary or contingent (whether free in Epictetus's sense or in Descartes's sense), the will nonetheless finds itself confronted with the pettiness of the self and, aside from grace or love, it alone can triumph over them. Generosity is this triumph, when will is its cause.

One might prefer, of course, for love to suffice. But if it could, would we need to be generous? Love is not in our power and never can be. Who chooses to love? What power does the will have over a feeling? Love doesn't come on command, it can't be ordered up.[14] Generosity is different: if we want to be generous, we can be. Love doesn't depend on us, that is its great mystery and why it lies outside the realm of virtue; love is a grace, indeed the only one. Generosity does depend on us, however, which is why it is a virtue and distinct from love even in the act of giving, in which it so resembles love.

Does being generous mean giving without loving? Yes, if it's true that love gives without needing to be generous! What mother feels generous for feeding her children? What father feels generous for showering his children with gifts? Parents are more likely to feel selfish for doing so much for their own children (out of love? Yes, but love doesn't excuse everything) and so little for other people's children, even when the latter are infinitely more unfortunate and destitute. Giving, when one loves, is within anyone's grasp. It isn't a virtue but a radiant grace, in other words, a surfeit of life or joy, a welcome excess, simplicity itself. Is it really giving, since nothing is lost? The communality of love makes common possession of all things; where is the generosity in it? True friends, Montaigne notes, "cannot lend or give anything to each other," "everything being in fact common as between them," just as laws "forbid gifts between husband and wife, meaning by that to imply that everything should belong to each of them, and that they have nothing to divide and part between them."[15] How could they demonstrate their generosity toward each other? I know the laws have changed and am glad of it, since couples so often outlast love, and individuals couples. But has love also changed so much, and friendship too, that even in love, even among friends, we still need to be generous?

"The union of two such friends being truly perfect," writes Montaigne, "it causes them to lose the sense of such duties, and to detest and banish as between themselves those words implying separation and difference—benefit, obligation, gratitude, entreaty, thanks, and their like."[16] Who can't see that generosity isn't another one of those words, a word that true friendship has no need of? What could I give my friend, since everything that is mine is his? One might object, rightly, that these considerations apply only to perfect friendships, like the ones Montaigne must have had, and that such friendships are so very rare. But that objection simply proves my basic point: we need to be generous only when we do not love enough, which is why we almost always need to be generous.

In its own way, generosity, like most other virtues, obeys the biblical commandment. But can we really love our neighbor as ourselves? If we could, what would be the point of generosity? And what good is it to make love a commandment if we are incapable of following it? Only actions can be commanded; therefore the commandment requires not that we love but that we act *as though* we loved—that we do unto our neighbor as we would unto our loved ones, and unto strangers as we would unto ourselves.[17] The commandment prescribes not feelings or emotions, which are not transferable, but actions, which are. For instance, if you loved that stranger who is suffering and hungry, would you stand there as you're doing and not come to his aid? Clearly he is in need: if you loved him, would you turn down his plea for help? If you loved him *as yourself*, what would you do? The answer, in all its maddening and ruthless simplicity, is the moral one: you would do what virtue demands—or would demand. Love has no need for generosity, but unfortunately only love can dispense with generosity and still be unselfish and virtuous.

We love love and do not know how to love; morality is born both of this love and of this inability to love, in what Spinoza might call an imitation of affections, but one in which each of us imitates primarily those affections he does not have.[18] Just as politeness is a semblance of virtue (to be polite is to behave as though one were virtuous), so all virtue—in any case, all moral virtue—is no doubt a semblance of love; to be virtuous is to act as though one loved. Not being virtuous, we make a pretense of virtue; this is called politeness. Not knowing how to love, we act as though we did; this is called morality. And children imitate their parents, who imitate theirs. All the world's a stage, and living means acting. But the roles and the players in this human comedy are not all equally good. Shakespearean wisdom: morality might well be a question of performance, but there is no good play that is not in some sense a morality play. Is anything more serious or more real than laughing or crying? We pretend, but it's not a game: the rules we follow are not there for our amusement; they make us what we are, for better or for worse. We each play a role, you might say, but that role is our own. And in truth, it is more than a role, it is our life, our history. There's nothing arbitrary or accidental in all this. We come to be who we are through our bodies, by way of desire; through our childhoods, by way of love and law. For desire primarily wishes to take, and love primarily to consume, devour, and possess. But the law forbids it, and so does the love that gives and protects. Freud's thinking may not be as remote as he thought from certain gospel truths. Suckling at our mother's breast, we tasted not only milk but love, just enough love to know that it was the only thing that could ever satisfy us and that we will miss it forever. Whence the virtues, these feeble approximations of love, which are the homage we pay to love when it is not there, the sign that it is still a valid demand, that it continues to reign where it no longer rules—that it remains a value and thus dictates even in its absence!

We miss love, as I said, and very often the lack of love is our most reliable experience of it.

We have made this lack a strength, or rather several strengths, and they are called virtues.

This is especially true of generosity. It becomes a requirement where love is lacking. Not completely lacking, however, since at least we love love (*"Nondum amabam et amare amabam,"* in Augustine's famous phrase—"I was not in love as yet, yet I loved to love": we are still at that point), sufficiently in any case for love to remain valid as a model or commandment whenever the feeling of love fails to triumph or blossom.[19] Since we wouldn't hesitate to give if we did love, generosity invites us to give in the absence of love to the very people we do not love and to give them more the more they need it or the better equipped we are to help them. Indeed, when love cannot guide us because we do not feel it, let us be guided by urgency and proximity. Some call this charity, mistakenly (since true charity is love and false charity condescension or pity). It should be called generosity, because it depends on us, solely on us, because in this sense it is free, because it is—in opposition to the bondage of instincts, possessions, and fears—freedom itself, in spirit and deed.

Love would be better, of course, which is why morality isn't everything or even the essential thing. But generosity is still better than selfishness and morality better than apathy.

■

Not that generosity is the opposite of selfishness, if we take this to mean that generosity is altogether free of self-interest. How could it be? Why should it have to be? "Since reason demands nothing contrary to Nature," says Spinoza, "it demands that everyone love himself, seek his own advantage, what is really useful to him, want what will really lead a man to greater perfection, and absolutely, that everyone should strive to preserve his own being as far as he can."[20] We remain within the confines of the pleasure principle since we remain within the confines of reality. But this doesn't mean that some pleasures aren't better than others. What makes them so? Joy and love.[21] What then is generosity? Spinoza answers: "By *nobility* [*generositas*] I understand *the desire by which each one strives, solely from the dictate of reason, to aid other men and join them to him in friendship*."[22] In this, *generositas* is, along with tenacity (*animositas*) or courage, one of the two instances of strength of character: "Those actions, therefore, which aim only at the agent's advantage, I relate to tenacity, and those which aim at another's advantage, I relate to nobility."[23] Note that in both cases, there is advantage for the agent himself. We remain within the confines of the self or, if we manage to transcend the self, we do so only on condition of accepting its first requirement, which is self-preservation to the extent possible—in other words, "to act, and to live."[24] That we cannot always do so, that sometimes we must die, that inevitably we must die, since the universe is stronger than we are—this is something that we all know and that Spinoza doesn't deny. But still we can choose. We can choose to die rather than betray, to die rather than disown, to die rather than desert, and in doing so we continue to assert our being, to use our vital power, our *conatus*, in a fight against death and ignominy. And as long as we live, we are victorious; as long as we fight and hold out, our struggle continues to serve. Spinoza reminds us again and again that virtue is an affirmation of self and seeks its own advantage.[25] But he also tells us that Christ, even on the cross, best exemplifies virtue so conceived.[26] Personal advantage is not about being more comfortable or living longer; it is about living as freely as we can, as authentically as we can. To live forever is not the point, since we cannot; the point is to live well. And how can we without courage or generosity?

Note that Spinoza defines generosity as a desire, not as a joy, which suffices to distinguish it from love or, as Spinoza also points out, from charity. That joy might be derived in addition, indeed that joy might even be an express aim, is rather clear, since friendship (which generosity tends to promote) is nothing other than shared joy. But that's just it: joy or love *can arise from* generosity, but they cannot be reduced to it and are not to be confused with it. To seek to benefit someone we love, we don't need the "dictates of reason" or, therefore, generosity either; love is enough, joy is enough![27] But when love is not there, when joy is not there or is not strong enough (and when we lack even the compassion that would make us benevolent),[28] reason remains and teaches us—since reason has no ego and therefore frees us of egoism—that to man "there is nothing more useful than man,"[29] that "hate can never be good,"[30] and finally that "men who are governed by reason . . . want nothing for themselves which they do not desire for other men."[31] And here is where the agent's advantage coincides with the advantage of others, and where desire becomes the desire to be generous. And so we must fight hate, anger, contempt, or envy—which are not only the source of sadness but sadness itself—with love, when it is present, or with generosity when it is not.[32] It may be that, in making the distinction between love and generosity, I am taking liberties with Spinoza's text, which is equivocal.[33] But not with its spirit, which is clear: "hate must be conquered with love," sadness with joy, and the function of generosity—as a desire and a virtue—is to strive toward love.[34] Generosity is the desire for love, the desire for joy and sharing, and it is joy itself since the generous person rejoices in this desire and, if nothing else, loves this love of love within himself. Let us recall Spinoza's powerful definition: "Love is a joy, accompanied by the idea of an external cause."[35] Consequently, to love love is to rejoice at the thought that love exists or will exist;[36] it is also a way of endeavoring to make love happen[37] and this endeavor is generosity itself: I would be inclined to say that being generous is striving to love and acting accordingly. Hence generosity is the opposite of hate (as well as of contempt, envy, anger, and probably also indifference), just as courage is the opposite of fear, or, more generally, strength of character the opposite of impotence and freedom the opposite of bondage.[38] Together these qualities still do not amount to salvation, since they can confer on us neither blessedness nor eternity; but nevertheless for us these virtues are "of the first importance."[39] They are part of what Spinoza calls "a correct principle of living," "sure maxims," or "the rule of reason,"[40] or, simply, "morality."[41] For it is not true that we must live beyond good and evil; we cannot.[42] Nor can we make do with the sad morality of the censorious or the unhappy.[43] The morality that Spinoza describes is a morality of generosity, which leads to an ethics of love.[44] "Act well and rejoice," Spinoza writes; love is the goal, generosity the road to it.[45]

According to Hume, if generosity were absolute and universal, we would have no need of justice; and as we have seen, such a state of affairs is indeed conceivable in the abstract.[46] On the other hand, it is clear that justice, even when it is accomplished, can't exempt us from generosity, which, though less necessary to society than justice, is more precious, it seems to me, to our humanity.

What good are these comparisons, you might ask, since we have so very little aptitude for either the one or the other? The fact is, this *very little*, in spite of everything, isn't trivial; it makes us sensitive to this minuteness and eager at times to increase it. Is there any virtue that isn't initially, if only in some small way, a desire for virtue?

As to whether generosity is a feeling that is implanted in our nature, as Hume conceives it, or develops out of desire and self-love (especially through imitation of the affects and the sublimation of drives), as Spinoza or Freud understand it, we can let the anthropologists decide; from the moral standpoint, the question is irrelevant.[47] The value of the virtues does not depend on their origin, nor can they be invalidated on the basis of their origin. We are mistaken if we think otherwise. I am personally convinced that they all stem from our animal nature and hence from what is—or seems—lowest in us (clearly, the matter and void out of which everything arises, including our nature, knows neither high nor low). But this is also to say that the virtues elevate us, which is why the opposite of any virtue is, no doubt, a form of baseness.

Generosity elevates us *toward others*, as it were, and toward ourselves as beings freed from the pettiness that is the self. He who is not at all generous, our language warns us, is low, cowardly, petty, vile, stingy, greedy, egotistical, squalid. Which we all are, but not always and never completely; generosity is what sets us apart—or, sometimes, frees us—from these impulses.

I conclude by observing that generosity, like all the other virtues, is multiple both in its content and in the names that we call it or that serve to describe it. Combined with courage, it turns out to be heroism. Joined by justice, it becomes equity. Coupled with compassion, it becomes benevolence. In league with mercy, it becomes leniency. But its most beautiful name is its secret, an open secret that everyone knows: accompanied by gentleness, it is called kindness.

8

COMPASSION

Compassion gets bad press: we don't like to be the object of compassion, and we don't particularly like to feel compassion either. This sets it quite apart from generosity, for example. To have compassion means *to suffer with*, and suffering is bad. How could compassion be good?

Yet, here again, language usage warns us not to reject compassion out of hand. Among the antonyms the dictionary gives for compassion are ruthlessness, cruelty, coldness, indifference, hard-heartedness, insensitivity. They make compassion attractive, at least by contrast. And its near synonym, or etymological doublet, is sympathy, which means in Greek exactly what *compassion* means in Latin, a fact worthy of note, especially in light of their *non*synonymy in modern usage, particularly in the Romance languages. In these languages, the word for sympathy—*sympathie* in French, *simpatia* in Spanish—in addition to conveying the same meaning as its English cognate and Greek origin, translates, indeed usually more appropriately translates, as *fellow feeling,* and the adjectival form—*sympathique, simpatico*—used in reference to someone or something that elicits that feeling, occurs about as frequently and conveys much the same idea as the word *nice* does in English when used to describe a likable person or an agreeable thing. Why, then, in a century in which this quality figures so ubiquitously and so positively, is this other quality, compassion, viewed so negatively? No doubt because we prefer feelings to virtues. But what does it mean for compassion if it belongs, as I will try to demonstrate, to both orders, the affective and the ethical? Doesn't part of its weakness and most of its strength reside in this ambiguity?

But first a word about sympathy as it is used in the Romance languages. Could there be a more appealing quality? Or a more pleasant feeling? The combination of meanings is itself unique and gives the concept something of its charm: sympathy is both a quality (in someone who arouses fellow feeling) and that feeling itself. And since, almost by definition, the quality and the feeling are responsive to each other, sympathy creates between two individuals a felicitous encounter, often from both sides. It is a smile from life or a gift of chance. Everyone knows, however, that sympathy—that is, likability, niceness—proves nothing, but what does that prove? Can a bastard be likable? Of course, initially, and even on second meeting. But as we have seen, bastards can also be polite, faithful, prudent, temperate, courageous... And sometimes generous and on occasion just. This possibility permits one to make the following distinction, between the complete virtues (as Aristotle would say), such as justice and generosity, by which we can know the value of an individual (the bastard can be just or generous only now and again, and at those times he ceases to be a bastard), and the partial virtues, those that, taken in isolation, are compatible with most sorts of vice and ignominy. Thus a bastard can always be loyal and courageous; but if he were always just and generous, he would no longer be a bastard. The possibility, which is not purely hypothetical, of the likable, sympathetic bastard proves simply that sympathy isn't a complete virtue. It remains to be seen whether it is a virtue at all.

What is sympathy? It is an emotional participation in the feelings of others (to be in sympathy with another person is to feel along with, or in the same way, or through him); it is also the pleasure and appeal that result from these feelings. Hence, as Max Scheler points out, sympathy has only as much value as these feelings may have; at any rate, sympathy cannot change their value. "It is certainly *not* moral to sympathize with someone's pleasure in evil . . . or with his hatred, malice or spite."[1] This is why sympathy, in and of itself, can never be a virtue: "mere fellow-feeling is, as such, quite regardless of the value of its objects. . . . Mere fellow-feeling, in all its possible forms, is in principle *blind to value*."[2] To sympathize is to feel or experience along with someone. It is certainly true that sumpathy can open the way to morality, since to share in another's feelings is already to leave behind the prison of the self, at least partially. But *what* we are sympathizing *with* still needs to be taken into account. To participate in another person's hatred is to be full of hate. To participate in another person's cruelty is to be cruel. Hence someone who sympathizes with a torturer, sharing his sadistic enjoyment, experiencing the excitement he experiences, also shares his guilt or at least his malignity. Sympathy in horror is a horrible sympathy!

One can see immediately that with compassion it is entirely different. Yet compassion is a form of sympathy; it is sympathy in pain or sadness—in other words, participation in the suffering of others.[3] But that's just the point: although the value of suffering is not always the same and suffering can even be low and vicious (as the suffering of an envious person at the happiness of others can be), it is still suffering, and all suffering deserves compassion. Note the asymmetry: pleasure is always a good but not always a moral good—far from it; usually it is morally neutral. Sometimes pleasure isn't even morally tolerable— think of the torturer's pleasure. Sympathy for pleasure thus has no more value than the pleasure in question, or if it can sometimes have greater value (when we participate in someone's morally neutral pleasure, our pleasure can be positively commendable, for it is the opposite of envy) it does so only to the extent that the pleasure is not morally perverse, in other words, not inspired by hatred or cruelty. Suffering, on the other hand, is always an evil, and always a moral evil. Which is not to say that suffering is always morally reprehensible (suffering is often innocent, and can even be virtuous or heroic). But suffering is a moral evil in that it is always morally regrettable; compassion is this regret, or rather this regret is compassion in its minimal form.

"Can we really suppose that a fellow-feeling such as that of rejoicing with A's pleasure at B's misfortune is morally valuable?" asks Max Scheler.[4] Of course not! But participating in B's suffering is!

Yet is participating in B's suffering still morally valuable if B's suffering is morally reprehensible, for instance, if it is caused by C's happiness? Compassion responds in the affirmative, and this is what makes it so merciful. Sharing in the suffering of another does not mean that one approves of him or shares whatever good or bad reasons he has for suffering; it means that one refuses to regard any suffering as a matter of indifference or any living being as a thing. This is why compassion is universal in its principle and the more moral for not being concerned with the morality of its objects (and it is in this unconcern that compassion leads to mercy). Here again, we have the same asymmetry between pleasure and suffering: to sympathize with the torturer's pleasure, with his malevolent joy, is to share in his guilt. But to have compassion for his suffering or his madness, for all that hatred, sadness, and wretchedness, is to be innocent of the evil that consumes him and to refuse, at the very least, to add hatred to hatred. Christ's compassion for his executioners, Buddha's for the wicked. Are these examples somehow oppressive? If so, it's not just that they are so lofty but that we perceive how high above us they stand. Compassion is the opposite of cruelty, which rejoices in the suffering of others, and of egoism, which is indifferent to that suffering. Surely, both are defects, just as compassion is assuredly a quality. But is it a virtue? For the Orient (particularly those parts of the Orient that are Buddhist), that answer is yes, it is, perhaps the greatest one.[5] As for the West, it holds a more qualified opinion, and this is what we must now briefly examine.

From the Stoics to Hannah Arendt (by way of Spinoza and Nietzsche), legions of thinkers have criticized compassion, or pity, to use the word most often employed by its detractors. Their criticisms are nearly always made in good faith and are quite often legitimate. Pity is the sadness one feels in response to the sadness of another: it does not spare the other person his own sadness but rather tends to add to it. Pity only increases the quantity of suffering in the world, and that is what damns it. What good is there in heaping sadness onto sadness, misfortune onto misfortune? The wise man feels no pity since he feels no sorrow.[6] Not that he doesn't want to help his fellowman, it is just that he doesn't need to feel pity in order to do so. "Why pity rather than give assistance if one can?" Cicero writes. "Or are we unable to be open-handed without pity? We are able for we ought not to share distresses ourselves for the sake of others, but we ought to relieve others of their distress if we can."[7] Actions rather than passions, the Stoic advises, and generous actions rather than acts of pity. Good advice, when generosity exists and in sufficient measure. But what if it doesn't?

Spinoza, in these areas, comes very close to the Stoics. His oft-cited condemnation of *commiseratio* has delighted some and offended others: "*Pity, in a man who lives according to the guidance of reason, is evil of itself and useless,*"[8] from which "it follows that a man who lives according to the dictates of reason, strives, as far as he can, not to be touched by pity."[9] What Spinoza is saying here goes to the heart of the matter. Pity is a sadness (born of our imitation of or our identification with the sadness of others),[10] whereas, in fact, it is joy that is good and reason that is just: love and generosity, not pity, should drive us to help our fellowmen. Pity is not necessary.[11] At least not for the wise man, which is to say, for the person who lives "under the sole guidance of reason," as Spinoza repeatedly says. This pure acceptance of truth, this love without sadness, this lightness, this serene and joyful generosity, aren't these the very hallmarks of wisdom? But who among us is wise? And so for the rest of us, or I should say, for all of us (because no one is completely wise), pity is better than its opposite and better, even, than the absence of pity: "Here I am speaking expressly of a man who lives

according to the guidance of reason," says Spinoza. "For one who is
moved to aid others neither by reason nor by pity is rightly called
inhuman. For he seems to be unlike a man."[12] Hence pity, without
being a virtue, "is still good,"[13] like shame and repentance,[14] because of
the part it plays in benevolence and human kindness or courtesy
(humanitas).[15] Spinoza's position here is actually the opposite of
Nietzsche's: the point is not to bring about a transvaluation of values or
an inversion of moral hierarchies[16] but simply to learn to practice in
joy—that is, moved by love or generosity—what decent people generally try to practice in sadness, moved by duty or pity. Alain, in some
very Spinoza-like remarks of his from 1909, comments that "there
exists a form of kindness that casts a gloom over life, a kindness that is
sadness, which we commonly call pity and which is one of the scourges
of our humanity."[17] True. As Montaigne and Spinoza observe, however, this sad kindness is still better than cruelty and egoism, a point
that Alain concedes: "Of course, in an unjust or completely unreflec-
tive person, pity is better than brutish insensitivity."[18] It is not yet a
virtue, however, merely a sadness and a passion. "Pity doesn't go far,"
Alain says later.[19] Yet it is better than nothing: though only a beginning,
at least it is a beginning. Here is where Spinoza is perhaps most enlightening. Between the moral behavior of the wise person and that of every
man, there is certainly an important affective difference: one acts out of
a sense of love and generosity, the other out of duty and pity.[20] Joy on
the one hand, sadness on the other. Morally, however, their actions are
the same. Love frees man from the law, not by abolishing it but, on the
contrary, by inscribing it in his heart.[21] What law is this? The only one
that Spinoza espouses, namely, the law of justice and charity.[22] The
wise man need not submit to that law, because he already is charitable
and just: reason and love make him so. As for the rest of us, we too can
become charitable and just—by way of pity. To think one might somehow get by without it is simply presumptuous.

I should also say that I'm not convinced that what I understand by
compassion is exhausted by the notions of pity or sadness. Might there
not be another kind of compassion, one that, if not joyful, is at least

positive, involving not sadness and passion so much as attentive openness, solicitude, patience, and listening? This sort of compassion may be what Spinoza meant by the word *misericordia*, ordinarily translated as "mercy" but closer to what I understand by compassion (in which notions of error and forgiveness, essential to mercy, do not figure). Of *misericordia* (of compassion, then), Spinoza writes that it "is love, insofar as it so affects a man that he is glad at another's good fortune and saddened by his ill fortune."[23] Now, compassion in the usual sense of the term applies only to ill fortune; good fortune does not call for compassion. And indeed, Spinoza seems to have some hesitation as to his definition, since he also tells us, oddly enough, that between *commiseratio* and *misericordia*—in other words, between pity and compassion (in our translation)—"there seems to be no difference . . . except perhaps that pity concerns the singular affect, whereas compassion concerns the habitual disposition of this affect."[24] I say "oddly enough" because one would have to assume that pity means not only sadness at another's ill fortune but also, like *misericordia*, joy in another's good fortune, which exceeds the ordinary—indeed the Spinozan—usage of the term. But after all, what does usage matter, as long as we agree on the definitions? What I find enlightening in the parallel definitions of compassion and pity is that pity (*commiseratio*) is defined as sadness, whereas compassion (*misericordia*) is defined as love, in other words, first of all, as joy.[25] To define compassion as joy does not take away from its sadness (we can prove this for ourselves: when we rejoice in someone's existence, which is to say, when we love that person, we are sad to see him or her suffer).[26] Rather it changes compassion's orientation and its value. For love is a joy,[27] and even if that joy gives way to sadness, in compassion as in pity, at least this sadness is devoid of hatred.[28] Or if there is hatred in it, the hatred is for unhappiness and not for the unhappy, whom we would rather help than scorn.[29] Life is too difficult and human beings are too unhappy for such a feeling not to be necessary and justified. Better a true sadness, I have often said, than a false joy. To which I should now add: better a saddened love—which is exactly what compassion is—than a joyful hatred.

But wouldn't a joyful love be better than either? Of course: wisdom and holiness would be better, too, and so would pure love or charity! "Compassion," Jankélévitch writes, "is a reactive or secondary charity which requires the other person's suffering in order to love; it needs its crippled dressed in rags, depends on the spectacle of his misery. Pity trails misfortune; pity loves no one except the pitiful, commiseration has no sympathy for anyone except the needy! True charity, on the contrary, is spontaneous. . . . It does not require tatters and misery in those whom it would love; after all, one's neighbor can and should be loved even if he is not unhappy."[30] But how difficult that is! Misfortune short-circuits envy, by definition, and pity short-circuits hatred. The path to love, to the wrenching closeness of the other, is cleared of that many more obstacles. Compassion, precisely because it is reactive and projective and identifies with its object, is the lowest form of love, perhaps, but also the easiest. Strange that Nietzsche should want to make us averse to it, as if we weren't put off by it already![31] As if to have done with it weren't our strongest, most natural, and most spontaneous desire! Isn't our own suffering quite enough for us? Wouldn't we all rather forget the suffering of others or at least not feel it? Vauvenargues is more lucid than Nietzsche: "The miser says to himself: Is the poor man's fortune my responsibility? And so he waves away pity, which annoys him."[32] We would be better off without pity, at any rate those who enjoy well-being now would be better off. But is this sort of well-being what we are after? Is the easy life, the comfortable life, our ethical norm? Why go to all this trouble philosophizing if what we want is to take the easy way out and be stroked for doing so? Schopenhauer, whose insight goes deeper than Nietzsche's on this question, sees compassion as the motive force behind morality, the origin of its value, ever-present and not susceptible to transvaluation.[33] The opposite of cruelty, the greatest of evils, and of egoism, the principle of all of them, compassion guides us far more dependably than any religious commandment or philosophical maxim. Can we even derive from compassion the virtues of justice and charity, as Schopenhauer tries to do? Not entirely, I think. But these are late-stage virtues, as it were, requiring considerable development on the part of humanity or civilization. Who knows if they would have come about without pity?

Let us note in passing—Schopenhauer again—that compassion holds for our relations with animals as well. Most of our virtues have humanity as their object: therein lies their greatness and their limitation. Compassion, on the contrary, sympathizes universally with all suffering beings; if we have duties with regard to animals, as I believe we do, they stem from or are part of compassion.[34] This is why compassion is perhaps our most universal virtue. One might object that we can also love animals and show them loyalty, even respect. Saint Francis of Assisi exemplifies this attitude in the Western tradition, and the Eastern tradition offers many other such models. Yet to treat our feelings for animals as though they had the same stature as the assuredly superior and more demanding feelings we owe human beings seems somehow wrong or at least inappropriate. We aren't faithful to our friends in the way that we are to our dogs; nor are we respectful of another human being, even a stranger, in the way that we are of a dog or a deer. When it comes to compassion, however, this distinction becomes less clear. Is it worse to slap a child or to torture a cat? If the latter is the more serious offense, as I tend to think, then one has to conclude that the unfortunate animal is more deserving of compassion. Pain, in this case, takes precedence over species and compassion over humanism. Compassion, therefore, is the one virtue that lets us open ourselves not just to all humanity but also to all living beings or, at the very least, to all suffering beings. A wisdom based on compassion, or nourished by it, would be the most universal wisdom, as Lévi-Strauss points out, and the most necessary.[35] The wisdom of Buddha, but also of Montaigne, it is the true wisdom, the wisdom of living beings, without which all human wisdom would be too human, which is to say, insufficiently humane.[36] Humanity, when we speak of it as a virtue, is nearly synonymous with compassion, a fact that says much about both. That we also can and should be humane toward animals constitutes our clearest claim to superiority over them, provided of course that we make good on that claim. To be utterly without compassion is

to be inhumane—in fact, inhuman—which only humans can be. Here
is an opportunity for a new humanism, a humanism that would consist
not in the exclusive possession of an essence and its attendant rights,
but in the exclusive awareness—until proof to the contrary—of the
demands or duties imposed on us by any victim of suffering. A cosmic
humanism: a humanism of compassion.

Schopenhauer cites Rousseau at length, and Lévi-Strauss acknowledges his debt to him explicitly.[37] In fact, it would be difficult to speak
of compassion without mentioning Rousseau, so essential is what he
has to say and so in line, moreover, with our contemporary sensibility.
It is worth rereading the beautiful passage in the *Second Discourse* in
which Rousseau demonstrates that pity, the favored term of his century
for compassion, is the first of all the virtues and the only natural one.[38]
Pity, he explains, is a feeling, a "natural sentiment," all the stronger for
deriving from self-love (through identification with others); it thus
tempers, in every man, "his ardor for well-being with an innate repug-
nance to see his kind suffer."[39] An unbounded compassion or one
bound only by pain, since compassion makes any suffering being a fellow creature of mine in some way. To have compassion is to commune
in suffering, and this incalculably vast community imposes on us, or
rather proposes to us, its own law, which is gentleness: "*Do your good
with the least possible harm to others.*"[40] Pity is thus what separates us
from barbarity, as Bernard Mandeville points out, but for Rousseau it is
also the mother of all virtues: "Mandeville sensed clearly that for all
their morality, men would never have been anything but monsters if
Nature had not given them pity in support of reason: but he did not see
that from this single attribute flow all the social virtues he wants to
deny men. Indeed, what are Generosity, Clemency, Humanity, if not
Pity applied to the weak, the guilty, or the species in general? Even
Benevolence and Friendship, properly understood, are the products of
a steady pity focused on a particular object; for what else is it to wish
that someone not suffer, than to wish that he be happy?"[41]

I wouldn't go quite so far as that, nor would I want to reduce all
virtues to a single one. But I am convinced that pity is the opposite of

cruelty, the evil of egoism at its worst. Which doesn't mean that pity is totally free of egoism, any more than generosity is. In fact, since Aristotle it has been a commonplace to regard pity "as a feeling of pain at an apparent evil ... which we might expect to befall ourselves or some friend of ours."[42] Pity, by this account, would merely be a projective or transferential egoism. In the words of Aristotle, "what we fear for ourselves excites our pity when it happens to others."[43] This may well be true, but what difference does it make? The pity we feel is no less real and extends, incidentally, to misfortunes that cannot befall us personally. The death of a child, and the parents' terrible suffering, will arouse the pity of a childless old man. Is this to say that pity is a selfless sentiment? I don't know and don't care. Selfless or not, the feeling is real and no less compassionate for perhaps not being selfless. The rest belongs to the subterfuges of self, worth only what such subterfuges are worth. One might as well disparage love or deny its existence, on the pretext that it is always associated with some sexual impulse. Freud knew better as regards love; shouldn't we, too, as regards compassion?

And what of the connection between compassion and cruelty? Though more paradoxical, it is not unthinkable: first, because there is ambivalence everywhere, even in the virtues, and, second, because pity itself can arouse, or give sanction to, cruelty. Hannah Arendt points this out in her discussion of the French Revolution ("Pity, taken as the spring of virtue, has proved to possess a greater capacity for cruelty than cruelty itself"), and though her observation is not absolutely damning of either pity or revolution, it does justify a certain vigilance toward both; the fact that pity can stand in the way of our worst impulses and even counter them does not prevent it from sometimes feeding them.[44] Pity is neither a guarantee nor a panacea. But what Hannah Arendt demonstrates is that during the Terror pity could justify violence and cruelty only by reason of its abstraction: pity for the unfortunate in general, that is, for the people, in the eighteenth-century meaning of the word, was fit cause for adding a few more individuals to the ranks of the unhappy. For Hannah Arendt, therein lies the distinction between *pity* and *compassion*, for unlike pity, compassion "can comprehend only the particular, but has no notion of the general and no capacity for generalization." Also, it "cannot reach out farther than what is suffered by one person" or "be touched off by the sufferings of a whole class."[45] Where pity is abstract, loquacious, and generalizing, compassion is concrete, silent, and specific (even were we to have, like Jesus, "the ability to have compassion for all men in their singularity, that is, without lumping them together into some such entity as one suffering mankind"—as pity does).[46] Hence the violence of pity and its occasional cruelty, in contrast to the immense gentleness of compassion. If one accepts this distinction, one could say that in the name of pity (for the poor in general), Robespierre and Saint-Just lacked compassion (for the revolution's opponents—or presumed opponents—as specific individuals). But then pity of this kind is only an abstract feeling (an imaginary one, Spinoza would say), and it is compassion that is the virtue.

I would like to suggest another distinction between these two notions, in addition to (rather than instead of) the one made by Hannah Arendt. Pity always entails, it seems to me, some degree of contempt, or at least a feeling of superiority on the part of the person who experiences it. *Suave, mari magno. . . .*[47] There is a self-satisfaction in pity that underscores the deficiency of its object. I take as proof the adjective *pitiful*, which formerly referred to the person full of or characterized by pity but today refers to the person who arouses or is fit to arouse this emotion. In this latter meaning, *pitiful* is a term of deprecation, roughly synonymous with *inferior, pathetic,* or *contemptible. Compassion* does not carry these negative connotations: *compassionate* describes only the person who feels or shows compassion; there is no corresponding passive adjective (like *compassionable*). Perhaps it is that compassion presupposes no particular value judgment with regard to its object; we can have compassion for someone we admire as well as for someone we disapprove of. On the other hand, it seems to me that compassion does entail respect, at least in some small measure; otherwise, according to my distinction, at any rate, it would no longer be compassion but pity. This distinction, I believe, is faithful to the spirit of the language. To someone who is suffering—from a serious illness, for example—we can convey our compassion or our sympathy. We wouldn't think of expressing our pity, which would be considered contemptuous or insulting. Pity comes, as it were, from the top down.[48] Compassion, on the contrary, is a horizontal feeling; it makes sense only among equals, or better yet, it realizes this equality between the suffering person and the person next to him, who becomes his equal by sharing his suffering. In this sense, there can be no pity without some measure of contempt and no compassion without respect.

This may be what Alain means when he writes that "the spirit has no pity and can have none; out of respect, it turns away from pity."[49] Not that the spirit is pitiless, of course, in the sense of ruthless and incapable of sorrow and regret. But how could it pity what it respects or reveres? This is why, as Alain also says, "pity is of the body, not the spirit"; the spirit (respectful and faithful) can only feel compassion.[50] Let us not, however, lapse into religion or spiritualism. Strictly speaking, it is not the spirit that has compassion or respect, it is respect and compassion that *make* the spirit. And the spirit is born of suffering, too—as courage, when the suffering is our own, and as compassion, when the suffering is that of others.

We should therefore avoid confusing compassion with condescension or with what has come to be caricatured as "good works," charity (in the sense of giving charity), philanthropy, or almsgiving. One can be of the opinion that, as Spinoza maintains, it is up to the state and not private persons to aid the poor[51] and that, consequently, in order to fight poverty, *political acts* are better than *acts of charity*. I would tend to agree. Even if I gave away everything I owned and became as poor as the poor, how would that change the fact of poverty? Social problems call for social solutions. Compassion, like generosity, can justify fighting for *higher* taxes and the better employment of those taxes, surely a more efficient way (and for many of us a costlier, hence more generous, way) of fighting poverty than giving a coin here and there. On the other hand, having a social approach to poverty does not mean our attitude toward the poor need not be one of fraternal closeness, respect, availability, and sympathy—in other words, compassion, which might also manifest itself (since politics is no panacea) in concrete acts of benevolence, as Spinoza defines the term, or of solidarity.[52] We each do what we can, or rather what we want to do, according to our means and what little generosity we are capable of. The ego dictates and decides. But not all by itself, and therein lies the meaning of compassion.

Virtue though it is, there's no getting around the fact that compassion is also very much a feeling; as such, it is something we either do or do not feel—it cannot be called up on command. This is why, as Kant reminds us, compassion cannot be a duty.[53] However, feelings are not destiny, which we must submit to. We cannot decide to love, but we can be taught to love. The same is true of compassion; it is not our duty to feel compassion, but, as Kant explains, it *is* our duty to nurture the capacity in us to feel it.[54] This is what makes compassion not just a feeling but a virtue—in other words, an effort, a capacity, and an excellence, all at once. The fact that it is both a feeling and a virtue, both a sadness and a capability[55] explains the privileged position it occupies for Rousseau and Schopenhauer, rightly or wrongly (more likely both rightly *and* wrongly). Compassion allows us to pass from one realm to the other, from the emotional realm to the ethical realm, from what we feel to what we want, from what we are to what we must do. Love, some will say, effects the same passage. Undoubtedly it does, but love isn't much within our reach, whereas compassion is.

Compassion, as I noted above, is the great virtue of the Buddhist East. We also know that charity—this time in the positive sense of the word, as love of benevolence—is the great virtue of the Christian West (at least in word if not in deed). Must we choose between the two? They are not mutually exclusive, so what would be the point? Were it necessary to make a choice, then I would say this: charity would certainly be better if we were capable of it, but compassion, which resembles charity (in its gentleness) is more accessible and might lead us to it.

Who can be sure of having ever experienced a true charitable impulse? Who can doubt ever having felt compassion? One must begin with what is easiest, and unfortunately our talent for sadness is much greater than our talent for joy. And so we all need courage. And compassion, for others and for ourselves.

Or to put it another way: Christ's message, which is love, is the more exhilarating, but Buddha's lesson, which is compassion, is more realistic.

Therefore, "love and do what you wish"—or be compassionate and do what you must.[56]

9

MERCY

Mercy, as I take this word to mean, is the virtue of forgiveness—or, better yet, its truth.

What does it actually mean to forgive? If, as the Christian tradition would have us understand, it means the wrong has been erased, is now to be considered null and void, then forgiveness is either a capacity that is beyond us or else a folly we had best avoid. The past is irrevocable, and all truth is eternal; even God, as Descartes observes, cannot make it so that what was done did not happen.[1] Nor can we, and no one can be held to the impossible. As for forgetting the wrong, aside from the fact that it would constitute a breach of faith with the victims—are we to forget the crimes of Nazism, must we put Auschwitz forever out of our minds?—it would also be folly and hence show a lack of prudence. If a friend has betrayed you, is it wise to continue trusting him? If a shopkeeper has cheated you, is it immoral to patronize another? Obviously not, and any claim to the contrary is either so much hot air or else a remarkable display of a very blind or very silly virtue. "*Caute*," Spinoza says, "take care," and he was in no way slighting mercy.

Spinoza's biographers also tell us how, having been stabbed by a fanatic, he kept the pierced jerkin all his life so as not to forget the event or, presumably, its lesson.[2] It is not that he had not forgiven (forgiveness, in some sense, is a demand of the Spinozan doctrine, as we shall see) but simply that to forgive does not mean to erase—or to forget. But then what does it mean? It means that one has ceased to hate, which is indeed the definition of mercy: the virtue that triumphs over rancor, over justified hatred (in this respect mercy goes beyond justice), over resentment, over the desire for revenge or punishment; the virtue that forgives not by expunging the wrong—an impossible charge, in any case—but by stilling the grudge we bear against the person who offended or harmed us. Mercy is not the same as clemency, which merely renounces punishment (one can hate without punishing, just as one can punish without hating), or compassion, which sympathizes only with suffering (one can be culpable without suffering just as one can suffer without being culpable), or absolution, if by absolution we mean the power—it would have to be a supernatural power—to nullify sins or wrongdoing. A singular and limited virtue yet sufficiently difficult, and sufficiently commendable, to make it one. For our misdeeds are too numerous, and we ourselves are all of us too wretched, too weak, and too vile for it to be unnecessary.

Let us return for a moment to the difference between mercy and compassion. Compassion, as we saw earlier, is concerned with suffering, and most suffering is innocent. Mercy, on the other hand, is concerned with wrongdoing, which is often painless, at least for those who wrong. Mercy and compassion are thus two quite different virtues, whose objects or beneficiaries generally do not coincide. It is true, however, that we more easily forgive someone who is suffering, even if his suffering is unrelated to his misdeed (or, specifically, to his repentance). Mercy is the opposite of resentment, which is a form of hatred. Now, as we saw in connection with compassion, it is almost impossible to hate someone whom we see suffering horribly: pity short-circuits hatred, which is why compassion, though not the same as mercy, can prepare the way for it. The converse is also sometimes true—it is easier to feel compassion when we have stopped hating. But in either case compassion, a more emotional, more natural, and more spontaneous virtue than mercy, almost always comes first. Mercy is the rarer virtue and more difficult.

The reason is this: mercy takes some reflection, whereas pity can quite easily get by without it. What does the merciful person think about? Does he reflect on himself and his own many sins? Quite possibly, and if he does, he may be dissuaded from casting the first stone, to lift a phrase from the Bible. But this kind of mercy, through identification, is possible only when identification is possible—when the wrong is one of which we know or can imagine ourselves capable. I can forgive the thief because I myself have on occasion stolen (books, during my youth). I can forgive the liar because I sometimes lie, the egoist because I am one, the coward because I could be one. But what about the rapist of children or the torturer? As soon as the offense exceeds a common limit, we stop identifying; indeed, the very idea of identification becomes implausible. Yet these crimes, and especially the most horrible among them, are the very ones that call for our mercy. What good is forgiveness if it only applies to trivialities? What good is mercy if it forgives only that which would be forgivable in its absence?

Mercy thus requires something other than identification, but what? Love? When love exists and survives the discovery of the wrong, obviously it leads to mercy, but then it also deprives mercy of its object. To forgive is to cease hating, to renounce vengeance, which is why love does not really need to forgive: it always already has and always will; if not, then it is not love. How can you cease hating when you do not hate? How can you forgive when you have no rancor in you to overcome? Love is naturally merciful and does not require mercy as a distinct and separate virtue. "We forgive so long as we love," says La Rochefoucauld.[3] But so long as we love, our forgiveness isn't mercy but love. Parents know this, and sometimes their children do too. I'm speaking not of infinite love, of which we are incapable, but of unconditional love, which, it would seem, can rise above any possible misdeed, any possible offense. "Is there anything I could do that you wouldn't forgive me for?" the child asks his parents. And they can think of nothing, not even the worst offense. Parents don't have to forgive their children: love supersedes mercy. It's children who have to forgive their parents, if and when they can. Forgive them for what? For too much love and egoism, for too much love and foolishness, for too much worry and distress . . . Or for too little love, in which case forgiveness will be just as necessary. Isn't this what becoming an adult is all about? There is a remark I am fond of in Oscar Wilde's *The Portrait of Dorian Gray:* "Children begin by loving their parents; as they grow up they judge them; sometimes they forgive them."[4] Fortunate are the children who can forgive their parents; fortunate are the merciful!

Outside the family, however, we are so little capable of love, especially in the face of wickedness, that love becomes an unlikely source of mercy. How could we love our enemies, or even tolerate them, without first forgiving them? How could love resolve a problem that only arises because of an absence of love? We are inept at love, and utterly so when it comes to the wicked. This is precisely why we need to be merciful! Not because there is love in our hearts but because there is not, only hate and anger! As for the good, they do not need our mercy; nor do we need, for our part, to have mercy on them. Admiration is sufficient and more appropriate.

So what *does* mercy require? Not a feeling, at least not at first, which is why mercy is a more difficult virtue than compassion. Consider: compassion is physical—we project ourselves into the suffering of another person and want to spare him the pain he feels. But so are anger, resentment, and hatred—the desire, the visceral craving for punishment and revenge. We might renounce these feelings if our adversary is suffering and pity comes to the aid of mercy. But if not? Something more, or less, than a feeling is required, namely, an idea. Like prudence, mercy is an intellectual virtue; at least it begins that way and remains so for some time thereafter. Mercy requires that we understand something. But what? That the other person is wicked, if indeed he is. Or that he is misguided, if such is the case. Or that he is ruled by passion or fanaticism, if his passions or his beliefs hold sway over him. Or in short, that he would be very hard pressed to act differently from what he is (how could he?) and to suddenly become good, gentle, reasonable, tolerant, and so forth.

To forgive is to accept. Not in order to stop fighting, of course, but in order to stop hating. "I die without any hatred in me for the German people."[5] Did the man who spoke these words as he faced the Nazi firing squad in Louis Aragon's poetic reconstruction of the event also have no hatred in him for his own executioners? That would have been harder, and whether he did or did not is something we can never know. Yet isn't it obvious that he is freer than they are? Indeed, even in his chains, he is freer than his murderers, who are slaves! Forgiveness registers or expresses this freedom, a freedom it shares with generosity (to *forgive* is also to *give*): forgiveness is like an overabundance of freedom. The forgiving person, knowing too well how unfree the guilty are to bear them unwavering resentment, does them the grace of understanding them, excusing them, and pardoning them for existing and being what they are. What bastard, after all, has freely chosen to be one? But does that make him innocent? We should rather say that it is not his fault if he is guilty; that he is a prisoner of his own hatred, stupidity, and blindness; that he did not choose to be what he is; that he did not choose his body or his history; that no one would freely choose to be in his place and be so evil and so wicked; that his guilt and wickedness have their causes; that it would be according him too great an honor to imagine him either free or beyond all comprehension; that if we hated him, we would be wronging ourselves; that it is enough to fight or resist him quietly, serenely, and joyously if we can and to forgive if we cannot. The point is to overcome our own hatred if we cannot make him overcome his; to achieve self-mastery if we cannot master him; to win at least this victory, over evil and hatred, and not add evil to evil; to avoid becoming his accomplice as well as his victim; to hold fast, if not to the good, then to love, which comes closest to it, or if not to love, then to mercy, or if not to mercy, then to compassion. As Epictetus says, "Man, if you must needs be affected in a way that is contrary to nature at the misfortunes of another, pity him rather, but do not hate him."[6] Or, as Marcus Aurelius says, "Men are born for each other's sake, so either teach people or endure them."[7] Or again, in the words of Christ, "Father, forgive them; for they know not what they do" (Luke 23:34).

Jankélévitch, when he cites these words, finds them a bit too "Socratic" for his taste. If they know not what they do, their misdeeds are errors, not crimes—is there even anything to forgive?[8] An error is always unintentional; it warrants not punishment but correction, not forgiveness but excuse. But then what is the point of mercy? No one is intentionally wicked, says Socrates; according to this thesis, called Socratic intellectualism, evil is merely an error.[9] But this is to make an error about evil. Evil is a matter of will, not ignorance; a matter of heart, not intelligence or mind; a matter of hatred, not stupidity. Evil is not an error, for errors are trivial; evil is selfishness, wickedness, cruelty. It is for this reason that it requires forgiveness, which error has no need of. "We *excuse* the ignorant; we *forgive* the wicked."[10] Only the will is or can be guilty; only the will is a legitimate object for rancor and hence for mercy. We bear no grudge against the rain for falling or lightning for striking, and consequently there is nothing to forgive them for. No one is *un*intentionally wicked, we might correct Socrates, and forgiveness applies only to the wicked. Only free acts can require forgiveness, just as forgiveness can arise only from a state of freedom: a freely bestowed grace for a freely committed wrong.

Yes, but what kind of freedom? Freedom of action, of course: it is the will that is guilty, and an action is culpable only if intentional. A dancer who inadvertently steps on your toes was not wicked but clumsy. To accept his excuses is not forgiveness but courtesy. Only someone who has done something *on purpose*—in other words, who has done what he wanted to do and acted *freely*—can need to be forgiven. Freedom of action: to be free, in this sense, means to do what one wants to do, to do as one intends. As for knowing whether a person was free not just to do what he did but also to want to do it, whether he could have wanted something else, that question is an undecidable one, having to do not with freedom of action, the existence of which we can all attest to, but with freedom of will (free will), which is beyond proof and (because the only way to test its existence would be to want something other than what we want) beyond experience. Except for occasional moments in Plato, this latter kind of freedom is something the ancient philosophers did not concern themselves with. They were not preoccupied with absolute guilt or eternal damnation. But, as my quotation from Epictetus should suggest, this did not prevent them from preferring pity to anger, justice to revenge, and mercy to rancor. Should we, simply because we are more preoccupied with our guilt than they were with theirs, lose our capacity to forgive? How can a decision depend on a question that cannot be answered one way or the other?

Here, as in my discussion of generosity, free will is not the issue. Virtue cannot depend on any particular metaphysical thesis. I will say only this: whether one believes the wicked person has freely chosen to be wicked or was fated to become so (by virtue of his body, his childhood, his education, or his personal history), he is wicked nonetheless and, having acted intentionally, he is responsible at least for his actions. One can punish him, if necessary, and even hate him if one so chooses. Yet punishment and hatred are two different matters. Punishment can be justified by its social or private usefulness; it can even be in keeping with certain ideas people have about justice ("He killed, therefore it is just to kill him"). But hatred? It is an added sadness, not for the culprit but for the person who hates.[11] What good does it do to hate? And above all, if the wicked person is what he is, his very wickedness, whether freely chosen or not, excuses him in some way: either by virtue of its causes, if his wickedness is predetermined, or, if we assume it to be free, then by virtue of a love of evil, a will toward evil. Is it his fault, then, if he is wicked? Yes, you will say, since he has chosen to be. But would he have made this choice if he hadn't already been wicked? For to assume that he chose evil while preferring the good is to assume that he is insane and thereby to exculpate him once again. In short, the wicked person is guilty of what he does, and if he is also guilty of being *what he is* (since he freely chose to be what he is), then his wickedness is only confirmed: he does evil for its own sake, or, as Kant would put it, because of his evil heart, or out of sheer selfishness, that is, for personal gain.[12] Mercy does not nullify this evil will, nor does it give up the fight against it; what mercy does do is refuse to partake of it, to add hatred to hatred, selfishness to selfishness, anger to violence. Mercy leaves hatred to the hateful, wickedness to the wicked, resentment to the resentful. Not because they are not really hateful, wicked, or resentful but *because they are.* (Even if a specific deterministic cause exists for their being the way they are, as I believe, determinism does not cancel the thing it produces.) As Jankélévitch puts it: "They are wicked, but for this very reason they must be forgiven—for their unhappiness is even greater than their wickedness. Or better yet, their very wickedness is a misfortune; the infinite misfortune of being wicked!"[13]

Nevertheless, we forgive more readily when we are aware of the causes determining an action or, especially, a personality. There is perhaps no crime more heinous, more unforgivable, than that of torturing a child. When we learn, however, that the abusive parent had himself been a victim of child abuse (as is often the case), our judgment of him changes somewhat: it is not that his crime is any less horrible but that our awareness of its cause helps us to understand his crime and, consequently, to forgive it. For how do we know we wouldn't have turned out just like him had we been brought up as he was in fear and violence? And if, having been brought up like him, we did not turn out like him, then isn't it because, despite the similarities, we are different from him? Did he choose to be the way he is? And did we choose not to be that way? Besides, how could we choose to be what we are, since every choice presupposes what we are and depends on it? How could existence precede essence? If it did, it would be existence of nothing— and therefore nonexistence. Such freedom to choose what we are amounts to nothingness—proving Sartre is right and at the same time wrong.

But I have allowed myself to be carried away by the topic of free will, which I had wanted to leave aside. My point is simply this. There may be two ways of forgiving, depending on whether one does or does not believe in the offender's free will: out of pure grace, as Jankélévitch would put it, if you believe in free will; out of true knowledge, as Spinoza would say, if you do not. But in either case, hatred disappears—that is the essence of mercy—and the misdeed, without being forgotten or justified, is accepted for what it is: a horror to be fought, a misfortune to be pitied, a reality to be endured, and ultimately the act of a person whom we should love, if possible. I have never been able to bring myself to believe in free will, but again this is not the place to go into my reasons.[14] I will mention only Spinoza's important observation, for each to make of what he will: people hate one another more if they imagine they are free and less if they know that they are determined.[15] It is in this sense that knowledge is merciful. "Passing judgment," says Malraux, "obviously means not understanding, since if we understood we could no longer pass judgment." Or, you might say, we could no longer hate, which is all that mercy requires of us—or rather all that it holds out to us.

Such is the meaning of one of Spinoza's most famous maxims: "Not to mock, lament, or execrate but to understand human actions."[16] This understanding is mercy itself, its only grace the grace of truth.[17] Is it still forgiveness? Not really: understanding abolishes the need for forgiveness (knowledge, like love, makes forgiveness both inescapable and superfluous). Then is it excusing? I don't wish to quibble over words. Everything can be excused, in a way, since everything has a cause. But to know that everything has a cause is not enough: forgiveness is the *enactment* of this idea, which otherwise would be merely an abstraction. We bear no grudge against the rain for falling or lightning for striking, as I said, and consequently there is nothing to forgive them for. Can't the same thing be said of the wicked, in the end, and isn't this the true miracle of mercy—which is no miracle at all? That at the very moment forgiveness is offered, it abolishes itself in mercy? That hatred is dispelled by truth? Man does not stand apart from the world: everything is real, everything is true, both good and evil, which is why good and evil do not exist independently of our love of the one and our hatred of the other. It is in this sense that God's mercy, as Spinoza would say, is truly infinite—it is truth itself and does not pass judgment.[18]

Only the wise man, the mystic, and the saint can approach these elusive realms, toward which mercy aims, toward which it leads us. But mercy aims for these realms, and leads us toward them. Mercy is the divine point of view within the hearts of men, the great peace of truth, the great gentleness of love and forgiveness. Love more than forgiveness, or forgiveness transformed by the gift of love. To forgive is to cease hating, hence to cease being able to forgive: when forgiveness has been accomplished, when it is complete, when there is nothing left but love and truth, there is no more hatred to bring to an end and forgiveness abolishes itself in mercy. This is why I began this chapter by saying that mercy isn't so much the virtue of forgiveness as its truth; mercy actualizes forgiveness but does so by doing away not with its object but with the misdeed, with hatred. In a sense, Spinoza's wise man has nothing to forgive, not because he can never suffer injustice or aggression but because he is never driven by hatred or misled by the illusion of free will.[19] Still, his wisdom is no less merciful, indeed it is more so— because hatred has well and truly vanished in him and with it all notion of absolute guilt (the responsibility not for acting but for being), because even love is again possible. This is why, in another sense, the wise man forgives everything. Are all of us innocent? Are all of us lovable? Certainly not for the same reasons. Though the works of good and of wicked people are both equally a part of nature and follow from its laws, Spinoza explains, "they do not differ from one another in degree only, but also in essence. A mouse no less than an angel, and sorrow no less than joy depend on God; yet a mouse is not a kind of angel, neither is sorrow a kind of joy."[20] Mercy neither annuls the misdeed, which remains, nor cancels out differences in value, which it assumes and demonstrates; nor does it do away with the need to fight.[21] But by eliminating hatred, it spares us the need to seek justification for hatred. By quelling anger and the desire for revenge, it allows for justice and, if necessary, serene punishment.[22] Finally, mercy makes conceivable the possibility that the wicked, who are a part of reality, can become an object of knowledge, understanding, and even love (a prospect mercy permits us to glimpse at least). All things are certainly not of equal value, but all that is real is true, the bastard just as surely as the decent man. Mercy on all, and peace to all, even as we carry on the fight!

The imagination rebels at this notion, and so does hatred. "If Spinoza had lived at the time of the mass exterminations," says Jankélévitch, "Spinozism would not have existed. Had Spinoza been a survivor of Auschwitz, he could not have said, '*Humanas actiones non ridere, non lugere, neque detestari, sed intelligere.*' After Auschwitz, to understand is not to forgive. Or rather, understanding is no longer possible; there is nothing left to understand. For the depths of pure evil are incomprehensible."[23] Yet can we be so sure? Aren't we giving those brutes too much credit in assuming that they are inexplicable or incomprehensible? Do we mean to say that we can explain Einstein, Mozart, or Jean Moulin but not the SS? That life is rational, but not hatred? That love is understandable, but not cruelty? By seeing the camps as consummately irrational, we justify the irrationalists who prepared the way for them and built them (true, only in this particular respect, but isn't that already excessive?). What good would reason be if it were capable of understanding only the reasonable? The fact that Nazism isn't *reasonable*, as is perfectly obvious, doesn't prevent its being *rational*, like anything else real; the fact that we cannot reasonably approve of it doesn't mean we cannot rationally know and explain it. Isn't that exactly what historians do? Indeed, how else can we fight it?

Here the distinction between forgetting and mercy is of the utmost importance. The Christian notion that *everything* can be forgiven is acceptable to even the most faithfully contemporary thinkers. As Jankélévitch says:

Forgiveness doesn't ask whether the crime is worthy of forgiveness, whether it has been sufficiently expiated, or whether resentment has gone on long enough. . . . There is no misdeed so serious that it cannot be pardoned in the end. Nothing is impossible for almighty forgiveness! Forgiveness, in this sense, knows no limits. Wherever sin abounds, says Saint Paul, forgiveness overabounds. . . . If some crimes are so monstrous that their perpetrators will never be able to expiate them, they can still be forgiven; indeed, forgiveness was devised precisely for these hopeless or incurable cases.[24]

None of this gives us leave to *forget* the crime, or our duty of fidelity toward the victims, or our obligation to fight today's criminals and those who take up the cause of the criminals of yesterday.[25] Yet a problem remains, like an open wound: can we and should we forgive those who have never asked forgiveness?[26] Jankélévitch replies in the negative:

Only the criminal's repentance, and especially his remorse, gives forgiveness its meaning, just as only despair gives meaning to grace. . . . Forgiveness is not intended for people smugly content in their good consciences or for unrepentant offenders. . . . Forgiveness is not intended for louts and their ilk. Before forgiveness can even be considered, the offender must cease challenging his guilt and acknowledge it, making no pleas in his own defense or calling on extenuating circumstances: above all, he must not blame his victims. For us to forgive, shouldn't we first be asked forgiveness? . . . Why should we forgive people who so little regret their monstrous infamies? . . . Though unexpiated crimes are precisely the ones that require forgiveness, unrepentant criminals are precisely the ones who do not.[27]

They do not need to be forgiven, but do we, for our part, need to forgive them? Hatred is always a sadness, and it is joy that is good. I am not saying that we must reconcile with monsters or tolerate their demands. But do we have to hate them in order to fight them? I do not mean that we must forget the past. But do we need to hate in order to remember it? Nor am I saying we should absolve the perpetrators of their sins—again, we cannot and must not (only their victims could legitimately think they are entitled to do so, but they are not here— they have been killed). The point is to eliminate hatred if we can and then to carry on the fight with joy in our hearts, if possible, or with mercy in our souls, when joy is impossible or inappropriate; the point is to love our enemies if we can or, if we cannot, then to forgive them.[28] Christ and Saint Stephen, according to tradition, exemplify this kind of forgiveness, a forgiveness without prerequisites or preconditions that does not insist that the wicked be less wicked—that is, that they regret having been so—before forgiving them; a forgiveness that is truly a gift and not an exchange (forgiveness for contrition); an unconditional pardon that operates at an utter loss, you could say, and yet is the greatest and perhaps only victory over hatred; a forgiveness that does not forget but understands, that does not erase but accepts; a forgiveness that gives up neither the fight nor the peace, that sacrifices neither itself nor the other, neither lucidity nor mercy![29] I am fully aware that these examples are beyond our reach, but does that prevent them from enlightening us?

I'm not suggesting that following the Scriptures can substitute for wisdom, or that in them we can find an answer for everything, or that I myself subscribe to them completely (even leaving aside the question of religion). I am hardly inclined to turn the other cheek, and in fighting violence I prefer the sword.[30] To love one's enemies it must be assumed one has enemies (how could one love something that does not exist?). But it does not follow that, having enemies, we must necessarily hate them. Love is a joy, not a form of powerlessness or surrender; loving one's enemies doesn't mean giving up the fight—it means fighting them joyously.

Mercy, then, is the virtue of forgiveness, its secret and its truth. It eliminates not the wrong but the resentment, not the memory but the anger, not the fight but the hatred. Mercy is not love but stands in for love when love is not possible or lays the foundation for love when love would be premature. A secondary virtue, you might say, but of the utmost urgency and hence so very necessary! The maxim of mercy is this: when you are unable to love, at least cease to hate.

Note that it is not only the wrongdoing but also the insult that occasions mercy. This qualification reveals our pettiness, which greets criticism with criticism and which considers any insult a misdeed and any affront reprehensible. That's the way things are and we should know it. Mercy on all, and on oneself as well.

Because hatred is a sadness, mercy (like the process of mourning, which it resembles and might even require, since to forgive is to bid farewell to our hatred) is on the side of joy. When it is not yet joyous, it is forgiveness; when it already is, it is love. A mediating, or transitional, virtue. In the end, however, for those who attain it, there is nothing left to forgive; the triumph of mercy resides in this peace—freed of hatred and anger—in which forgiveness culminates and dissolves. Mercy, like evil, is infinite or should be, which is why it is probably beyond our capacities. But to strive toward it is itself a virtue; mercy is that path which accommodates even those who fail to reach its end. Forgive yourself, O soul of mine, for your hatred and your anger.

Can one forgive oneself? Of course, since one can hate oneself and overcome self-hatred. What hope would there be for wisdom otherwise? Or for happiness? Or for peace? We must forgive ourselves for being merely what we are. And also forgive ourselves—when we can do so without injustice—for feeling hatred or pain or anger so strong that we cannot forgive. Fortunate are the merciful, who fight without hatred or hate without remorse!

10

GRATITUDE

Gratitude is the most pleasant of virtues, though not the easiest. And why would it be easy? There are pleasures that are difficult or rare and that are no less pleasing, indeed are perhaps even more pleasing for being so. Still, in the case of gratitude, the surprising thing is not the pleasure so much as the difficulty. After all, who wouldn't rather accept a gift than receive a blow? Or express thanks than show forgiveness? Gratitude is a second pleasure, one that prolongs the pleasure that precedes and occasions it, like a joyful echo of the joy we feel, a further happiness for the happiness we have been given. Gratitude: the pleasure of receiving, the joy of being joyful. What could be easier? That gratitude is a virtue, however, should suffice to indicate that it cannot be taken for granted, that it is something we can be lacking in, and that consequently, in spite of or perhaps because of the pleasure, there is merit in experiencing it. But why? Gratitude is a mystery, not because of the pleasure it affords us but because of the obstacles we must overcome to feel it. It is the most pleasant of virtues and the most virtuous of pleasures.

But what about generosity and the pleasures of giving that we hear so much about? The interested nature of that argument—it has become a staple of advertising, after all—should put us on our guard. Were there really such pleasure in giving, why would we need advertisers to remind us to give? If generosity were a pleasure, or rather, if it were only a pleasure or primarily a pleasure, why would we be so lacking in it? Giving always involves loss, which is why generosity is the opposite of and counter to selfishness. But receiving? Gratitude takes nothing from us: it is a gift given in return with no loss and almost no object or objective. Gratitude has nothing to give, except this pleasure of having received. What lighter, brighter, what more *Mozartian* virtue, I am inclined to say, and not just because Mozart inspires it in us but because he celebrates it and incarnates it, because he carries within him this joy, this boundless gratitude for who knows what—for all and everything—this generosity of gratitude. What happier and more humble virtue, what easier and more necessary grace than that of *giving thanks* with a smile or a dance step, with a song or with happiness itself? The generosity of gratitude. This expression, which I owe to Mozart, I find particularly enlightening: if so often we lack gratitude, might it not be more because we cannot give than because we cannot receive, more because we are selfish than because we are insensitive? To thank is to give; to be gracious means to share. This pleasure that I owe to you is not for me alone. This joy, this happiness, they belong to both of us. The egoist enjoys receiving; but his enjoyment is his alone and he keeps it for himself. Or if he shows his pleasure, it is because he wants to make others envious, not because he wants to make them happy: he displays his pleasure, but it is *his* pleasure. He has already forgotten that others might have had something to do with it. But what does he care about others? The egoist is ungrateful not because he doesn't like to receive. He is ungrateful because he doesn't like to acknowledge his debt to others and gratitude is this acknowledgment; because he doesn't like to give in return and gratitude is giving thanks in return; because he doesn't like to share and he doesn't like to give. What does gratitude give away? It gives away itself, like a joyful echo, as I said;

and in this it is love, it is sharing, it is a gift. It is pleasure upon pleasure, happiness upon happiness, gratitude upon generosity. Aware only of his own satisfactions and his own happiness, hoarding them as a miser hoards his coin, watching over them as a miser watches his purse, the egoist cannot be grateful. Ingratitude is not the incapacity to receive but the inability to give back—in the form of joy or love—a little of the joy that was received or experienced. This is why ingratitude is so pervasive a vice. We absorb joy as others absorb light, for egoism is a black hole.

Gratitude is a gift, gratitude is sharing, gratitude is love: it is a joy accompanied by the idea of its cause, as Spinoza would say, when the cause is another person's generosity, or courage, or love.[1] Joy in return is love in return. Strictly speaking, therefore, gratitude can be addressed only toward living persons. Nevertheless, it is worth asking ourselves whether any gotten joy, whatever its cause, might not be the object of this joy in return for which is gratitude. How could one not be grateful to the sun for existing? To life, to flowers, to birds? I could feel no joy were it not for the rest of the universe (since without the rest of the universe, I would not exist). In this respect all joy, even a purely internal or introspective one (Spinoza's *acquiescentia in se ipso*), has an external cause that is the universe, God, or nature—in other words, all and everything.[2] No one is the cause of himself or, in the end, of his own joy. All causal chains, of which there are an infinite number, are themselves infinite: all things are interrelated, and related to us, and flow through us. All love, taken to its logical extreme, should therefore love all things: all love should be a love of everything (the more we love individual things, Spinoza might say, the more we love God),[3] a universal gratitude, then, one that, though certainly not undifferentiated (how could we have the same gratitude for birds as for snakes, for Mozart as for Hitler?), would nevertheless be comprehensive or at least thankful for everything. Excluding nothing and rejecting nothing, not even the worst of things, this gratitude would have to be a *tragic* gratitude, in the Nietzschean sense, since the real must be accepted or rejected as is, since the real in its totality is the only reality.[4]

Gratitude is gratuitous in that one cannot ask of it, or for it, any recompense whatsoever. Gratitude may be a duty, or in any case a virtue, but, as Rousseau notes, it cannot be demanded as a right and nothing can be demanded in its name.[5] Gratitude is love, not a quid pro quo. It is responsive and inclined to act in behalf of the person who inspires it, not as an exchange of one favor for another (this would no longer be gratitude but barter)[6] but because love wants to delight the person who delights us. It is in this way that gratitude almost invariably fosters generosity, which in turn fosters gratitude. Whence Spinoza's characterization of gratitude as a "reciprocal love," an "eagerness of love." "*Thankfulness* or *gratitude* is a desire or eagerness of love, by which we strive to benefit one who has benefited us from a like affect of love."[7] Here is where we go from a purely affective gratitude (to use a Kantian term) to an active gratitude, from joy in return to action in return.[8] To my mind, Spinoza does not so much define gratitude here as describe its consequences (we can, for example, be grateful to someone who is dead and whom we cannot benefit). But the distinction is unimportant. What is certain is that gratitude differs from ingratitude precisely in its ability to see in the other the cause of its joy (unlike self-love, which sees the cause of its joy only in the self).[9] This is why ingratitude is dishonorable[10] and why gratitude is good and makes us good.

"All things excellent are as difficult as they are rare," Spinoza writes.[11] In the case of this excellent thing called gratitude, it is the strength of self-love that accounts for its rarity or difficulty. We all tend to see the love we have received as reason for self-congratulation rather than as cause for gratitude, which is love for the other.[12] "Pride refuses to owe, self-love to pay," writes La Rochefoucauld.[13] How could pride be anything but ungrateful, if it can only love, admire, and extol the self? There is humility in gratitude, and humility is difficult. Is it a sadness? According to Spinoza it is, a point we will return to in the next chapter. What gratitude teaches us, however, is that there is also such a thing as joyful humility, or humble joy, humble because it knows it is not its own cause or its own principle and, knowing this, rejoices all the more (what a pleasure to say thank you!); because it is love, and not primarily love of self; because it knows it is indebted, or rather—since there is nothing to repay—because it knows it has all it could wish for and more, more than it had hoped for or could have expected, all thanks to the existence of the very person or thing responsible for this joy—God if you are a believer, or the world, or a friend, or a stranger, or anything at all. Gratitude is humble because it knows it is graced, graced by existence, or by life, or by all things, and gives in return, not knowing to whom or how, simply because it is good to offer thanks— to give grace—in return, to rejoice in one's own joy and love, whose causes are always beyond our comprehension but which contain us, make us live, and carry us along. The humility of Bach, the humility of Mozart, each so different (the former gives grace with unequaled genius; the latter, we might say, is grace itself) but both overwhelming in their happy gratitude, their true simplicity, their almost superhuman power; even in anguish and suffering, they have a serenity to them that stems from the knowledge of being an effect and not a cause, an effect contained in the very thing they sing, to which they owe their existence and which carries them along. Clara Haskil, Dinu Lipatti, or Glenn Gould could express this, it seems to me, at least when they were at their best, and the joy we feel in listening to them reveals to us what gratitude essentially is, namely joy itself, in as much as it is something received and received undeservedly (yes, even for the best of us!), a state of grace that is always giving itself over to an even higher state of grace, the grace of existing, or rather of existence itself, the essence of being, the principle behind all existence, all beings, all joy, all love. Yes, what we read in Spinoza's *Ethics* we can also hear in music; best of all, it seems to me, in the works of Bach and Mozart (in Haydn what we hear is more on the order of politeness and generosity, in Beethoven courage, in Schubert gentleness, in Brahms fidelity). And so we see how lofty a virtue gratitude is, a virtue more for giants than for dwarfs. Not that we are thereby exempted from it: let us be grateful for grace, and first of all to those who reveal it to us by celebrating it.

No man is the cause of himself: the spirit, Claude Bruaire says, "is in debt for its being."[14] That is not quite accurate, however, for no one ever *asked* to come into being (it is the loan, not the gift, that results in a debt), and no one could ever repay such a debt. Life is not a debt: life is a state of grace, and being is a state of grace; therein lies gratitude's highest lesson.

■

Gratitude rejoices in what has taken place or in what is. It is therefore the opposite of regret or nostalgia (which aches for a past that never was or is no more); it is also the opposite of hope or apprehension, one desiring, the other fearing (both of them desiring *and* fearing) a future that is yet to come and in fact may never be but that tortures by its absence. Gratitude or anxiety, the joy of what is or was, versus the dread of what could be. "The fool's life," says Epicurus, "is empty of gratitude and full of fears; its course lies wholly toward the future."[15] Those who are incapable of gratitude live in vain; they can never be satisfied, fulfilled, or happy: they do not live, they get ready to live, as Seneca puts it.[16] Or as Pascal would say, they hope to live[17] and then regret the life they lived or, more often, the life they did not live. They miss the past as well as the future. The wise man, on the contrary, takes delight in living and also rejoices in having lived. Gratitude (*charis*) is this joy of memory, this love of the past—it neither suffers over what no longer is nor regrets what has been but joyfully recalls what was. It is time regained—the past recaptured, if you will—"the grateful recollection of what has been," says Epicurus—by which we understand that the idea of death is made immaterial, as Proust says, for even death, take us though it will, cannot take from us what we have lived.[18] These are immortal blessings, observes Epicurus, not because we do not die but because death cannot nullify what we have lived, lived fleetingly but definitively.[19] Death deprives us only of the future, which does not exist. Gratitude frees us from death, through the joyous knowledge of what was. Gratitude is acknowledgment, which is to say, knowledge (whereas hope is merely imagination); this is why gratitude touches on truth, which is eternal, and inhabits it. Gratitude is the enjoyment of eternity.

Yet someone will say, in answer to Epicurus, that the recollection, however grateful, of what has been will not give us back the past or return what we have lost. But what can? Gratitude does not abolish grief; it completes it. "We must heal our misfortunes by the grateful recollection of what has been and by the recognition that it is impossible to make undone what has been done."[20] Is there any more beautiful formulation of the mourning process? Mourning is about accepting what is, hence also what no longer is, and loving it as such, in its truth, in its eternity, so that we can go from the unbearable pain of loss to the sweetness of remembrance, from unfinished mourning to its completion ("the grateful recollection of what has been"), from amputation to acceptance, from suffering to joy, from love rent apart to love appeased. "Sweet is the memory of the departed friend," says Epicurus: gratitude is this sweetness itself, when it becomes joyous. Yet suffering at first is the stronger: "How awful that he should have died!" How can we ever accept it? That is why mourning is necessary, and so difficult and so painful. But joy returns in spite of everything: "How fortunate that he should have lived!" The process of mourning is a process of gratitude.

Kant and Rousseau think gratitude a duty.[21] I'm not convinced. Moreover, I don't really believe in duties. But that gratitude is a virtue, in other words, an excellence, of this we find ample proof in the obvious baseness of those who are incapable of gratitude and in the mediocrity of all of us, who are lacking in it. How easily hatred outlasts love! How much stronger resentment is than gratitude. Gratitude sometimes even turns into resentment, so exquisitely sensitive is self-love. As Kant writes, ingratitude toward one's benefactor "is an extremely detestable vice in the public judgment, yet man is so notorious for it, that one thinks it not unlikely to make an enemy even by rendering a benefit."[22] The greatness of gratitude, the pettiness of man.

And yet for all that, gratitude itself can sometimes warrant suspicion. La Rochefoucauld sees it as mere disguised self-interest,[23] and Chamfort observes, correctly, that "there is a base kind of gratitude"—

a disguised servility, a disguised egoism, disguised hope.[24] Sometimes we offer thanks only so that we might continue to receive (we *say* "thank you" but we *think* "more!"). This is not gratitude but flattery, obsequiousness, mendacity. It is not a virtue but a vice. In fact, even sincere gratitude cannot exempt us from any other virtue or justify any wrongdoing. It is a secondary, though not a second-rate, virtue and must be kept in its proper place: justice or honesty might warrant a breach of gratitude, but gratitude never warrants a breach of justice or good faith. Suppose someone has saved my life: am I therefore obliged to give false testimony on his behalf and cause an innocent person to be condemned? Of course not! Whatever we may owe someone, we do not become ungrateful by keeping in mind what we owe everyone else, and ourselves. He is not ungrateful, writes Spinoza, "who is not moved by the gifts of a courtesan to assist her lust, nor by those of a thief to conceal his thefts, nor by those of anyone else like that. On the contrary, he shows firmness of mind who does not allow any gifts to corrupt him, to his or to the general ruin."[25] Gratitude is not connivance; nor is it corruption.

Again, gratitude is joy; it is love. In this respect it borders on charity, which Jankélévitch has likened to "an inchoate gratitude, an unfounded, unconditional gratitude, just as gratitude is a secondary or hypothetical charity."[26] Joy upon joy; love upon love. Gratitude, then, is the secret of friendship, not because we feel indebted to our friends, since we owe them nothing, but because we share with them an overabundance of common, reciprocal joy. "Friendship goes dancing round the world," says Epicurus, "proclaiming to us all to awake to the praises of a happy life."[27] *Thank you for existing*, friends say to one another, and to the world and all the universe. This kind of gratitude is certainly a virtue, for it is the happiness of loving, the only happiness there is.

11

HUMILITY

Humility is a humble virtue, so much so that it even doubts its own virtuousness: to pride oneself on one's own humility is to lack it.

Which proves nothing, however: virtue is nothing to be proud of, and that is what humility teaches us. Humility makes the virtues discreet, unself-conscious, almost self-effacing. Humility is not, however, a lack of awareness; it is the extreme awareness of the limits of all virtue and of one's own limits as well. This discretion is the mark—a discreet mark—of perfect lucidity and unwavering standards. Humility is not contempt for oneself, or if it is, it is informed contempt, deriving not from ignorance of what we are but from the knowledge, or rather the acknowledgment, of all that we are not. This acknowledgment is its limit, since humility is concerned with a kind of nothingness. But that is also what makes humility human. "However much of a sage he may be, after all, he is a man; what is there more unable to support itself, more miserable, more nearly nothing?"[1] The wisdom of Montaigne, the wisdom of humility. It is absurd to want to surpass our humanity; we cannot and must not.[2] Humility is a lucid virtue, always unsatisfied with itself; if it were not, it would be more unsatisfied still. Humility is the virtue of the man who knows he is not God.

And so it is the virtue of saints, a virtue that the wise, apart from Montaigne, sometimes seem utterly without. Pascal criticized philosophers for their arrogance, and not without reason: some have taken the idea of their own divinity quite seriously. Saints are not so easily deluded and invariably reject any suggestion that they are divine. Indeed, anyone who truly believes he is divine either knows nothing about God or else does not know himself. At the very least, humility refuses this second type of ignorance, and it is essentially in this refusal that humility is a virtue. Being humble means loving the truth and submitting to it. Humility means loving truth more than oneself.

Hence all thought that deserves to be so described presupposes humility; humble thought, which is to say, real thought, is the opposite of vanity, which is not thought at all but a form of belief—a belief in the self. Humility, on the other hand, doubts everything, particularly itself. Human, all too human. Could it be that humility itself masks a very subtle form of pride?

But let me first try to define it.

"Humility is a sadness born of the fact that a man considers his own lack of power, or weakness," writes Spinoza.[3] This kind of humility is less a virtue than a feeling: it is an emotion, Spinoza says, and therefore a state of mind. Whoever contemplates his own lack of power finds his spirit "saddened."[4] We have all had this experience, and it would be wrong to claim it as a strength. Now, for Spinoza, strength is precisely what virtue is—strength of mind and always joyous. Thus humility, from his perspective, is not a virtue,[5] and the wise man has no need of it.

The problem, however, may simply be one of nomenclature. For although Spinoza does not consider humility a virtue, he does allow that it "brings more advantage than disadvantage"[6] (it can help the person who practices it to come to the point where he can "live from the dictate of reason," and the prophets were right to commend it).[7] But more important, Spinoza expressly envisions another affect, this one positive, which corresponds precisely to a humility I would call virtuous. "If we suppose," he writes, "that the man conceives his lack of power because he understands something more powerful than himself, by the knowledge of which he determines his power of acting, then we conceive nothing but that the man understands himself distinctly *or* that his power of acting is aided."[8] Such humility is indeed a virtue, for great strength can come from the mind's having adequate knowledge of itself (the opposite of humility is pride, and all pride is ignorance), from its knowing that there exists something greater than itself. Can this knowledge come without sadness? Why not, if one ceases to love oneself only?

Let us not confuse humility with Aristotle's *micropsuchia*, which, certain translations notwithstanding, is better rendered by the term *lowliness*. What is involved here? Recall that, for Aristotle, all virtue is a mean between two vices. So it is with magnanimity or nobility of soul: to exceed this mean is to succumb to vanity; to fall short of it is to succumb to servility, to lowliness. Being lowly means forsaking one's true worth, underestimating one's true value, to the point of not allowing oneself to undertake any higher action, which one assumes to be beyond one's capabilities.[9] Lowliness corresponds rather well to what Spinoza calls *abjectio*, which he distinguishes from humility (*humilitas*). Lowliness, he writes, means "thinking less highly of oneself than is just, out of sadness."[10] Obviously, lowliness can be born of humility, which is why humility can take on the qualities of a vice.[11] But it need not: we can be sad about our powerlessness without thereby exaggerating it—this is what I call virtuous humility—and we can even find in this sadness an added measure of strength with which to fight our powerlessness. It may be said that I am departing from Spinozism here. I am not sure that I am, nor do I care, of course.[12] We know from experience, it seems to me, that sadness can sometimes be a source of inner strength or can help us to muster the strength we already have within us; this is something Spinoza himself recognizes and it counts for more than any philosophical system.[13] There is a courage that comes from despair and a courage, too, that comes from humility. Besides, we do not choose the source of our courage. Better a true sadness than a false joy.

Humility, as a virtue, is this truthful sadness of being merely oneself. And how could one be anything else? We must be merciful toward ourselves: mercy, which tempers humility with a bit of gentleness, teaches us to be content with what we are, which we could not otherwise be without also being vain. Mercy and humility go hand in hand and complement each other. Self-acceptance—but without illusions.

"Self-esteem," says Spinoza, "is really the highest thing we can hope for."[14] Let us say in turn that humility is the highest thing we can despair of, then all will have been said.

◼

Well, maybe not quite, and not yet, for we have still to consider the most important question: what is the *value* of humility? I have said it is a virtue, but how important a virtue is it? What is its status? What is it worth?

The problem is obvious: if humility deserves respect or admiration, isn't it groundlessly humble? And if it is rightly humble, how could we rightly admire it? It seems humility is a contradictory virtue, whose value comes only at its own expense.

"I am very humble" is a performative self-contradiction.

"I lack humility" is a first step toward humility itself.

But how can a subject's value arise from self-depreciation?

Which brings us, basically, to the two perhaps most important critiques of humility, those of Kant and Nietzsche. Let us look at what they wrote. In *The Metaphysical Principles of Virtue*, Kant legitimately opposes what he calls "false humility" (or servility) to the duty of respecting in oneself the innate dignity of man as a moral being: *servility* is the opposite of *honor*, he explains, and the former is a vice as surely as the latter is a virtue.[15] Of course, Kant hastens to add that there does exist a true humility (*humilitas moralis*), which he defines beautifully as "the consciousness and feeling of the insignificance of one's moral worth in comparison with the *law*."[16] Far from violating the dignity of the subject, this latter form of humility presupposes dignity (there would be no reason to subject to the law an individual incapable of such internal legislation: humility implies a certain moral elevation); it also attests to that dignity (to submit to the law is to fulfill a moral duty, here the duty of humility).

Nevertheless, Kant holds humility to very narrow bounds, far narrower, I might add, than those prescribed by Christian (or perhaps only Catholic?) custom. In doing so, he excludes a spiritual disposition that, at least for those who take seriously what mystics, Western as well as non-Western, have to say, is valued. "Kneeling down or groveling on the ground, even to express your reverence for heavenly things, is contrary to human dignity," writes Kant.[17] Well put, but is it true? Clearly one should be neither servile nor sycophantic. But must one therefore—and in opposition to the highest and most recognized spiritual traditions—also condemn begging, for instance? Did Saint Francis of Assisi or the Buddha compromise their own—or our—humanity?[18] One might allow that "bowing or scraping before another seems in any case unworthy of man."[19] But aside from the fact that humility differs from humiliation and has no need of it (only the proud or the perverse find good in it), should we take entirely seriously the *sublimity*—to use the Kantian term—of our moral constitution, when it comes to ourselves? Wouldn't we thereby in fact be demonstrating a lack of humility, of lucidity—and of humor? Man in the system of nature (*homo phaenomenon*, *animal rationale*) is a being of little importance, Kant explains, but man as a person, as a moral being (*homo noumenon*), possesses absolute dignity. "His insignificance as a human animal," he writes, "cannot injure the consciousness of his dignity as a rational man."[20] Perhaps. But what if the two are really one? The materialists are more humble and never forget the animal within them. Human beings are children of the earth (*humus*, whence the word *humility*) and forever unworthy of the heaven they invent for themselves. And as for "comparing oneself with other men," is it really reprehensible or lowly to bow before Mozart?[21] "Whoever makes himself a worm cannot complain when he is then trampled underfoot," writes Kant, proudly.[22] But whoever would make of himself a statue—be it for the glory of man or the sake of the law—cannot complain when he is suspected of being hard-hearted or assuming a pose. Better the sublime beggar who washes the sinner's feet.

As for Nietzsche, he is, as always, right about everything and wrong about everything, and what he says about humility is part of this maelstrom. Who can take issue with the idea that humility often involves a fair amount of nihilism and resentment? How many people reproach themselves solely in order to better reproach the world or life—and thereby excuse themselves? How many negate themselves only because of their inability to affirm—or to do—anything? Or as Spinoza puts it, "those, who are believed to be most despondent [*abjectio*] and humble are usually most ambitious and envious."[23] All that is true. But is it true of everyone? There is a humility in Cavaillès, Simone Weil, Etty Hillesum—and even in Pascal and Montaigne—in comparison with which Nietzschean greatness rings of empty hyperbole. Nietzsche takes up the same image as Kant, the image of the worm: "The trodden worm curls up. This testifies to its caution. It thus reduces its chances of being trodden upon again. In the language of morality: Humility."[24] But is this all there is to humility? Is it what is essential? Do we really believe that this sort of psychologism can account for the humility of Saint Francis of Assisi or Saint John of the Cross? "The most generous people are usually also the most humble," writes Descartes, who was anything but a worm.[25]

One would also be wrong to treat humility as merely the flip side of a kind of self-hatred or confuse it with bad conscience, remorse, or shame. The point is to pass judgment not on what we have done but on what we are. And we are so insignificant. Is there even anything within us to judge? Remorse, bad conscience, or shame presupposes that we might have done things differently and better. "Could do better": this stock phrase, so dear to teachers, accuses rather than encourages. Remorse says the same. Humility says, "Is what he can be." Too humble to accuse or excuse, too lucid to blame unequivocally. Again, humility and mercy go hand in hand. Remorse is an error—because it assumes free will—rather than a failing; the Stoics and Spinoza challenge it on that ground. Is humility more a science—a form of knowledge—than a virtue? A sad science? Perhaps, but it is more useful to man than blissful ignorance. Better to look down on oneself than to misjudge oneself.

Without confusing shame and humility, one might apply to the latter what Spinoza says of the former: "Though a man who is ashamed of some deed is really sad, he is still more perfect than one who is shameless, who has no desire to live honorably."[26] Even sad, the humble man is more perfect than the impudent braggart. Better the decent man's humility than the bastard's self-satisfied arrogance: this everyone knows, and it proves Nietzsche wrong. Humility is the virtue of slaves, he says; the masters, "noble and brave," have no use for it: to them, all humility is worthy of contempt.[27] Granted. But isn't contempt more contemptible than humility? And is "self-glorification," that mark of the aristocrat, compatible with the lucidity that elsewhere Nietzsche correctly takes to be the philosophical virtue par excellence?[28] "I know myself too well to pride myself on anything," the humble man protests; "I need all the mercy I am capable of just in order to put up with myself." What could be more ridiculous than playing at being a superman? Why bother to stop believing in God if it is only to be so utterly self-deceived? Humility is atheism in the first person: the humble man is an atheist with respect to himself, just as the nonbeliever is an atheist with regard to God. Why destroy all idols if it is only to glorify this one last effigy (the self) and worship it? "Humility equals truth," said Jankélévitch: how much truer, and more humble, a notion than Nietzschean *glorification*![29] Honesty and humility are sisters: "Pitiless, lucid honesty, an honesty without illusions, is for those who are honest a continual lesson in modesty; and, conversely, modesty, for the modest, is an aid to honest self-regard."[30] Psychoanalysis operates in this same spirit (in psychoanalysis, Freud says, "his majesty the self" loses his throne), wherein lies its principal merit. Love the truth or love thyself. All knowledge is a narcissistic wound, a blow to our self-esteem.

Is it therefore necessary to hate ourselves, as Pascal would have us do? Certainly not. To do so would be to lack charity, to which everyone (including oneself) has a right, or rather which gives everyone, above and beyond all questions of right and deserts, the love that illuminates him, like a grace, gratuitous and necessary, unjustified but nevertheless due—the small measure of true love, even for ourselves, of which we are sometimes capable!

Love thy neighbor as thyself, and thyself as thy neighbor; "Wherever there is humility," says Augustine, "there is also charity."[31] This is because humility leads to love, as Jankélévitch reminds us,[32] and all true love presupposes humility; without humility, the self comes to occupy all the available space and sees the other person as an object—not of love but of concupiscence!—or as an enemy. Humility is the effort through which the self attempts to free itself of its illusions about itself and—since these illusions are what constitute it—through which it dissolves. Therein lies the greatness of the humble, who penetrate the depths of their pettiness, misery, and insignificance—until they reach that place where there is only nothingness, a nothingness that is everything. Behold, they are as we all are: alone, naked, and revealed, exposed to love and to the light.

Love without illusions, love without lust—are we even capable of such a thing? Which is to say, are we capable of charity?

I shall not try to answer that question just yet. But even supposing that charity were beyond our capabilities, there is always compassion, its humblest face and common approximation.

In speaking of humility, Jankélévitch rightly observes that "the Greeks hardly knew this virtue."[33] Could it be that they did not give themselves a God so great that man might appear as small as he really is? One cannot be sure, however, that they were mistaken as to their own greatness. (Jankélévitch, in my opinion, misunderstands "Stoic pride," just as Pascal does: there is in Epictetus a form of humility through which the self knows it is not God and knows it is nothing.)[34] It could be that they had less narcissism to fight against or at least fewer illusions about themselves to dispel. Whatever the case, our God (the God of the Jews, the Christians, and the Muslims), whether we believe in him or not, offers all of us, in his difference, an invaluable lesson in humility. The ancients defined themselves as mortal; death alone, they believed, set them apart from the gods. Ours is a different perspective, and we now know that even immortality could not, alas, make us different from what we are (and would for that reason probably be an unbearable prospect). Who is there that does not sometimes long for death in order to be freed from the self?

Humility, in this respect, may well be the most religious of virtues. How one yearns to kneel down in churches! Why deny oneself? Speaking only for myself, I would say it is because I would have to believe that God created me—and that pretension, at least, is one of which I have freed myself. What little things we are, how weak and how wretched! Humanity makes for such a pathetic creation: how can we believe a God could have wanted *this*?

So it is that humility, born of religion, can lead to atheism.

To believe in God would be a sin of pride.

12

SIMPLICITY

Humility, the virtue that makes the self an object for its own appraisal, can sometimes be lacking in simplicity. To judge oneself is to take oneself very seriously. The simple person has fewer questions about himself. Is this because he accepts himself as he is? Not exactly: he neither accepts himself nor rejects himself. Nor does he question or think about or study himself. Neither self-glorifying nor self-hating, the simple person is what he is, simply, straightforwardly, unaffectedly; or perhaps I should say—since *being* is a term he would find too grand for his own small existence—he does what he does, like all the rest of us, but sees in his actions no cause for commentary, discussion, or even reflection. He is like the birds in the woods, always silent and weightless, even when singing or sitting on a branch. Reality is sufficient unto itself and simplicity is reality itself. Such is the simple person: a real individual, reduced to his simplest expression. The simplicity of song but more often of silence, and always of life. The simple person lives as he breathes, as effortlessly as he breathes, as unremarkably and as shamelessly as he breathes. Simplicity is not a virtue supplemental to existence; it is existence itself, inasmuch as existence is all there is and cannot be supplemented. It is also the lightest of virtues, the most transparent, and the rarest. The very opposite of literature, simplicity is life plainspoken, without lies, exaggeration, or grandiloquence. It is life in all its insignificance and all its truth.

Simplicity is also the opposite of duplicity, complexity, and pretension. This is why it is so difficult. Isn't consciousness always double, being always consciousness of something? Isn't reality always complex, by virtue of the network of causes and functions that, by definition, it contains? Don't all of us necessarily become pretentious as soon as we try to think? If simplicity is not stupidity, unawareness, nothingness, what then is it?

That the simple man need not ask himself these questions neither invalidates them nor resolves them for us. Simplicity is not simplemindedness. But neither do these questions invalidate simplicity as a fact or as a virtue. Intelligence is not abstruseness, complication, or snobbery. Of course the real is complex, no doubt infinitely so. No one will ever definitively or exhaustively describe or explain a tree, a flower, a star, a pebble . . . This does not prevent them from being simply what they are—yes, very simply and exactly what they are, in all their perfection, straightforwardness, and unpretentiousness—or compel anyone to pursue the hopelessly infinite task of complete description or comprehension. Everything is complex and everything is simple. "The rose has no why attached to it, it blooms because it blooms, has not thought of itself, or desire to be seen."[1] What could be more complicated than a rose for someone who wants to understand it? What could be simpler for someone who wants nothing? The complexity of thinking, the simplicity of beholding. "Everything is both simpler than we can imagine," says Goethe, "and more entangled than we can conceive."[2] The complexity of causes, the simplicity of presence; the complexity of the real, the simplicity of being. "The opposite of being is not nothingness but duplicity," writes Clément Rosset.[3] The opposite of the simple is not the complex but the false.

Simplicity in man—simplicity as a virtue—need not negate consciousness or thought. What characterizes simplicity is its capacity to transcend these, to free itself from them and be undeceived by them yet not repudiate them. True, all consciousness is double, since it is consciousness of an object (intentionality) and consciousness of being conscious (introspection). But this doubleness has no bearing on the simplicity of the real, or of life, or even of pure preintrospective and prepredicative consciousness, without which predication and reflection would not be possible. Simplicity is not unawareness, simplicity is not stupidity: the simple soul is not a simpleton! Simplicity constitutes rather "an antidote to introspection"[4] and to intelligence; it prevents them from deluding themselves, from getting lost within themselves and losing contact with reality, from taking themselves seriously, and from obscuring and ultimately standing in the way of the very thing they claim to reveal or disclose. Simplicity learns to unlearn its attachments, or rather it *is* this detachment from everything, including itself. "Letting go," as Christian Bobin puts it, "accepting what comes, without keeping anything for oneself."[5] Simplicity is nakedness, dispossession, poverty, its only wealth everything, its sole treasure nothingness. Simplicity is freedom, lightness, transparency. Simple as air, free as air: simplicity is airiness of thought, a window open to the grand breath of the world, to the infinite and silent presence of all things. What could be simpler than the wind? What could be airier than simplicity?

Intellectually, simplicity is possibly nothing more than good sense or sound judgment unencumbered by knowledge or belief and thus open to reality and its simplicity, confronting it each time as though for the first time. Simplicity is reason undeceived by itself, lucid reason, embodied reason, minimal reason, if you wish, but still the precondition for all forms of reason. When forced to choose between two proofs, two hypotheses, or two theories, scientists are wont to favor the simplest, wagering on the simplicity of the real and not on the power of the human mind. This choice, the validity of which cannot itself be proved, is merely good sense. Complication not of the real but of thought is a bad sort of complication. Better a "simple, artless truth," as Montaigne put its, one that, though tailored to the complexity of the real when it needs to be, does not complicate reality with the muddle of our minds or mistake itself for reality.[6] Intelligence is the art of making complex things simpler, not the opposite. The intelligence of Epicurus, Montaigne, Descartes ... And of contemporary scientists. What could be simpler than $E=mc^2$? Simplicity of the real, even when complex; clarity of thought, even when difficult. "Aristophanes the grammarian," writes Montaigne, "was all at sea when he criticized in Epicurus the simplicity of his words and the aim of his oratorical art, which was solely perspicuity of language."[7] Why make something complicated when we can make it simple, long when we can make it brief, murky when we can make it clear? If a thought cannot be clearly stated, of what value is it? It is said of our contemporary Sophists that they affect obscurity. I disagree: they affect profundity, which requires that they in fact be obscure. Shallow waters can seem deep only if they are turbid. Their arguments would be more convincing if they were clearer. But if they really were convincing, would they need to be so murky?

This problem is not new. Scholasticism knows no age, or rather every age has a scholasticism of its own. Every generation has its Sophists, its show-offs, its *précieux ridicules*, its pedants. What Descartes said of the Sophists of his time holds for those of today: "This manner of philosophizing is very convenient for those with only mediocre minds, for the obscurity of the distinctions and principles which they use makes it possible for them to speak about everything as confidently as if they knew it, and to defend all they say against the most subtle and clever thinkers without anyone having the means to convince them that they are wrong."[8] Obscurity and complexity protect. To them Descartes opposes the "very simple and evident" principles that he uses, principles that make his philosophy comprehensible to all and open to discussion. The point of thinking is not self-protection. Simplicity, then, is also an intellectual virtue.

But first it is a moral virtue, indeed a spiritual one. Openness of gaze, purity of heart, sincerity of speech, rectitude of soul and conduct ... It would seem we can approach simplicity only indirectly, by something other than itself. For simplicity is not the same as purity, honesty, or rectitude. Fénelon notes, for example, that "many people are honest without being simple: they say nothing that they do not believe is true; they want to be seen only for what they are but are in constant fear of being taken for what they are not; they are forever observing themselves, controlling their every word and thought, and reexamining all they have done in the fear of having done or said too much."[9] In short, they are too preoccupied with themselves, even if their motives are good, and such self-concern is the opposite of simplicity. Not that we should avoid thinking about ourselves. For, as Fénelon writes, "in trying to be simple ... we stray farther from simplicity."[10] The point is to avoid affectations, even affectations of simplicity. Simple selfishness is better than affected generosity, and simple fickleness is better than affected fidelity. Again, it is not that simplicity can be reduced to honesty or to the absence of hypocrisy or mendacity. It is rather that simplicity is devoid of calculation, artifice, or affectation. A simple lie is better than calculated honesty. "These people are honest," Fénelon continues, "but they are not simple; they are ill at ease with others, and others are ill at ease with them; in their presence, nothing is easy, free, artless, or natural; one would rather they be less consistent and more imperfect, and thus less affected. Such is the preference of men, and of God, too: he wants souls that are not concerned with themselves and forever striking poses in the mirror."[11]

Simplicity is spontaneity; it is joyous improvisation, unselfishness, detachment, a disdain for proving, winning, impressing. Hence the impression it gives of freedom, lightness, happy artlessness. "Simplicity," Fénelon writes, "is a rectitude of the soul that sheds all useless reexamination of the self and its actions.... It runs a free course, because it does not pause to affect an image."[12] Simplicity is carefree but not careless; it concerns itself with the real, not with itself. It is the opposite of self-love. Fénelon again: "In shedding all attempts at self-examination, one becomes mentally disengaged from oneself and thus acts more naturally. This kind of true simplicity can sometimes seem careless and lax, but it has a marked penchant for candor and truth and

an artless, gentle, innocent, merry, peaceful quality that charms immediately when viewed from up close with pure eyes."[13]

To be simple, then, is to forget about oneself, and that's what makes
simplicity a virtue: not the opposite of egoism, which is generosity, but
the opposite of narcissism, pretension, self-importance. Is generosity
the worthier virtue? Yes, but only because the ego is so dominant. Yet
not all generosity is simple, whereas absolute simplicity is always generous. (What self-importance in Descartes! What generosity in Saint
Francis!) For the self is nothing more than the set of illusions it has
about itself. Narcissism is not a by-product of the ego but its principle.
Generosity overcomes narcissism, simplicity dispels it. Generosity is
an effort; simplicity is repose. Generosity is a victory; simplicity, a
grace.

Jankélévitch is perceptive in seeing that simplicity is essential to all
the virtues.[14] Affected gratitude is not gratitude, affected humility is
not humility, and courage that is there merely for display is not courage
at all. Modesty without simplicity is false modesty. Simplicity is the
truth of virtues; a virtue can be a virtue only if unfettered from any
concern for appearances, even from any concern for *being* (yes—unfettered from itself!), hence only if it is devoid of affectation, artifice, and
pretension. A person who is courageous, generous, or virtuous only
publicly is not really courageous, generous, or virtuous. And a person
who is simple only publicly is simply mannered (this happens—there are
people who are intimate with strangers and distant from themselves).
"Simplicity put on is a subtle imposture," said La Rochefoucauld.[15] A
lack of simplicity will corrupt any virtue, leaving it empty, or rather,
filled with self. Conversely, while true simplicity does not rid a person
of his faults, it makes us more tolerant of them; someone who is simply
selfish, simply cowardly, or simply unfaithful can still be an appealing,
likable person. On the other hand, who can tolerate the pretentious
imbecile, the devious egoist, or the grandstanding coward? Or the
playboy who passes himself off as a romantic? Simplicity is the truth of
the virtues and it excuses faults; it makes for the grace of saints and the
charm of sinners.

Obviously, however, simplicity does not excuse everything; in fact, it is not so much an excuse as a seduction. But anyone who would use it to that end would be lacking in simplicity.

◾

The simple person is a person without pretensions, unconcerned with himself, his image, or his reputation; he doesn't calculate, has no secrets, and acts without guile, ulterior motives, agendas, or plans. So is simplicity the virtue of childhood? Not really. Rather, it is childhood as a virtue, but childhood rediscovered and recaptured, as though liberated from itself, from its need to imitate adults, from its impatience to grow up, from the seriousness with which it approaches life. Simplicity can be learned only gradually. Witness Clara Haskil's performances of Mozart or Schumann. No child could ever play the C Major Variations, or the *Scenes from Childhood* with the same grace, poetry, lightness, and innocence as this elderly lady. Hers is the spirit of childhood, to which children rarely have access.

The fact that the word *simplicity* can also serve to designate a form of stupidity says much about how we think of intelligence and the uses we ordinarily put it to. But this synonymy cannot obscure the essential thing, which is that simplicity is a virtue and a grace. "Look at the birds of the air ," say the Gospels, "they neither sow nor reap nor gather into barns, and yet your heavenly Father feeds them. . . . Consider the lilies of the field, how they grow; they neither toil nor spin."[16] Prudence will remind us that we cannot always live like the birds of the air. Prudence, however, is an intellectual virtue, while simplicity is a spiritual one. Anyone can see that prudence is more necessary, and simplicity higher. The heavenly Father is not very good at feeding his children, and it is prudent not to live like a bird. But it is also wise to bear in mind the bird's wisdom, that of simplicity. It's the poet's wisdom: "We wander here and there seeking joy, and everywhere there are only crumbs of joy; in the hopping of the sparrow is our only chance to taste these scatterings of God on earth."[17] For God, everything is simple; for the simple person, everything is divine—even work and even effort. "So do not worry about tomorrow, for tomorrow will bring worries of its own. Today's trouble is enough for today."[18] There is nothing wrong with sowing and reaping. But why worry about the harvest when one is sowing? Why repent of having sowed when one is reaping? Simplicity is virtue in the present, here and now, which is why no virtue is real unless it is simple. Nor is there anything wrong with planning, scheduling, and calculating. But simplicity, and thus virtue as well, always eludes them. Complication exists only in the future. The present is simple.

Simplicity means forgetting oneself, forgetting one's pride and fear: tranquillity versus restlessness, joy versus worry, lightness versus seriousness, spontaneity versus reflection, love versus self-love, truth versus pretense. The self persists, but as if lightened, purified, liberated (*"unfettered,"* Bobin says, *"bound no more to any kingdom"*).[19] It has long since given up the quest for salvation and no longer cares about its loss. Religion, and even morality, is too complicated for it. It sees no point in perpetual self-examination. The human capacity for self-scrutiny, self-appraisal, and self-reproach knows no bounds. Our best actions are suspect, our best sentiments ambiguous. The simple person knows this and does not care. He is not interested enough in himself to judge himself. Mercy takes the place of innocence for him, or perhaps it is innocence that takes the place of mercy. He does not take himself seriously or give tragic dimensions to himself or to his life. He goes his merry way, lightheartedly and peacefully. No goal before him, he feels no longing for the past, no impatience about the future. The world is his kingdom, the present his eternity, and that is enough for him. He has nothing to prove, since he does not seek to impress. He seeks nothing at all, since everything is there for him. What could be simpler than simplicity? What could be lighter? Simplicity is the virtue of wise men and the wisdom of saints.

13

TOLERANCE

Several times over the years, French high school students have faced the following question on their baccalaureate examination: "Is it necessarily a sign of intolerance to think that certain things are intolerable?" Or else, in a different version: "Does being tolerant mean tolerating everything?" The answer to both questions, of course, is no, at least if we want tolerance to be a virtue. Must we deem virtuous someone who tolerates rape, torture, or murder? Who could find virtue in a disposition to tolerate the worst? But if the answer can only be negative (something of a drawback for an essay question), the arguments supporting that response nevertheless bring out enough issues of definition and delimitation to keep students sufficiently occupied for the entire four-hour test. An essay examination is not an opinion poll. To be sure, both require answers, but the answer to the former is only as good as the arguments offered in its support. To philosophize is to think without the benefit of proof (if proofs exist, it is no longer philosophy), which is not to say that any thought and all ways of thinking are, philosophically speaking, equally valid. Indeed, to think carelessly or sloppily is not to think at all. In philosophy, reason commands, as it does in the sciences, but without recourse to confirmation or refutation. But then why bother to venture beyond the sciences, where proof is possible? Because we must: the sciences provide no answers to any of the fundamental questions we ask ourselves, not even those they force us to ask. The question "Should we pursue mathematics?" has no mathematical answer. Nor does the question "Are the sciences true?" have a scientific answer. And, of course, there are no mathematical or scientific answers to questions about the meaning of life, the existence of God, or the validity of our values. But how could we keep from asking such questions? The point is to think to the very reaches of our lives, hence as far as possible, beyond the limits of what we know. Metaphysics is the truth of philosophy, even in epistemology and even in moral or political philosophy. Everything holds together and holds us to it. A philosophy is a set of reasonable opinions—something more difficult, and more necessary, to achieve than one might think.

But what does all this have to do with tolerance? Philosophizing, I said, means thinking without proofs, and it is here that tolerance enters the picture. When a truth is known with certainty, tolerance is irrelevant because it has no object. One would not tolerate an accountant's refusal to correct mistakes in his calculations. Nor would one tolerate a physicist's standing fast by a hypothesis of his that experiments have disconfirmed. The right to error applies only *a parte ante:* once an error has been proven, the right no longer applies; to persevere in error, *a parte post,* is no longer an error but a fault. This is why mathematicians have no use for tolerance: proof is all they need. As for those who seek to prevent scientists from doing their work or expressing their findings—as did the Church, for instance, in persecuting Galileo—it is not tolerance they lack so much as intelligence and love of truth. Knowledge must be the priority. The truth demands nothing other than that we pursue it. Scientists need not tolerance but freedom.

That tolerance and freedom are not the same thing is easy to see. No scientist would ask for, or even accept, tolerance of his mistakes, should he make them, or of his incompetence in his own field of study, should he demonstrate it. But nor would he accept being told what to think. The scientist can accept no constraints other than those imposed by experience and reason and an at-least-possible truth: we call this *intellectual freedom*. How does it differ from tolerance? Tolerance comes in only when knowledge is lacking; intellectual freedom is more like knowledge itself in that it frees us from everything, including our own selves. Truth is not obedient, says Alain; this is why it is free, albeit necessary—and why it makes us free. Accepting or rejecting the proposition "The earth revolves around the sun" does not, from a scientific standpoint, involve tolerance in any way whatsoever. A science advances only by correcting its mistakes; it cannot be asked to tolerate them.

The problem of tolerance arises only in matters of opinion, which is why it arises so often, indeed almost constantly. We know far less than we do not know, and everything we know depends, directly or indirectly, on something we do not know. Who can prove beyond a doubt that the earth exists? Or that the sun exists? And if they do not exist, what does it mean to say that one revolves around the other? A proposition that does not involve tolerance from a scientific point of view might involve it from a philosophical, moral, or religious standpoint. Take Darwin's theory of evolution: those who demand that the teaching of it be prohibited have not understood what makes it a scientific theory;[1] yet those who would impose it in an authoritarian manner as the absolute truth about man and his genesis would be demonstrating intolerance. The truth of the Bible can be neither proven nor refuted; therefore, one must either believe in it or tolerate that others believe in it.

This brings us back to where we started. If we must tolerate the Bible, why not *Mein Kampf*? And if we tolerate *Mein Kampf*, why not racism, torture, and extermination camps?

Such universal tolerance would of course be morally reprehensible: it would mean forgetting the victims, abandoning them to their fate, and perpetuating their martyrdom. To tolerate means to accept what could be condemned or allow what could be prevented or combated. It means renouncing some of one's power, strength, or anger. Thus we tolerate the whims of a child or the positions of an adversary, but such forbearance is virtuous only if it involves self-control, the overcoming of personal interest, personal suffering, or personal impatience. Tolerance has value only when exercised against one's own interests and for the sake of someone else's. We cannot claim tolerance when we have nothing to lose, much less when we have everything to gain, by putting up with—in other words, by doing nothing about—what we might otherwise choose to combat or resist. "We all have strength enough to endure the troubles of others," says La Rochefoucauld.[2] Perhaps, but no one would regard this capacity as tolerance. To tolerate is to take upon oneself; a tolerance that comes into being on the backs of others is no longer tolerance. To tolerate the suffering of others, to tolerate an injustice of which we are not a victim or an atrocity that we are spared is not tolerance but selfishness, indifference, or worse. Tolerating Hitler meant becoming his accomplice, at least by omission or neglect; this kind of tolerance was already a form of collaboration. Hatred, rage, and violence are all preferable to this sort of passivity in the face of horror, to this shameful acceptance of the worst. Tolerating everything would mean tolerating atrocity—an atrocious tolerance.

But universal tolerance would also be self-contradictory in practical terms and thus not just morally reprehensible but also politically doomed. Karl Popper and Vladimir Jankélévitch, in different contexts, both speak to this point. Taken to the extreme, Jankélévitch argues, tolerance "would end up negating itself" since it would give free rein to those who seek to destroy it.[3] Tolerance, therefore, can only apply within certain boundaries, which maintain and preserve the conditions that make it possible. Popper calls this "the paradox of tolerance": "If we extend unlimited tolerance even to those who are intolerant, if we are not prepared to defend a tolerant society against the onslaught of the intolerant, then the tolerant will be destroyed, and tolerance with them."[4] This qualification of tolerance is valid only to the extent that humanity is the way it is—prone to conflict, passion, and division. And that is why it is in fact valid. A society in which unlimited tolerance was possible would no longer be a human society; moreover, it would have no need for tolerance.

Unlike love and generosity, which have no inherent boundaries or finitude except those imposed by our own personal incapacities, tolerance is instrinsically limited; an infinite tolerance would mean the end of tolerance! Should there be freedom for the enemies of freedom? Things are not so simple. Virtue cannot be confined to a community of the virtuous; a person who is just solely with the just, generous solely with the generous, and merciful solely with the merciful is neither just nor generous nor merciful. Similarly a person is not tolerant if he is tolerant only of other tolerant people. If tolerance is a virtue, as I believe it is and as it is ordinarily seen to be, it must be applicable unilaterally and include people who do not practice it themselves. Morality is neither a transaction nor a mirror. It is true, of course, that intolerant people would have no right to complain if they were treated with intolerance. But why would a virtue depend on the point of view of those who are lacking in it? As John Rawls observes, the just must be guided by the "principles of justice and not by the fact that the unjust cannot complain."[5] The same applies to the tolerant, who must be guided by the principles of tolerance. Though one must not tolerate everything, since to do so would be to ensure the downfall of tolerance, one cannot refuse to extend any tolerance whatsoever toward those who do not themselves respect it. A democracy that would ban all nondemocratic parties would be insufficiently democratic, just as a democracy that would allow them complete latitude would be overly, or rather badly, democratic—and therefore doomed: it would not defend freedom with force when force was necessary; nor could it defend the law through the imposition of constraints.

The criterion here is not moral but political. Whether a specific individual, group, or behavior should be tolerated depends not on whether they themselves are tolerant—if it did, then all the extremist groups of our youth would have been banned and thereby vindicated—but on how dangerous they really are: an intolerant action or group should be banned if and only if it genuinely threatens freedom or the conditions that make tolerance possible. When a republic is strong and stable, democracy, tolerance, or liberty will not be endangered by a demonstration against them: hence such a demonstration need not be banned and to seek such a ban is to lack tolerance. But if institutions are fragile, if civil war threatens or has already begun, if seditious groups threaten to take power, the same demonstration can become a genuine danger. It then may be necessary to prohibit it, even by force, and not to do so would be to lack resolve or prudence. In short, circumstances vary, and this "casuistry of tolerance," as Jankélévitch calls it, is one of the major problems of our democracies.[6] After presenting the paradox of tolerance, according to which tolerance is weakened if extended ad infinitum, Karl Popper continues:

In this formulation, I do not imply, for instance, that we should always suppress the utterance of intolerant philosophies; as long as we can counter them by rational argument and keep them in check by public opinion, suppression would certainly be most unwise. But we should claim the *right* to suppress them if necessary even by force; for it may easily turn out that they are not prepared to meet us on the level of rational argument, but begin by denouncing all argument; they may forbid their followers to listen to rational argument, because it is deceptive, and teach them to answer arguments by the use of their fists or pistols. We should therefore claim, in the name of tolerance, the right not to tolerate the intolerant. We should claim that any movement preaching intolerance places itself outside the law, and we should consider incitement to intolerance and persecution as criminal, in the same way as we should consider incitement to murder, or to kidnapping, or to the revival of the slave trade, as criminal.[7]

Democracy is not weakness. Tolerance is not passivity.

Reprehensible morally and doomed politically, a universal tolerance would be neither virtuous nor viable. Or to put it another way, some things are intolerable, even—or especially—for a tolerant person. Morally intolerable is suffering of others, injustice, and oppression, when they could be prevented or fought against by means of a lesser evil. Politically intolerable is anything that actually threatens the freedom, peace, or survival of a society (determining whether such a threat is real means assessing risks, always an uncertain enterprise). Any threat to tolerance is therefore also politically intolerable, provided the threat is not simply the expression of an ideological position—which can be tolerated—but a genuine danger—which must be fought, if necessary through force. This formula leaves room for casuistry in the best of cases and bad faith in the worst.[8] It also leaves room for democracy, for its uncertainties and risks, which are nonetheless clearly preferable to the comfort and certitudes of totalitarianism.

What is totalitarianism? It is the complete power of a party or the state over the whole of society. The differences between totalitarianism and dictatorship are to be found above all in the former's ideological dimension. Never just the power of one man or group, totalitarianism is also, perhaps primarily, the power of a doctrine or ideology (often with scientific pretensions), of a "truth" or so-called truth. Every type of government has its guiding principle, says Montesquieu; monarchy operates on the principle of honor, republicanism on virtue, despotism on fear, and totalitarianism, adds Hannah Arendt, on ideology or (seen from within) on "truth."[9] This is why totalitarianism is intolerant: because truth is not a matter of debate (though it *is* a matter *for* debate); it doesn't require elections or take individual preferences or opinions into account. Totalitarianism is like a tyranny of truth. This is also why all intolerance tends toward totalitarianism—or, in religious matters, toward fundamentalism: only in the name of the supposed truth of one's point of view can one pretend to impose it on others, or rather, only by supposing its truth can one claim justification for its imposition. Dictatorship that governs through force is despotism; if it governs through ideology it is totalitarianism. Naturally, most totalitarian regimes are also despotic (force must come to the rescue of ideology, if need be) and in modern societies, which are mass-media societies, most despotic regimes tend toward totalitarianism (force must be justified by ideology). Indoctrination and the police state go hand in hand. The fact remains that the question of tolerance, for a long time solely a religious question, now tends to permeate the life of society as a whole, or perhaps I should say, conversely, that sectarianism, formerly a religious phenomenon, is now omnipresent and multiform and governed by politics much more than by religion: whence terrorism, when sectarianism is in the opposition, and totalitarianism, when sectarianism finds itself in power. Perhaps human history will one day escape these recurrent patterns. What we shall never fully escape, however, is intolerance, fanaticism, and dogmatism. With each new "truth," they make their reappearance. What is tolerance? Alain's answer is this: "A wisdom that overcomes fanaticism, that baleful love of truth."[10]

Must we therefore stop loving the truth? To do so would be to do totalitarianism a great favor and deprive ourselves of the means to fight it. "The ideal subject of totalitarian rule," notes Hannah Arendt, "is not the convinced Nazi or the convinced Communist, but people for whom the distinction between fact and fiction (*i.e.*, the reality of experience) and the distinction between true and false (*i.e.*, the standards of thought) no longer exist."[11] Sophistry plays into the hands of totalitarianism: if nothing is true, how can we oppose its lies? If there are no facts, how can we accuse totalitarianism of concealing or distorting them, and how can we reply to its propaganda? For while totalitarianism lays claim to the truth, it inevitably, whenever the real truth disappoints its expectations, invents another, more manageable one. I need not dwell on this point: the facts are well known. Totalitarianism begins as dogmatism (it claims that the truth legitimizes it and justifies its power) and ends as sophistry (it calls "truth" whatever legitimizes it and justifies its power). First "science," then brainwashing. Clearly, totalitarian truths and totalitarian sciences are ersatz truths and pseudosciences (like Nazi biology or Stalinist history), but that is not the essential problem with them. A regime whose power rested on real science—a tyranny of physicians, for example—would nonetheless be totalitarian if it pretended to govern in the name of its truths: truth never governs, never dictates what to do or prohibit. Truth does not obey, as Alain reminds us, and that makes it free. Nor does it give orders, and that makes us free. It is true that we will die, but that truth does not make life condemnable or murder justifiable. It is also true that we lie, that we are selfish, unfaithful, and ungrateful, but that does not excuse us or prove wrong those who are sometimes faithful, generous, or grateful. Truth is of a different order from good and evil. Knowledge is no substitute for will, either for communities or for individuals (no science, not even a true science, can take the place of either democracy or morality).[12] Therein lies the failure, at least the theoretical failure, of totalitarianism: contrary to its claims, truth cannot justify it or legitimize its power. That the truth does not govern does not mean it can be put to a vote. It cannot be, and therefore all government can and must be.

Not that one must renounce the love of truth in order to be tolerant; quite the contrary, it is this very love—stripped of its illusions—that provides us with our main reasons for being. The first of these reasons is that loving truth means recognizing that we can never know it absolutely and with utter certainty. The problem of tolerance, as we have seen, arises only in matters of opinion. And what is an opinion, if not an uncertain belief or, at any rate, a belief whose only certainty is subjective? A Catholic may be subjectively certain of the truth of Catholicism, but if he is intellectually honest—if he loves truth more than certitude—he will have to admit that he cannot convince a Protestant, an atheist, or a Muslim of that truth, even though they may be as cultured, intelligent, and sincere as he is. Every believer, however convinced he is that he is right, must acknowledge that he cannot prove that he is right, must recognize that his position is no different from that of any of his adversaries, who are just as convinced as he is and just as incapable of convincing him. Tolerance, as a practical capacity or virtue, is based on our theoretical powerlessness—in other words, on our inability to attain the absolute. Montaigne, Bayle, Voltaire all recognize this. "It is placing a very high value on one's conjectures," says Montaigne, "to cause a man to be burned alive because of them." "Obviousness is a relative quality," says Bayle. And Voltaire in pedal point: "What is toleration? It is the prerogative of humanity. We are all steeped in weaknesses and errors: let us forgive one another our follies, it is the first law of nature."[13] Here is where tolerance verges on humility, or rather follows from it, just as humility follows from honesty and good faith; to love truth all the way is to accept the doubt in which truth, for man, must culminate. Voltaire again: "But it is even clearer that we should tolerate each other because we are all weak, inconsequential, subject to mutability and to error. Would a reed laid into the mud by the wind say to a neighboring reed bent in the opposite direction: 'Creep in my fashion, wretch, or I shall petition to have you torn up and burned'"?[14] Humility and mercy go hand in hand and, together, in matters of thought, lead to tolerance.

The second reason has more to do with politics and the limits of the state than with either morality or knowledge. Even if a sovereign had access to absolute truth, he would lack the power to impose it on anyone, because an individual cannot be compelled to think other than what he thinks or be made to believe true what looks false to him. Spinoza and Locke recognized this fact, a fact that the various forms of totalitarianism in the twentieth century confirm.[15] One can prevent a person from expressing his beliefs, but one cannot prevent him from having them, unless one were to suppress thought itself and weaken the state accordingly. There can be no intelligence without the freedom to come to one's own judgments, and no society can prosper without intelligence. A totalitarian state must therefore resign itself to either stupidity or dissidence, to either poverty or criticism. The recent history of Eastern Europe demonstrates that although totalitarianism can steer between these shoals for a long time, eventually they spell disaster for it—a disaster that is as unavoidable, sooner or later, as its shape is unpredictable. Intolerance makes people stupid just as stupidity makes people intolerant. This is fortunate for our democracies and may account in part for their strength, which many have found surprising, or for the ultimate weakness of totalitarian states. Neither would have surprised Spinoza, who anticipates totalitarianism in the following description:

> But let it be granted that freedom may be crushed, and men so bound down, that they do not dare to utter a whisper, save at the bidding of their rulers; nevertheless this can never be carried to the pitch of making them think according to authority, so that the necessary consequences would be that men would daily be thinking one thing and saying another, to the corruption of good faith, that mainstay of government, and to the fostering of hateful flattery and perfidy, whence spring stratagems, and the corruption of every good art.[16]

In short, a state's intolerance (and therefore also what we call totalitarianism) must weaken the regime sooner or later, by weakening the social fabric and individual conscience. In a tolerant regime, on the other hand, the strength of the state makes for the freedom of its constituents, and their freedom makes for its strength. "If governments are to retain a firm hold," Spinoza concludes, everyone must submit "to the control of authority over his actions" (the authority of the people, in a democracy); yet, he adds, "it is imperative that freedom of judgment should be granted, so that men may live together in harmony, however diverse, or even openly contradictory their opinions may be."[17] What is it that Spinoza is describing here if not secularism? And what is secularism if not tolerance as an institution?

The third reason, which I alluded to first, is perhaps the most recent to enter our spiritual universe and the least widely accepted: it has to do with the disjunction between truth and values, between the true and the good (or let us say, with their mutual independence). If truth commands, as Plato, Stalin, or John Paul II believes, then the only virtue is submission to truth. And since truth is the same for us all, we must all submit identically to the same values, rules, and imperatives; a single truth, a single morality, a single politics, and a single religion for all! There can be no salvation outside the truth, and no truth outside the

Church or the Party. Pragmatic dogmatism, which treats value as though it were truth, leads to clean consciences, complacency, exclusion of or contempt for others—it leads to intolerance. John Paul II, for example, writes that all those who do not submit to "the *truth* about moral good and evil," a truth "indicated by the 'divine law,' *the universal and objective norm of morality*," live in sin, and though we must certainly feel sorry for such people and love them, we cannot acknowledge their right to a different opinion: to do so would be to lapse into "subjectivism, relativism, and skepticism" and thereby to forget that "there can be no freedom apart from or in opposition to the truth."[18] Since truth does not depend on us, morality does not either: "moral truth," according to John Paul II, compels recognition by all and cannot derive from cultures or history or from any autonomy of man or reason.[19] And this truth, of course, is "revealed truth," as transmitted by the Church, and by the Church alone. Never mind the countless Catholic couples who use condoms or the Pill, never mind the countless Catholic homosexuals and modern-thinking theologians: "The fact that some believers act without following the teachings of the Magisterium, or erroneously consider as morally correct a kind of behavior declared by their Pastors as contrary to the law of God, cannot be a valid argument for rejecting the truth of the moral norms taught by the Church."[20] Nor can individual or collective conscience be: *"The Church's reply contains the voice of Jesus Christ, the voice of truth about good and evil."*[21] Truth compels recognition by all; therefore so does religion (since it is the *true* religion) and so does morality (since it is "founded upon truth").[22] This philosophy is like a Russian doll: one must obey the truth, therefore God, therefore the Church, therefore the pope. Atheism and apostasy, for example, are mortal sins—in other words, sins that if unrepented lead to "eternal damnation." That makes me already twice damned, even without counting my other transgressions, which are innumerable. John Paul II calls this "the consoling certainty of the Christian faith."[23] *Veritatis terror!*

I do not wish to dwell on this encyclical, which hardly matters. Since historical circumstances make any return to the Inquisition or a moral order implausible (at least in the West, in the near or not too distant future), the Church's positions, intolerant though they are, must of course be tolerated. As we have seen, only the potential danger of an attitude, not its own degree of tolerance or intolerance, ought to determine whether one should tolerate it or not. What fortunate times are these, what lucky countries we live in, now that even the churches have ceased being dangerous! Gone are the days when the Church could have Giordano Bruno burned at the stake, Calas tortured, and the Chevalier de La Barre guillotined (at nineteen). I brought up the encyclical merely as an example of how pragmatic dogmatism always leads to intolerance, however attenuated. If values are true and known, they are not subject to discussion or choice. Those who do not share them are simply wrong and deserve only such tolerance as one might show the ignorant or the mentally challenged. But is this sort of attitude still tolerance?

For those who recognize that values and truth belong to two different orders (the latter to that of knowledge, the former to that of desire), this disjunction provides an additional reason for being tolerant: even if we had access to absolute truth, everyone would not be obliged to respect the same values or live the same way. Knowledge, which concerns itself with how things are, has nothing to say as to how things should be; knowledge does not pass judgment and does not dictate! Knowledge compels recognition, but it compels nothing else. Even if God existed, why would we always have to approve of him? Whether he exists or not, on what grounds could I impose my desires, will, or values on people who do not share them? Because we need to have common laws? Certainly we need them, but only in areas where commonality exists! Why should I care about other people's erotic peculiarities so long as they are practiced between consenting adults? As for laws that apply to all, they are certainly necessary (to prevent the worst and protect the weak), but it is up to politics and culture to see to them. Always relative, contentious, and mutable, they cannot be derived from some absolute truth that would compel recognition and that we could thereby legitimately compel others to accept. The truth is the same for all of us, but desire and will are not. I do not mean to say that our desires and wills can never bring us closer; it would be most surprising if they did not, since we all have essentially the same body, the same faculty of reason (which, though not wholly responsible for morality, does play an important part in it, of course), and, increasingly, the same culture. The confluence of desires, the communion of wills, the convergence of civilizations, when they occur, are not the result of any particular knowledge; they are the work of history, desire, civilization. Christianity has played a major role in these developments, as we all know. This fact does not excuse the Inquisition, of course, but neither is it erased by it. *"Love, and do what you wish ..."* Can we still have this morality of love without the dogmatism of Revelation? Why not? Do we need complete knowledge of the truth in order to love it? Do we need a God in order to love our neighbor? *Veritatis amor, humanitatis amor ...* Against the splendor of truth (why assume it is splendid?) and the weight of dogmas and churches, let us have the gentleness of tolerance.

And so to conclude, we might ask ourselves if the word *tolerance* is appropriate; it has something condescending, even contemptuous, about it that is disturbing. Paul Claudel, playing on a French euphemism for brothel, once said: "Tolerance? There are houses for that!" The quip reveals much about Claudel, and about tolerance. When we tolerate other people's opinions are we not implying that we consider them inferior or erroneous? Strictly speaking, we can only tolerate something that we would have the right to prevent: if opinions can be freely held, as they should be, then they do not fall under the purview of tolerance! Therein lies yet another paradox of tolerance, one that seems to invalidate the notion. If we are entitled to freedom of belief, opinion, expression, and religion, then these freedoms need to be not tolerated but respected, protected, and honored. Only "the insolence of a dominating religion," as Condorcet notes, "could call tolerance, that is, a permission granted by men to other men," what should be seen as a respect for mutual freedom.[24] A hundred years later, at the beginning of this century, contributors to Lalande's *Vocabulaire technique et critique de la philosophie* express the same reservations. "It is a misnomer to call the respect for religious freedom tolerance," writes Charles-Bernard Renouvier, "for it is nothing other than justice and entirely an obligation." Louis Prat, another contributor, says: "We should not say *tolerance* but respect; otherwise we insult moral dignity. In our language, the word *tolerance* all too often connotes politeness, or pity, or indifference; this may be why the idea of respect owed to honest freedom of thought is distorted in most minds."[25] All these observations are justified, but they have been of no avail against usage. I note, moreover, that the adjective *respectful*, in French, evokes not the notion of respect for other people's freedom, or even for their dignity, but rather that of a kind of deference or regard that we often find suspect and that certainly does not belong in a treatise on the virtues.

On the other hand, in philosophical as well as everyday language, *tolerance* is the standard term to designate the virtue that stands counter to fanaticism, sectarianism, authoritarianism—in short, to intolerance. This usage does not seem unreasonable to me, for it reflects the intolerance of which each of us is capable in the very virtue that overcomes it. As I said earlier, strictly speaking we can only tolerate something that we would have the right to prevent, condemn, or forbid. But this *right*, which we do not have, we almost always feel we have. Are we not right to think what we think? And if we are right, then aren't those who think otherwise necessarily wrong? How, except through tolerance, could truth ever accept the existence or persistence of error? Dogmatism will always be with us, for it is simply an illusory and egoistical love of truth. Were we more lucid, generous, and just, what we call tolerance we would call respect or sympathy or love. *Tolerance* is therefore the appropriate word, given our lack of love, our lack of sympathy, our lack of respect.

The word bothers us only because tolerance is not beyond our natures, or not too far beyond—for once! A minor virtue, says Jankélévitch, because it resembles us.[26] "Tolerance is obviously not an ideal," F. Abauzit notes. "It is not a maximum but a minimum."[27] True, but it is better than nothing and certainly better than its opposite! It goes without saying that respect or love would be better still. But if *tolerance* has become the standard term, it is probably because we all feel so very incapable of love or respect toward our adversaries—those toward whom tolerance is most necessary. "While awaiting the day when tolerance will become loving," concludes Jankélévitch, "we will say that tolerance, prosaic tolerance, is the best we can do! Tolerance—though the word is hardly exalting—is therefore a passable solution; while awaiting better—that is, until men become capable of loving one another, or simply of knowing and understanding one another—let us count ourselves fortunate if they can at least suffer each other. Tolerance, then, belongs to the interim period."[28] Let us hope that this interim can endure: if it does not, its likely successor will be barbarism, not love! Tolerance, like politeness, is a small virtue, and it may well play the same role in the life of the collectivity that politeness plays in our interpersonal relationships.[29] Tolerance is only a beginning, but at least it is that.

This is to say nothing of the fact that one must sometimes tolerate things that one wants neither to respect nor to love. Disrespect is not always wrong—far from it—and there are hatreds that come close to being virtues. Some things are intolerable, as we have seen, and must be fought; other things are tolerable even though contemptible and detestable. Tolerance reveals this range or at least allows it. This small virtue suits us; it is within our reach, which is not so usual, and some of our adversaries, we feel, deserve no better . . .

Just as simplicity is the virtue of the wise and the wisdom of saints, tolerance is wisdom and virtue for all those—like ourselves—who are neither wise nor saintly.

A small but necessary virtue. A small but accessible wisdom.

14

PURITY

Purity, if in fact a virtue, is perhaps the most difficult to grasp or apprehend. We must have some experience of it, however; otherwise, how could we know anything at all about impurity? But the experience of purity is at first a foreign and questionable one. The purity of young girls, of certain young girls, has always greatly affected me. Who is to say whether their purity was real or feigned, or rather whether it wasn't simply an impurity that differed from mine and that troubled it only because of its difference, as two colors will sometimes enhance each other by contrast, though both are colors still. Could it be that I, who have loved nothing more intensely than purity and desired nothing more intensely than the impure, do not know what either of them is? It may well be. What Augustine said of time may hold for purity as well: so long as no one asks me to explain it, I know what it is; but if someone asks me to explain it and I try to do so, I no longer know.[1]

I mention young girls. The fact is that in our day purity tends first to be understood in sexual terms. Because sex is impure? That remains to be seen. The girls I am thinking of, several of whom brightened my adolescence, were of course no less feminine than others, nor were they less desirable (sometimes they were more so), nor perhaps any less desiring. But they had the virtue (yes, virtue), or so it seemed, of inhabiting their sexual and mortal bodies in bright daylight and of radiating something of an inner light, as though neither love nor blood could defile them. Indeed, how could they? Love and blood are the purity of the living and represent life itself. Such purity beats within their veins like a peal of laughter.

Other young girls, as you might guess, attracted me (and I suppose others as well) by a suggestion of impurity that one would be hard put to describe. They seemed to inhabit night, not day; they stopped the light (as certain men can do) or rather reflected it (which few men can do), and yet could see into themselves as well as into you. They seemed to live on the same level as the desire of men, with its violence, coarseness, and fascination with obscenity or darkness, and they had just the right touch of vulgarity and joyful perversion that attracts men or reassures them.

As girls like these grow older, it becomes much harder to tell the two apart. Or if one can, it is only by the quantity of love of which they are capable: love has no use for purity, or is the only purity of any value. Women know this better than girls, and that is why they frighten us more.

But let us return to purity. The first meaning of the word, both in Latin and in French, is physical: what is pure is clean, spotless, unsoiled. Pure water is unmixed water, water that is nothing but water. Note that such water is actually dead, a fact that says a lot about life and about a certain nostalgia for purity. Whatever lives also soils, and all that cleans kills. Thus we add chlorine to our swimming pools. Purity is impossible; we can only choose between different varieties of impurities, and the practice of this choice we call hygiene. How can one make a moral system of it? The wars in Serbia, Bosnia, and Croatia gave us the term *ethnic cleansing*, and the horrors it represents will be the eternal shame of those who have made it a political principle. There are no pure or impure populations. Every group is a mixture, as is every organism and all life. Purity, at least this sort of purity, is on the side of death or nothingness. Water is pure when it contains no germs, chlorine, calcium, or mineral salts and is nothing but water—in other words, a water that does not exist, or rather that exists only in laboratories. Such water, odorless and tasteless, would kill us if we drank nothing else. Furthermore, it is pure on only one level. If the hydrogen molecules could speak, they could protest their contamination by oxygen, and each nucleus could complain of being forced into an impure association with an electron. Only nothingness is pure, and nothingness is nothing: whatever exists is a stain on the infinite void, and all existence is impure.

Agreed. Still, all religions, or nearly all, make a distinction between that which the law dictates or allows—the pure—and that which it forbids or punishes—the impure. The sacred in the first instance is what can be profaned, and perhaps that is all it is. Purity, conversely, is what allows a person to approach sacred things without defiling them or being destroyed by them. Hence the prohibitions, taboos, and purification rites that religions seem to generate in such profusion. We are only at the surface, but one must begin somewhere. Still, we would be short-sighted indeed if we reduced all religious notions of purity to hygiene, prudence, and disease prevention. Religious dietary prohibitions, those of Judaism, for example, might certainly have played that role. But were that the end of it, the world's debt to the Jewish people would not be what it is—enormous, decisive, forever ineradicable—and we could dispense with morals altogether in favor of dietetics, as would have pleased Nietzsche. But does anyone really take such ideas seriously? Is hygiene all that monotheism amounts to, all that it has bequeathed to us? Is maintaining our precious health, cleanliness, and wholesomeness all we care about and all we need to care about? True masters, of course, have always said the opposite. Rituals are not the essential thing; what is essential is what they suggest or engender. Kashrut is not about health, it is about keeping or not keeping kosher! Sanctity is not a matter of sanitation. Clean and pure are not the same. Instead of reducing ritual to hygiene, we would do far better to seek out in each the elements that transcend and justify them. All living religions do this. From the very beginning, they learn to give prescriptions for external behaviors a primarily—even exclusively—symbolic or moral meaning. The function of ritual is not hygienic but pedagogic and is pedagogic for spiritual, not sanitary, ends. Religious purity is a first step toward moral purity—and even toward another, completely internal purity next to which morality itself might appear superfluous or squalid. Morality is something that only the culpable need worry about; for the pure, purity takes the place of morality or exempts them from it.

Some will say, however, that morality is therefore more necessary, and I will agree; or that the purity of which I am speaking is a myth, and of course I cannot prove that it is not. Let us not give Pascal and his ilk—all those who would like to imprison us in our sinful natures— more than their due. Purity is not incorporeity. The body can be pure and it can be innocent, even in orgasm: *pura voluptas*, says Lucretius, pure pleasure, next to which morality seems somehow obscene.[2] I do not know how confessors manage; I suppose by now they have probably given up quizzing, judging, and condemning. They must know that most of the time the impurity evinced in the confessional would come from their side of the screen and that lovers have no use for their morality.

Yet let us not rush too far ahead, too fast. Women who have been raped, when they are able to describe what happened, all report the feeling of having been dirtied, defiled, and humiliated. And wouldn't many wives, if they were truthful, admit that they submit to their husbands' irksome or brutal impurity only halfheartedly? Halfheartedly: the word is revealing in itself. Only the heart is or can be pure; only the heart purifies. Nothing is pure or impure in itself. Spittle and kisses contain the same saliva; sexual desire can be expressed by rape as well as by love. Sex is not impure, but force and coercion are (Simone Weil puts it this way: love "neither exercises force nor submits to it. That constitutes the only purity"), as is anything that humiliates or demeans, desecrates or debases, that lacks respect, gentleness, or consideration.[3] Conversely, purity resides not in the ignorance or the absence of desire (were such a state possible, which I doubt, it would be a disease, not a virtue); it resides in desire that is nonoffensive and nonviolent, in desire that is accepted and shared, that elevates and celebrates. I know that transgression, violence, and guilt can also heighten desire, sometimes even more than purity can. But that is just the point: purity is an exaltation of the opposite kind. It is the gentleness of desire, its peace and innocence. Look how chaste we are after lovemaking, how pure we can be in our sexual pleasure. No one is absolutely innocent or guilty. Thus the "despisers of the body," to use Nietzsche's expression, are wrong, as are those who devote themselves to the body too zealously or exclusively.[4] Purity is not an essence; nor is it an attribute that one either has or lacks. Purity can never be absolute; purity is not pure; purity is a certain way of not seeing evil where there is no evil to be seen. An impure person sees evil everywhere and takes pleasure in the fact. A pure person sees evil nowhere, or rather sees it only where it exists—in selfishness, cruelty, spitefulness—and it grieves him. Whatever we do with an evil heart, or heartlessly, is impure. This is why we are impure, almost always, and why purity is a virtue: the self is pure only when it is purified of itself. The ego befouls whatever it touches. "To assume power over is to soil," writes Simone Weil. "To possess is to soil."[5] Conversely, "to love purely is to consent to distance"—in other words, to nonpossession, to the absence of power and control, to joyful and disinterested acceptance.[6] "You will be loved," Cesare Pavese confides in his diary, "the day when you will be able to show your weakness without the person using it to assert his strength." He wanted to be loved purely, which is to say, to be loved.

Love that takes is impure; love that gives or contemplates is pure.

To love, to love truly and purely, is not to take; to love is to look, to accept, to give and to lose, to rejoice over what we cannot possess, over what we lack (or would lack if we sought to possess it), over what makes us infinitely poor; and it is our only possession and our only wealth. The absolute poverty of a mother at her child's bedside: she possesses nothing since her child is all and she does not possess him. "My treasure," she whispers. And she feels destitute. The poverty of the lover and the saint: they have placed all they have in what cannot be possessed or consumed and have made of themselves a kingdom and a desert for an absent god. Their love is pure loss—it is love itself, or the only love that is pure. Who would love only in the hope of profit, gain, and advantage? Egoism may still be love, certainly, but it is an impure love, "the very source of evil," Kant says.[7] One does not commit evil for the sake of evil, only for the sake of pleasure, which is a good. What corrupts "the purity of motives," to use Kant's terminology again, is not the body or some malignant will (that would desire evil for evil's sake) but "the cherished self" that we always come up against.[8]

Not that we are not entitled to love ourselves, of course; if we did not, how could we love our neighbor *as we love ourselves* (assuming we can)? The self is not detestable, or rather, only selfishness makes it so. There is nothing wrong with loving oneself, what is wrong is loving *only* oneself, being indifferent to the suffering of others, to their desire and freedom, being prepared to hurt them for one's own benefit or humiliate them for one's own pleasure, wanting to use them for one's own pleasure instead of loving them, using them for pleasure instead of taking pleasure in the fact that they exist, or rather taking pleasure only in one's own pleasure and thereby, once again, loving only oneself.[9] This is the first impurity, possibly the only one there is. Not an excess of love but a lack of love. It is neither by chance nor merely out of prudery that sexuality has been considered impurity's privileged domain, presided over as it is by what scholastic theologians used to call concupiscent love (loving another person for one's personal benefit), which they contrast to benevolent love, the love of friends (loving another person for his own benefit). One can love another person as an object, wanting to possess, consume, and enjoy him as one would a wine or a good cut of meat, in other words, loving him only for one's own self: this is Eros, a love that takes or devours, and Eros is a selfish god. Or one can love the other person truly, as a subject and a person, respecting and defending him, if only against one's own feelings of desire: such love is Philia or Agape, the love that gives and protects, the love of friendship, kindness, and, if you wish, charity; a pure love, yes, and the only purity, indeed the only god.[10]

What is a pure love? Fénelon describes it well: it is disinterested love, the kind we have, or should have, for our friends; Fénelon understands that many friendships "are merely self-love subtly disguised," but still, he maintains, we have in us "this idea of a pure friendship" that alone can satisfy us. Indeed, who would accept to be loved, or to love, only out of self-interest? Pure love is also love "without hope," to use his words again, love liberated from the self "such that we forget ourselves and count ourselves as nothing, in order to give ourselves entirely to the other person."[11] In short, what Saint Bernard calls "an unadulterated love unstained by personal pursuit": it is love itself and the purity of pure hearts.[12]

The term *purity*, we would do well to recall at this point, has meaning in other than sexual contexts. An artist, a political activist, a scholar can also be pure, each in his or her field. And in these three fields, no matter how they differ in other respects, the pure are the ones who are selfless and give themselves entirely to a cause, seeking neither money nor glory. They are those who "forget themselves and count themselves as nothing," as Fénelon would say. In each of these three instances, purity is the opposite of self-interest, egoism, covetousness, and all the squalidness of the self. I note in passing that the love of money cannot be a pure love, a fact that says much about both money and purity. Nothing that can be owned is pure. Purity is poverty, dispossession, renunciation. It begins where the self ends, where the self does not venture, where it ceases to exist. Pure love is the opposite of self-love. If sex can afford us a "pure pleasure," as Lucretius maintains and our own experience sometimes confirms, it is because sex sometimes frees itself, and us, from the prison of narcissism, egoism, and possessiveness: for pleasure, like love, is pure only when disinterested, only when it escapes the ego, which is why, Lucretius says, passionate pleasure is never pure,[13] why "wandering Venus" (sexual freedom)[14] or "marital

Venus" (the couple)[15] is often purer than our mad, exclusive, all-consuming passions. The phenomenon of jealousy reveals quite clearly the role that hatred and egoism can play in the amorous state.[16] The wise know jealousy for what it is, and even if they succumb to it, they are never fooled by it. Jealousy, they know, is not the most important thing about love, and while it is often love's most violent form—as everyone knows from experience—it is not its purest or highest form. Consider the description Plato gives of it, in the *Phaedrus*, before rescuing it with religion.[17] Eros is a dark god, as Pieyre de Mandiargues puts it, a jealous, possessive, egoistic, concupiscent god. Eros is an impure god.

It is easier to love friends or children purely, because we expect less from them or because we love them enough not to expect anything from them—enough, at any rate, not to make our love conditional on what we expect from them. Such love Simone Weil calls chaste love: "Every desire for enjoyment belongs to the future and the world of illusion, whereas if we desire only that a being should exist, he exists: what more is there to desire? The beloved being is then naked and real, not veiled by an imaginary future. . . . Thus in love there is chastity or lack of chastity according to whether the desire is or is not directed towards the future."[18] Weil, who is not out to please anyone, adds the following, which may shock the gullible but gives one something to think about: "In this respect, and on condition that it is not turned towards a pseudo-immortality conceived on the model of the future, the love we devote to the dead is perfectly pure. For it is the desire for a life which is finished, which can no longer give anything new. We desire that the dead man should have existed and he has existed."[19] What she describes is the successful outcome of the mourning process, when all that remains is the gentleness and joy of remembrance, the eternal truth of what once was, and feelings of love and gratitude. But the present is just as eternal. Accordingly, one might add that the love we feel for bodies, living bodies—provided it is not directed toward a pseudo-consumption conceived on the model of the future—can also sometimes be perfectly pure. This kind of love, after all, is the desire for the life that is present before us and thus perfect: we desire that this body exist and it does. What more can we ask?

I am well aware that things are not usually so simple, that need, violence, and lust play their part (how many men think they desire a woman when all they really want is an orgasm?). I know all about the obscurity of desire, about the murky and unsettling play of transgression and desecration (the sacred, as I said, is whatever can be profaned, and the human body is sacred). I know about that uniquely human fascination one can have with one's own animal nature and with that of others, the interplay of life and death, pleasure and pain, the sublime and the shameful—everything, in short, that pertains strictly to Eros rather than to love (or Agape!) in two bodies meeting or seeking each other. But all of this is impure or seems impure solely in reference to something else: bestiality holds allure only for human beings, perversion attracts only by virtue of the law that it transgresses, and turpitude only because it offends the sublime. Without Philia or Agape, Eros would be impossible, or in any case would have nothing erotic about it—only mindless drive would remain, and what a bore that would be. I tend to agree with Freud that the converse is true as well: without desire, what would we know about love? And what good would desire be without love? Without Eros, there would be no Philia or Agape, but without Philia or Agape, Eros would have no value. We must therefore learn to inhabit them simultaneously or to inhabit the gulf that separates them. To do so is also to inhabit oneself as a human being who is neither a beast nor an angel but an impossible, necessary combination of the two. "The sexual organs," says Nietzsche, "are the reason why man has trouble taking himself for a god." So much the better: man is and remains human only on that condition.

Sexuality, then, is also a lesson in humility, a lesson we never tire of gleaning more from. How verbose and presumptuous philosophy seems by comparison! How silly religion seems! The body teaches us more than books, and books have value only so long as they do not lie about the body. Purity is not the same as prudery. "Extreme purity," writes Simone Weil, "can contemplate both the pure and the impure;

impurity can do neither: the pure frightens it, the impure absorbs it."[20] The pure person is afraid of nothing; he knows that "nothing is impure in itself" or that "everything is pure to those who are pure" (which amounts to the same thing).[21] This is why, as Simone Weil also says, "purity is the power to contemplate defilement."[22] Purity dispels defilement (since nothing is impure in itself): lovers make love by the light of day and obscenity itself is a sun.

Let me sum up. To be pure is to be unadulterated, which is why purity does not exist and is not human. The impure within us is not absolute, or definitive, or equal; to know that we are impure presupposes, at the very least, a certain idea or ideal of purity, an ideal of which art sometimes makes us aware (think of Dinu Lipatti's renditions of Mozart or Bach, certain paintings by Vermeer, or poems by Eluard) and that we ourselves sometimes approach in our own lives (in our love for our children, for our friends, for close ones who have died). This purity is not an eternal essence; it results from a process of purification—Freud would say of sublimation—whereby love comes into being by freeing itself from itself: the body is the crucible, desire is the flame (which "consumes everything that is not pure gold," says Fénelon), and what remains—if anything remains at all—is sometimes "an act of pure and entirely selfless love," liberated, as Fénelon says, from all hope as well.[23] Purity is not a thing or even a property of the real; it is a certain modality of love—or it is nothing at all.

A virtue? No doubt, or that which allows love to be one and to take the place of all the others. One must therefore not confuse purity with continence, prudery, or chastity. Purity exists whenever love ceases to be "mixed with self-interest,"[24] or rather—since purity is never absolute—only insofar as love displays disinterestedness: truth, justice, and beauty can be loved purely, as can—why not?—that man or that woman present before you who gives of himself or herself and whose existence (far more than his or her possession) is enough for you. Purity is love without covetousness.[25] We love in this way the beauty of a landscape, the fragility of a child, the solitude of a friend, and, some-times, the man or the woman that our entire bodies covet nonetheless. There is no absolute purity, but there is also no complete or definitive impurity. It can happen that love, pleasure, or joy frees us from our-selves, from our own avidity and egoism; it is even possible for love to purify love (it seems to us we have experienced or sensed as much), to the point where the subject gets lost and flees, when there is nothing but joy, when there is nothing but love (love "freed from all belong-ing," as Christian Bobin puts it)—when there is nothing but everything and the purity of everything. *"Blessedness,"* writes Spinoza, *"is not the reward of virtue, but virtue itself; nor do we enjoy it because we restrain our lusts; on the contrary, because we enjoy it, we are able to restrain them."*[26] This is the last proposition in *The Ethics*, which shows how great the path is that separates us from what those words describe.

But though the path may be filled with turpitude, to the pure gaze it is already pure.

15

GENTLENESS

Gentleness is a feminine virtue. That is why it is especially pleasing in men.

One might object, however, that virtues have no gender, and it is true they do not. But we do, and it stamps all our gestures and all our feelings, and even extends to our virtues. Virility, regardless of its suggestive etymology, is not a virtue, nor is it the basis of any. Still, we can be virtuous in a more or less virile or a more or less feminine way. A man's courage is not that of a woman, nor is his generosity, or his love. Look at Simone Weil or Etty Hillesum: no man will ever write, or live, or love as they did. Only truth is absolutely universal and hence asexual. But truth has no morality, no feelings, no will. How could it be virtuous? There is no virtue that does not partake of desire, and what desire is not bound up with the sexual? "There is a bit of the testicle," Diderot writes, "at the bottom of our most sublime reasonings and most refined tenderness."[1] *Testicle*, in his day, was the term used for the ovaries as well, which is not to say the two are precisely the same. If, as I believe, value only exists for and through desire, it would follow that

all our values are somehow sexually marked.[2] Not in the sense that each
value belongs exclusively to one or the other of the two sexes—God
forbid—but rather in the sense that every individual lives his or her values, or lacks them, in a way that tends to be either masculine or feminine (and not simply for biological reasons). "It would be disastrous,"
Todorov states, "if everyone aligned with the masculine values"![3] It
would mean the triumph of war and of ideas (a dismal prospect even if
all wars were just and all ideas generous). The essential thing would be
missing, and that essential thing is love (I cannot but think that for both
the individual and the species, love begins with the mother) and life and
gentleness. I hope, for pity's sake, that no one raises the objection that
women have ideas as well: it is not something that I have failed to
notice. But nor have I failed to notice that women are less often fooled
by ideas than men are, and this, of course, is to their advantage. Few
women, I believe, would have consented to write *The Critique of Pure
Reason* or Hegel's great *Science of Logic*, for reasons having to do with
the fact that these books, works of genius though they be, are nonetheless ponderous and dull; they require an intellectual gravitas, a faith in
ideas and a worship of concepts, to a degree that a little femininity—
even in a man—renders unlikely and almost laughable were these
books not so deadly. What could be more impoverished and lifeless
than an abstraction? What could be more ridiculous than taking an
abstraction altogether seriously?

As for violence in women, it is not something I have never encoun-
tered. Does anyone believe, however, that coincidence alone accounts
for the fact that nearly all crimes involving bloodshed are committed
by men? That only little boys play at war? And that it is men, almost
exclusively, who wage war and sometimes find pleasure in it? This tendency, you will say, is a matter of nurture as much as, or even more
than, of nature. Perhaps it is, but what difference does that make? I
have never said that femininity and masculinity were exclusively biological. Sexual difference is too important and too ubiquitous to be
explainable without reference to both our bodies and our education, to
both culture and nature. Culture is a part of reality too. "We are not

born women but become women," we've been told. Obviously it is not that simple. We are born women, or men, and then become what we are. Virility is neither a virtue nor a fault. It is, however, a strength, just as femininity is a rich resource (in men too) and a strength as well, but of a different kind. Everything about us is sexually defined except truth (a fact worth repeating), and a good thing that is, too. What difference could be richer and more desirable?

But let us return to gentleness. What is, or seems to be, feminine about it is its courage without violence, its strength without harshness, its love without anger. These qualities we hear so clearly in Schubert, feel so vividly in Etty Hillesum. Gentleness is, to begin with, a kind of peace, either real or desired: it is the opposite of war, cruelty, brutality, aggressiveness, violence. An inner peace, the only kind that is a virtue. It can be pierced by anguish and suffering (as in Schubert) or brightened by joy and gratitude (as in Etty Hillesum), but it is always devoid of hatred, harshness, and insensitivity. "There is a difference between [being] hardy and [being] hard," notes Etty Hillesum in 1942.[4] Gentleness is what distinguishes one from the other. Gentleness is love in a state of peace, even in times of war, and is all the stronger when it is hardy, and all the more gentle. Aggressiveness is a weakness; anger is a weakness; even violence, when unmastered, is a weakness. And what can better master violence, anger, and aggressiveness than gentleness? Gentleness is a strength, which is what makes it a virtue; it is strength in a state of peace, serene and gentle, full of patience and leniency. A mother's gentleness toward her child. Christ's gentleness, or Buddha's, toward all. No virtue—not even generosity, not even compassion— more resembles love. Gentleness should not be confused with either of these other two, though all three usually go together. Compassion suffers at the suffering of others; gentleness refuses to produce or increase suffering. Generosity seeks to do good; gentleness refuses to do harm. This would seem to be to the greater credit of generosity, and perhaps it is. Yet so often our acts of generosity vex, our good deeds intrude, overwhelm, and even offend. Wouldn't a touch of gentleness lighten them and make them more pleasant? And let us not forget that gentleness makes us generous, for when we do not perform the good deed asked of us or extend the generosity that is within our capabilities, we do harm. Gentleness goes beyond compassion, since it anticipates suffering and can exist in the absence of another's pain. More negative, perhaps, than generosity, which is entirely affirmative, but more positive than compassion, which is entirely reactive, gentleness lies somewhere in between. In speaking of purity, I cited Pavese's remarkable statement from his diaries: "You will be loved the day when you will be able to show your weakness without the other person using it to assert his strength." A desire to be loved purely, I said, but it is also a desire to be loved with gentleness—in other words, to be truly loved. Gentleness and purity almost always go together, since violence is the preeminent evil, the preeminent obscenity, since evil harms, and egoism, in its avidity, tactlessness, and brutality, corrupts everything. Conversely, what consideration, what gentleness, what purity are contained in a lover's caress! A man's violence, his brutality, and his obscenity all dissolve in it. "My gentle heart," he says: these are words of love, perhaps the truest and gentlest that can be uttered.

Though values tend to be distributed along gender lines, Todorov notes, all individuals are necessarily heteroclite beings, imperfect and incomplete; accordingly, the way to a more complete and thus more human humanity can be found only in androgyny or within the constellation of the couple.[5] It is a man's feminine side that almost always rescues him from the worst. Think of the utter boor who lacks this feminine side, think of trains packed with soldiers—the horror of men among men, all the vulgarity and violence. I cannot say the same holds for women, that they are in equal need of a masculine side. "Women," Rilke says, "are closer to the human than men." Androgyny, in women as in men, can be a rich resource, a charm and a strength. But do women need it? Is it a virtue? All too often we confuse femininity with hysteria, which is merely (in men and women alike) a pathological caricature of femininity. The hysteric wants to seduce, to be loved, to attract attention. This is not gentleness or love; it is narcissism, trickery, thwarted aggressiveness, control ("The hysteric," Lacan says, "seeks a master to rule over"), and certainly seduction, but in the sense that seduction exploits or (as its etymology suggests) misleads. Hysteria is love as war and thus the opposite of love; it is the art of conquest and thus the opposite of giving; it is the art of show and thus the opposite of truth. Gentleness is the reverse: receptiveness, respect, openness. A passive, submissive, acquiescent virtue? Perhaps it is, but it is all the more essential for that very reason. Can wisdom, love, or even action exist without passivity? Such notions, which may surprise or even shock a Westerner, are taken for granted in the East. Perhaps it is because the East, as Lévi-Strauss suggests, is woman, or at any rate is not so taken in by masculine values.[6] Action is not activism, agitation, or impatience. Nor is passiveness inaction or laziness. Let yourself be carried by the current, says Swami Prajnanpad, swim with it, inside it, instead of exhausting yourself against the stream or allowing yourself to be swept away.[7] Gentleness yields to reality, to life, to becoming, to the imperfections of daily life, for it is the virtue of flexibility, patience, devotion, adaptability. It is the opposite of the "pretentious and impatient male," as Rilke puts it, the opposite of rigidity, haste, and relentless or dogged force. Effort is not always appropriate or adequate, nor is action. "By a necessity of nature," Thucydides says, "every being always exercises all the power he has." Gentleness is the exception that proves the rule: it is power over and, if need be, against oneself. Love is a retreat, as Simone Weil demonstrates, a refusal to exercise one's force or power, to use one's violence; love is gentleness and giving.[8] It is the opposite of rape, of murder, of conquest, of seizing control. It is Eros freed from Thanatos and from the self. A supernatural virtue for Simone Weil but not for me: cats are gentle with their kittens, dogs with their puppies. Humanity does not invent gentleness. But humanity cultivates it, is sustained by it, and it makes humanity more human.

The wise person, says Spinoza, acts "kindly, generously" (*humanite et benigne*).[9] This kindness or gentleness is Montaigne's *bénignité*, which we owe even to animals, he says, indeed to trees and plants.[10] It is the refusal to inflict suffering, to destroy unnecessarily, to devastate. It is respect, protection, benevolence. It is not quite charity—loving one's neighbor as oneself—for charity presupposes, as Rousseau understands, that we adopt as our own the "sublime maxim": "Do unto others as you would have them do unto you."[11] Gentleness does not set its sights so high. It is a form of natural and spontaneous kindness whose maxim, "much less perfect but much more useful than the first," would be the following: "Do your good with the least possible harm to others."[12] This maxim of gentleness, certainly less lofty, demanding, and exalted than that of charity, is also more accessible and hence more useful and necessary. The whole history of humanity testifies to the fact that one can live without charity. But one cannot live without a modicum of gentleness.

The Greeks, particularly the Athenians, prided themselves on having brought gentleness to the world. They saw gentleness as the opposite of barbarism and therefore as more or less synonymous with civilization. Ethnocentrism is nothing new. Yet if our civilization is indeed Greek, then our gentleness must owe something to theirs. And what was gentleness (*praotēs*) for the ancient Greeks? The same as it is for us: the opposite of war (the first attestations of the word are of the verb, which means to appease), the opposite of anger, violence, or harshness.[13] It is not so much a virtue, to begin with, as the conjunction of several virtues or their common source:

> In its most modest sense, gentleness denotes kindness of manner, benevolence toward others. But it can occur in much nobler contexts. Gentleness toward the unfortunate begins to resemble generosity or kindness; toward the guilty, it becomes leniency and understanding; toward strangers, or human beings in general, it becomes humanity and verges on charity. In political life, similarly, it can be tolerance or clemency, depending on whether it concerns relationships toward citizens or subjects or a defeated population. Nevertheless, at the origin of these different values we find the same tendency, that of receiving the other person as someone whose welfare one wishes to promote—insofar as one can, at least—without failing in some other duty. And the fact is, the

Greeks sensed this common origin, since all those so very different values can on occasion be used to designate the word *praos*.[14]

Aristotle will make of it a full-fledged virtue: gentleness, in anger, stands as the mean between the two faults of irascibility and spinelessness.[15] The gentle person occupies the middle ground between the "hot-tempered, difficult, and savage man" and the man who by virtue of his impassiveness or excessive placidity is "servile and dumb."[16] For there is just and necessary anger, as there are just wars and justified acts of violence; gentleness must decide and act accordingly. Aristotle is ill at ease with this definition and acknowledges that his virtue of *praotēs* "err[s] rather in the direction of deficiency."[17] For if the gentle man is "angry at the right things and with the right people and, further, as he ought, when he ought, and as long as he ought" and never more often, longer, or to any greater extent than he ought, this still does not settle the question of criteria and limits.[18] The gentle man is so called only because he is gentler than his fellow citizens, but who knows how far his gentleness might go? Who is to determine the legitimate object, scope, or duration of a man's anger? And so one can oppose gentleness, as Aristotle does, to magnanimity, just as one can oppose Greek pride to Judeo-Christian humility: "To endure being insulted and put up with insult to one's friends is slavish."[19] Alexander's teacher was no more accustomed to turning the other cheek than was his student.[20] There is a form of gentleness, a gentleness taken to an extreme, that can be seen either as contemptible or as sublime, depending on one's point of view, and that calls to mind the temptation of Christ. Is such gentleness a form of cowardice? No, since gentleness is gentleness only so long as it owes nothing to fear. It is simply that one must choose between two logics, that of honor and that of charity, and we all know which way gentleness inclines.

Does gentleness therefore require that one advocate nonviolence? The matter is not so simple, since nonviolence, if taken to the extreme, would prohibit us from fighting effectively against criminal or barbarous violence, not just when it is aimed at us but also when it targets the defenseless and the innocent. Whereas charity might allow or justify nonviolence in the former circumstances, neither charity nor justice could tolerate it in the latter. Who would not fight to save the life of a child? Who would not be ashamed to have failed to do so? Simone Weil puts it very well: "Nonviolence," she writes, "is no good unless it is effective."[21] Which is another way of saying that the choice depends not on principle but on circumstance. If equal or superior in effectiveness to violence, nonviolence of course is preferable, a fact that gentleness reminds us of and one that Gandhi understood. But calculating the relative effectiveness of the two alternatives is a matter of prudence, which cannot be sacrificed when someone else's security is at stake, lest we lack charity. What should I do, for example, if I witness a woman being attacked? "Use force," replies Simone Weil, "unless you are such that you can defend her with as much chance of success without violence." Of course whether one can or cannot depends on the person, on the situation, and, adds Weil, "on the adversary."[22] Nonviolence may be appropriate against British troops. But against Hitler and his panzer divisions? Violence is better than collusion, than weakness in the face of horror, than spinelessness and accommodation in the face of the worst.

We must make a clear distinction, therefore, between the *peaceable*, who are prepared to defend peace even with the use of force, and *pacifists*, who oppose war in whatever circumstances and against anyone. To espouse pacifism is to make of gentleness a system or an absolute and to deny oneself the possibility of effectively defending, at least in certain circumstances, the very thing one claims as a principle—namely, peace. Max Weber speaks of this stance as an ethic of conviction, but it is an ethic that can also be irresponsible in being so convinced. There is no such thing as an absolute value—or in any case, gentleness cannot be one; there is no such thing as a moral system or a single, all-sufficing virtue. Even love does not justify or excuse everything: it cannot take the place of prudence or justice. All the more reason why gentleness is a virtue only on condition that we not practice it at the expense of justice and love, which, need I recall, we owe first of all to the weakest among us, to victims more than to their tormentors.

Under what circumstances, then, does one have the moral right (or even the duty) to fight and, particularly, to kill? Only when fighting and killing are necessary in order to prevent a greater evil, such as more deaths, more suffering, or more violence. One might object that each person has his own way of determining such necessity and that such a principle therefore offers no guarantee. But what guarantee could we be given? We never confront general cases, only individual, specific ones, and no one can make these decisions for us. Can capital punishment be justified? Why not, if it were effective? In these areas, the problem is not moral so much as it is technical and political. Suppose one could demonstrate that the death penalty for people who murdered children would save children—by its deterrent effect or by precluding the possibility of repeat offenses—and would do so in numbers greater than, equal to, or even slightly smaller than the number of perpetrators of this crime who would die as a result. Who, then, could find fault with this punishment? Or must respect for human life be regarded as an absolute? Again, why not? But then we would also be obliged to condemn abortion—all abortion: why accord greater protection to someone who has murdered a child than to a child in gestation? But in that case, one had no right to kill the Nazis during the Second World War, and the judges who sat at Nuremberg are therefore to be regarded as guilty for having sentenced Göring, Ribbentrop, and others to death. What is absolute brooks no qualification and is by definition independent of circumstances or individuals. I personally do not believe in absolutes (what can be more relative than life, and the value of life?), and so for me, the problem of capital punishment is entirely one of opportuneness, fitness, and effectiveness, as I said; hence the relevant virtue is not gentleness so much as prudence—or if gentleness, then gentleness checked by prudence and charity. The point is not so much to punish as it is to prevent. On the question of capital punishment, in matters of common law, I have no opinion, nor would I dwell on them: is imprisonment for twenty or thirty years so very preferable? Marcel Conche suggests a reasonable solution that I could find acceptable. Instead of *abolishing* capital punishment, he argues, let us *suspend* it, so that it might be "reinstated, for example, if we were again confronted with public enemies like those that were judged at Nuremberg."[23] But I will never be persuaded that we should never kill under any circumstances or that Hitler, had he been caught alive, or any successor to him should have ended his days in prison. Prisons are too inadequately guarded, too unreliable, and the victims—past and future—have the right to ask for more.

A political problem, as I said, or a technical one. This leaves the moral question unresolved. If we accept that sometimes it can be legitimate to kill, in order to fight a greater evil, the individual value of the act will nevertheless vary with the individual, as it always does, even in situations of supposedly collective action and responsibility (war, for instance). In all circumstances, each person must make his own evaluation, but how? Some criterion is needed. Simone Weil, with her usual rigor, proposes one that is both filled with gentleness and extremely demanding:

> War. To keep the love of life intact within us; never to inflict death without accepting it for ourselves.
>
> Supposing the life of X . . . were linked with our own so that the two deaths had to be simultaneous, should we still wish him to die? If with our whole body and soul we desire life and if nevertheless without lying, we can reply "yes," then we have the right to kill.[24]

Very few of us will ever be capable of such gentleness, and only those who are will be capable, sometimes, of completely innocent violence. For the rest of us, who are not there yet, this does not mean that violence is never justified (it is, when an absence of violence would be worse); it simply means that, for us, violence is never innocent.

Blessed are the gentle.[25] They never asked for such fortune, yet only they, but for mercy, could ever come by it innocently.

For the rest of us, there is gentleness to limit our violence as much as it can, to the necessary or acceptable minimum.

A feminine virtue, by which alone humanity is human.

16

GOOD FAITH

A word escapes me: what do we call the virtue that governs our relationship to truth? *Sincerity* came to mind initially, then I thought about *truthfulness*, *honesty*, or *veracity*, before pondering for a while over *authenticity*. In the end, I have settled on *good faith*, though I realize that this usage might exceed the conventional understanding of the concept.

What is good faith? It is both a psychological fact and a moral virtue. As a fact, it consists of the agreement of our acts and words with our inner life, of our inner life with itself. As a virtue, it consists of love or respect for truth, in my opinion, the only faith worth having. An *alethic* virtue (from *alētheia*, the Greek word for truth), it has truth itself as its object.[1]

I don't mean to say that good faith is the equivalent of certitude or even truth (it rules out mendacity but not error); it's simply that someone of good faith says what he believes, though he may be wrong, and believes what he says. This is why good faith is a faith, in both senses of the term—belief and fidelity. It is true belief, being true to what we believe. At least for as long as we believe it to be true. Earlier, in speaking of fidelity, I pointed out that it needed first of all to be faithful to truth; this condition defines good faith as well. Being of good faith does not mean that one always speaks the truth, since one can make mistakes, but it does mean at the very least that one speaks the truth about what one believes, and this truth, even if what one believes is false, is no less true for all that. Good faith, in this sense, is what we call sincerity (or truthfulness or candor) and is the opposite of mendacity, hypocrisy, and duplicity, in short, the opposite of bad faith, in all its private and public forms. But good faith goes beyond sincerity, and so I offer the following distinction: sincerity means not lying to others; good faith means lying neither to others nor to oneself. Robinson Crusoe's solitude on his island spared him the obligation of being sincere and even made this virtue pointless. Good faith, however, remained every bit as necessary, praiseworthy, and obligatory. To whom did he owe it? To himself, and that is enough.

Good faith is a sincerity that is both transitive and reflexive. It sets to right our relationships with others as well as with ourselves—or can, at any rate, in seeking to establish both among people and within the individual as much truthfulness and authenticity and as little fakery and pretense as possible. There is no such thing as absolute sincerity, or absolute love or justice, but this does not prevent us from aspiring to such absolutes, and making the effort to approximate them. Good faith is this effort, which is itself already a virtue. An intellectual virtue, if you wish, since it is concerned with truth, yet it involves the totality of the individual, his body and soul, his wisdom and folly (for everything is true—even our mistakes, which are truely false, and our illusions, which are truly illusory). It is Montaigne's virtue and counts among his first words: "*Loe a book in good faith, reader . . .*"[2] It is also, or should be, the foremost virtue of intellectuals and, particularly, of philosophers. Those who are inordinately deficient in it or who claim to be exempted from it are unworthy of that name, to which they bring discredit even as they flatter themselves with it. Thinking is not just an occupation or an amusement. It is a human requirement and may be the species' primary virtue. It's been said, though not often enough, that the invention of language does not in itself create any truth (since truths are all eternal); yet it does bring something new into the world, namely, the possibility not just of animal cunning and deception but of mendacity. *Homo loquax: homo mendax.* Man is a creature who can lie and does. This is what makes good faith logically possible and morally necessary.

Some will say that good faith proves nothing, and I have to agree. After all, the world abounds in sincere bastards, in horrors perpetrated in good faith. And is there anyone less hypocritical than the fanatic sometimes is? The Tartuffes are legion, but not as numerous or as dangerous as the Savonarolas and their disciples. A Nazi who acts in good faith is still a Nazi: who cares if he is sincere? An authentic bastard is still a bastard: what's his authenticity to us? Good faith is no more a sufficient or complete virtue than fidelity or courage is. It does not take the place of justice, generosity, or love. But what would something like bad-faith justice amount to? Or bad-faith love or generosity? Not justice, love, or generosity as we understand them but, at best, some corrupt imitation based on hypocrisy, blindness, and lies. No virtue is true, or truly virtuous, without this virtue of truth. Virtue devoid of good faith is bad faith and not virtue.

"Sincerity," writes La Rochefoucauld, "is an openheartedness that shows us as we are; it is a love of truth, a loathing for disguise, and a desire to make up for our faults and even lessen them by the credit of admitting to them."[3] It is the refusal to mislead, dissemble, or embellish, and if this refusal is itself sometimes merely an artifice, a seduction like any other, it isn't always, as even La Rochefoucauld concedes.[4] Therein lies the difference between love of truth and love of self: self-love may often get the better of us, but it can sometimes be overcome by our love of truth. Good faith means loving truth more than oneself. Like all the other virtues, it is the opposite of narcissism, of blind egoism, of the self's enslavement to itself. In this respect, good faith is intimately related to generosity, humility, courage, justice: justice in contracts or exchanges (it is bad faith to deceive a buyer in selling him goods, for instance by failing to advise him of some hidden flaw, and it is also unjust); courage of thought and expression; humility in the face of truth; generosity toward others . . . Truth does not belong to the self; the self belongs to truth, which contains it, traverses it, and dissolves it. The self is always deceitful, illusory, bad. Good faith is disenamored of the self, and that is what makes it good.

Must we therefore always speak our hearts, give voice to every thought and every feeling? No, because we cannot. There is too little time, and decency and gentleness forbid it. Sincerity is not exhibitionism; it is not tactlessness. One has the right to remain silent and indeed quite often one must. Good faith forbids not silence but deception (or silence only when it would be deceitful), and the latter not always, as we shall see. Truthfulness is not the same as foolishness. The fact remains that truth, as Montaigne puts it, is "the principal and fundamental part of virtue"; all the other virtues depend on it and it depends, in its principle, on none.[5] Truth need not be generous, loving, or just in order to be true, valid, and due; whereas love, generosity, and justice are virtues only on condition of first being true (of being truly what they seem), on condition, then, of being performed in good faith. Truth is uncompliant, even to justice or love; it brings no advantage or consolation and it doesn't pay. This is why, says Montaigne, "it must be loved for itself."[6] The love of truth for its own sake is the sine qua non of good faith: "He who speaks the truth because he is elsewise so compelled, and because it is useful, and who does not fear to tell a lie when it matters to no one—he is not sufficiently truthful."[7]

Good faith is not about telling all, it is about speaking only the truth, at least to the best of our belief—unless a higher duty intervenes. There is room here for a form of casuistry—in the good sense of the word—that will not mislead those of good faith. What is casuistry? It is the study of *moral dilemmas*, in other words, of the moral difficulties that result, or can result, from the application of a general rule (for example: "One should not tell a lie") to specific situations often more fertile or more equivocal than the rule itself, which remains valid all the same. The rule is well stated by Montaigne, and it is a rule of good faith: "Everything must not always be said, for that would be folly; but what one says should be what one thinks; otherwise it is knavery."[8] I will return to the exceptions to this rule; they are valid, as exceptions, only because of the rule they presuppose and cannot negate. Good faith is the virtue that makes of truth a value (which is to say, since value does not exist in and of itself, good faith is the virtue that makes truth an object of love, respect, and will) and submits to it. One must be faithful to the truth first, lest all fidelity be mere hypocrisy. One must love truth first, lest all love be mere illusion or deception. Good faith is this fidelity, this love, in both spirit and deed. I can put it a better way: in being a love that commands our acts, our words, and even our thoughts, good faith is the love of truth and the virtue of the truthful.

What is a truthful person? According to Aristotle, he is someone "who loves truth" and consequently refuses to lie, whether by over-statement or understatement, fabrication or omission.[9] He observes "the mean" between boastfulness and dissemblance, braggadocio and reticence, vainglory and false modesty.[10] He "calls a thing by its own name, being truthful both in life and in word, owning to what he has, and neither more nor less."[11] A virtue? Of course: "falsehood is *in itself* mean and culpable, and truth noble and worthy of praise."[12] How for-tunate and noble were the Greeks, for whom this manifest truth never became outdated or relativized! Even so, they had their Sophists, just as we have ours, who smile at this naïveté, as they call it. It is their loss. What value does a thought have, apart from the truth it contains or seeks after? I call *sophistry* any thought that is subordinate to some-thing other than truth or that subordinates truth to something other than truth itself. Philosophy is sophistry's opposite in theory, just as good faith is its opposite in practice. The point is to live and think *truthfully*, as much as possible, even at the cost of anguish, disillusion-ment, or misfortune. Fidelity to truth first; true sadness is better than false joy.

That good faith is primarily concerned with boastfulness, which it resists, is something that Aristotle sees quite clearly, and this position confirms his objection to narcissism or vanity.[13] Did he object to self-love? Not at all: for Aristotle, the truthful person is loveable, self-love is a duty, and to feign an impossible indifference toward oneself would be to lie.[14] But the truthful man loves himself as he is, as he knows himself to be, not as he wishes to seem to himself or appear to others. Truthfulness is what distinguishes self-love from vanity, or pride, as Aristotle defines it, from conceit. The proud man, says Aristotle, must "be open in his hate and in his love (for to conceal one's feelings, i.e., to care less for truth than for what people will think, is a coward's part), and must speak and act openly; for he is free of speech because he is contemptuous, and he is given to telling the truth, except when he speaks in irony to the vulgar."[15]

Is this kind of pride lacking in charity? Yes, but not because of the truth it entails. Better true nobility than false humility. Does it care too much about honor?[16] It does, but not so much that it would lie to preserve it. Better true pride than vainglory.

The truthful person is governed by what Spinoza calls the *standard of the true idea as given,* and I would add, *or as possible:* he says what he knows is true or believes is true, never what he knows or believes to be false. Does good faith therefore disallow any lie? It would seem so, almost by definition: how could one lie in good faith? Lying assumes one's knowing the truth or believing that one knows it and deliberately saying something other than what one knows or believes. This is what good faith forbids or refuses to indulge in. To be of good faith is to say what one believes is true; it is being faithful (in words and deeds) to one's belief, and yielding before the truth of what one is or thinks. Any lie would therefore be in bad faith and thereby blameworthy.

This rigid moral standard, which I feel is difficult to uphold, seems nevertheless to have been adopted by both Spinoza and Kant. The concurrence of two such prominent figures deserves to be examined.

"A free man always acts honestly, not deceptively."[17] The free man is indeed one who is guided only by reason, which is universal; if reason allowed deception, then it would allow it always, and any human society would be impossible.[18] Fine. But suppose the life of some individual is at stake? This changes nothing, Spinoza replies serenely: reason, being one and the same for everyone, cannot be made to depend on the interests, not even the vital interests, of particular individuals. Hence we read the following surprising scholium:

> Suppose someone now asks: What if a man could save himself from the present danger of death by treachery? Would not the principle of preserving his own being recommend, without qualification, that he be treacherous?
>
> The reply to this is the same. If reason should recommend that, it would recommend it to all men. And so reason would recommend, without qualification, that men should make agreements to join forces and to have common laws only by deception—that is, that really they should have no common laws. This is absurd.[19]

I have never been able to reconcile to my satisfaction this scholium with propositions 20 through 25 in part 4 of *The Ethics*, in which the effort to preserve one's being is said to be "the first and only foundation of virtue," as well as its gauge and its purpose.[20] I notice, however, that Spinoza does not categorically forbid deception but simply states that reason, which alone is free, cannot prescribe it. Why this distinction? Reason is not man's sole attribute; it is not even the most essential of his attributes—love and desire are.[21] No one is completely free or utterly rational; nor must anyone be so or want to be so.[22] The proposition does specify that it is the "free man" who never acts deceptively.[23] Well and good. It also states that for this reason deceit and treachery can never be virtues in and of themselves. Well and good again. But quite often it would be unreasonable to listen solely to reason, blameworthy to love only virtue, and disastrous to freedom to seek to act only *as a free person*. Good faith is a virtue, but so are prudence, justice, and charity. If it is necessary to lie in order to survive, or in order to hold out against barbarism, or in order to save the life of someone we love, someone worthy of love, then there is no doubt in my mind that we should lie when there is no other way or when any other way would be worse, and I think Spinoza would likely agree. Reason certainly cannot recommend a lie, since reason is universal and lying can never be: if everyone lied, there would be no point in lying, since no one would believe anyone else. Indeed, what would be the point of speaking? But reason is purely abstract unless desire takes possession of it and makes it live. Desire, however, is always unique and concrete, and that is why it is possible to lie, as Spinoza recognizes in *A Political Treatise*, without violating either natural right or—and this amounts to the same thing—the interests of each and all.[24] Will, not reason, commands; desire, not truth, dictates its law.[25] The desire for truth, which is the essence of good faith, thus remains subject to the truth of desire, which is the essence of man;[26] being faithful to truth does not free one from the obligation to be faithful to joy, love, and compassion[27] or, as Spinoza says, to justice and charity, which are the whole law and true fidelity.[28] Being faithful to truth first means also being faithful to the truth of desire within ourselves: if our choice is either to deceive another or betray our own selves, to deceive the wicked or abandon the weak, to be false to our word or to betray our love, then fidelity to truth—the truth that is each of us, that each of us carries within us and loves—can sometimes compel us to lie. It is in allowing for this possibility that Spinoza, at least in my reading of him and notwithstanding that strange scholium of proposition 72—differs from Kant. Good faith is a virtue, of course, which lying simply cannot be, but that does not mean that all lies are blameworthy or that we must always abstain from lying. No lie is free, of course; but who can be free at all times? Indeed, how could we be in the face of the wicked, the ignorant, the fanatical, when they are stronger and when to be sincere with them would be a form of complicity or suicide? *Caute* . . . Lying is not ever a virtue, but neither is foolishness or suicide.[29] One must sometimes accept a lesser evil, and lying can be just that.[30]

Kant, however, goes much further and for him the question of lying is far more clear-cut. Not only is lying never a virtue, it is always an offense, a crime, an indignity.[31] This is because veracity, its opposite, is "an *unconditional duty* which holds in all circumstances" and as such cannot tolerate any possible exceptions "from a rule which in its nature does not admit of exceptions."[32] Benjamin Constant objects that this amounts to saying "that to tell a falsehood to a murderer who asked us whether our friend, of whom he was in pursuit, had not taken refuge in our house, would be a crime."[33] But Kant is not swayed by such considerations. It would indeed be a crime, he says, since humanity turns on this very notion of truth in utterances, truthfulness being "a sacred unconditional command of reason [which is] not to be limited by any expediency," not even if the life of another or one's own life is at stake.[34] Intention does not enter the picture at all. For Kant, there are no white lies, or rather all lies are blameworthy, even white lies or generous lies: "Its cause may be mere levity or even good nature; indeed, even a really good end may be intended by lying. Yet to lie even for these reasons is through its mere form a crime of man against his own person and a baseness which must make a man contemptible in his own eyes."[35]

Even if this assessment were correct, I can't help thinking that to subscribe to it would be to attach a great deal of importance indeed to one's own person. What kind of virtue is so self-involved, so concerned with its own scrap of integrity and dignity, that to preserve itself it is prepared to hand over an innocent person to murderers? What is this duty that has no prudence, compassion, and charity in it? Lying is an offense? Of course it is, but so is hardness of heart, and a graver one at that! Truthfulness is a duty? So be it, but giving aid to someone in danger is a duty too, and the more pressing of the two. Woe to him who favors his own conscience over his fellowman!

Shocking as it already was in the eighteenth century, as Benjamin Constant's objection makes plain, Kant's position has become completely untenable today. For barbarism has assumed other dimensions, next to which any rigid moral standard is ludicrous if its sole concern is conscience or heinous if it ends up helping the torturers. You are sheltering a Jew or a Resistance fighter in your attic. The Gestapo is looking for him and starts to ask you questions. Are you going to tell them the truth? Are you going to refuse to answer their questions (it comes down to the same thing)? Of course not! Anyone with a sense of honor or courage, or even a sense of duty, will feel not only entitled to lie but obligated to do so. And I mean lie. For a lie is still what it is, a statement that is intentionally false. "Lying to the German police when they ask us whether we are hiding a patriot in our house," writes Jankélévitch, "is not lying, *it is telling the truth*; to answer, 'There's no one here,' when there is someone there is the most sacred of duties [in this situation]."[36] I grant the second proposition, obviously; but how can one accept the first except unthinkingly, since what it asks us to do is not consider the very problem it claims to resolve. Lying to the German police is lying, obviously, which simply proves (since lying, in this instance, is definitely virtuous) that, whatever Kant may have thought, truthfulness is not an absolute, unconditional, or universal duty and possibly that there are no absolute, universal, unconditional duties (and thus no duties at all, in the Kantian sense), only values that are more or less noble and only virtues that are more or less commendable, urgent, or necessary. Again, truthfulness is such a virtue. But it is less important than justice, compassion, and generosity and certainly less important than love; to put it another way, truthfulness, as love of truth, is less important than love of one's fellowman, or charity. Besides, one's fellowman is also true, and this truth of flesh and blood, this suffering truth, is more important—much more important—than the truthfulness of our utterances. Fidelity to truth first, but to the truth of feelings more than to the truth of our statements, to the truth of suffering more than to the truth of our words. When we make good faith an absolute, we lose it, for it is no longer good; it is hardened and deathly, a hateful truthfulness. It is no longer good faith but literalism; no longer a virtue but fanaticism: theoretical, disembodied, and abstract fanaticism, the fanaticism of philosophers who love truth *madly*. But madness is never good; fanaticism is never virtuous.

Here is another, less extreme example. Should one tell a dying person the truth of his condition? Always, says Kant, at least if the dying person inquires, since truthfulness is an absolute duty. Never, says Jankélévitch: to do so would be to inflict on the person "the torture of despair" for no reason.[37] It seems to me that the problem is more complicated. Telling a dying peson the truth, if he inquires and is able to bear it, can be a way of helping him to die lucidly (to lie to a dying person is, as Rilke says, to rob him of his death); it can help him die as he lived and wanted to live, in peace and dignity and truth, not amid illusions and denials. Jankélévitch writes that "someone who tells a dying person that he is going to die lies: first, literally, because he simply doesn't know, because only God knows, because no man has the right to tell another man he is going to die," and then "in spirit, because he is harming him."[38] As for the literal lie, here Jankélévitch confuses good faith and certitude, sincerity and omniscience: what prevents the person's physician or relatives from telling him truthfully what they know or believe, including the limits of all knowledge and belief when it comes to such matters? As for lying in spirit, Jankélévitch attaches too little value to truth and underestimates the spirit. To value hope more than truth, lucidity, and courage is to value hope too highly. What is hope worth if it comes at the cost of lies and illusion? "Poor, lonely people should not be made to suffer," says Jankélévitch, "this is more important than anything else, including truth."[39] If the pain is excruciating, if the poor, lonely person is unable to bear it, if his illusions alone sustain him, then, yes, I agree. But is this inevitably the case? What is the point of philosophy or even of honesty if they retreat at the approach of death, if truth is good only when it reassures us and carries no risk of pain? I tend to be wary of people who say *never* in these domains, as I am of those who say *always*. Naturally I agree that it is possible to lie out of love or compassion and that it is sometimes necessary to do so. What could be more idiotic or cowardly than to impose on others a degree of courage that we are not sure we ourselves are capable of? Yes, the dying person must first decide, if he can, just how important truth is for him, and if he cannot decide, no one can decide in his place. In such cases, gentleness must take precedence over violence, compassion over truthfulness. But truth remains a value nonetheless, and we cannot withhold it from another without very powerful and carefully considered reasons, especially if he asks for it. Comfort and well-being are not everything. Physical suffering, of course, has to be eliminated as much as possible, and physicians need to do more in this direction. But must moral suffering, anguish, and fear be eliminated as well, when they are part of life itself? "He was lucky," people say. "He didn't know he was dying." But is that really a medical victory? For nevertheless he died, and the task of physicians, as far as I know, is to cure us when they can and not to conceal from us that they cannot. "If I tell him the truth, he will kill himself," a physician said to me. But suicide is not always a disease (it is also a right, one that the patient in this case is being denied); depression, however, is a disease and should be treated. Physicians are supposed to treat disease, not decide for their patient whether his life—and death—is worth living or not. Physicians must beware of paternalism; they are in charge of their patients' health, not their patients' happiness or serenity. Does a dying person not have the right to be unhappy? To experience anguish? What is it about this unhappiness and anguish that so frightens us all?

As always, such considerations are, or ought to be, tempered by compassion, gentleness, tenderness. It is better to lie than to torture, better to lie than to terrify. Truth cannot take the place of everything. But nor can virtue take the place of truth or be completely valid without it. The best death, from a moral, spiritual, and human standpoint, is the most lucid one, the most serenely lucid one; and moreover it is our duty to accompany the dying, when necessary and when they are capable of it, toward that ultimate truth. Who would dare lie to Christ or Buddha, to Socrates or Epicurus, to Spinoza or Simone Weil, in their final moments? But such individuals, you will say, are the exception. Undoubtedly. Still, we must be aided in our efforts to emulate them, even if in a small way; the inclination, though poignant, and the possibility, though painful, should not be denied us ahead of time. Truthfulness still applies, even at a dying person's bedside. Again, not just truthfulness: compassion and love also apply, even more. Flinging the truth at someone who never asked to hear it, who cannot bear to live with it, who is pained or crushed by it is not an act of good faith but an act of brutality, of insensitivity, of violence. Truth is a value and honesty a virtue, and therefore we must speak the truth, or as much truth as possible, but not recklessly or indiscriminately. We must speak the truth as much as possible, as much as we can or as much as we should—in other words as much as we can without thereby failing in some higher or more urgent virtue. Here I join paths with Jankélévitch, who writes, "Woe to those who place above love the criminal truth of informing! Woe to the brutes who always speak the truth! Woe to those who have never lied!"[40]

Truthfulness, however, is a qualified obligation only where others are involved, for although one can legitimately prefer the interests of another, particularly when he is weak or suffering, to one's own truthfulness, one cannot legitimately accord oneself that same preference. Good faith thus goes beyond sincerity and, within the realm of the intrapersonal, is a universal obligation, valid for all and at all times. It is sometimes legitimate, even from a moral standpoint, to lie to another person rather than tell him the truth. But one cannot legitimately lie to oneself, for to do so is to value oneself more than the truth, to value one's comfort or good conscience more than one's mind. It would be a sin against truth and against the self. All sins, of course, deserve to be treated with mercy: we all do what we can, and life is too hard and too cruel for us to condemn anyone for failing in this area. Does anyone know what he himself would do if faced with the worst and how much truth he could bear under such circumstances? I do not mean to suggest that all actions are equally commendable or that indulging in bad faith with oneself can ever be considered morally neutral or a matter of indifference. Lying to the wicked can be legitimate—for example, if my own life is at stake—but the reason it is legitimate is not because I value myself more than the truth, since even under those circumstances, there is nothing to prevent me from loving, respecting, and acknowledging the truth, at least inwardly. Indeed, one lies to a murderer in the name of what one holds to be true, and in this sense the lies one tells are told in good faith. In such cases, one must draw a distinction between sincerity, which is directed toward others and allows for a wide range of exceptions (good faith as transitive and conditional), and reflexive good faith, which is directed solely toward oneself and is therefore universally valid. That it is sometimes necessary to lie to others, out of prudence or compassion, is something I have already discussed and need not delve into again. But what could justify our lying to ourselves? Prudence? This would mean we prefer comfort to lucidity, the ego to the spirit. Compassion? It would mean we lack courage. Love? But without good faith, love is mere self-love and narcissism.

Jean-Paul Sartre, in a philosophical context that is different from mine, argues that bad faith, as "a lie to oneself," betrays (that is, indissolubly both expresses and denies) an essential dimension of human consciousness that prevents it from ever being fully congruent with itself, as might a thing or a fact.[41] To believe that one is a waiter or a professor of philosophy or that one is sad or cheerful, as fully as one believes that a table is a table, or even to believe that one is absolutely sincere in the same way that one believes that one is blond or dark-haired, is to be of bad faith, always. For it is to forget that one is in a state of becoming (in other words, that we are not yet or definitively what we are), and it is to deny our angst, our nothingness, our freedom. Hence bad faith is a "permanent threat" to consciousness.[42] But it is a threat that we must meet head-on and cannot transform into a fatality or an excuse except through more bad faith. Bad faith is not a state of being, a thing, or a destiny but the "thingifying" of what we are, or think we are, or would like to be, in the necessarily artificial form of the in-itself-for-itself, which would be God but is nothing. Nor is the opposite of bad faith a state of being (we lie to ourselves if we think we *are* of good faith), a thing, or even a quality; it is an effort, a demand, a virtue. What Sartre calls authenticity and everyone else calls good faith is this: consciousness not being congruent with itself in ossified self-satisfaction, but constantly wrenching itself away from lies, from serious-mindedness, from the roles one plays or is—in short, from bad faith and from the self.[43]

At its most general, good faith is nothing other than love of truth. This is why it is the philosophical virtue par excellence. I do not mean to say that it is the exclusive domain of anyone but rather that a philosopher, in both the strongest and most ordinary sense of the term, is someone who, when it comes to himself at least, sets truth above all things, above honor or power, happiness or systems, and even virtue or love. He would rather know that he is evil than pretend that he is good; he would rather stare love's absence in the face when it occurs or his own egoism when it prevails (which is almost always) than persuade himself falsely that he is loving or generous. He knows, however, that truth without charity is not God.[44] But he also knows, or thinks he knows, that charity without truth is just another lie and not charity. There is a kind of joy that delights in knowledge regardless of its object; this joy of knowing Spinoza calls *an intellectual love of God* ("The more we understand singular things," he writes, "the more we understand God"), for everything is in God and God is everything.[45] And if no truth is God, if all the truth in the world does not amount to God, if no God is true—what then? Spinoza's point essentially still holds: love of truth is more important than religion, lucidity is more precious than hope, and good faith is more valid and more valuable than faith.

Psychoanalysis shares this spirit ("truth, and more truth," writes Freud); if it did not, it would be just another form of sophistry, which it often is; only the "love of truth," as Freud says, which "precludes any kind of sham or deceit," allows it to be something else.[46]

Such is the spirit of our times, when it still has spirit and has not lost it along with faith.

An eternal and fleeting spirit that, as Alain observes, "makes light of everything," even of itself.[47] Of truth? Sometimes, but this is another way of loving it. To venerate truth, idolize it, or make it into a god would be to lie. All truths are of equal value and have no value at all; it is not because truth is good that we must love it but, as Spinoza says, because we love it that we deem it good; and it is indeed good for those who love it.[48] Truth is not God; it has value only for those who love it, and through them; it has value only for the truthful who love it without worshiping it and who submit to it without being taken in by it. Love comes first? Yes, but only to the extent that it is true; hence love is first in value but second in being.

Good faith is the spirit of the mind, which prefers sincerity to deception, knowledge to illusion, laughter to solemnity.

Thereby does good faith lead to humor, just as bad faith leads to irony.

17

HUMOR

That humor is a virtue ought not surprise us. Taking oneself completely seriously is always a fault. Humor prevents us from doing so and, beyond the pleasure it affords us, is valued for that reason.

If "seriousness is that intermediate position of a man who stands midway between despair and futility," as Jankélévitch nicely puts it, then humor, by contrast, may be said to opt resolutely for the two extremes.[1] The "politesse of despair," Boris Vian calls it, and thus, in a sense, of futility too. It is impolite to assume an air of self-importance. It is ridiculous to take oneself seriously. To lack humor is to lack humility, lucidity, and lightness; the humorless person is too full of himself, too self-deceived, too severe, or too aggressive and thus lacks generosity, gentleness, and mercy . . . Too much seriousness, even about virtue, is somehow suspect and disturbing: scratch the surface and you expect to find illusions or fanaticism beneath it. Humorless virtue thinks much of itself and is thereby deficient in virtue.

One mustn't exaggerate the importance of humor, however. A bastard can have a sense of humor, and a hero can lack one. But as we have seen, the same is true of most virtues, and as an argument against humor it proves nothing, except of course that humor itself proves nothing. But if it were out to prove something, would it still be humor? A subsidiary virtue, if you like, or a composite one, light and unessential—a funny virtue, in a way, since it is irreverently indifferent to morality and satisfied simply with being funny. Even so, it is a great and precious quality: a decent man can lack it certainly but not without losing something of our esteem, even our moral esteem. A humorless saint is a sad saint. A humorless sage is something other than wise.[2]

To hold that humor is a virtue does not mean that we should not take others seriously or can make light of our obligations, commitments, and responsibilities to them. Nor does it mean we should not be serious about the way we lead our lives. What it does rule out is self-deception and self-satisfaction in the conduct of our lives and our relations with others. Vanity of vanities: with a bit of humor, the Ecclesiast might have made this important point better. A bit of humor and a bit of love—a bit of joy—even if for no reason or against reason. Virtue is sometimes not so much a happy medium as the capacity to embrace, in a single smile or smiling gaze, these two extremes of despair and futility between which our lives unfold and which humor brings together. For the lucid eye, what isn't cause for despair? And for the despairing eye, what isn't futile? We can still laugh about it all; in fact, that's probably the best we can do. What good is love without joy? What good is joy without humor?

Whatever is not tragic is laughable, lucidity teaches us. And with a smile, humor adds that things are not so tragic after all.

The truth of humor. The situation is hopeless but not serious.

Philosophy has traditionally opposed Democritus's laughter to Heraclitus's tears: "Democritus and Heraclitus," Montaigne recalls, "were two philosophers, the former of whom, deeming the human state vain and ridiculous, never appeared in public but with a mocking and laughing countenance; Heraclitus, having pity and sympathy for that fate of ours, wore an unchangeably sad visage, and his eyes were full of tears."[3] Certainly there are reasons enough to laugh or cry. But which is better? There is no fact of the matter: reality neither laughs nor cries. This doesn't mean that the choice is ours to make or that it somehow depends on us. Instead I would say that we are this choice, are traversed by it—laughter or tears, laughter and tears, we oscillate between the two poles, some of us inclining one way, the rest of us the other. Melancholy versus cheerfulness? Things are not so simple. Montaigne had his moments of sadness, despondency, and disgust yet preferred Democritus: "I like best the first humor, not because it is more agreeable to laugh than to weep, but because it is more contemptuous and condemns us more than the other; and it seems to me that we can never be despised as much as we deserve."[4] A sad state of affairs, indeed, but not lamentable: to cry over it would be to take ourselves too seriously. Better to laugh about it: "I do not think that we have so much ill fortune as inconstancy, or so much bad purpose as folly, we are not so full of evil as we are of inanity; we are not so wretched as we are base. . . . Our peculiar condition is as ridiculous as risible."[5] Why cry so over little (over the little that we are)? What good is it to hate ourselves ("for what we hate, we take too seriously"), when we can simply laugh?[6]

But there is laughter and there is laughter, and here a distinction must be made between humor and irony. Irony is not a virtue but a weapon, one that is almost invariably turned against others. Irony is bad laughter, sarcastic and destructive, mocking and wounding; it is the laughter of hatred and conflict, a laughter that can kill, the kind of laughter Spinoza disavows (*"non ridere, non lugere, neque detestari, sed intelligere"*).[7] Is it useful? Of course, and sometimes necessary. What weapon is not? But no weapon is peaceful, and no irony humorous. Language can be deceiving. Those whom we call, or who call themselves, humorists are often only ironists or satirists. And while we definitely need such talents, the best among them combine both genres. The French comedian Guy Bedos is a case in point: more the ironist when speaking about the right, more the humorist when speaking about the left, he is a humorist pure and simple when speaking about himself and about us all. How sad it would be if we could only laugh *at*! And how seriously we would be taking ourselves, if we could only laugh about others! Yet irony is just that: a laughter that takes itself seriously, excludes itself from its mockery of others, and is always at someone else's expense. Even when irony is directed against the self (in what we call self-mockery), it remains external and injurious. Irony scorns, disparages, censures. It takes itself seriously and questions only *other people's* seriousness, even if it has to speak about the self "as about a third party," as Kierkegaard notes.[8] More than one great wit has been humbled, or hobbled, by this stricture of irony. This is not to say that irony or self-irony is a form of humility. Quite the contrary, to mock others one must take oneself very seriously indeed. Even self-contempt requires a certain arrogance! Irony is that form of seriousness in whose eyes everything is ridiculous. Irony is that pettiness in whose eyes everything is petty.

Rilke has a remedy: "Seek the depths of things: thither irony never descends."[9] But humor does, and therein lies a first difference between the two. A second and more significant difference between them has to do with humor's self-reflexiveness and inwardness, with what I am tempted to call its immanence. Irony laughs at others (or when it is self-mockery, at the self as though it were another); humor laughs at the self, or at another as though it were the self; it always includes the self in the nonsense it brings about or exposes. I do not mean to say that the humorist takes nothing seriously (humor is not frivolousness). Simply, he refuses to take himself, his laughter, or his anguish seriously. Irony is self-assertive, humor self-effacing, Kierkegaard points out.[10] Humor can never be permanent or systematic; if it were, it would be a defense like any other and would no longer be humor. Our era perverts humor by dint of celebrating it. What could be sadder than cultivating humor for its own sake, using it as a tool of seduction or turning it into a monument to the glory of narcissism? Making a profession out of it is one thing: we all have to earn a living one way or another. But to make it one's religion or ambition is both to betray it and to betray a lack of it.

When true to itself, humor leads rather to humility. Arrogance requires serious-mindedness, and serious-mindedness a certain arrogance. Humor is the nemesis of both; it undermines the former by deflating the latter. It is for this reason that humor needs to be self-reflexive or at least self-inclusive in the laughter it provokes or in the smiles—sometimes bittersweet—that it inspires. It is not so much a question of content as one of frame of mind. The nature of a quip or a joke can change, depending on how the person making it situates himself with regard to what he says: what is ironic in the mouth of someone who excludes himself can be humorous coming from someone who includes himself. When Aristophanes makes fun of Socrates in *The Clouds*, he is being ironic; but Socrates—a great ironist at other times—displays humor when he laughs as heartily as the next man during the performance.[11] Humor and irony can, of course, be so enmeshed as to be indistinguishable, except by tone and context. Remember this line by Groucho Marx: "I've had a perfectly wonderful evening, but this wasn't it"? Directed toward his hostess after an unsuccessful dinner party, the remark is ironic; delivered to his audience at the close of a performance, it is humorous. Even in the first, however, there can be a touch of humor if Groucho makes his remark by way of acknowledging his own share of responsibility for the evening's failure, just as there can be a touch of irony in the second if the audience has demonstrated its own ineptness, as audiences sometimes will do. One can joke about anything—failure, war, death, love, disease, torture. But the laughter needs to add a bit of joy, gentleness, or lightness to the world's misfortunes, not more hatred, suffering, or contempt. One can also laugh at anything, but it all depends how. A Jewish joke is never humorous when told by an anti-Semite. Laughter isn't everything and excuses nothing. Moreover, when it comes to evils that one can prevent or combat, one must not content oneself with making jokes. Humor is no substitute for action, and unresponsiveness to another person's suffering is wrong. But it would also be wrong if, in our action or inaction, we took too seriously our own fine feelings, our own virtues, fears, and outrage. Lucidity properly begins with the self.

Hence humor, the virtue that can make us laugh at anything provided we first laugh at ourselves.

"The only thing I regret," says Woody Allen, "is not being someone else." In the act of saying so, however, he accepts himself for what he is. Humor is a kind of mourning (it has us accept precisely that which makes us suffer) and therein lies a third difference between humor and irony: where irony wounds, humor heals; where irony kills, humor makes it easier to live; where irony seeks to dominate, humor frees. Irony is merciless, humor merciful. Irony is humiliating, humor humble.

But humor does more than serve humility. It is also valuable in its own right; it transmutes sadness into joy (and hence hatred into love or mercy, as Spinoza would say), turns disillusionment into comedy, despair into delight. It pulls the rug out from under seriousness and thus defuses hatred, anger, resentment, fanaticism, totalizing systems of thought, mortification, and even irony. Laugh at yourself first, but without hatred. Or laugh at everything, but be sure you understand and accept the fact that you are part of the joke yourself. Irony says no (often while pretending to say yes); humor says yes, assenting to everything in spite of it all, accepting even that which the humorist as an individual cannot accept. Are irony and humor therefore duplicitous? Irony almost always is (there can be no irony without sham, without some degree of bad faith); humor almost never is (how could humor expressed in bad faith still be humor?).[12] Humor is ambivalence, contradiction, fracture, but accepted, overcome, transcended, and transformed. It is Pierre Desproges announcing he has cancer: "If your cancer is worse than mine, you're dead!" Or Woody Allen making a spectacle of his fears, failures, and neuroses. Or Pierre Dac confronting the human condition: "To those three eternal and heretofore unanswered questions, 'Who are we? Where do we come from? Where are we headed?' my answer is as follows: 'As for me personally, well, I'm me, I've come from home, and that's where I'm headed.'" I have noted elsewhere that there is no such thing as a comic philosophy; this no doubt is a limitation of laughter (it cannot take the place of thought), but it is also a limitation of philosophy, which is no substitute for laughter, joy, or even wisdom.[13] How sad are totalizing systems of thought, how ponderous are concepts, when they cannot make light of themselves! A little humor is the antidote: Montaigne and Hume have it; Kant and Hegel do not. "Not to mock, lament, or execrate, but to understand," Spinoza says.[14] Yes, but what if there is nothing to understand? Then we can only laugh—not *at* (irony) but *about* and *with* (humor). We are at sea, and our ship is going down: better to laugh about it than to cry. Such is the wisdom of Shakespeare and Montaigne, the only true wisdom there is.

Freud, oddly enough, speaks of humor as a "triumph of narcissism."[15] He goes on to point out, however, that this victory is achieved at the expense of the ego, relegated to its proper place, as it were, by the superego.[16] A triumph of narcissism, perhaps, but a triumph over narcissism as well (being "the victorious assertion of the ego's invulnerability," through its taking pleasure in the very things that distress it and that it overcomes).[17] Freud also speaks of humor as a triumph "of the pleasure principle."[18] But that triumph is possible only if one accepts, laughingly, reality as it is and will always remain. Humor "means: 'Look! Here is the world, which seems so dangerous! It is nothing but a game for children—just worth making a jest about!'"[19] "The rejection of the claims of reality" is humorous only if humor rejects its own claims as well (otherwise it would not be humor but madness) and thereby acknowledges the reality that it pokes fun at, makes light of, or comes to terms with.[20] Freud offers the example of the criminal who, as he is led to the gallows on a Monday, remarks: "Well, the week's beginning nicely!"[21] In humor there is courage, as well as nobility and generosity. Humor frees the ego from itself. It "has something liberating about it; but it also has something of grandeur and elevation."[22] In this respect humor differs from the other forms of the comic[23] and involves virtue.

This, then, is another difference between humor and irony: the latter is always denigrating, never sublime or generous. "Irony is an expression of greed," writes Bobin. "The ironic intelligence grits its teeth lest a single word of praise escape its lips. Humor, conversely, is an expression of generosity; to smile at what we love is to love it twice as much."[24] Twice as much? I couldn't say. What I will say, however, is that what we love smilingly we love better, in a lighter, more intelligent, and therefore freer way. Irony, on the other hand, can only hate, criticize, and scorn. Dominique Noguez may be stretching the point a bit, though he is on the right track, when he characterizes the relation between humor and irony as follows: "Humor and irony both rest on a noncoincidence of language and reality. In the former, however, the discrepancy is experienced affectionately as a brotherly greeting to the thing or person in question, whereas in the latter, it is the expression of a shocked, scornful, or malevolent opposition. Humor is love; irony, contempt."[25] At any rate, there can be no humor without a modicum of sympathy, as Kierkegaard plainly sees: "But just because there is always a hidden pain in humor, there is also a sympathy. In irony there is no sympathy."[26] Sympathy in pain, in dereliction, fragility, anguish, futility, in the universal insignificance of all things.

Humor has to do with absurdity, with nonsense, with despair. I am not suggesting that absurd statements are always amusing; in fact, they never are (if by "absurdity" one means that which makes no sense at all). We can laugh only at meaning. But meaning is not always amusing; most meaning, of course, is not. Laughter arises neither from sense nor from nonsense; it arises out of the transition or passage from the one to the other. Humor occurs in the vacillation of meaning, in its self-negation, in the evanescent flourish of its appearance-disappearance (suspended in the air, as it were, and caught in passing by laughter). When Groucho Marx, for example, takes a patient's pulse and says, "Either this man is dead or my watch has stopped," the remark does mean something—otherwise, it would not be funny. But as a meaningful statement it refers to a situation that is neither possible (except in the abstract) nor even plausible; its meaning self-destructs at the moment of its production, or rather is produced in the very process of self-destruction (if it were completely destroyed, we would not laugh). Humor involves a flickering or wavering of meaning, or sometimes its explosion; in short, it is always a movement, a process, albeit condensed and compact. Humor can tend in one of two directions, either toward its source (the seriousness of meaning) or toward its natural outcome (the nonsense of absurdity), bringing out any one of an infinite number of nuances or modulations, as we all know. But whichever the direction in which it tends, toward seriousness or toward absurdity, humor always lies somewhere in between them, in the sudden shift (seized in flight, as though momentarily frozen) between sense and nonsense. Too much meaning is not yet humor (it can often be irony); too little meaning is no longer humor (it is merely absurdity). And so we have before us once again a quasi-Aristotelian golden mean: humor is neither seriousness (in which everything is meaningful) nor frivolousness (in which nothing is) but rather an unstable, equivocal, or contradictory golden mean that reveals the frivolous side to all seriousness as well the serious side to all frivolity. The man of humor, as Aristotle would say, laughs appropriately, neither too much nor too little, at the right time and at the right things. But the question of appropriateness is for humor alone to decide, for it can laugh at anything, including Aristotle, the golden mean, and humor itself.

The best or most profound humor plays on meaning that touches important areas of our lives, drawing into its wake and shaking up larger fields of significance, our beliefs, values, illusions—in short, our seriousness. Sometimes humor seems to bring about an implosion of thought, as Lichtenberg famously does when he talks about his "bladeless knife with a missing handle." At other times it is the vanity at the root of some contemporary ambition or another that implodes—for example, the pursuit of speed in all things and at all costs: "I read all of *War and Peace* in twenty minutes," says Woody Allen of a speed-reading course. "It's about Russia." At other times, humor zeroes in on the very meaning of our behavior or reactions, shaking their foundations and calling them into question, scrambling our values, pretensions, and points of reference. Woody Allen again: "I always wear a sword for self-defense. In case I get attacked, I press the pommel and the sword changes into a white cane. Then people come to my rescue." Note that in this last example, the movement is not from sense to nonsense but from one sense to another (the sword as symbol of virile swagger—here is a man poised to fight—is shown, via the somewhat cowardly ruse of a white cane, to be essentially a crutch of masculinity). But this shift from one meaning to another, from respectability to ridiculousness, undermines both and sides with nonsense, at least potentially. At other times—the following examples are all from Woody Allen—humor expresses angst, but absurdly, as a way of exorcising it or keeping it at bay: "I'm not afraid of death, but I'd rather be somewhere else when it happens." In other instances, our feelings are set in contrast with one another, made relative, and put into perspective: "Is it better to be the lover or the loved one? Neither, if our cholesterol is over six hundred."[27] At other times, finally—I say *finally* because I will stop here though I could go on forever, since meaning can always be challenged and seriousness constantly undermined—at other times, then, humor scrutinizes our hopes and reveals what it is about them that is problematic ("Eternity is a long time, particularly toward the end"), squalid ("If only God would give me some clear sign! Like making a large deposit in my name at a Swiss bank"),[28] or improbable ("Not only is there no God, but try getting a plumber on weekends!").[29] I believe Woody Allen's humor would have appealed to Freud, who was particularly fond of a certain advertisement for an American funeral parlor, whose slogan was "Why live, if you can be buried for ten dollars?" He offers the following commentary: "The moment one inquires about the sense or value of life one is sick, since objectively neither of them has any existence."[30] This inherent senselessness and valuelessness of life is what humor expresses but finds amusing rather than lamentable.

This brings us back to Kierkegaard: "Weary of time and its infinite succession, the humorist runs away and finds a humorous relief in positing the absurd."[31] But for Kierkegaard, it is not so much its truth as its "falsification," "retraction," or "revocation" that allows humor to betray its true vocation, which is to lead us from the ethical to the religious.[32] Humor is "the last stage of existential inwardness before faith"; it is even, as Kierkegaard put it, the *incognito* of the religious in the ethical, just as irony is the *incognito* of the ethical in the aesthetic.[33] I don't share these convictions, of course. While it is true that humor challenges the seriousness of the ethical, makes it suspect, puts it in perspective, pokes fun at its vanity and pretensions and so forth, humor also challenges the seriousness of a certain kind of aesthete (the snob, the lady's man), as well as the more common and fundamental seriousness of the religious person. To laugh at the ethical by invoking a higher meaning (faith, for example) would be irony, not humor. Humor is far more likely to poke fun at the ethical (or the aesthetic or religion) by invoking a lower meaning, which it does in the name of nonsense or simply in the name of truth. Pierre Desproges, for example, on selflessness: "The Lord said, 'Love thy neighbor as thyself.' Personally I prefer myself, but I won't let my personal opinions enter into the discussion." Or Woody Allen on eternity: "Still obsessed by thoughts of death, I brood constantly. I keep wondering if there is an afterlife and if there is, will they be able to break a twenty?"[34] Truth alone is funny or, in any case, humorous, or is capable of being so, which is why nonsense is often so amusing: nothing is true, where meaning is concerned, except by virtue of the seriousness we ascribe to it. Humor does not do away with this seriousness (for we cannot and must not joke all the time, and humor depends on meaning somehow being preserved so that we may laugh at it); rather, it lightens it, puts it in perspective, keeps it at a judicious distance and destabilizes it, and ultimately frees us from it (for anything can be joked about) without destroying it altogether (for humor leaves reality unchanged, and since our desires, beliefs, and illusions are part of that reality). Humor is a form of joyful disillusionment. This is why it is doubly virtuous or can be: as disillusionment, it verges on lucidity (hence on good faith); as joy, it verges on love and is all-embracing.

The spirit, to come back to Alain's comment, makes light of everything. When it mocks what it hates or scorns, we have irony. When it laughs at what it loves or respects, we have humor. What do I love and what do I respect above all else? "Myself," as Desproges says. An apt testimonial to humor's nobility and uncommon distinction. How could it not be a virtue?

18

LOVE

Sexuality and the brain are not muscles, nor can they be. From this fact important consequences ensue, not the least of which is this one: we do not love what we want to love, we love what we desire; we love what we love, not what we choose to love. How could we choose our desires or loves—or even among them—since we choose according to them? Love does not command and thus cannot be a duty.[1] Is its inclusion in a treatise on virtues therefore problematic? Perhaps. But virtue and duty are not the same (duty is a constraint, virtue a freedom); both are necessary and each depends on the other, yet their relationship is one of complementarity, indeed symmetry, rather than similarity or identity. So it is with any virtue: the more generous one is, for instance, the less charity seems a duty—that is, a constraint.[2] And so it is a fortiori with love. I would not go so far as to say, as Nietzsche does, that "what is done out of love always takes place beyond good and evil."[3] But beyond duty and taboo, yes, almost always, and so much the better! Duty is a constraint (a "yoke," says Kant); it is a sadness, whereas love is joyous spontaneity.[4] "What one does from constraint does not come about from love," Kant observes.[5] The converse is also true: what one does out of love one does not do from constraint or out of duty. This we all know, just as we all know that some of our most patently ethical experiences have nothing to do with morality, not because they go against it but because they simply have no need of its obligations. What mother feeds her child out of duty? As for conjugal duty, what a mortifying expression! Who needs duty where there is love, where there is desire? Conjugal *virtue* on the other hand is not a contradiction in terms, nor is maternal virtue, and neither is incompatible with pleasure or love—quite the contrary. One can nurse or nurture or love or caress with more or less generosity, more or less purity, more or less fidelity, more or less prudence if need be, and with varying degrees of humor, simplicity, good faith, and love. What else could it mean to feed one's child or make love *virtuously,* in other words, excellently? There is a way of making love that is mediocre, selfish, and sometimes malevolent. And there is a way, or rather a number of ways—as many as there are individuals and couples—of making love well. To make love well is to do good and hence is a virtue. Physical love is merely one example, and it is as absurd to overvalue it, as many do today, as it is to have demonized it for centuries. Love may have its roots in sexuality, as Freud thought and as I fully believe, but it cannot be reduced to sexuality; in any case, it goes far beyond our erotic pleasures, great and small. Our lives—private and public, domestic and professional—have value only in proportion to the love we invest in them and find in them. How could we be selfish or self-centered, if we did not love ourselves? Why would we work, unless we loved money, comfort, or our work? Why would we study philosophy, unless we loved wisdom? And if I did not love philosophy, why all these books? Why this one, unless I loved the virtues? And why, dear reader, would you be reading it unless you shared one of these loves? Love cannot be commanded, for it is love that commands.

The same applies, of course, to our moral or ethical lives. Let me repeat, we need morality only for want of love, which is why we need it so! Love commands, but we do not love; and so love commands in the absence of love, commands by its very absence. Duty expresses and reveals this truth: it obliges us to do that which we would do simply out of love, if in fact we loved. How can love, which cannot be commanded, command something other than itself, or at any rate something other than what resembles it? Only actions can be commanded, and here we come to the heart of the matter: morality does not prescribe love; instead, it asks us to perform out of duty the very same action that, if we loved, we would have accomplished for love alone. Hence duty's maxim: Act as though you loved.

This obligation comes down to what Kant calls practical love. Love "towards men is no doubt possible," he writes,

> but cannot be commanded, for it is not in the power of any man to love anyone at command; therefore it is only *practical love* that is meant in that pith of all laws. . . . To love one's neighbour means to like to practise all duties towards him. But the command that makes this a rule cannot command us to have this disposition in actions conformed to duty, but only to *endeavour* after it. For a command to like to do a thing is in itself contradictory.[6]

Love is not a command; it is an ideal ("an Ideal of holiness," Kant says), one that guides and enlightens us.[7]

We are not born virtuous, we become virtuous. How? Through education: through politeness, morality, and love. Politeness, as we saw, is a semblance of morality: to act politely is to act as though one were virtuous. Morality thus starts at the bottom, by imitating the virtue it lacks and yet approaches and, through education, makes us approach. In a life well led, politeness gradually loses importance as morality takes on a larger and larger role in our conduct. Adolescence is essentially the discovery of this fact, one that adolescents are quick to remind us of should we ever forget it. But that process marks only the beginning of a farther-reaching trajectory. If politeness is a semblance of morality, morality is a semblance of love: to act morally means to act as though one loved. Morality comes into being and continues to exist by imitating the love it lacks, the love we all lack, the love that morality itself, through habit, internalization, and sublimation, approaches and draws us toward, sometimes even to the point of negating itself in this love that attracts, justifies, and dissolves it. To act well at first means to do as is done (politeness); then it means to do what ought to be done (morality); and finally, it is to do what one wants to do—that is, provided one loves (ethics). Just as morality frees us from politeness by having already achieved the latter's ends (only the virtuous man no longer needs to act *as though* he were), so love in its turn, in already fulfilling through acts of love what morality prescribes as duty, frees us from morality: only he who loves no longer needs to act *as though* he loved. "Love, and do as you wish," the Gospels say.[8] Or as Spinoza explains, if Christ frees us from the law, it is not by abolishing it (as Nietzsche, stupidly, wants to see) but by fulfilling it ("Think not that I have come to abolish the law and the prophets; I have come not to abolish them but to fulfill them")[9]—in other words, by "confirm[ing] and establish[ing]" the law, by having us take it into our hearts.[10] Morality is that semblance of love which makes possible the love that frees us from morality. Morality is born of politeness and tends toward love; it leads us from the one to the other. This is why we love morality, austere and off-putting though it may be.

Yet must we also love love? Of course we must, but the fact is that we do (for at the very least, we love being loved), or if we do not, then morality can do nothing for us. Without this love of love we are lost, and therein perhaps lies the true definition of hell, by which I mean damnation or perdition in the here and now. We must either love love or love nothing, love love or be lost. Constraint, morality, ethics—how could they be, what would they be, if we did not love love?[11] Without love, which of our virtues would remain? And what good would they be if we did not love them? In this regard, Pascal, Hume, and Bergson are better teachers than Kant: morality stems from feeling rather than from logic, from the heart rather than from reason, and reason commands morality (through universal imperatives) or serves it (through the dictates of prudence) only to the extent that we so desire.[12] The Kantian ambition to battle egoism or cruelty through the principle of noncontradiction strikes one as somehow amusing. As though a person ready to lie, kill, or torture would stop to consider whether his action could or could not be established without contradiction as a universal law. What does he care about contradiction or universality? We have need of morality only because we cannot love. But we are capable of it only because of that pittance of love, if for no one but ourselves, that we have been given and managed to preserve, dream, or rediscover.

Love, therefore, is first: not absolutely, of course (for then it would be God), but in relation to morality, duty, and the law. It is the alpha and omega of all virtue. First the mother and her child, the warmth of bodies and hearts, hunger and milk, desire and pleasure, the calming or consoling caress, the protective or nurturing gesture, the reassuring voice. First the obvious—a mother nursing—then this surprise, a man watching over a sleeping child, all his native violence left at the door. Had love not preceded morality, would we know anything of morality at all? And what does morality offer that might be better than the love from which it arises, the love that it lacks and that both drives and attracts it? That which makes morality possible is also that toward which it tends and which frees it. A circle? If you wish, but not a vicious circle, since it would seem not to be the same love at the beginning as at the end. One is the condition for law, its source and origin. The other is, as it were, its effect, its transcendence, its most beautiful and successful outcome. The alpha and omega of virtue: two different letters, two different loves (two at the very least!), with an entire alphabet between them to be lived. A circle, then, but a virtuous one, a circle that makes virtue possible. We never step outside this circle, this love, for desire circumscribes our lives. But though love does not change in its nature, it does change its object, transforming itself in the process and us along with it. For this reason, we must take our distance from it before we can consider love as a *virtue*.

What is love? That is the great question. I would like to propose three answers that are not so much at odds with one another (though to some extent they are, as we shall see) as complementary. None of them are of my own invention: love is not so unknown nor is tradition so blind that new definitions are needed. All there is to say has perhaps already been said. What we must now do is try to understand it.

Eros

The first definition, which will serve as my point of departure, is that of Plato, from *The Symposium*. Undoubtedly his most famous work (at least once we leave the ranks of professional philosophers, who prefer *The Republic*), it owes its popularity largely to the object with which it is concerned. Love interests everyone, more than anything else. Besides, what subject would interest anyone, were it not for the love we bring to it or seek within it?

Let us recall the argument, as one would say about a play, which basically is what this book is. A few friends have gathered at Agathon's house for a banquet—a *symposion*—to celebrate the poet's success a few days earlier in a tragedy competition. Everyone is eating and drinking and, above all, conversing. The topic of conversation? Love (*erōs*). No one is really trading confidences, or not many, at any rate. This is a drinking party for men, and love is glaringly conspicuous by its absence, or, let us say, is brilliantly present as an idea: they are after a definition of love, each man seeking to grasp its essence by praising it or to praise it by saying what it is. This approach is rather telling in itself and suggests that it is of the essence of love to be good or, in any case to be loved, celebrated, and glorified. Prudence is therefore necessary. For what does glory prove? Too much confusion can muddle the mind, as we see happening here. Socrates reproaches his friends: they have sacrificed truth to praise, whereas it ought to be the other way around.[13] This is basic philosophy. It is philosophy itself. The truth is subject to nothing, and everything else, all praise and all blame, must bow to it. Socrates has not digressed from the topic at hand, for as he repeatedly reminds his companions, love is the philosopher's subject par excellence, the only one in which he, Socrates, has any interest or expertise.[14] But when it comes to discourse or thought, the love of truth must take precedence over any

other love, including the love of love, lest argument become mere elo-
quence, sophistry, or ideology.

But enough said. The first speeches are not very important, and
I mention them only as a reminder: Phaedrus's, which attempts to
demonstrate that Eros is the oldest god (since he has no father or
mother) and the most useful for both man and the state (since we tend to
emulate what we love); Pausanias's, which draws a distinction between
the transient passions of the vulgar man, who loves the body and its per-
ishable beauty rather than the soul, and the enduring heavenly love of
him who loves the soul more than the body and "will remain faithful
all his life" because he has united himself to something everlasting;
Eryximachus's, which celebrates Eros as a universal force, a power "so
great, so wonderful, and all-embracing," from which, Eryximachus,
physician that he is, derives a kind of pan-eroticism of medical as well as
aesthetic and cosmological dimensions, probably inspired by Hesiod,
Parmenides, or Empedocles; and, finally, Agathon's, in which Eros is
extolled for his youthfulness, sensitivity, loveliness, gentleness, righ-
teousness, temperance, valor, suppleness—all the virtues, in short, since
he is the author of them all."[15] These speeches, some of which are bril-
liant, are of unequal interest and tend to be overlooked. When people
speak of *The Symposium,* it is almost always in reference to the two
speeches I have not yet mentioned—that of Aristophanes, with its
famous (though erroneously designated) "myth of the hermaphrodites," and of course that of Socrates. Needless to say, it is the latter
who, according to Plato—and here he is not alone—speaks the truth
about love. Strangely enough, Aristophanes' speech is the more often
cited of the two, and the only one, I have often observed, that the reading public recalls and praises, usually for its profundity, poetry, and
truth. Imagine forgetting Socrates and Plato! This is no accident, however. Aristophanes tells us exactly what we would all like to believe
about love, describing the kind of love we dream of, fulfilled and fulfilling, a happy, gratifying passion; whereas Socrates gives us love as it is,
destined to remain unfulfilled, incomplete, and unhappy and thus

dooming us to misery or religion. But let us examine the arguments in a little greater detail.

First, Aristophanes' speech.[16] It is a poet who speaks. "In the beginning," he explains, "we were nothing like we are now." Our ancestors were double, at least by comparison with what we are today, yet they embodied a perfect unity that we now lack: "Each of these beings was globular in shape, with rounded back and sides, four arms and four legs, and two faces, both the same, on a cylindrical neck, and one head, with one face one side and one the other, and four ears, and two lots of privates, and all the other parts to match." The genital duality in particular accounts for there being at the time not two sexes but three: males, who had two male organs, females who had two female ones, and androgynes who, as the term implies, had one of each. The males, as Aristophanes explains, were descended from the sun, the females from the earth, and the androgynes, or hermaphrodites, from the moon, which has something of the nature of both sexes. All three—the males, the females, and the hermaphrodites—were beings of such exceptional strength and valor that they attempted to scale the heights of heaven and do battle with the gods. To punish the would-be usurpers, Zeus decided to cut them in half, from top to bottom, as one slices an egg. That marked the end of completeness, unity, happiness. Everyone since has been reduced to seeking *his other half,* as they say, an expression meant to be taken literally here: formerly, "we were a complete whole . . . we were one"; now we are "separated from ourselves," ceaselessly yearning to regain the *whole* we once were.

This quest, this desire, is what we call love, and its fulfillment is the prerequisite for happiness. Love alone can heal "our dissevered nature by finding each his proper mate." We are given to understand that we are homosexual or heterosexual depending on the nature of the oneness we lost: those whose lost oneness was male or female are homosexual in their present existence, whereas those whose lost oneness was androgynous are heterosexual. Aristophanes accords no special status to heterosexuality—far from it (one might suppose that it is better to be descended from the moon than from the earth, but surely nothing can equal a solar origin)—and so it is a mistake, from that standpoint, to talk about the myth of the hermaphrodites, who make up but a part of the original race of mankind, and certainly not the best. But no matter. What people generally retain from Aristophanes' myth, and rightfully so, is that it validates the myth of love, by which I mean the love we talk about, dream about, and believe in—love as religion, as fairy tale, the one true love, total, permanent, exclusive, unconditional. "When this boy lover—or any lover, for that matter—is fortunate enough to meet his other half, they are both so intoxicated with affection, with friendship, and with love, that they cannot bear to let each other out of sight for a single instant." What do they desire? "To be merged . . . into an utter oneness with the beloved." What Aristophanes describes is the very definition of fusional love that would restore us to what he calls our "primeval oneness" and free us from our solitude (since, "welded together," the lovers would never part); there could be "no more happier fate" in this life or the next.

The love he describes is an absolute, unconditional love, since it is simply one's self that one loves, a self at last restored to its original completeness, unity, and perfection. It is an exclusive love, since each person, having by definition a single other half, can experience but one love. And finally, it is a permanent love, since the original oneness antecedes us and, once restored, will fulfill us to the day we die and even, Aristophanes says, in the hereafter. (Love's errancy, by his account, is simply error: we have found ourselves with the wrong partner, who, by definition, is not our one true love.) Indeed, there is nothing in our wildest dreams of love that this myth leaves out or fails to justify.

But what store do we set by our dreams? And what does a myth prove? These same values, beliefs, and illusions we can find in romance fiction as well, which proves no more in one case than in the other. Aristophanes describes love as we sometimes dream of it, as we may have experienced it either in our mothers' arms—this is what Freud suggests, at any rate—or (who is to say?) inside their wombs.

Nevertheless, it is a love that we will never experience again, not today, except as a sickness or a lie, and not tomorrow, unless by some miracle or in madness. Have I begged the question here, postulating what needs to be demonstrated? So be it. I understand that I have Aristophanes and romance fiction against me on this issue. But I have Plato, who hated Aristophanes,[17] on my side, as well as Lucretius (and Pascal, Spinoza, and Nietzsche, and all of philosophy . . .) and Freud, Rilke, and Proust. Have I forgotten that what is in books is not what is essential? Not at all. But where are the real-life counterinstances? And what do they prove? Every now and then I hear of a man and a woman who love each other with this sort of love, who live together in absolute and complete oneness. I also hear of people who have seen the Virgin Mary, and I attach no greater importance to these latter reports. On the subject of miracles, Hume says all that needs to be said, and what he says applies no less to the miracle of absolute love. Any testimony is merely probable and must therefore be compared with the likelihood of what it states: if the attested event is more improbable than is the testimony's falsehood, the very reasons that would have us believe the testimony (its likelihood, of whatever degree) must cause us to doubt its veracity (since the likelihood that the testimony is true does not outweigh the greater improbability of the fact in question). This formula applies, by definition, to all miracles; hence we cannot reasonably believe in them.[18] I am not digressing here: what could be more improbable, miraculous, and contrary to our daily experience than two beings merging into one? I trust bodies more than books or witnesses. It takes two people to make love (at least two!), and this fact explains why coitus, far from abolishing solitude, only confirms it. Lovers know this. Souls could merge, if they existed, but it is bodies that touch each other, that love each other, that have orgasm, and that are still there when it has passed. Here is Lucretius's description of the oneness that is often sought but never found in the lovers' embrace—or, if found or thought to be found (in the seeming obliteration of the ego), is immediately lost:

Lastly, when clasped body to body they enjoy the flower of their age, at the moment when the body foretastes its joy and Venus is on the point of sowing the woman's field, they cling greedily close together and join their watering mouths and draw deep breaths pressing teeth on lips; but all is vanity, for they can rub nothing off, nor can they penetrate and be absorbed body in body; for this they seem sometimes to wish and to strive for.[19]

The lovers' quest for oneness always results in failure and often in sadness. They wanted to be but one, and now more than ever they are *two*. "From the very fountain of enchantment rises a drop of bitterness to torment even in the flowers," Lucretius writes.[20] The futility and sadness, the bitterness in which this quest for oneness inevitably ends does not gainsay pleasure when it is pure or love when it is true. But it does argue against the illusion of oneness that pleasure itself refutes just when it thinks it has reached it. *Post coitum omne animal triste . . .* The animal that we are is sad because he has returned to himself, to his solitude and banality, to the vast emptiness inside him where desire once was. Or if we are spared this sadness, as we sometimes are, it is through the wonder of pleasure, of love, of gratitude—in short, through an encounter, which presupposes duality, and never through the fusion of two beings or the obliteration of their differences. The truth of love: it is better to make love than to dream about it. The simultaneous orgasm of two lovers (not the most frequent occurrence, but let us not dwell on that) makes for two different pleasures, each mysterious to the other, two spasms, two solitudes. The body knows more about love than poets know, at least more than those poets who lie about the body— which is to say, almost all of them. What is it they fear? What are they trying to make themselves feel better about? Themselves, perhaps, the power and irrationality of desire (or its insignificance afterwards?), their own animality, the swiftness with which the dizzying depths of their passion are filled (pleasure being shallow after all, a glorified stream), the deathlike peace that comes so suddenly once they are. Solitude is our lot in life, and that lot is the body.

I doubt that Socrates would agree on every point, which is not to say he agrees with Aristophanes. Quite the contrary. But if my ideas do not represent those of Socrates (at least not those of Plato's Socrates) on the subject of love, whose "truth" he is about to tell us, neither are they, strictly speaking, his own.[21] For early on in this speech, Socrates informs us that all he knows about love he owes to a woman, Diotima, whose words he is simply relating (and it is probably not insignificant that in matters of love Socrates, as was scarcely his wont, casts himself as the disciple of a woman). And what does Diotima say? Or, rather, what does Socrates say she said to him? First of all, that love is not God or a god. For all love is love of something, something desired and lacking,[22] and what could be less godlike than to be lacking in the very thing that makes us exist or live? Aristophanes has it all wrong. Love is not completeness but incompleteness. Not fusion but quest. Not perfect fulfillment but all-consuming want. Any understanding of love must proceed from this critical starting point: love is desire and desire is want. Are love, desire, and want therefore synonymous? No, not entirely. Desire exists only where want is perceived and experienced as such (we do not desire what we do not realize we lack). And love exists only where desire, indeterminate in itself (like the feeling of hunger unaccompanied by a desire for a particular food), focuses on a specific object (hence the love of meat, or fish, or pastries). It is one thing to eat because we are hungry, quite another to love what we eat or to eat what we love. The desire for a woman that is not a desire for a particular woman is one thing (it is desire); the desire for a *specific* woman is another (it is love, even if, as sometimes happens, this love is purely sexual and transitory). Being in love is something other than and more than being sexually aroused. Yet can one be in love without desiring in one way or another the person one loves? Probably not. If not all desire is love, all love (at least this kind of love, *erōs*) is indeed desire, the determinate desire for a certain object as an object that is lacking *in particular*. Love, writes Plato, "is the love of something which [one] hasn't got, and consequently lacks."[23] If not all want is love (it is not enough to be ignorant of the truth in order to love it, we must also know we are

ignorant and desire not to be), all love, according Plato, is indeed want: love is nothing other than this want—a conscious want, experienced as such—for a specific object. Socrates drives the point home: "whoever feels a want is wanting something which is not yet to hand, and the object of his love and of his desire is whatever he isn't, or whatever he hasn't got—that is to say, whatever he is lacking in."[24] If love loves beauty and goodness, and we know from experience that it does, the reason is that it is lacking in them. How then could love be a god?

But to say that love is not a god is not to say that it is bad or ugly, as Socrates makes clear: it occupies an intermediate position, midway between mortal and immortal, between god and man. Love is a daemon, Diotima says—in other words, a mediator between the gods and men. This daemon, or spirit, may be the greatest of all, but it is his fate to be always in want. Is he not the son of Penia and Poros—of Need and Resource? He is always poor, Diotima observes, barefoot and homeless, forever in pursuit of the beautiful and the good, always hunting and seeking, always troubled, ardent, resourceful, craving, and avid . . . We are a long way from Aristophanes' round completeness, the restful comfort of restored oneness! Eros never rests. Incompleteness is his destiny, since he is defined by want: "Sleeping on the naked earth, in doorways, or in the very streets beneath the stars of heaven, and always partaking of his mother's poverty. . . . In the space of a day he will be now, when all goes well with him, alive and blooming, and now dying, to be born again by virtue of his father's nature, while what he gains will always ebb away as fast."[25] Nevertheless he is rich in everything he lacks and forever in want of the object of his pursuit—neither rich nor poor, then, or both, always midway between the two, between wealth and poverty, knowledge and ignorance, happiness and misfortune. A gypsy child, if you wish, always on the move, on the run, always yearning. "Ever insatiable," as Plotinus says of *erōs* in his commentary on Plato, never fulfilled or satisfied, and for good reason: love "is like a goad; it is without resource in itself; even winning its end, it is poor again."[26] This love is no longer the love of our dreams, fulfilled and fulfilling, the love served up by romance fiction; it is love as bounteous suffering,[27] a

strange comingling of "joy and anguish," as the *Phaedrus* describes it,[28] an insatiable, solitary love, always longing for what it loves, always yearning for its object; it is love as passion in its true sense, terrifying and rending passion that starves and tortures, elates and imprisons. How could it be otherwise? We desire only what we lack, what we do not have: how could we have what we desire? There are no happy loves, and this want of happiness is love itself. "How happy I would be if she loved me," the man tells himself. "If only she were mine!" But if he were happy, he would no longer love her, or at any rate his love would no longer be the same.

Here, of course, I am departing from Plato, or at least I am modernizing him a bit, drawing certain lessons from him. If love is lack, and insofar as it is, it precludes completeness by definition. Lovers know this, and their knowledge proves Aristophanes wrong. Want, once satisfied, ceases to be want; passion cannot long outlast happiness, nor happiness passion, no doubt. Hence the great suffering that is love, so long as want holds sway. And the great sadness that is the couple when it no longer does. Satisfaction kills desire, which therefore must be unsatisfied or dead, missed or missing, unhappy or spent. Can we ever escape this predicament? Plato suggests two solutions, but neither, I am afraid, will make our love lives any easier. What does it mean to love? It means to lack that which we love and to want to possess it forever.[29] Love, then, is selfish, at least this kind of love is, selfish and yet perpetually driven outside itself. It is "ex-tatic," Lacan says,[30] and in this sense ecstasy (the ecstasy of oneself in another) aptly defines passion as a decentered selfishness, an egoism torn apart and overflowing with absence, replete with the void of its object and of itself, as though it were that very void. How can love possess forever since it will die, and how could it possess anything at all since it is lack? It can, Plato says, by bringing "forth upon the beautiful, both in body and in soul,"[31] in other words, through creation or procreation, art or the family. This first solution is the most accessible and the most natural. We see it at work already in the world of animals, Diotima explains, when they are seized with the desire to procreate, when love is on their brain, when they sacrifice themselves for their offspring. That reason plays no part in all this suffices to prove that love precedes or transcends reason. But then where does this love come from? According to Diotima, it comes from the fact "that the mortal does all it can to put off mortality. And how can it do that except by breeding, and thus ensuring that there will always be a younger generation to take the place of the old?"[32] Procreation is the cause or principle of love, thanks to which mortals, who are constantly becoming other than what they are, nonetheless tend to perpetuate themselves and partake of immortality, insofar as they can. Eternity and divinity through replacement. Hence the love that mortals have for their children, and their love of glory: it is life they love, immortality that they pursue—and death that haunts them.[33] Love is life itself—life perpetually in want of itself, seeking to preserve itself yet unable to do so, gnawed at by death and doomed to nothingness. Love can escape absolute want, absolute deprivation, and absolute misfortune only by *bringing forth,* as Plato puts it: some bring forth through the body, others through the soul—that is, through the family or through creation, be it in art, politics, or science.[34] A solution perhaps, but not a salvation, for no matter what we do, death remains and will carry us all off—us, our children, and our works—and the lack that is love will always torment us, unless we cease to love. The family, as everyone knows, is the future of love and its natural outcome, but that fact has never been able to save love, the couple, or the family. And, indeed, how could our creations—our works of art, philosophies, political institutions—save love if our acts of creation themselves depend on love? Or if they do not depend on it?

It is perhaps for this reason that Plato offers another solution, more difficult and demanding than the first. This second solution is that of the famous ascending dialectic, with which Diotima's speech concludes. What does it consist of? An ascent, to be sure, but a spiritual one, an initiatory journey, one might say, and literally a salvation. A journey of love and a salvation through beauty. How can we follow the path to love without losing our way, how can we make it our master without becoming its slave? There is a way, Plato says. We can mount the rungs of love one by one: first we love the beauty of one individual body; next we love all lovely bodies, since they all partake of the same beauty; then we love the beauties of the soul, which are superior to those of bodies; and afterwards the beauty of laws and institutions, followed by the beauty of the sciences, and finally the very soul of beauty, everlasting and supernatural, subsisting of itself and by itself, the beauty of which all lovely things partake, from which they all originate and receive their beauty.[35] This ultimate beauty, to which love leads us, saves love and saves us. In other words, Diotoma's secret, and Plato's, is that religion alone can save love: if love is want, then its own logic impels it ever onward toward what it lacks, toward what it lacks more and more or entirely—thus, toward the good (of which the beautiful is merely a dazzling manifestation) or toward transcendence, or God, toward the point at which love abolishes itself, finally satiated, finally appeased, finally happy—and dead![36] Is this love still love if it no longer lacks anything? I do not know. Plato would say, perhaps, that in love's final completion and abolition nothing remains but beauty, just as Plotinus will say that nothing remains but the One, and the mystics that nothing remains but God. But if God is not love, what good is God? And what could God possibly lack?

We must leave Plato here, right where he leaves us. He has taken us from the dream of fusion (Aristophanes) to the experience of want (Socrates), and finally from want to transcendence or faith (Diotima). Quite a journey for such a small book, which shows how great a book it is. But is Plato's solution accessible to us today? Is it credible or even acceptable? Christians will no doubt answer yes, but not all of them. For lovers, whether they believe in God or not, know that not even he can save them if they cannot first, on their own, save the love they have within them and for one another. What good is faith if we do not know how to love? And why would we need it if we knew?

But the truth, of course, is that we do not know how to love. Couples live this truth continually, painfully, and with difficulty; it dooms them to failure, perhaps, while justifying their existence. How can we love without learning? How can we learn without loving?

I recognize that other forms of love exist, and I plan to discuss them. But this one is the strongest, or in any case the most violent (parental love is stronger for some but calmer), and it is the greatest source of suffering, failure, illusion, and disillusionment. Eros is its name, want is its essence, and passionate love is its culmination. Want necessarily means suffering and possessiveness. I love you means I want you (in Spanish, as we know, the two expressions are identical: *te quiero*). The scholastic philosophers call this love *concupiscent love*; the troubadours speak of it as an affliction, *le mal d'amour;* Plato describes it in *The Symposium*, as we have seen, and also, more cruelly, in the *Phaedrus:* it is a jealous, avid, possessive love, and far from always rejoicing over the loved one's happiness (as would a generous love), it suffers dreadfully whenever this happiness threatens its own or draws the loved one away.[37] The lover is irksome and jealous as long as he loves, unfaithful and deceitful when he stops loving. His "attentions . . . carry no good will; they are no more than a glutting of his appetite, for 'As wolf to lamb, so lover to his lad.'"[38] Concupiscent love, then, clearly: being in love means loving the other person for one's own benefit. This kind of love is not the opposite of egoism; it is egoism's passionate, relational, transitive form, an egoistical transference or a transference of egoism.[39] It has nothing to do with virtue but often a great deal to do with hatred. Eros is a jealous god. He who loves wants to possess his beloved and keep her for himself alone. If she is happy with someone else, you would rather see her dead! If he is happy with someone else, you would rather have him unhappy with you. What a fine love this, which is but love of self.

But let her leave you and see how you miss her! How you desire her! How you love her! How deeply you suffer! Eros has you in his grip and tears you apart; you love what you do not have, what you lack: these are the pangs of love.

But look, now she loves you again, she always loved you, she is with you now, she's here for you, she's all yours! What frenzy in your reunion, what eagerness in your embraces, what savagery in your pleasure! And afterwards? Peace, a quieting ebb, a sudden emptiness. She senses you are less present, less urgent. "Do you still love me?" she asks. Naturally, you answer yes. But in fact, you *want* her less. The feeling will return, for the body is made thus. Yet by dint of her being there every day and every night, every evening and every morning, you will in time come to want her less and less, less strongly and less frequently, and finally you will want someone else or want your solitude more than you want her. Eros has been calmed, Eros is bored: you are no longer in want of what you have and this state is what is called being in a couple.

A woman friend said to me, "Men rarely die of love; they fall asleep first." A killing sleep sometimes, for women.

Am I painting too bleak picture of love? Let us say that I am oversimplifying, by necessity. Some couples experience something better, far better, than this benumbing of passion, this disenamorment that dare not speak its name. But others can experience much worse, even hate, violence, and madness. How it is that happy couples do exist is something that Plato fails to explain but that we must try to understand. If love is want, how can it survive after it has been fulfilled; how can it continue once it has been satisfied; how can we make love without unmaking it, without consuming it? Isn't pleasure the end (that is, not just the goal but also the termination) of desire? Isn't happiness the end of passion? How can love be happy if its object can only be "not yet to hand"?[40] How can love last if it is happy?

"Just think of a Mrs. Tristan!" writes Denis de Rougemont.[41] We all know what he means: that her passion would not have survived that fate, that without the sword that lay between her and Tristan, between her and happiness, Isolde could not have remained in love—in short, that love is passionate only if it feels want, that love is this very want, focused by its object, fueled by its absence, and that therefore passion can last only in and through suffering, and possibly only for the sake of suffering. Want is suffering, passion is suffering, the two—suffering and passion—are one and the same, or perhaps passion is merely a hallucinatory or obsessional exacerbation of the suffering of love (love, says René Allendy, is "a normal obsessional syndrome"),[42] brought about by the lover's concentration on a determinate object that (because want is indeterminate) thereafter is indeterminately overvalued. Hence all the intense excitations often associated with love, Stendhal's "crystallization" and Breton's *amour fou*."[43] Hence, no doubt, romanticism itself and perhaps religion, too (God what is lacking in the most absolute sense).[44] Hence, in any case, this love that is only as strong as it is frustrated and unhappy. "'Passion' triumphs over desire," writes Denis de Rougement. "Death triumphs over life."[45] Remember Truffaut's *Adele H*. How one wishes she would stop being in love, stop waiting for him, stop suffering, and get over it! But she prefers death or madness. It's the same old story, it's Tristan's song, again and again: "'The olden ditty once more tells me: / 'Tis yearning and dying! . . . / Yearning now calls / for death's repose.'"[46]

If life is want, what does she want that she does not have? Another life, or death. Such is the logic of nothingness ("real life is absent": being is elsewhere, being is what is lacking!), the logic of Plato ("philosophers . . . are half dead already"),[47] the logic of Eros: if love is desire and desire is want, we can love only what we do not have and suffer from this lack; yet we can have only that which we do not lack and which thereafter we can no longer continue to love (since love is want). Passion or boredom, then. Albertine present, Albertine gone. When she is there, he dreams of other things, of what he is missing out on ("comparing the mediocrity of the pleasures that Albertine afforded me to the richness of the desires she prevented me from realising," Proust writes), and so she bores him.[48] But as soon as she leaves, passion instantly reawakens in want and suffering! "Very often," Proust observes, "in order that we may discover that we are in love, perhaps indeed in order that we may fall in love, the day of separation must first have come."[49] The logic of passion is the logic of want: the couple is its prospect (in dreams) and its death (in reality). How could we lack what we have? How could we love passionately what we do not lack? Speaking of Tristan and Isolde, Denis de Rougement notes: "Their need of one another is in order to be aflame, and they do not need one another as they are. What they need is not each other's presence, but each other's absence!"[50] Hence this salutary sword between them, this chastity they choose as if a symbolic suicide: "What they desire they have not yet had—this is Death—and what they had is now being lost—the enjoyment of life."[51] Eros as Thanatos: "Unawares and in spite of themselves, the lovers have never had but one desire—the desire for death!"[52] For they loved love more than life, loved lack more than presence and passion more than happiness or pleasure. "My Lords, if you would hear a high tale of love and of death . . ." *The Romance of Tristan and Iseult* begins with these words but so could *Romeo and Juliet*, *Manon Lescault*, and *Anna Karenina*.[53] Yet they apply only in the best of cases, by which I mean when there is real passion and not its imitation—not a hope or nostalgia for passion—which also imprisons and also kills but without grandeur. For every Isolde, how many Emma Bovarys?

Let us not make too much of passion or make it out to be more beautiful than it is; let us not confuse it with the novels written about it (besides, the best of them are those that are least taken in by it: think of Proust, Flaubert, Stendhal . . .). I remember once telling a writer how little I liked novels about great, all-consuming, absolute, sublime passions, the kind that are found only in books—for example, in hers. She responded to my comment by mentioning a mutual friend of ours who, she said, really and truly had had a great and tragic love affair. I had no idea, and my curiosity was aroused. A few days later I ran into the friend of whom she had spoken and asked him. He smiled: "You know, in the end, it was just a rather ordinary fiasco." We ought not confuse love with the illusions we have about it when we are in love or with how we imagine it when we are not in love and want to be. Memory is more real than dreams and experience more real than imagination. What is being in love, in fact, if not harboring certain illusions about love, about oneself, and about the person with whom one is in love? Usually these three streams of illusions converge, forming a river that sweeps us away. To where? To where all rivers go, where they end or get lost: in the ocean of time or the sands of everyday life. "It is of the essence of love," notes Clément Rosset, "to profess to love forever but in fact to love only for a time."[54] Thus it is of the essence of love (in any case, of this kind of love, passionate love) to be illusory and ephemeral. Truth itself is fatal to love, which is why those who celebrate love would like to do away with truth: some will freely admit their preference for dreams or illusions. But dreams and illusions are usually not enough to save them or to save love. They want to prove that reality is wrong, but then reality catches up with them and proves them wrong. They want to save passion, make it last, and keep it alive. But how could they, since their passion does not depend on them; since, when it is happy, the passage of time kills it and since the idea of keeping passion alive is antithetical to passion? Every want, if it does not kill, eventually subsides. It subsides because it has been satisfied, because we have grown accustomed to it, because it has been forgotten. If love is want, it is doomed to failure (in life) or can succeed only in death.

Some will say that, indeed, love can only fail and that therefore Plato is right. So be it. But is this love the only kind of which we are capable? Do we know only how to want and to dream? What sort of virtue would it be that can lead only to suffering or religion?

Philia

I promised three definitions of love, and now it is time to discuss the second. According to Spinoza, no one can desire virtue without also desiring to act and to live.[55] But how can life be an object of desire, given that one can desire life only on the condition of having a life, of being alive? If we follow Plato (and accept our lot as one of unhappiness or dissatisfaction), there is no contradiction here: the life we desire is always some other life than the one we have. If desire is lack, and to the extent that it is, life necessarily leaves us wanting. If we desire only what we do not have, we can never have what we desire and hence can never be happy or satisfied.[56] Our very desire for happiness keeps us from attaining it. "I would be so happy, if only I were happy!" Woody

Allen says, apparently siding with Plato, who insists that we can only desire "something which is not yet to hand"—something, in other words, that does not exist.[57] We desire not this particular woman, who is real, but the possession of her, which is not. We desire not our works, the accomplishment of our creative efforts, but the glory we hope to attain through them. Not the life that we have, but another one that we do not have. We can desire only nothingness, only death. And how could we love that which does not exist? If love is lack, then all love is imaginary love—and we never love anything but phantoms.

But is love always a lack? Is it never anything more? In *The Symposium*, Socrates tries to counter his own argument: Can't a healthy person desire health? he asks. And in desiring health, would he not in fact be desiring the very thing he has and not something he lacks? Not at all, Socrates says, for the health he desires is not the same as the health he has; what he has is a present state of health, whereas what he desires is its continuation, in other words, a future state of health, which he does not have.[58] The response is revealing, more so than Plato perhaps intended, for it points to a critical confusion of desire with hope. For the sad truth about hope is that I cannot hope to have what I have or to be what I am or to do what I am doing: in what sense can I at this moment hope to be alive, since I am alive, or hope to be sitting, since I am sitting now, or hope to be writing as I put these words to paper? One can hope only for that which one does not have; hope is forever consigned to a fate of unreality and lack and consigns us to that fate as well. But is all desire hope? Can we desire only what does not exist? If so, how could we ever love what is?

To these questions Plato can supply no answers, nor can those who follow in his footsteps. Not only Sartre, for whom desire is both "the being of human reality" and "a lack of being," but indeed all existentialisms, atheist and Christian alike, offer nothingness or transcendence as our only alternative.[59] We cannot love, they tell us, except in frustration (when the other is absent) or in failure (when the other is present: "pleasure is the death and failure of desire").[60] Like Plato, they all confuse desire with hope, and love—in all its forms—with want. They mistake the part for the whole, accident for essence. It is true, I said, that one can hope only for what one does not have: hope is want itself, want in the face of our ignorance of, and powerlessness to control, the future. We can hope only for that which we do not possess, do not know, or cannot bring about on our own power.[61] Accordingly, says Spinoza, hope is fear, ignorance, and incapacity;[62] it is not desire or love. Or rather, not all desire and not all love are forms of hope. When someone is out for a stroll, what is it he desires if not to stroll, if not the very steps he takes at the very instant he takes them? How could he feel as though he lacked them? And how could he walk without the desire to do so? Suppose he desired only the steps he has yet to take or only the landscape that has yet to come into view; in that case we would have to say either that he is not really strolling or that he has no notion of the true pleasures of this pastime. The same holds for all of us, once we stop hoping. Why would I be sitting if I had no desire to? How could I write unless I wanted to? And why would anyone believe that I desire only the words that I have yet to write and not those I am now writing? Am I anticipating the words that will follow these? Yes, but I am not hoping for them! I imagine them, sense them, search for them, summon them, choose them . . . How can I hope for what depends on me? Why would I hope for what does not? The writing present, like any living present, is future-oriented, but not always or principally because of want or hope. A great gulf separates *writing* from *hoping to write,* the same gulf that separates desire as want (hope or passion) from desire as capacity or enjoyment (pleasure or action). For things that depend on us, volition is desire in action: how could its object be lacking since we are accomplishing it? For things that do not depend on us, pleasure is desire fulfilled: how could its object be wanting since it is being enjoyed? Desiring what we do, what we possess, or what is, is called willing, acting, enjoying, or taking delight, and thus even our littlest actions, pleasures, or joys are a refutation of Platonism. For when do action, pleasure, and joy take place? The answer is simple: whenever we do, have, or are what we desire, whenever what we desire exists—in short, whenever we desire something that we are not lacking. And every time we do, Plato is wrong—which says a great deal about Platonism! Drinking when we are thirsty, eating when we are hungry or when the food on our plate is appetizing, strolling when we care to, talking with friends, admiring the landscape, listening to music we love, writing the words we choose, accomplishing the acts we wish to accomplish . . . where is the want? In hunger and thirst? Perhaps. But note first that music, friendship, or action can be enjoyed without one's lacking them beforehand. And second, that we can eat and drink with pleasure when we have good things to eat and drink, without feeling any want at all. And finally, that it makes little sense to speak of want in the case of someone who has something to eat and drink. Hunger is one thing, it is the feeling that tortures the famished; appetite is another, it allows the eater to enjoy his food; taste is something else again, it brings happiness to the gourmet. Want can blend with pleasure, but it cannot by itself cause pleasure or explain it. Even in the domain of sexuality, is it at all clear that Eros reigns alone and supreme? Perhaps it does in passion, suffering, and frustration. But in love? In pleasure? In action? If we desired only what we do not have, either because it does not exist or because it is not ours, our sexual life, it seems to me, would be even more complicated than it is and far less enjoyable.

What on earth do a man and woman who love and desire each other lack when they are making love? Each other? No, they are already there for each other, entirely available, giving of themselves wholeheartedly. An orgasm? No, an orgasm is not what they are after, since they will have one soon enough, since desire is fulfillment enough, and since love, the very act of making love, is itself a pleasure! That there is tension in desire and that this tension calls for release, no one will dispute. But it is the tension of a force, not of a lack, a joyous, affirmative, vital tension that has nothing to do with frustration and everything to do with the experience of one's capacity and plenitude. How alive they are when they make love! How present! How fulfilled each is by the other, fulfilled in the here and now! When sex is accompanied by love and pleasure, when lovers make love lovingly, they lack nothing, and that is why they feel so good and so happy, giving pleasure to each other, taking pleasure in themselves and in each other, in their desire and their love. But their desire is of another kind, for it lacks nothing, and their love is of another kind as well, since it is happy. Or if the two forms of love can sometimes mix, as they often do, this fact confirms again that they are different. There is the love that we suffer from, which is passion, and there is the love that we make and give, which is action. Do you really regard an erection as a lack? Is it really your experience that all love is suffering?

One can cite other examples. To be a father, Socrates observes, is necessarily to be *somebody's* father.[63] Fine, but then the father loves his child even though he does not lack one! He may very well have loved his child before having him; he may have desired him and hoped for him; he may even have desperately wanted a child, loved the child he did not have, suffered from the passion to beget, from the paternal Eros. In that case, his love is an imaginary love, with an imaginary object. He loved the child he dreamed of, and his love was merely the dream of love. A happy dream, as long as it envisions its own fulfillment, but a painful one, if it lasts too long. How great is his suffering and frustration if the child does not come! But if he does come, if he is here? Does the father stop loving his child because he is no longer lacking? Sometimes, but usually not. Most fathers learn to love their child differently, for real—in other words, as he is, as he lives, grows, and changes, as a child who is no longer lacking . . . To learn to love the real child and not the child one has dreamed of is a never-ending process.

All parents know that this process is both necessary and difficult, that there can be no love (of the real) without a degree of mourning (for the imaginary), that in fact one does not shift one's love from the one to the other, from the dreamed-of child to the real child; rather the two loves intermix, each adding to the other, yet without merging completely. For we continue to imagine; we continue to want. We do not escape Plato or Eros so easily. Every father wants, as Plato would say, "to go on having" what he already has.[64] He therefore desires what he does not have (since by definition the future is lacking). A father wants his child to live up to his hopes, a desire to which the child is utterly indifferent; but above all, far above all, a father desperately wants his child to live, and to this desire life is indifferent. What father does not feel hope and anguish, is not gripped at times by fear and passion, by an Eros that will not release his hold on him? But clearly, these feelings do not encompass the extent of his love, or its best part, or the part that is liveliest, truest, freest, and happiest. Poor father, poor love (and poor son!), if the father loved only the son to be, the *preservation* of the son, as Plato would say[65]—in other words, the very thing of which death can deprive him at any moment—or, I should say, of which it will necessarily deprive him ("If one of us must die, then let it be me!" thinks the father), of which it already deprives him, since the son *is* lacking, the nonexistent, dreamed-of son, the son as nothingness, anguish, the son felt as a gaping hole at the heart of being or in the bosom of happiness, as a knot in the throat and a sudden desire to cry . . .

I shall say it again. Such love does indeed exist: a father's passionate love for his son, with its hopes and fears that imprison, as all passions do, and that threaten to imprison the son as well, dooming them both to anguish, the imaginary, and nothingness. This kind of love exists, but it is not the only kind; for the father also loves his child as he is, the child he no longer lacks, the actual, present, living child, against whom anguish, nothingness, and death are powerless, the child whose very fragility has something indestructible or eternal about it, even in the face of death or time, something utterly simple and living, which the father at times knows enough to merely accompany and which, oddly enough, appeases and reassures him, indeed, reassures him and delights him.

Against anguish, reality. Against want, joy. This too is love, but no longer Eros. What kind of love is it then?

And what about the love we have for our friends? How sad it would be if we loved them only in their absence. But the very opposite is true, and for this reason friendship is quite distinct from passion. In friendship there is no want, anguish, jealousy, or suffering. We love our friends as they are, not for their absence but for their being with us. It is no accident that Plato has nothing noteworthy to say about friendship. Aristotle, on the other hand, says all that is most important to say on the subject, in two sublime books of the *Nicomachean Ethics*. He says that life without friendship would be a life of error, that friendship is a precondition of happiness, a refuge from misfortune, at once useful, pleasant, and good. That friendship is "desirable in itself" and "seems to lie in loving rather than in being loved." That friendship cannot exist without equality, which either precedes it or results from it. That friendship is better than justice and includes it, being at once its highest expression and its transcendence. That friendship is neither want nor oneness but rather community, sharing, fidelity. That friends delight in one another and in their friendship. That one cannot be a friend to all or to many. That the highest form of friendship is not a passion but a virtue. And finally, in a statement that sums up all the others, that "loving [is] the characteristic virtue of friends."[66] Indeed, friendship is love (a friend for whom we feel no love would not be a friend) but not want or Eros. What kind of love then is it?

And so we need another definition, for which I turn to Spinoza. Love, for Spinoza, is of course desire, since desire is the very essence of man.[67] Desire, however, is not lack but a capacity or potency,[68] and love is a joy.[69] It is here that we must begin, or rather begin anew.

The fact that in ordinary language we speak of something called "sexual potency" tells us something important. It tells us that desire, whether lacking its object or not, cannot be reduced to lack, that it is also and in the first instance a force, an energy, or, to use Spinoza's term, a capacity: it is the capacity to enjoy and the enjoyment of our capacities. Not just sexual desire but all desire, says Spinoza, is a capacity for action and the power to exist ("*agendi potentia sive existendi vis*"), hence the capacity to live and life itself as capacity.[70] Otherwise, how could pleasure, or love, or even life exist? Death would be easier, so something must keep it at bay. If hunger is a lack of food, and hence suffering, appetite is the power to eat (both in the presence and in the absence of food) and the enjoyment of what we eat. Some will object that appetite is merely a mild form of hunger, in which want remains the essential element. But the dead are not hungry: hunger presupposes life, want presupposes a capacity. To reduce desire to want is to mistake the effect for the cause or the outcome for the precondition. Desire is first, capacity is first. It is the anorexic who is lacking in something, not the person who eats with a hearty appetite. It is the melancholic person who is lacking in something, not the person who loves life and plunges into it with gusto. It is the impotent person who is lacking something, not the happy and avid lover. Anyone who has lived long enough has experienced moments of disgust, depression, and impotence. What was missing at those times? Not always an object or the desire for an object (for that object could just as easily be present as absent, there for us to enjoy as not). What was missing was desire, taste, the strength to enjoy or love. Lack and desire are not the same: we lack when the object of our desire is absent (frustration) or when our desire has grown tired of it (disgust).[71] Lack is not the essence of desire; it is its accident or its dream, the deprivation that irritates it or the phantom it conjures up for itself.

Just as there are different desires for different objects, so too, if love is desire, there should be different loves for different objects of our love. Such is indeed the case: one can love wine or music, a woman or a country, one's children or one's work, God or power.[72] What all these different loves have in common, and what justifies the use of the same word for all of them, is the pleasure, as Stendhal would say, or the joy, as Spinoza would say, that the various objects of our love give us or give rise to within us. "To love," writes Stendhal, "is to derive pleasure from seeing, touching and feeling through all one's senses and as closely as possible, a lovable object who loves us."[73] Strike the final relative clause, which applies only to interpersonal relationships, add that one can derive pleasure or joy from the mere thought of the object (since absent persons or abstractions can be loved), and we have an adequate definition: to love is to take pleasure in seeing, touching, feeling, knowing, or imagining.

The broad scope of this definition, excessively broad perhaps for some, is in keeping with the word's polysemy or, to be exact, with the multiplicity of its referents. A definition is helpful only insofar as it helps us say what we mean or mean what we say or understand what we see, and everyone ultimately is master of his vocabulary. Yet one must not do too much violence to the language. Personally, I would suggest the following definition, which seems to me both easier (to understand) and wider (in scope) than Stendhal's, which it supports and extends: *to love is to be able to derive pleasure or joy from something*. Hence someone who loves oysters as opposed to those who do not. Someone who loves music as opposed to all those who are indifferent to or bored by it. Someone who loves women, or a particular woman, as opposed to someone who tends to derive pleasure (physical love) or joy (spiritual love—the two, of course, can go together and combine with each other) from men or from boys, like the guests at Plato's symposium. The objects of love are infinite in number, as are the causes for pleasure and joy or the different ways of loving that these objects give rise to or allow. I love oysters, Mozart, Brittany, a certain woman, my children, my friends. Let us imagine for the moment that none of these are missing: I am in Brittany with my children, the woman I love, and my best friends; we are eating oysters as we gaze at the sea and listen to Mozart. What do these different loves have in common? Certainly not want or even the fulfillment of a want. I hardly ever feel in want of Mozart, oysters, or Brittany; nor do I feel in want of my friends, unless we have been separated for a very long time—the mere fact that they exist, even if they are far away, makes me joyful. What these different forms of love have in common is love itself: an inner happiness, the capacity to derive pleasure or joy (or both) from something that I might also feel in want of (if I were very hungry, or in need of a woman, or of children, or of friends) but of which want is neither the essence, nor the content, nor even the precondition (since in the example I gave, I love precisely people and things that are not lacking). One might object that none of this is very erotic. True enough, if we think of Plato's Eros and my anodyne example. But lovers know well how sensual, voluptuous, and intense it is to make love in joy rather than want, in action rather than passion, in pleasure rather than suffering, in the fulfillment rather than the frustration of our capacity—in other words, to desire the love we are *making* rather than the love we dream of, do not make, and are obsessed by.

The definition I just proposed owes a great deal to another, which is Spinoza's: "Love is a joy, accompanied by the idea of an external cause."[74] To love is to derive joy, or more precisely (since love presupposes the idea of a cause) to *derive joy from*. To derive joy or pleasure, I said earlier, but pleasure is love, in the strongest sense of the term, only if it brings joy to the soul, and this is especially true of our interpersonal relationships. The flesh is sad when there is no love or when we love only the flesh. As Spinoza says, love is joy added to pleasure, illuminating and reflecting it, like a mirror of the soul, announcing, accompanying, or following it, like a promise or echo of happiness. Is this the ordinary meaning of the word? I believe it is; at least it gets at its most essential and best aspect. If someone says to you, "I rejoice in the thought that you exist," or, "When I think that you exist, it fills me with joy," or again, "There is joy within me, and the reason for this joy is the thought that you exist," you would interpret these statements as declarations of love and, of course, you would be right. But you would also be extremely lucky, not just because few are so fortunate as to receive a Spinozist declaration of love but also, and above all, because it is a declaration of love that—surprisingly—asks for nothing in return! I know that the statement "I love you" does not appear, at least on the face of it, to ask for anything at all. Yet whether it actually does or does not depends on the kind of love the speaker feels. If love is want, to say "I love you" is indeed to ask for something. You are asking not just that the other person answer, "Me too"; you are asking for *the other's self*, since you love or lack him or her, and, by definition, lack always wishes to possess what it longs for.[75] What a burden on the loved one's shoulders! What anguish! What a prison! To delight in the beloved, on the other hand, is not to ask for anything at all but rather to celebrate a presence, an existence, a grace. What lightness for you and for your beloved! What freedom and happiness! Who does not love to declare his love when he is joyful? Joyful love, then, is a gift, an offering, a grace offered in return. Who does not love being loved? Who does not delight in the joy he provides? And when we do, love nurtures love and intensifies it;[76] the fact that this love is without want makes it all the stronger, all the lighter, and, as Spinoza would say, all the more *active*.[77] This lightness has a name, and that name is joy. It has proof, as well, and that proof is the happiness of lovers. I love you: I am joyful that you exist.

In its Spinozist form, this kind of declaration is rare. No matter. There are other simpler and more common ways of saying the same thing. For example: *"Thank you for existing, thank you for being what you are, for being real and not a figment of my imagination!"* This declaration is one of fulfilled love. Sometimes a mere look, a smile, a caress, or a joy can say the same thing. Gratitude, as I said, is the happiness of loving (see chapter 10). But it is more: it is love itself, as happiness. What would love lack and why, since it derives joy from what is and since it is this very joy? As for *"the will of the lover to join himself to the thing loved,"* writes Spinoza in critiquing the Cartesian definition, it *"expresses a property of love, not its essence"* and does so moreover in a very obscure and equivocal manner. "It should be noted," he says,

> that when I say it is a property in the lover, that he wills to join himself to the thing loved, I do not understand by will a consent or a deliberation of the mind, *or* free decision [since there is no free will, since no one can decide to love or desire]. Nor do I understand a desire of joining oneself to the thing loved when it is absent or continuing in its presence when it is present. For love can be conceived without either of these desires [in other words, without want]. Rather, by will I understand a satisfaction in the lover on account of the presence of the thing loved, by which the lover's joy is strengthened or at least encouraged.[78]

Love, in itself, is lacking in nothing. If it lacks an object, as it sometimes will, the reasons are external or contingent: the loved one's departure, absence, or perhaps death. But it is not because the loved one is gone that he is loved. Love can be frustrated, can suffer or grieve. If the cause of my joy disappears, how could I not be unhappy?[79] But love resides in joy—wounded or severed though it may be and for all its dreadful pain when torn from us—not in the absence that sunders it. I do not love because I lack; I love, and that which I love I sometimes lack. Love comes first; joy comes first. Or rather desire is first, capacity is first, and love is the joyful affirmation of the two. Good-bye, Plato and his daemon! Good-bye, Tristan and his sorrow! If one considers love in its essence—in other words, if we take it for what it is—there is no unhappy love.

Nor can there be any happiness without love. If love is a joy accompanied by the idea of an external cause, if all love therefore is in its essence joyful, the converse is also true: all joy has a cause (as does everything that exists)[80] and therefore all joy is loving, if not actually, when it is fully conscious of itself and thus has knowledge of its cause, then at least potentially (for a joy that cannot love is unfathomed and unfathomable, ignorant, obscure, and truncated).[81] Hence love is transparent joy, its light, its known and acknowledged truth. This is Spinoza's secret and the secret of wisdom and happiness: love exists only as joy and there is no joy other than love.

Am I painting too rosy a picture of love? I think not. I am certainly simplifying and schematizing, as I did with Plato and must do here, but I am not misrepresenting love or embellishing the truth. If one cannot recognize in the picture I describe the more nuanced, confused, and blurred colorings of our lives, it is because in real life joy and sadness intertwine, of course, and we ourselves are forever hesitating, oscillating, fluctuating between the two affects and the two truths (Plato's and Spinoza's), between want and capacity, hope and gratitude, passion and action, religion and wisdom, between the love that desires only what it does not have and wants to possess (*erōs*), and the love that, since it desires only what is, has everything it desires and finds pleasure and joy in it. What shall we call this kind of love?

Just that—*love*. To love another being means to desire that he exist when in fact he does (otherwise one is only hoping for him), to enjoy his existence and presence and the pleasures and joys he offers. But, as we have seen, the same word is used for want or passion (for *erōs*) and this dual sense of the word can lead to confusion. The Greek is clearer in its unequivocal use of the verb *philein* (*to love*, regardless of the love object) and the noun *philia*, especially for interpersonal relationships. Doesn't *philia* mean *friendship*? Yes, but friendship in its broadest— and also strongest and noblest—sense. For Aristotle, the model of friendship is first of all "the delight mothers take in loving";[82] it is also the love (*philia*) "between man and wife," especially when "each has its own virtue and they will delight in the fact."[83] It is the love of parents, brothers, or children,[84] but it is also the love of lovers, which *erōs* cannot entirely contain or exhaust.[85] And finally, it is perfect friendship, the friendship of the virtuous, "who wish well to their friends for their sake," whereby they are "most truly friends."[86] Let us say the word: *philia* is love in all its forms when it flourishes between human beings,[87] whenever it is not reduced to want or passion (*erōs*). The word, therefore, has a narrower range than the word *love* (which can be used in reference to an object, animal, or god) but wider than the word *friendship* (which is hardly ever used with reference to the parent-child relationship).

Let us say that *philia* is love-as-joy, inasmuch as it is, or can be, reciprocal: the joy of loving and being loved,[88] mutual or potentially mutual goodwill,[89] the will to live together,[90] a choice we take on ourselves, a reciprocal pleasure and trust.[91] In sum, *philia* is active love,[92] thereby standing in contrast to *erōs* (love-as-passion), which is not to say they cannot converge or go hand in hand. What lovers do not become friends if they are happy together? How could they be happy if they did not? Aristotle sees the love (*philia*) "between man and wife" as a form of friendship, no doubt the most important kind (since "man is naturally inclined to form couples—even more than to form cities"), and he understands, of course, that it includes the sexual dimension as well.[93] It is in Aristotle that I find justification for my borrowing the word *philia* in order to distinguish, in our love lives, between love-as-joy (love according to Spinoza) and love-as-want (love according to Plato); another justification is his completely Spinozist formulation, *"To love is to feel pleasure."*[94] The same cannot be said of want, and this distinction suffices to differentiate the two forms of love.

At least in theory. In practice, the boundaries between these two feelings can disappear, as we have seen, and almost always do, particularly in relations between men and women. We can take delight (*philia*) in the very person we want (*erōs*) and wish to possess (*erōs*), in the very person whose existence is already a source of joy (*philia*); in other words, we can love passionately and joyously at the same time. It is not a rare thing at all, in fact it is quite common among couples, especially in the beginning. To be in love is almost always to want, to seek to possess, to suffer at the prospect of one's love not being returned or in the fear of no longer being loved, to regard one's happiness as dependent entirely on the love, presence, and possession of the other person. And truly it is a great happiness when we are loved, when we possess and enjoy the very person we were lacking! Love may be the most powerful thing we can experience, apart from horror; it might also be the best thing we can experience, apart from wisdom. A happy, passionate relationship is the springtime of couples, their youth, the avid joy of lovers smooching on public benches, as George Brassens puts it in his song; they are indeed a friendly sight to see, as he also says, or a touching one, in their combination of enthusiasm and silliness. But how could this stage last? How long can one go on lacking what one has (in other words, lack what is not lacking)? How can we passionately love the person with whom we have been sharing our daily life for years, or continue to idolize someone we have come to know so well, or dream what is real; how can we stay *in* love—a crucial nuance—with our spouse? Crystallization, to use Stendhal's terminology, is an unstable state that has trouble outlasting the stability of a couple. At first everything about the other person seems marvelous; then he appears as he is. In time, as Claude Nougaro reminds us in his song, "the wicked husband kills Prince Charming." They are the same individual: Prince Charming is simply the husband you lacked, the husband you dreamed of, desired, and hoped to find and marry one day; and the husband is the Prince Charming you married and now possess and know and no longer lack. The first is radiant in his absence, the latter tarnished in his presence. As Nietzsche understands, if marriage can be a demanding and beautiful adventure, more often than not it is a shabby and ordinary routine:

> Alas, this poverty of the soul in pair! Alas, this filth of the soul in pair! Alas, this wretched contentment in pair! . . .
> This one went out like a hero in quest of truths, and eventually he conquered a little dressed-up lie. His marriage he calls it. . . .
> Many brief follies—that is what you call love. And your marriage concludes many brief follies, as a long stupidity.[95]

That "high tale of love and death" turns out to have a different ending. And Mrs. Tristan, Mrs. Romeo, and Madame Bovary? Day by day and year by year, they will come to resemble one another more and more as their marriages drag on and settle into a state of morose conjugality. As for the husband, he thinks increasingly about sex and work and less and less about love or his wife; or if he does think of her, it is for the worries she causes him, her moods, reproaches, and attitudes. He wants peace and pleasure; she wants happiness and passion. And they blame each other for not being, or for no longer being, what they had hoped for, desired, and loved, each of them regretting that the other is merely what he or she is. How could it be otherwise, and whose fault is it if passion is no more than a dream from which we must awaken? "I loved her because she had that air of mystery about her," he says to himself, admitting in essence that he loved her because he did not know her and no longer loves her now that he does. "We love a woman for what she isn't," Serge Gainsbourg said, and "leave her because of what she is." Women love men, and leave them, for the same reasons. There is almost always more truth in falling out of love than in being in love—at least when it comes to this kind of love, fascinated with mystery, with what it longs for and does not understand. A strange love that loves only what it is ignorant of.

But what of those other, more successful couples, the kind we tend to envy for the happiness and love they seem to have managed to preserve even with the passing years? Has their passion survived intact, is it stronger today than it was yesterday but not as strong as it will be tomorrow? I don't believe it for a minute; and even if a couple could preserve its passion, even if some couples actually did, it would be so rare, so miraculous, and so independent of our will that we could never reasonably base our life choices or even pin our hopes on the possibility. Moreover, the actual experience of the happy couple does not correspond to the picture we imagine. They are anything but lovebirds, they will tell you, and were you to compare them to Tristan and Isolde, they would laugh at you. The "secret" of their success is simply that they have continued to desire each other, and, if they have been living together for years, their desire is definitely capacity rather than want, pleasure rather than passion; they have managed to transform the passion and ardor they had in the beginning into joy, gentleness, gratitude, lucidity, and trust, into happiness in being together—in other words, into *philia*.

Is it tenderness perhaps? Tenderness is one of its dimensions, but it has others: complicity, loyalty, and humor, an intimacy of body and mind, pleasure visited and revisited again and again ("the fulfilled love of a desire that remains desire," as René Char puts it). Animality is part of their love as well, an animality that is both accepted and tamed, triumphant and defeated. There is closeness and mutual respect, the attentiveness of two solitudes, each inhabited and sustained by the other; there is also that buoyant and simple joy, the familiarity, matter-of-factness, and sense of peace; the glint in the eye, the heedful silence; the strength, openness, and fragility of being two. And oneness? They have long since rejected the idea of becoming one, if they ever believed in it at all. They love their duet far too much, with its harmonics, counterpoint, and occasional dissonances, to want to transform it into an impossible monologue! Their mad love has become wise love, and one would have to be crazy to think that they have lost something in the process, that their love has diminished or become banal when, on the contrary, it is deeper and more loving and more truthful, the genuine exception in emotional life. What could be easier to love than a dream? What could be harder to love than reality? What could be easier than to seek to possess? What could be harder than to learn how to accept? What could be easier than passion? What could be harder than being a couple? Anyone can be in love, but not everyone is capable of loving.

I once attended a colloquium on love where I heard this surprising admission: "I would rather experience a small passion than a great friendship."[96] How sad, how self-centered, how narrow this passion for passion! Passion is merely love of the self (and not of the other). It is the love of one's own love, of one's own little narcissistic palpitations. In one fell swoop, friends become nothing more than stopgaps between two passions and the world is reduced to a single being, a single gaze, a single heart. Passion has something monomaniacal about it; it is like an intoxication with love. That is what makes it strong, beautiful, and noble as long as it lasts. Certainly we should live our passion when we encounter it! All love is good, and passionate love, which is the easiest kind, might teach us to love more, and better. What could be more ridiculous than to condemn passion? To do so when we feel it is futile, to do so when we do not is pointless. We should live and enjoy our passion but not make ourselves its dupe or prisoner, if possible. And why would it not be possible? The truth is, we need not choose between passion and friendship, we can have both: we all know that passion does not require that we forget our friends and that passion itself invariably ends in death or suffering, in oblivion, rancor . . . or friendship. Passion does not last, it cannot; love either changes or dies. Wanting to be faithful to passion at all costs means being unfaithful to love and to becoming; it means being unfaithful to life, which cannot be reduced to the experience of a few months of happy passion (or a few years of unhappy passion). And to subject our love to the vagaries of passion is to be unfaithful ahead of time to those we love, passionately or otherwise. Denis de Rougemont draws this apt distinction: "To be in love is a state; to love, an act."[97] Now, acts depend on us, at least in part; they can be willed, prolonged, maintained, shouldered, and committed to. But a state? A promise to remain in love is a contradiction in terms. One might as well promise that one will always run a fever or always be insane. A committed love, whatever its object, must commit to more than just passion.

In this regard, language usage today is entirely Aristotelian: how does one member of an unmarried couple refer to his or her other half when speaking to a third party? "My companion" sounds puritanical or old-fashioned. "My partner" is simply ugly. To call someone "my lover" or "mistress" usually implies an adulterous, or at least a transgressive, relationship. What is left? Within the confines of the couple the first name is all that is needed or else some term of endearment—for example, "my love." But outside the couple, in speaking to someone to whom a first name would be meaningless? One simply says, "my friend," and everyone knows what one means. The friend is a person we love; and in the singular, as an absolute, it is the person with whom we share our life or, at the very least, the person with whom we make love, not once or every now and then as with an occasional "partner" but regularly and over a (more or less extended) period of time, for as long as the couple lasts. How could friendship not become an important part of desire over the course of time? How could it not gradually replace the consuming passion (or mere love-struck state) that preceded it and in fact prepared it?

The same is true of marriage—of a happy marriage, that is—and it is only linguistic conventions that tend to obscure this fact. In speaking of the person to whom one is married, one says "my wife" or "my husband" rather than "my friend." Fortunate are those married couples for whom these terms are merely a question of usage, of different words that express the same thing. And what is that same thing? Love, no longer merely dreamed of but achieved. A woman in her forties once said to me, speaking of the man with whom she had been living for ten or twelve years and with whom she had had two children whom they were bringing up together, "Of course, I am no longer in love with him. But I am still sexually attracted to him and he is my best friend." In this quiet statement, which still moves me, I recognized at last the truth about happy couples and I also understood that they live something that is sexually very strong, gentle, and arousing. People who have never made love with their best friend are ignorant, it seems to me, of something essential about love and the pleasures of love, of something essential about the couple and the sensuality of couples. One's best friend is the person one loves the most, yet without suffering or yearning, without the sense of lack, the feeling of want; he or she is the person we know best and who knows us best, the person on whom we can rely and with whom we share memories, projects, hopes, and fears, our fortunes good and bad. Isn't it clear that this description is precisely that of two people in a couple, married or not, who have been together for some time—provided their bond is not one of mutual self-interest or convenience but one of intimacy and love and strength and truth? Montaigne has a nice term for this state. He calls it "marital friendship," and this category of relationship far better describes the happy long-standing couples I have known than do those of want, passion, or mad love.[98]

Most young girls reading such a description would regard it as an insipid, disappointing step backward. But women who have been down this road know otherwise or, at any rate, that it is good to step back from dreams we should abandon anyway—so that we can finally move *forward*. Better a little true love than the dream of love. Better a real couple than a dreamed-of passion. Better a little true happiness than a happy illusion. For the sake of what? For the sake of good faith (love of truth), for the sake of life and happiness—for passion does not and cannot last, or can only last as unhappiness. "Passion means suffering, something undergone, the mastery of fate over a free and responsible person. To love love more than the object of love, to love passion for its own sake, has been to love to suffer and to court suffering—all the way from Augustine's *amabam amare* down to modern romanticism," observes de Rougement.[99] To love passion for its own sake is to

show a "secret preference for what is unhappy," for another life, a supposedly "real life," to use the poet's phrase, that "is elsewhere" always,
since it is impossible and exists only in death.[100] How we must fear life
to prefer passion! How we must fear truth to prefer illusion! A couple,
on the other hand, when happy (when more or less happy, for happiness is never absolute), is a place of truth, of life shared, of trust, of
peaceful and gentle intimacy, reciprocal joys, gratitude, fidelity, generosity, humor, love. So many virtues to make a couple! But they are
happy virtues, or at least they can be. The couple is also a place where
the body can find its fill of bold pleasures and discoveries that, for
many, only the couple makes possible. And then there are the children,
the children that couples make, for which—at least biologically speaking—they are made and who justify their existence.

A word or two on this subject, then, since the family is almost always
the future of the couple, hence the future of love, as well as its beginning. What would we know of love if we had not first been loved? Or of
the couple, without the family? If all love is transference, as Freud
believes, it is in part because all love begins as something received and
only later is something we learn to give. Or, to put it a better way (since
these two loves are neither of the same kind nor directed toward the
same object), the grace of being loved precedes the grace of loving and
prepares us for it. This preparation is the family, despite its failings, and
is also the family's great achievement. "Families, I hate you!" Gide
famously says.[101] Yet to hate the family in this way is still to be faithful
to it, if this hatred is based on love—on a wider, more open, more generous, and freer love. Certainly one must love outside of the family, outside of oneself, outside of everything. But the family enables that love,
which it both imposes (through the incest prohibition) and results in
(through the creation of a new couple and new children). Freud says
essentially the same thing. First the mother and child: love received,
prolonged, and sublimated, at once forbidden (as *erōs*) and saved (as
philia); first the flesh and fruit of the flesh: the child, protected, preserved, educated. "Ultimately," Alain writes, "it will be the couple that
saves the spirit."[102] Yes, but out of fidelity to the child they once were

and will one day make, perhaps. It is through the child, then, that they will save the spirit, and nearly always for the child who may or may not save the couple but whom the couple saves, or tries to save, and in fact does save in losing him, by letting him go. Such is the iron rule of the family and the golden rule of love: "You will leave your father and your mother."[103] We do not have children in order to own them or keep them. We have them so that they will leave us and love elsewhere, in a different way; so that they will have children who will in turn leave them; so that everything might die, so that everything might live, so that everything might continue. Thus humanity begins and thus it reproduces itself, generation upon generation.

The scholastic philosophers distinguished between concupiscent or covetous love (*amor concupiscentiae*) and benevolent love—or, as Thomas Aquinas also calls it, love of friendship (*amor benevolentiae sive amicitiae*).[104] Although this distinction does not exactly coincide with the *erōs/philia* opposition that I have tried to work through, one could say that covetous love is faithful to Plato ("when a human being is lacking in something and finds what he is lacking, he covets it")[105] whereas benevolent love is faithful to Aristotle (for whom, Aquinas reminds us, "to love is to wish good to someone").[106] We can divide love this way, Aquinas says: "That which is loved with the love of friendship is loved simply and for itself; whereas that which is loved with the love of concupiscence is loved, not simply and for itself, but for something else."[107] In short, concupiscent or covetous love, though not necessarily blameworthy, is a selfish love that loves the other for its own benefit. Benevolent love, on the other hand, is a generous love—it loves the other for the other's benefit.

Aquinas knows, of course, that usually our love is a mixture of both these loves.[108] Nevertheless, there is a difference between the two, a difference that their combination at once presupposes and confirms. I love oysters and I also love my children, but these two loves are not the same: I do not love oysters for their benefit; nor is it solely for my own benefit that I love my children. I doubt that any human love is entirely devoid of covetousness. But sometimes covetousness alone prevails (when I love oysters, money, women ...), and then love, even if intense, is at its lowest. But when covetousness is mixed with benevolence (when I love my children, my friends, the woman I love), then the stronger my benevolence the more elevated my love. Aristotle is manifestly moved by those mothers who have to give away their babies at birth for the children's good and never see them again yet who for the rest of their lives will continue to love them, unrequitedly and hopelessly, more concerned for their children's well-being than for their own and ready to sacrifice the latter to the former, if such a distinction can even be made.[109] Such love is pure benevolence and is noble ("it is noble to do well by another without a view to repayment").[110] But it is not the rule. Usually benevolence and covetousness combine with each other, fortunately for those of us who are not saints—in other words, for all of us, since it allows us to seek our own good while doing a bit of good, to mix egoism with altruism, in short, to be a friend to our friends (whom we wish well) as well as to ourselves (whom we also wish well).[111]

So it is with the couple: what could be more natural than to love (*philia*) the woman or man whom we ardently desire (*erōs*)? What could be more normal than to wish the one who is good to us well; to love benevolently and joyously the one who brings us sexual pleasure; to be the friend, in short, of the one whom we covet and possess. *Erōs* and *philia* almost always combine, and their combination makes for what we call a couple or a lasting romance. But *erōs* is consumed as it is satisfied, or else (since the body has its needs and limitations) it reawakens only to die again, reawaken and yet again die, each time with less violence, less passion, and less want (hence with less *erōs*, which is not to say less power) than the time before; whereas *philia*, in a happy couple, never ceases to intensify, deepen, and flourish. Such is the logic of life and the logic of love. At first we love only ourselves: the lover throws himself on the loved one like the newborn upon his mother's breast—or the wolf upon the lamb. This is want or concupiscence. Hunger is a desire and desire a hunger: a love that takes and devours. *Erōs* is egoism. Then (in a family, in a couple) we learn to love the other person as well, for himself or herself: this is joy, friendship, benevolence. We go from carnal love, as Saint Bernard de Clairvaux calls it, to spiritual love, from self-love to love of the other, from a love that takes to a love that gives, from violence to gentleness—from *erōs* to *philia*. Here as in *The Symposium* we have an ascent, an ascent of love, through love. For carnal love comes first, of course, as Saint Bernard perceives: "Since nature is too fragile and too weak, necessity commands it to place itself first in its own service. Hence carnal love, in which man begins by loving himself out of pure self-love, as Saint Paul says: *The animal part came first, and then the spiritual part.* This is not a commandment but a fact inherent to nature."[112] From carnal love, says Saint Bernard, we must strive to reach the second degree of love (to love God out of self-love), then the third (to love God for himself), and finally the fourth (to love oneself only for the sake of God).[113] This path is no longer ours. Nevertheless it has something important to tell us, which is that the body is the necessary starting point, from which the spirit arises or invents itself. This path is a path of love, and love itself is a path. We first love only ourselves or for our own sake (when we love what we are lacking). Within each of us there is a newborn who seeks the breast and covets it, who would keep it forever. But we cannot and must not. The incest prohibition obliges us to love differently, to love precisely what we cannot possess, take, or consume, precisely what we cannot enjoy sexually; and so another kind of love awakens, in this (at first, imposed) submission of desire to the law, and this love is love itself.

I repeat: desire, or the drive, comes first, and we experience it as want. *Erōs* comes first. As Freud would say, in the very beginning we are only the id: a living, avid body. But in his human environment, the little mammal notices that something has preceded him, welcomes him, and protects him, that a breast is there to satisfy his desire and give him pleasure, indeed far more than a breast, far more than pleasure. What is it? Love—the kind that covets (what mother did not desire to have a child for her own benefit?) but also the kind that gives (what mother does not place her child's welfare above her own?). *Erōs*, therefore, but also *philia*, for the two are inextricably mixed, intertwined, commingled, yet different, one arising from the other, benevolence from concupiscence and love from desire, love merely being desire's joyous, fulfilled sublimation. This kind of love, Aquinas notes, following in the steps of Aristotle, is not a passion but a virtue: wanting the good of another is goodness itself.[114]

Look at a mother and her newborn infant. What avidity there is in the child! What generosity in the mother! In the child, one sees little more than desire, drive, animality. In the mother these are hardly discernable anymore, so transformed are they by love, gentleness, and benevolence. One can already see this transformation in animals, it seems to me, at least in mammals, but humanity has gone much further in this direction than any other known species. This is where humanity invents itself, in inventing, or rather reinventing, love. The child takes; the mother gives. Pleasure for him; joy for her. Eros comes first, since every mother was once a child. Yet love precedes us, almost always (since every child is born of a mother), and teaches us to love.

It is in this love that humanity and the spirit invent themselves. There is no other God than this, the God of love. Alain, good atheist though he was, and because that is what he was, expresses this idea well:

In the presence of the child there can be no doubt. We must love the spirit without expecting anything from it. Certainly there is a charity of the spirit toward itself, and that charity is thought. But look at the image; look at the mother.

Look at the child again. That weakness is God. That weakness which needs all of us is God. That being who would cease to exist without our care is God. Such is the spirit, in relation to which even truth is an idol. Because truth is dishonored by power; Caesar enlists it, and pays it well. The child pays nothing; he demands and goes on demanding. It is the iron rule of the spirit that the spirit pays nothing, and that no man can serve two masters. But how shall we say strongly enough that there is a truth of truth, which experience can never negate? The less proof a mother has, the more intent she is on loving, helping, and serving. This human truth, which she carries in her arms, may be nothing that exists in the world. Nevertheless she is right, and she will be right even when every child has proved her wrong.[115]

Yes. But the child does not know this; he will learn it only in learning to love.

Agape

Are joy and desire all there is to love? If only it were so, or could be so, if only love were sufficient unto itself! But unfortunately it is not so, because we barely know how to love ourselves and those close to us, because our desires are almost always egoistical, and finally because we have to share our lives not just with our close ones, whom we love, but also with our neighbor, whom we do not love.

Friendship is not a duty, for love cannot be commanded; but it is a virtue, for love is an excellence. What would we think of someone who loved no one? Conversely, as Aristotle remarks, "we praise those who love their friends"; friendship is thus "not only necessary but also noble."[116] For Epicurus, too, "all friendship is desirable in itself (*aretē*)," in other words, a virtue, from which all the others arise or would if we knew how to practice it fully.[117] To be stingy toward one's friends is to show not just a lack of generosity but also a lack of love. Similarly, to be cowardly in the face of those who would attack them or to be merciless in judging them is to show a lack of love as much as or more than a lack of courage or of mercy. For if courage, mercy, and generosity are universal standards, with or without love, they become all the more necessary, as virtues, when we do not love. Hence what I have called morality's maxim: *Act as though you loved*. When we do love, however, the other virtues follow spontaneously, as though naturally, so much so that they can cease to be specific virtues or specifically *moral* virtues. The mother who gives her child everything she possesses is not being generous and does not need to be generous in order to do so: she loves her child more than her own self. The mother who would die for the sake of her child is not being courageous, or rather her courage is, as it were, supplementary: she loves her child more than life. The mother who is prepared to forgive her child for anything at all and accepts him unconditionally as he is, regardless of what he has done or might do, is not merciful; she loves her child more than justice or the good. Mothers are not alone in loving this way. But other exemplars of this kind of love—Jesus Christ and the saints are two that come to mind—tend to be historically questionable or difficult to interpret. Did Christ really exist? What was his life really like? To what extent were the saints really saintly? What can we know of their intentions, motivations, and feelings? Their lives are too bound up with legend, their times too remote from our own. The love of parents, of mothers particularly, is at once more manifest, no less exemplary, and closer to our own experience. If parental love has its own myths—what doesn't?—at least we can hold them up to observable reality. And what do we see when we do? We see that vis-à-vis their children mothers have most of the virtues that we (and they) ordinarily lack. Or rather, that love nearly always takes their place and obviates them—since almost all these virtues are *morally* necessary only for lack of love. What could be more faithful, prudent, courageous, merciful, gentle, sincere, simple, pure, compassionate, and just (yes, more just than justice itself) than this kind of love? I know that mothers are also capable of madness, hysteria, possessiveness, ambivalence, pride, violence, jealousy, anguish, sadness, and narcissism. Yet even in these "maternal vices" there is love. That love does not negate them, but they do not negate it either. One can speak only of individual cases: I have known mothers who were admirable, others who were insufferable, still others who were sometimes admirable, sometimes insufferable, sometimes both at once. Yet who could deny that in no other sphere of human activity does what exists so often approach what ought to be, so often in fact that it sometimes attains or even surpasses everything one could legitimately expect, demand, or require? Unconditional love may exist nowhere else, but it does sometimes exist—in the love of a mother or of a father for that mortal god whom they have begotten (not created), for this son of man (for this daughter of man) born of woman.

A virtue? Of course, since it is a disposition, a power, an excellence. Earlier I said of virtue that it is "human capacity, the power to be human,"[118] and no virtue is more crucial than this disposition to love, this capacity to love, this excellence of love in parents, thanks to which our animal nature opens itself to something other than itself, something that can be called spirit or God but whose true name is love and that, not once and for all but with each new generation, each birth, and each childhood, makes of mankind something other than a biological species.

Yet this kind of love remains trapped within itself and within us.

Why do we love our own children so much and those of others so little?

Because they are ours and because through them we love ourselves.

And why do we love our friends, if not because they love us and because we love ourselves? Self-love comes first, as Aristotle and others point out,[119] and it remains foremost; friendship is like its projection, extension, and refraction on those who are close to us. Self-love both makes friendship possible and restricts its scope. The same inclination that makes us love our friends (the love we have for ourselves) prevents us from loving our enemies or even, by definition, those toward whom we feel nothing at all. We can escape egoism and narcissism only through self-love, which we never escape.

By this account, love would be the virtue that is noblest in its effects but also poorest, narrowest, and most restrictive in its possible objects. Of all the living beings we know, how many bring us joy or bring us enough joy to allow us to overcome our own egoism (if even through a displaced or sublimated self-love)? Our children, a few relatives, a handful of real friends, a lover or two. In other words, for each of us there is in the best of cases perhaps a total of ten or twenty people whom we are more or less capable of loving, which leaves somewhere in the neighborhood of six billion others who are beyond the reach of this kind of love! For them, should we be content with morality, duty, and the law? I believed as much for a long time, and sometimes I still believe it; certainly it is clear to me that our inability to love more than a few individuals is what makes morality necessary. But does that make it sufficient? Does nothing lie between friendship and duty, between joy and constraint, between power and submission? What of what Spinoza calls the spirit of Christ?[120] In other words, what of that love which is at once singular and universal, demanding and free, spontaneous and respectful, that love which cannot be erotic, since it loves that which it does not lack (how could we lack our neighbor, someone who by definition is there beside us, in our midst or in our way)? What of that love which has to be more than a love of one's friends since its distinguishing feature, its specific difference and particular excessiveness, is its being *the love of one's enemies*?

"You have heard that it was said, 'You shall love your neighbor and hate your enemy.' But I say to you, Love your enemies and pray for those who persecute you."[121] Whether or not Christ existed and whatever he really said or did, which we will never know, who can deny that the Gospels' message, as it has come down to us, far surpasses the capacities not only of *erōs* but also of *philia*? To love what one lacks is within anyone's capabilities. To love one's friends (those who are not absent, who do us good and love us), though difficult, is still an accessible goal. But to love one's enemies? To love those whose existence is a matter of indifference to us? To love those whom we can just as well do without and who do not bring us joy? To love those who thwart us, who bring sorrow or misfortune upon us? How could we? How could we even admit the possibility of such a love? A stumbling block to Jews and folly to Gentiles, Saint Paul calls it,[122] and, as a matter of fact, it is beyond both the Law and common sense.

Yet, even if nothing more than an ideal or a figment of the imagination, this love beyond love (beyond *erōs* and *philia*), this sublime and maybe impossible love deserves at least a name. Usually, it is called *charity*. But that word has been so corrupted, cheapened, and defiled (by two thousand years of clerical, aristocratic, and ultimately bourgeois condescension) that we would do better to return to its etymological origins and—with *erōs* and *philia* as our precedent—keep speaking Greek. This love that is neither want nor capacity, neither passion nor friendship, this universal and disinterested love that would have us love even our enemies, is what the Greek of the Scriptures—from the Septuagint Bible to the Letters of the Apostles—calls *agapē;* hence in The First Letter of John, "God is love, *o Theos agapē estin.*"[123] (The word was most likely pressed into service because no prior claims had been made to it. Virtually unknown in the secular literature, at least as a noun, it derives from the verb *agapan;* one can find it in classical Greek, for example in Homer and Plato, where it means to welcome in friend-ship, to love, and to cherish. In the Vulgate it is usually rendered as *caritas*—love or affection—from which the word *charity* derives, inde-pendently of and prior to the "tainted" meanings it came to acquire.) *Agapē*, then, is our third definition of love, or rather the third form of love or term for love, which now requires definition. If God is love, then this love—*agapē*—cannot be defined by want or lack, since God is lacking in nothing. Nor can it be friendship, since no being can be the cause of God's joy or expand his existence: God engenders and creates being, even though in this act of creation his joy, power, and perfection are not increased—again, they cannot be—but, on the contrary, are sev-ered, wounded, and crucified. Here is where we must begin our inquiry: with the creation and the cross. So that we might seek God? Not at all. So that we might seek love. *Agapē* is divine love, if God exists, and per-haps is even more divine if God does not exist.

Why does the world exist? The existence of God, far from explain-ing the world, as some believe, actually makes it harder to explain. God is supposed to be absolutely perfect, and this supposition, as Descartes and Leibniz demonstrate, serves as a definition for him—or rather for us.[124] God is the maximum being and value possible. He therefore can-not be lacking in anything. To postulate that God created the world or human beings for his own benefit, because there was something he lacked—for example, a work, or glory, or beings to extol or worship him—in short, to postulate an *erotic* justification for creation, is to utterly misunderstand the Western idea of God—in other words, of God as absolute perfection. If God is perfect, then everything in the world may lack God and tend toward him (as in Aristotle, where God is a final cause, that is, a love object or *erōmenon* that moves everything without being moved either physically or emotionally by anything), but he himself lacks nothing, tends toward nothing, and hence, as Aristotle explains, does not move.[125] God thinks himself, Aristotle says, his thought is thought thinking itself, and this act of contemplation is his joy in its entirety, his eternal joy that has no need of creation or love.[126] The same is true of Plato's good-in-itself, which, though the ultimate object of all desire, want, or *erōs*, experiences none. If love is the desire for the good, as Plotinus says, and if desire is lack, how could the good be love, since it would have to be lacking in itself?[127]

Nor can the world be explained any better by divine *philia*. Not only would it be a bit ridiculous, as Aristotle notes, to believe oneself a friend of God,[128] but friendship remains subject to the law of being, self-love, and potentiality.[129] Spinoza puts forth this same idea more explicitly. What is love? A joy accompanied by the idea of its cause. What is a joy? The passage to a greater perfection or reality (the two words are synonymous in Spinoza).[130] To rejoice is to exist more fully, to feel one's capacity increased, to persevere triumphantly in one's being. To be sad is, by contrast, to exist less, to feel one's power diminish, to draw closer in some way to death or nothingness. It is for this reason that everyone desires joy (since every being strives to persevere in its being, to exist as much as possible) and hence love (since love is a joy and therefore an added measure of existence or perfection). In short, love is but one occurrence among many of the *conatus* or, as Spinoza also says, of power.[131] Spinoza does not flinch before the logical consequences of his propositions: God, he explains, "is not affected with any affect of joy or sadness. Consequently, he also loves no one and hates no one."[132] Not because he lacks the power to hate or love, as one might imagine but, to the contrary, because his power, which is absolutely infinite, is immutable: it cannot be increased (joy or love) or diminished (sadness or hatred) by anything.[133] Spinoza's God is too full of being, too full of power, too replete with itself to love or even let exist anything other than itself.[134] Nor does he create, since everything that is, is within him and remains so.

Traditional monotheistic conceptions of a personal God do not make the problem of creation any easier, at least so long as one remains within this logic of fulfilled joy, perfection, and power. Why would God go creating anything, since he himself is all possible being and good? How can being be added to infinite being? Or goodness to absolute good? Creation makes sense, within this logic of power, only if the original state of affairs can be improved upon, however slightly. But not even an all-powerful God can improve on the original state of affairs, since, being God itself, it is absolutely infinite and perfect! Some might imagine that before the creation God was dissatisfied with himself, like an enormously conscientious student who in the margin of his homework, or his divinity, writes, "Can do better." But God cannot surpass himself in his creation, he cannot even create his own equivalent (for he would have to create himself and hence would not be creating anything—such is perhaps the meaning of the Trinity). If God wants to create something other than himself, which is to say, to create, he can only create something inferior to himself. Let me put it a better way (which will probably make matters worse): God, being all possible good already and therefore unable to increase it, can only create evil! Hence this world of ours. But then why the devil did he create it?

The problem has a long tradition behind it. But of all those who have grappled with it, none has grasped it more clearly or resolved it better, to the extent that it can be resolved, than Simone Weil. What is the world, she asks, if not God's absence and withdrawal, his distance (which we call space), his awaiting (which we call time), his imprint (which we call beauty)? God could create the world only by withdrawing from it (otherwise there would be only God), or if he does remain in the world (if he did not, there would be nothing, not even the world), it is in the form of absence, secrecy, and withdrawal—like a trace left in the sand at low tide by a stroller who has since passed, this empty sign the sole proof of his existence and disappearance . . . What Weil postulates, then, is something of a "negative" pantheism, one that impugns all authentic or positive pantheisms, all idolatry of the world or reality. "This world, in so far as it is completely empty of God, is God himself,"[135] and it is for this reason that "God is absent,"[136] forever absent, as in the famous prayer "Our Father which art in Heaven . . ." Simone Weil takes the statement seriously and draws the logical conclusion: "He is our Father who is in heaven—not elsewhere. If we think to have a Father here below it is not he, it is a false God."[137] A spirituality of the desert, where praying meets only "the formidable, all-pervasive absence," to use the words of Alain, who was Weil's teacher.[138] And she replies, "We have to be in a desert. For he whom we must love is absent."[139] But why this absence? Why this creation-disappearance? Why this "good broken up into pieces and scattered throughout evil,"[140] if all possible good exists already (in God), if evil exists only because of the scattering of good and the absence of God—because of the world? "One can only accept the existence of affliction by considering it at a distance," Weil also says.[141] So be it. But why this distance? And since this distance is the world itself, inasmuch as it is not God (and it can be the world, of course, only on condition of *not being* God), why should the world exist? Why creation?

Weil answers: "God created through love and for love. God did not create anything except love itself, and the means to love."[142] But this love is not an addition of being, joy, or power. Quite the opposite: it is a diminution, a weakness, a renunciation. The clearest, most crucial text is the following one:

> On God's part creation is not an act of self-expansion but of restraint and renunciation. God and all his creatures are less than God alone. God accepted this diminution. He emptied a part of his being from himself. He had already emptied himself in this act of his divinity; that is why Saint John says that the Lamb had been slain from the beginning of the world. God permitted the existence of things distinct from himself and worth infinitely less than himself. But through this creative act he denied himself, as Christ has

told us to deny ourselves. God denied himself for our sakes in order to give us the possibility of denying ourselves for him. This response, this echo, which it is in our power to refuse, is the only possible justification for the folly of love of the creative act.

The religions which have a conception of this renunciation, this voluntary distance, this voluntary effacement of God, his apparent absence and his secret presence here below, these religions are true religion, the translation in different languages of the great Revelation. The religions which represent divinity as commanding wherever it has the power to do so seems false. Even though they are monotheistic they are idolatrous.[143]

Here again, love is passion, but in an altogether different sense: not the passion of Eros or of lovers but that of Christ and the martyrs. Here once again, love is folly, but of a completely different sort: not the folly of lovers but that of the cross.

This love, Weil explains, is the opposite of violence, in other words, the opposite of force and power as a means of control. She cites Thucydides: "By a necessity of nature, every being invariably exercises all the power of which it is capable."[144] Such is the law of *conatus*, of power, and not only in war and politics; it is the law of the world, the law of life. "Children," a friend once remarked to me, "are like water: they invariably fill all available space." But not God: were he to do so, there would be only God and no world. And not parents: sometimes, not always (after all, parents, too, have to protect their living space), but more often than one might think, parents withdraw, step back, cede their space to their children, and refrain from exercising all the power at their disposal. Why? Because they love them, because they want to leave them the space, power, and freedom to become who they are, because they do not want to crush them with their presence, power, and love. And parents are not alone in this respect. Who is not careful with a newborn child? Who does not check his own strength and abstain from violence? Who does not curb his own power? Weakness commands, and that is the meaning of charity. "It happens," says

Simone Weil, "although extremely rarely, that a man will forbear out of pure generosity to command where he has the power to do so. That which is possible for man is possible also for God."[145] Out of pure generosity? Let us say out of pure love, from which generosity follows. But what kind of love? Not *erōs*, for God is wanting in nothing, nor are parents wanting in children, nor is the adult wanting in the weakness he protects. Not *philia* either, at least not as it has been so far presented, for God's joy cannot be increased, for joy is not the only source of parental love, nor can it fully explain the gentleness an adult will feel toward a stranger's child—a gentleness that gives him a sense of peace or of something more perhaps than peace. Benevolence and joy are in this love, but they are there in the space they create but do not occupy, their presence attested to above all by that force which is not exercised, by this withdrawal, gentleness, thoughtfulness, by that power which seems to empty itself of itself and check itself of its own accord and which chooses to deny itself rather than assert itself, to retract rather than expand, to give rather than keep or take, and even to lose rather than possess. This love, one might say, is the exact opposite of water, of children, of the *conatus*, of life asserting itself while consuming what it desires. It is the opposite of heaviness and the opposite of force. It is what Simone Weil calls grace and love.

The love of couples sometimes approaches what I am describing. In it there is *erōs*, which desires, takes, and possesses. And there is *philia*, which rejoices and shares and is like a combination of strengths, a capacity intensified by the capacity, the joy, and the existence of the other. And who does not love to be desired and loved? Yet by dint of seeing how strong, happy, and satisfied the other person is in his love for you, how your "relationship" agrees with him, how love agrees with him, how easily he takes up all available space and all available life; by dint of seeing him assert his power, his existence, and his joy and persevere so triumphantly in his being, you can find yourself overcome by an immense fatigue, a weariness or weakness. You feel assailed, crushed, and overwhelmed, that you are less and less alive, that he is suffocating you, and all you want to do is run away or cry. You back away? He advances, just like water, just like children, just like armies, and this incursion he calls "his love," or "your relationship." And suddenly you would rather be alone.

I will cite Pavese's moving aphorism once more: "You will be loved the day when you will be able to show your weakness without the person using it to assert his strength." This kind of love is the rarest of loves, the most precious and miraculous. You take a step back? He takes two steps back. Why? Simply to give you more room, to avoid crowding you, invading you, or crushing you, to give you more space and freedom and to let you breathe, and the weaker he feels you are, the more freedom he gives you. He steps back so as not to impose on you his power, or even his joy or love, so as not to take up all available space, all available being, or all available power. One who forbears in this way is the precise opposite of the *salaud*, the dirty bastard, whom Sartre thinks can be defined as someone possessed by "the fat fullness of being." If one accepts this definition, which is as good as any, one would have to say that charity, were anyone capable of it, would be the opposite of this dirtiness of being oneself. To be charitable is to renounce the fullness of the ego, of power and potency. It is to renounce God as well, who "emptied himself of his divinity," as Weil says,[146] and in doing so makes the world possible and faith bearable. "The true God is the God we think of as almighty, but as not exercising his power everywhere."[147]

Charity is real love, or rather (since *erōs* and *philia* are real too), it is the divinity that love sometimes contains. "Love consents to everything and commands only those who consent to it. Love is abdication. God is abdication."[148] Love is weak, "God is weak" though all-powerful, since he is love.[149] Weil could find this theme in Alain: "It must be said of God that he is weak and small, and forever dying, between two thieves, at the will of the paltriest police force. Always persecuted, slapped, humiliated; always defeated; always reborn on the third day."[150] In this notion of God, says Alain, resides the true essence of Jansenism, which "takes refuge in a hidden God, a God who hides himself out of pure love or, as Descartes says, pure generosity; who has nothing to give except spirit; who is absolutely weak and absolutely proscribed, who serves no purpose, but on the contrary must be served, and whose kingdom has not yet come."[151] A purifying atheism, as Simone Weil will describe it, purified of religion.[152] Love is the opposite of force, like the spirit of Christ, the spirit of Calvary: "When people tell me about an all-powerful god," Alain insists, "my answer is that he is a pagan god and an outdated god. The new god is weak, crucified, humiliated. . . . Do not say that the spirit will triumph, will gain power and victory, have guards and prisons, in short a crown of gold. No. . . . He will have a crown of thorns."[153]

This weakness of God, or this divinity of weakness,[154] is an idea that Spinoza or Aristotle would never have thought of, yet it is one that speaks to our fragility, to our weariness, and even, it seems to me, to the strength within us that is so light and so rare, to that little bit of truly selfless love of which we are sometimes capable or think we are capable or for which, at the very least, we feel a nostalgia or a need. No longer, then, is love want, passion, or covetousness (*erōs*), a joyous and expansive capacity, a shared affirmation of a mutually augmented existence, self-love redoubled by love of the other (*philia*); rather, it is withdrawal and gentleness, the thoughtfulness of existing less, of asserting oneself less, of reining in one's being; it is the self-limitation of one's capacity, strength, and being, the sacrifice of one's own pleasure, comfort, or self-interest; it is the love that lacks nothing but is not full of itself or of its strength (it lacks nothing because it has relinquished everything); it is the love that does not increase power but limits or negates it (it is an abdication, Simone Weil says, the opposite of egoism and violence); it is the love that does not add to self-love but offsets it and dissolves it, that does not comfort the ego but liberates it; it is disinterested and gratuitous love, pure love, as Fénelon puts it;[155] it is the love that gives (as *philia* does) but gives at a dead loss, and not to a friend (giving to a friend is not losing; it is a different way of possessing, of enjoying) but to a stranger, an unknown person, an enemy . . .

Anders Nygren, who spells out the distinguishing features of Christian *agapē*, describes it as a spontaneous and gratuitous love, groundless, disinterested, and even unjustified.[156] These features set it apart from *erōs*, the love that is always avid, egoistical, motivated by what it lacks, forever deriving its value, reason, and hope from the other. But they also set it apart from *philia*, which is never completely selfless (since my friends' interests are my own), never completely gratuitous (since it gives me pleasure to please my friends—they love me more, and I love myself more, when I do), never completely spontaneous or free (since it is invariably determined by the fortuitous encounter of two egos, the harmonious combination of two egoisms: "Because it was he, because it was I").[157] God's love for us, according to Christianity, is by contrast perfectly selfless, perfectly gratuitous, and perfectly free: God has nothing to gain from it since he is infinite and perfect; quite the contrary, he sacrifices himself for us, limits himself for us, crucifies himself for us, and for no reason other than a love that has no reason, for no other reason than love, for no other reason than that he has chosen to relinquish being everything. God's love for us has no justification: he loves us not because of what we are, not because we might be lovable, good, and just (God also loves sinners and even gave his son for them), but because he is love and love, at least this kind, needs no justification. "God's love is always spontaneous," writes Nygren, "it is not called out by anything outside itself. Hence, when it is said that God loves man, this is not a judgment on what man is like, but on what God is like."[158] God loves man not because man is lovable but because God is love. This love comes first, absolutely; it is absolutely active (and not reactive) and absolutely free; it is not determined by the value of what it loves, by a value that it is lacking in (*erōs*) or that would bring it joy (*philia*). Rather, it determines the value of its object by loving it. It is the source of all value, all want, and all joy. *Agapē*, writes Nygren, is not "conditioned by the worthiness of its object"[159] since it creates this worth:

> *Agapē is creative.* . . . It is not that God loves that which is in itself worthy to be loved; but, on the contrary, *that which in itself is without value acquires value by the fact that it is the object of God's love.* Agape is the direct opposite of that love which is called out by

the worthiness of its object and so may be said to be a recognition of the value and attractiveness of its object. The man whom God loves has not any value in himself. His value consists simply in the fact that God loves him.[160]

But how does all this relate to us, to our lives and loves, if God does not exist? It relates if nothing else by its difference, and that difference can clarify. When Denis de Rougemont, who draws on Nygren, nevertheless tries to oppose Christian marriage—an instance of *agapē*, according to him—to the passion of lovers, whom he sees as in the thrall of *erōs*,[161] he forgets that we do not marry just anyone, that the love we have for our husband or wife is neither gratuitous nor disinterested, and that, indeed, no one suggests that we ought to marry our enemies. The contrasting dyad of *erōs* and *agapē* is far too simple and schematic to explain love as we know it and live it: human love (particularly in the couple, whether Christian or not) owes nearly as much to *erōs* as to *philia*, and no doubt far more to *philia* than to *agapē*. Hence the tripartite division I am suggesting, which, though still inevitably schematic, nevertheless can perhaps account more accurately for our true feelings and how they develop, the way one kind of love constantly changes into another. Nygren, too, no doubt errs in insisting on a break between *erōs* and *agapē* that is so radical and definitive as to preclude any passage from one to the other, any synthesis between them. Augustine, Bernard of Clairvaux, and Thomas Aquinas were more nuanced, more realistic, and more human in their views of love and thus could demonstrate how one can go from self-love to love of the other, from selfish love of the other to selfless love of the other, from covetousness to benevolence, and from benevolence to charity—in sum, from *erōs* to *philia* and then, sometimes, at least a little, as a distant possibility, from *philia* to *agapē*.[162] Charity is not altogether divorced from want (one could say that charity is the want within us for the good, that charity is the good itself as the object of our attraction), nor is it unrelated to friendship (it is like a universal and selfless friendship, unfettered by preference for a specific person, which is always egoistical or, in any case, ego-related). It is closer, of course, to *philia* than to *erōs*. The love within us that wants God, as Saint Francis of Sales would say, being a purely selfish love, is not yet charity (since charity, as Saint Paul says, "does not insist on its own way");[163] it is mere covetousness, mere hope![164] Charity only really begins with our *philia*—the expansive, self-affirming love that friends feel for one another—for God; indeed charity is this very friendship, as it lights up our whole life and is reflected onto our fellowmen.[165] Aquinas describes the crucial transition clearly: charity is a benevolent love (a friendship) that transcends friendship properly speaking and breaches its boundaries, going beyond an affective or—to use Kantian terminology—pathological determination, beyond a merely reactive or preferential spontaneity. By what process? Through a kind of transference, as we would say today, through the "transitivity" or generalization of love: "Indeed, so much do we love our friends, that for their sake we love all who belong to them, even if they hurt or hate us; so that, in this way, the friendship of charity extends even to our enemies, whom we love out of charity in relation to God, to Whom the friendship of charity is chiefly directed."[166] But, again, what does this leave us with if God does not exist?

It leaves us perhaps with a certain idea of humanity in which all men are bound together: the Greeks called it *philanthropia*, which they defined as a "natural tendency to love men, a way of being which incites to charity and benevolence towards them."[167] Charity, then, would simply be a very wide friendship, as some have interpreted Epicurus to say,[168] less intense perhaps than the love of God but broader in its scope and richer in its objects, as though open to the universal and "dancing around the world"[169] like a light of joy and gentleness shining on all men, known and unknown, near and far, in the name of a common humanity, a common life, a common fragility. How can we not love, even if only a little, someone who resembles us, who lives and suffers as we do, and who, like us, will die? Friends or enemies, lovers or rivals, we are all brothers in the face of life, all brothers in the face of death; charity would be like a brotherhood of mortals, and this is certainly no small thing.

And perhaps it also leaves us with a certain idea of love, one in which love is not determined by the value of the love object but instead generates that value and lies at its source. "Spontaneous love," Nygren says, "uncaused, creative." This love is love itself. We do not desire something because we deem it to be good, Spinoza explains, we deem something to be good because we desire it.[170] This capacity to generate value, Nietzsche says, is the power of desire to make treasures and jewels out of all esteemed things.[171] It is the power of love as well, indeed it is love's peculiar power. We do not love something because it is lovable; it is lovable because we love it. Thus do parents love their children before knowing them, before being loved by them, regardless of what they are or what they become. This love transcends *erōs* and *philia*, at least as we ordinarily experience them or think of them (as subject to or determined by the prior worth of their object). Love is first, which is not to say it precedes being (for then love would be God); rather, it precedes all value: what is valuable is what we love. No doubt it is in this respect that love is the supreme value, the alpha and omega of living, as I said, the starting point and destination of all our judgments. But then love is valuable, too, provided we love it, and the more we love it the more valuable it is. It is not because people are lovable that we must love them, it is insofar as we love them that they are lovable (to us). Charity is that love which does not wait to be deserved, that basic, gratuitous, indeed, spontaneous love which is the truth of love and its ever-distant prospect.

Yet in its opposition to egoism, self-love, and the *conatus*, this self-less love can seem mysterious, even of dubious existence. Can one actually love one's neighbor as oneself? Probably not. But the injunction to do so points us in a certain direction, toward love. And if in friendship love lies in the direction of life, joy, and the realization of our capacities, charity enjoins us to proceed in precisely the opposite direction, as though one had to renounce oneself in order to allow the other to exist. Mystics speak of this renunciation as dying to one's self; Simone Weil calls it *decreation*: just as God in creating the world renounces his being everything, so "we should renounce being something."[172] Once again, the exact opposite of Spinoza's *conatus*:

He emptied himself of his divinity. We should empty ourselves of the false divinity with which we were born.

Once we have understood we are nothing, the object of all our efforts is to become nothing. It is for this that we suffer with resignation, it is for this that we act, it is for this that we pray.

May God grant that we become nothing.[173]

One might look on this desire as a triumph of the death instinct and ascribe it to what may be pathological (this time in the ordinary sense of the term) in Simone Weil's personality. But supposing it is, we still need to know what we ourselves are to do about this death instinct, or, as they say, about our aggression. For what Freud says or at least implies, and what we tend to forget, is that the death instinct inevitably triumphs, since life itself is subject to it, and that in any case we can never simply rid ourselves of it once and for all.[174] Is there any desire that is not also a desire for death? Is there any life that is not a form of violence? For many, love is simply the denial of this desire, this violence, this aggression that is life. But Simone Weil can hardly be said to practice denial. What we see in her rather is the introversion of death, violence, and negativity, or, to use words that are not hers, the turning back of the death instinct onto the self, which liberates the life instinct and makes it available to others. Desire remains (since "we are made of desire"),[175] joy remains (since "joy and the sense of reality are identical"),[176] and love remains (since "belief in the existence of other human beings as such is *love*"),[177] but now they are freed of egoism, hope, and possessiveness[178]—and we, in turn, are as though freed from ourselves, from "the prison of the self,"[179] lighter, more joyful, and more luminous since the ego, having ceased absorbing into itself all the available love and attention, no longer stands in the way of reality or joy.

This buoyancy, joy, and luminosity is the common hallmark of wisdom and sainthood. Simone Weil may not have attained either—she never claimed to have done so. Nevertheless she helps us to grasp what wisdom and sainthood are. "The sin in me says 'I,' " she writes.[180] And elsewhere: "I must love being nothing. How horrible it would be if I were something. I must love my nothingness, love being a nothing-ness."[181] An expression of resentment, an idealization of asceticism, self-hatred? One could put it that way. Such things can and do exist. But if they were the sole content of this love, would Simone Weil move us so? Would she enlighten us so? But there may be something else to this love, an inversion of the life and death instincts, or rather (since these two instincts in all likelihood are but one) a permutation of their objects at the two poles of a single ambivalence. To put our life in God, Simone Weil explains, is "to put our life into that which we cannot touch in any way." And she adds, "It is impossible. It is a death. That is what is required."[182] Eros and Thanatos. In most people, or in all people most of the time, Eros centers on the self (and is projected on others to the extent that we lack them or that they bring us joy—to the extent that they can be useful to us), whereas Thanatos focuses more on others; it is easier to love oneself than others, easier to hate others than oneself. What Simone Weil calls decreation, which according to her expresses itself in charity, could perhaps be thought of (in Freudian terms, if not her own) as these two forces or their objects turning toward each other, intersecting with each other, the self relinquishing its monopoly on the life instinct, ceasing to absorb the positive energy, and focusing the entire death instinct, or all the negative energy, not on the other but on itself. There is room here, it seems to me, for a nonreligious reading of Simone Weil, which could perhaps integrate into a materialistic theory (for example, a Freudian one) some elements of the notion of decreation, which she also calls this "reversal of the positive and the negative":

For we are wrong side upward. We are born thus. To re-establish order is to undo the creature in us.

Reversal of the objective and subjective.

Similarly, reversal of the positive and the negative. That is also the meaning of the philosophy of the Upanishads.

We are born and live in an inverted fashion, for we are born and live in sin which is an inversion of the hierarchy. The first operation is one of reversal—Conversion.

Except the seed die . . . It has to die in order to liberate the energy it bears within it so that with this energy new forms may be developed.

So we have to die in order to liberate a *tied up* energy, in order to possess an energy which is free and capable of understanding the true relationship of things."[183]

And what is the true relationship of things? Absolute equality—since nothing has value without love, and all things have value through love. Whereby charity is nothing other than justice ("The Gospel," notes Simone Weil, "makes no distinction between the love of our neighbor and justice"),[184] or, rather, differs from justice only through love (we can be just without loving, but we cannot love universally without being just); charity is like love freed of the injustice of desire (*erōs*) and friendship (*philia*), hence it is like a universal love, without preference or choice, a dilection without predilection,[185] a love without limits and even devoid of egoistical or affective justifications. Charity, therefore, cannot be reduced to friendship: friendship always presupposes a choice, a preference, a special relationship, whereas charity sees itself as universal,[186] and applies particularly to enemies or people we do not care about (since, for anyone else, friendship suffices). As Ferdinand Prat notes, "one never says in Latin or even in Greek, '*Amate (phileite) inimicos vestros*'—this would be asking the impossible—but always, '*Diligite (agapate) inimicos vestros.*'"[187] How could we be the friend of our enemies? How could we rejoice in their existence, when it hurts us and kills us? They must therefore be loved differently. As for *erōs*, the word does not appear anywhere in the New Testament, nor does any word of the same root.[188] How indeed could we feel a want for our enemies? How could we expect good, pleasure, or happiness from them?

Agapic love, then, is unique, precisely because it claims to be universal. Being in love with one's fellowman, in other words with everyone and anyone, all the more so with one's enemies, would be a patent absurdity. And those who have many friends, Aristotle notes, "are thought to be no one's friend."[189] Charity, therefore, is something else: "love transfigured into virtue," as Jankélévitch puts it.[190] Or rather (if friendship is already a virtue, as I believe it is), charity is love "become permanent and chronic, extended to the universality of men and the totality of the person."[191] It can certainly also be directed toward the person who is our lover or friend, but it addresses itself to all human beings, good and evil, friends or enemies, which does not prevent us from preferring our friends or fighting our enemies (if we can fight without hatred—if hatred is not the sole motivation for fighting). Still, it introduces into the sphere of human relations that distant goal of universality which was already suggested by compassion and justice, albeit negatively and formally for the most part, and infuses it, to the extent possible, with a positive and concrete content. Charity is the joyful acceptance of the other, of any other, as he is or whatever he may be.

Since it is universal, charity includes the self among its objects but in no way preferentially. (When Pascal writes that we must hate ourselves, he lacks charity toward himself: what would be the sense in loving one's neighbor as oneself if one was not supposed to love oneself?)[192] "To love a stranger as oneself," Simone Weil writes more accurately, "implies the reverse: to love oneself as a stranger."[193] Here, Pascal supports her view: "In a word, the Self has two qualities: it is unjust in itself since it makes itself the centre of everything; it is inconvenient to others since it would enslave them; for each Self is the enemy, and would like to be the tyrant of all others."[194] Charity is the antidote to this tyranny and injustice, which it fights through a decentering (or, as Simone Weil would say, through a decreation) of the self. The self is hateful only because it does not know how to love others—and itself—as it should. Because it loves only itself or for itself (through covetousness or concupiscence). Because it is egoistical, unjust, and tyrannical. Because, like a spiritual black hole, it absorbs all joy, all love, all light. Charity, which is not incompatible with self-love (which, on the contrary, it includes and purifies: "to love oneself as a stranger"), nevertheless stands opposed to this egoism and injustice—to the tyrannical slavery of the self. In this distinction may reside the best definition: a love that is freed of the ego and that frees us from it.

Even if it were impossible to live by the dictates of charity, we would still be obliged to conceive it as an idea, in order to know what we are lacking and what we are missing.

For this love is at least something we desire, and our lack of it, the need we feel for it, suffices to make us aware of its value, or to make it a value, and thus to make love "this thirst that invents sources" and that source itself.[195] Charity is a want that would free us from all want or a power that would free us from power. For we want love, for love makes us rejoice: *agapē* is also an object or an ever-distant goal for *erōs* and *philia*, preventing them from remaining imprisoned within the self, or self-satisfied. *Agapē*, as Plato notes, leads them to seek their satisfaction beyond all possible object, all possible possession, all possible preference; leads them into those regions of the spirit or being where nothing is wanting anymore and everything brings joy, that zone which Plato called the Good and others for two thousand years have called God and which is perhaps nothing other than this love that beckons us to the precise extent—but only to the extent—that we beckon it, that we love it and sometimes live by it, if not in its presence, of which we can never be certain, then at least in its absence or at least by its requirements or commandments. Love cannot be commanded, I said, since it commands and is therefore, as Saint Paul says, the whole law[196] and more precious even than science, faith, or hope, which have value—when and if they do—only through love or because of love. It may be appropriate at this point to cite the most beautiful text that has ever been written on charity and for which this long chapter is merely an excuse:

> If I speak in the tongues of men and of angels, but have not charity,
> I am a noisy gong or a clanging cymbal. And if I have prophetic
> powers, and understand all mysteries and all knowledge, and if I

have all faith, so as to remove mountains but have not charity, I am nothing. If I give away all I have, and if I deliver my body to be burned, but have not charity, I gain nothing.

Charity is patient and kind; charity is not jealous or boastful; it is not arrogant or rude. Charity does not insist on its own way; it is not irritable or resentful; it does not rejoice at wrong, but rejoices in the right. Charity bears all things, believes all things, hopes all things, endures all things.

Charity never ends; as for prophecies, they will pass away; as for tongues, they will cease; as for knowledge, it will pass away. For our knowledge is imperfect and our prophecy is imperfect; but when the perfect comes, the imperfect will pass away. When I was a child, I spoke like a child, I thought like a child, I reasoned like a child; when I became a man, I gave up childish ways. For now we see in a mirror dimly, but then face to face. Now I know in part; then I shall understand fully, even as I have been fully understood. So faith, hope, charity abide, these three; but the greatest of these is charity.[197]

Faith, hope, and charity are traditionally the theological virtues (because they have God as an object). The first two I have not included in this treatise because they have no plausible object, it seems to me, other than God, in whom I do not believe. Moreover, one can do without these two virtues: courage suffices in the presence of danger or the future, just as good faith suffices in the presence of truth or the unknown. But how could one do without charity (at least as an idea or ideal)? And who would dare pretend that its only object is God, when everyone feels (and Paul explicitly says) just the opposite, namely that it can exist completely only in the love of one's neighbor?[198] Augustine and Aquinas, in their commentaries on this paean to charity, demonstrate that of the three theological virtues charity is not only "the greatest of these," as Paul says, but also the only one that still makes sense in God, in what they call the kingdom of God. Faith passeth (for what does it mean to believe in God when one *is* in God?), hope passeth (for in the kingdom of God, there will be nothing more to hope for), and so it is said that charity alone "will endure": in the kingdom of God there will be only love, without hope and without faith.[199] The kingdom of Heaven is very much like the kingdom of Earth in this respect: faith and hope have left us; we live without them. Only desire, joy, and charity remain. To reject hope and faith is not necessarily to betray Christ's spirit or to part completely from his path. "In Christ," Aquinas notes, "there was neither faith nor hope," and yet "in him was perfect charity."[200] Clearly we can never attain that perfection. But must we therefore renounce that pittance of pure, gratuitous, selfless love—of charity—of which we might perhaps be capable?

I say "perhaps" because there can be no guarantee that such love is possible. But the same can be said of any virtue, as Kant shows,[201] and thus the fact that nothing guarantees that we can be charitable refutes neither the possibility of nor the need for this love. Is it within our capabilities? Can we experience it? Can we come close to it? There is no way of knowing or of proving that we can or cannot. Charity is perhaps "this love that is missing in every love," as Christian Bobin puts it,[202] yet it is missing nothing, and we miss it for that reason, and it attracts us. Even in its absence it lights the way for us, for the absence of love is still love.

"To love," says Alain, "is to find one's riches outside oneself."[203] This is why love is poor, always, and the only wealth. But there are several ways of being poor in and through love, or rather of being rich in one's poverty: through want, which is passion; through received and shared joy, which is friendship; and finally through the joy that is given and given at a loss, the joy that is both given and given up, which is charity. To summarize and simplify matters, there are therefore three types of love, or three degrees to love: want (*erōs*), joy (*philia*), and charity (*agapē*). It could be that the last is really nothing more than a halo of gentleness, compassion, and justice that tempers the violence of want or joy or comes to moderate or ease the too brutal or overweening aspects of our other loves. There is a kind of love that is like hunger and another that resonates like laughter. Charity is more like a smile, when it is not a desire to cry, as it sometimes is. I do not see that this condemns it. Our laughter can often be cruel; our tears rarely if ever are.[204] And compassion? It may well be the principal content of charity, its truest affect, indeed its real name. In any case, compassion is what charity is called in the Buddhist East, in this respect more lucid and realistic, as I have suggested, than the Christian West.[205] It may well also be that friendship—purified friendship, that is, as if rarefied in proportion to its expansion—is the only generous love of which we are capable; such is the objection an Epicurean might have made to Paul or the first Christians. Yet charity, if it is possible, might be recognizable (and surpass compassion) in this: it does not need the suffering of the other in order to love him, it is not "in tow to misfortune," as Jankélévitch puts it, it is like a basic, nonreactive compassion.[206] Similarly, charity might be distinguishable from simple friendship and surpass it in its not needing to be loved, or potentially loved, in order to love, in its having nothing to do with reciprocity or self-interest,[207] in its being like a basic and nonreactive friendship, like compassion freed from suffering and, again, friendship freed from ego.

The absence of charity, though there may be no remedy for it, is what makes the virtues necessary; love (nonegoistical love), when it exists, frees us from the law and, when love is lacking, makes it enter our hearts.[208]

That love is more often absent than not, that indeed it may always be absent, is what justifies the present treatise: what would be the point of discussing morality were it not for the fact that love is absent? "A short and true definition of virtue," said Augustine, "is a due ordering of love."[209] But more often than not, love is glaringly conspicuous in its absence; hence the brightness of the virtues and the darkness of our lives. A secondary brightness, an essential but not total darkness. The virtues are nearly all justified only by our lack of love; in other words, they are fully justified. Yet they cannot fill the void that illuminates them; the very thing that makes them necessary makes it impossible to believe that they might suffice.

Love commits us to morality and frees us from it. Morality commits us to love, even in its absence, and must yield before it.

Notes

PROLOGUE

1. Aristotle, *Nicomachean Ethics*, I, 6, 1097b22–1098a20, in *The Basic Works of Aristotle*, ed. Richard McKeon, Random House, 1941.

2. Michel de Montaigne, *The Essays of Montaigne*, trans. George B. Ives, Harvard University Press, 1925, vol. 4, book 3, ch. 13, p. 350.

3. Benedict de Spinoza, *The Ethics*, IV, D8, in *A Spinoza Reader: The Ethics and Other Works*, ed. and trans. Edwin Curley, Princeton University Press, 1994, p. 201.

4. *The Essays of Montaigne*, book 2, ch. 36, and Spinoza, *The Ethics*, IV, prop. 50, schol.

5. See, in particular, my *Vivre*, vol. 2 of *Traité du désespoir et de la béatitude*, PUF, 1988, ch. 4 ("Les labyrinthes de la morale"), and *Valeur et vérité*, PUF, 1994.

6. The formulation is Aristotle's, of course, in the *Nicomachean Ethics*, II, 4–9, 1105b–1109b, and *Eudemian Ethics*, II, 3, 1220b–1221b. The concept is sometimes called the golden mean, which is not mediocrity but its opposite: "Hence in respect of its substance and the definition which states its essence virtue is a mean, with regard to what is best and right an extreme" (*Nicomachean Ethics*, II, 6, 1107a–5–7, p. 959. See also my discussion in *Vivre*, ch. 4, pp. 116–18).

1. POLITENESS

1. Immanuel Kant, *Education*, trans. Annette Churton, University of Michigan Press, 1966, pp. 2, 6.

2. Immanuel Kant, *Anthropology from a Pragmatic Point of View*, trans. Victor Lyle Dowdell, Southern Illinois University Press, 1978, § 14, p. 39.

3. Immanuel Kant, *The Metaphysical Principles of Virtue* (part 2 of *The Metaphysics of Morals*), trans. James W. Ellington, Library of Liberal Arts, Bobbs-Merrill, 1964, § 48, p. 140.

4. Aristotle, *Nicomachean Ethics*, II, 1, 1103a33, in *The Basic Works of Aristotle*, ed. Richard McKeon, Random House, 1941, p. 952.

5. Ibid., 1103b1, p. 952.

6. Kant, *Education*, pp. 2–3.

7. Jean de la Bruyère, *The Characters of Jean de la Bruyère*, trans. Henri van Laun, Brentano's, 1929, 32, p. 114.

8. Kant, *Education*, p. 105.

9. Kant, *Anthropology from a Pragmatic Point of View*, § 14, p. 35.

10. Immanuel Kant, "The Discipline of Pure Reason in Polemics," 2, AK. 3, in *Critique of Pure Reason*, trans. J. M. D. Meiklejohn, Prometheus Books, 1990, p. 420.

11. Ibid.

12. Kant, *Anthropology from a Pragmatic Point of View*, § 14, p. 39.

13. Aristotle, *Nicomachean Ethics*, II, 1, 1103b21, p. 953.

14. Alain, *Définitions*, in *Les arts et les dieux*, Bibliothèque de la Pléiade, p. 1080 (definition of politeness).

15. Alain, *Quatre-vingt-un chapitres sur l'esprit et les passions*, in *Les passions et la sagesse*, Bibliothèque de la Pléiade, p. 1243.

2. FIDELITY

1. Augustine, *Confessions*, trans. R. S. Pine-Coffin, Penguin Books, 1961, book II, esp. ch. 20, p. 269.

2. Friedrich Nietzsche, "History in the Service and Disservice of Life," trans. Gary Brown, in *Unmodern Observations*, ed. William Arrowsmith, Yale University Press, 1990, p. 90.

3. François George, "D'un critère nouveau en philosophie," *L'âme et le corps*, ed. M. P. Haroche, Plon, 1990.

4. Vladimir Jankélévitch, *L'imprescriptible*, Seuil, 1986, p. 55.

5. Aristotle, *Ethica Eudemia*, VII, 2, 1237b37–40; *Nicomachean Ethics*, IX, 3, 1165b32–36, in *The Basic Works of Aristotle*, ed. Richard McKeon, Random House, 1941, p. 1081.

6. Vladimir Jankélévitch, *Les vertus et l'amour*, vol. 2 of *Traité des vertus*, Champs-Flammarion, 1986, p. 140.

7. Ibid., pp. 140–42.

8. Ibid., pp. 142–43. In fidelity, Jankélévitch notes in the same passage, "the Stoics would have recognized the *Constantia sapientis*" (the constancy of the sage).

9. Ibid., p. 141.

10. Blaise Pascal, *Pensées*, trans. W. F. Trotter, Modern Library, 1941, no. 123, p. 45.

11. Marcel Conche, *Montaigne et la philosophie*, Mégare, 1987, pp. 118–19. See also Michel de Montaigne, *Apology for Raymond Sebond*, in *The Essays of Montaigne*, trans. George B. Ives, Harvard University Press, 1925, vol. 2, book 2, ch. 12, pp. 401–02.

12. Jankélévitch, *Les vertus et l'amour*, p. 154. For Jankélévitch, this is "fidelity par excellence."

13. Jankélévitch, *L'imprescriptible*, p. 60.

14. Marcel Conche, *Orientation philosophique*, PUF, 1990, p. 106.

15. Henri Bergson, *The Two Sources of Morality and Religion*, trans. E. Ashley Audra and Cloudesley Brereton, University of Notre Dame, 1977, p. 281.

16. Jean Cavaillès, "Education morale et laïcité," *Foi et vie*, no. 2 (Jan. 1928), p. 8. See also my essay "Jean Cavaillès ou l'héroïsme de la raison," *Une éducation philosophique*, PUF, 1989, pp. 287–308.

17. Benedict de Spinoza, *The Ethics*, III, 27, exp., in *A Spinoza Reader: The Ethics and Other Works*, ed. and trans. Edwin Curley, Princeton University Press, 1994, p. 192.

18. Friedrich Nietzsche, *The Will to Power*, book 3, § 498.

3. PRUDENCE

1. The others are courage (or fortitude), temperance, and justice. This classification (in which prudence is sometimes called *practical wisdom*) seems to date back to the sixth century B.C. We find it in Plato, or at least something close to it (see, for example, *The Republic*, IV, 427e, and *Laws*, I, 631c), and then in its classical form in Stoicism (see, for example, Diogenes Laertius, VII, 126). It later turns up in Christian thought (via Cicero primarily), especially in Ambrose, Augustine, and Thomas Aquinas. See Pierre Aubenque, *La prudence chez Aristote*, PUF, 1970, pp. 35–36; G. Rodis-Lewis, *La morale stoïcienne*, PUF, 1970, pp. 72–86; and Thomas Aquinas, *Summa Theologica*, Ia–IIae, quest. 61, *The "Summa Theologica" of St. Thomas Aquinas*, trans. Fathers of the English Dominican Province, R. & T. Washbourne, 1915. See also Alain, *Propos du 19 janvier 1935* (*Propos*, Bibliothèque de la Pléiade, vol. 1, pp. 1245–47), as well as the beautiful definition of virtue (*Définitions*, in *Les arts et les dieux*, Bibliothèque de la Pléiade, p. 1098).

2. See, for example, Immanuel Kant, *Fundamental Principles of the Metaphysics of Morals*, in *Kant's Critique of Practical Reason and Other Works on the Theory of Ethics*, trans. Thomas Kingsmill Abbott, Longmans, Green, 1948, p. 33. See also *Critique of Practical Reason*, I, I, ch. 1, schol. 2; *Religion within the Limits of Reason Alone*, II; and *The Metaphysical Principles of Virtue*. See also Pierre Aubenque, "La prudence chez Kant," *Revue de métaphysique et de morale* (1975), pp. 156–82.

3. Immanuel Kant, *On a Supposed Right to Tell Lies from Benevolent Motives*, in *Kant's Critique of Practical Reason and Other Works on the Theory of Ethics*, pp. 361–66.

4. See Max Weber, *Politics as a Vocation*.

5. Aristotle, *Nicomachean Ethics*, VI, 5, 1140a–b, in *The Basic Works of Aristotle*, ed. Richard McKeon, Random House, 1941, p. 1026.

6. Aquinas, *Summa Theologica*, Ia–IIae, quest. 57, art. 5, and quest. 61, art. 2. See also IIa–IIae, quests. 47–56 (especially quest. 47, arts. 5–8). See also Etienne Gilson, *Saint Thomas moraliste*, Vrin, 1974, pp. 266ff. (*The Christian Philosophy of St. Thomas*, trans. L. K. Shook, Random House, 1956).

7. Indeed, we deliberate not about ends but about means (*Nicomachean Ethics*, III, 3, 1112b11–19). See also Aquinas, *Summa Theologica*, Ia–IIae, quest. 57, art. 5: "In order to perform an act well, it is not merely what a man does that matters, but also how he does it, namely, that he acts from right choice and not merely from impulse or passion. Since, however, choice is about means to an end, rightness of choice necessarily involves two factors, namely, a due end and something suitably ordained to that due end. . . . Consequently, an intellectual virtue is needed in his reason to complement it and make it well adjusted to these things. This virtue is prudence."

8. Aristotle, *Nicomachean Ethics*, VI, 12, 1144a6–9, p. 1034: "Again, the work of man is achieved only in accordance with practical wisdom as well as with moral virtue; for virtue makes us take aim at the right mark, and practical wisdom makes us take the right means." See also X, 8, 1178a18, p. 1106: "Rightness in morals is in accordance with practical wisdom."

9. See, for example, the testimony of Stobaeus, *Eclogues*, II, 59, 4, in the *Stoïcorum veterum fragmenta*, III, 262 (cited by Aubenque, *La prudence*, p. 33, and n. 1). See also Pierre Aubenque's paper "La 'phronèsis' chez les stoïciens," *Actes du VIIᵉ Congrès de l'Association Guillaume Budé*, Les Belles Lettres, 1964, pp. 291–92.

10. Aristotle, *Nicomachean Ethics*, VI, 5, p. 1026. When modern sciences take on the subject of chance—in probability theory, for example—it is in order to find what is necessary in it. It is valid only for large numbers (which again proves Aristotle right), when choice and action exist only on a one-time basis.

11. See Aubenque, *La prudence*, p. 78.

12. Epicurus, *Letter to Menoeceus*, 130, in Diogenes Laertius, *Lives of Eminent Philosophers*, trans. R. D. Hicks, Loeb Classical Library, Harvard University Press, 1991, vol. 2, pp. 655, 132, 657. See also the *Sovran Maxims*, V–X, as well as *Sentence Vaticane* 71.

13. Epicurus, *Letter to Menoeceus*, 129, p. 655.

14. Cicero, *The Laws*, XXIII.

15. See Cicero, *Republic*, VI, 1; *On the Nature of the Gods*, II, 22, 58; and *The Laws*, I, 23. See also Aubenque, *La prudence*, p. 137.

16. Aubenque, *La prudence*, p. 137.

17. Immanuel Kant, "The Analytic of Pure Practical Reason," in *Kant's Critique of Practical Reason and Other Works on the Theory of Ethics*, p. 126.

18. Aristotle, *Nichomachean Ethics*, VI, 13, 1144b31, p. 1036.

19. Augustine, *De Moribus Ecclesiae Catholicae*, § 15: *"Prudentia, amor ea quibus adjuvatur ab eis quibus impeditur, sagaciter seligens"* ("Prudence is love that chooses with sagacity between that which hinders it and that which helps it").

20. See Hans Jonas, *The Imperative of Responsibility: In Search of an Ethics for the Technological Age*. See also J.-M. Besnier, *L'humanisme déchiré*, Descartes & Cie, 1993, pp. 111–21. Let us note in passing that J.-M. Besnier obviously errs in using Hans Jonas against me on this point (p. 111). That ethics can only be of the present does not prevent all ethics from having—as prudence would require—the future as its preoccupation, including (especially today, because of the unprecedented power of our technologies) the future of generations to come. Only the living can have duties, but they also have them—as Jonas's book demonstrates—toward human beings who are not yet living, toward the humanity to come, whose existence we cannot compromise without culpability. For my part, I have of course never thought we should or even could exempt ourselves from all relations with the future. Indeed, I have clearly and frequently written to the contrary (see, for example, *Le mythe d'Icare*, PUF, 1984, pp. 149–50; *Vivre*, PUF, 1988, pp. 214–24; *Une éducation philosophique*, PUF, 1989, pp. 350–52; *L'amour la solitude*, Paroles d'Aube, 1992, p. 26; *Valeur et vérité*, PUF, 1994, pp. 145–46 and 158–60). What I have attempted to demonstrate, as against the seductions of hope and the dangers of utopia, is simply that any stance with regard to the future can be politically and morally responsible only to the extent that the future in question is taken to be one *that depends on us*—in other words, only to the extent that the relationship is one that is determined by will and not by hope. Such is prudence: the will in the present (like all other will) to prepare for or safeguard the future—our own, insofar as we can, and that of others, insofar as we must.

21. *Caute quia spinoza,* "Take care, I have thorns," was the motto on Spinoza's seal.

4. TEMPERANCE

1. Benedict de Spinoza, *The Ethics*, IV, P45, schol., in *A Spinoza Reader: The Ethics and Other Works*, ed. and trans. Edwin Curley, Princeton University Press, 1994, p. 224.

2. Ibid.

3. Aristotle, *Nicomachean Ethics*, II, 7, 1107b4–8, and III, 14, 1110a–5–20, in *The Basic Works of Aristotle*, ed. Richard McKeon, Random House, 1941. On virtue as the mean between two opposing vices, "that which depends on excess and that which depends on defect," see also II, 5 and 6, esp. 1107a1–7.

4. Epicurus, *Letter to Menoeceus*, in Diogenes Laertius, *Lives of Eminent Philosophers*, trans. R. D. Hicks, Loeb Classical Library, Harvard University Press, 1991, vol. 2,

p. 655. Compare with what Aristotle writes about temperance (*Nicomachean Ethics*, III, 13–15). On Aristotle's *autarkeia*, see I, 5, 1097b8ff.

5. On the meaning of this distinction, see my essay "Morale ou éthique?" in *Valeur et vérité*, PUF, 1994, pp. 183–205. On the care of the self, see Michel Foucault, *The History of Sexuality*, trans. Robert Hurley, esp. vols. 2 (*The Use of Pleasure*, Vintage, 1990) and 3 (*The Care of the Self*, Vintage, 1988).

6. On natural and necessary desires, and those that aren't, see Epicurus, *Letter to Menoeceus*, as well as *Principal Doctrines*, 29, in *The Essential Epicurus*, trans. Eugene O'Connor, Prometheus Books, 1993, p. 55. On the classification of desires in Epicureanism, see Marcel Conche, *Epicure, Lettres et maximes*, PUF, 1987, pp. 63–69.

7. "*Et finem statuit cuppedinis atque timoris*" (Lucretius, *De Rerum Natura*, VI, 25, trans. W. H. D. Rouse, Loeb Classical Library, Harvard University Press, 1982).

8. Michel de Montaigne, *The Essays of Montaigne*, trans. George B. Ives, Harvard University Press, 1925, vol. 4, book 3, ch. 13, p. 350.

9. Epicurus, *Letter to Menoeceus*, p. 657.

10. Lucretius, *De Rerum Natura*, V, 1117–19.

11. Arthur Rimbaud, Letter to Paul Demeny, May 15, 1871, *Complete Works*, trans. Paul Schmidt, Harper & Row, 1976.

12. Thomas Aquinas, *The "Summa Theologica" of St. Thomas Aquinas*, trans. Fathers of the English Dominican Province, R. & T. Washbourne, 1915, IIa–IIae, quest. 141, art. 8.

13. Ibid., art. 4.

14. Ibid., IIa–IIae, quest. 142, art. 1. See also Aristotle's *Nicomachean Ethics*, II, 7, 1107b4–8, and III, 14, 1119a–5–21.

15. Spinoza, *The Ethics*, P56, schol., pp. 184–85, and V, P42 and schol., p. 264.

16. Ibid., and IV, D8, p. 201.

17. Alain, *Définitions,* in *Les arts et les dieux*, Bibliothèque de la Pléiade, p. 1094 (definition of temperance).

18. Montaigne, *Essays*, I, 30, p. 262, and Kant, *The Metaphysical Principles of Virtue* (part 2 of *The Metaphysics of Morals*), trans. James W. Ellington, Library of Liberal Arts, Bobbs-Merrill, 1964, Introduction, XVII.

5. COURAGE

1. I cannot find the reference, but the same idea turns up in *Rome sauvée, ou Catilina*, V, 3: "Undaunted courage, in the hearts of mortals, / Makes for great heroes or great criminals" (*Oeuvres complètes*, vol. 5, Garnier-Frères, 1877, p. 264).

2. Aristotle, *Nicomachean Ethics*, III, 6, 1115a, and *Ethica Eudemia*, III, 1, 1229b; Thomas Aquinas, *The "Summa Theologica" of St. Thomas Aquinas*, trans. Fathers of the English Dominican Province, R. & T. Washbourne, 1915, IIa–IIae, quest. 123, arts. 4 and 5; and Vladimir Jankélévitch, *Les vertus et l'amour*, vol. 2 of *Traité des vertus*, Champs-Flammarion, 1986, pp. 134–35.

3. Immanuel Kant, *Religion within the Limits of Reason Alone*, trans. Theodore M. Greene and Hoyt H. Hudson, Open Court, book 1, p. 41. See also *Critique of Practical Reason*, I, theorem 4, schol. 2, and *Fundamental Principles of the Metaphysics of Morals*, II.

4. René Descartes, *Treatise on Passions*, II, art. 59, and III, art. 171; Immanuel Kant, *The Metaphysical Principles of Virtue*, trans. James W. Ellington, Library of Liberal Arts, Bobbs-Merrill, 1964, book 1, pp. 77–105. For Kant "pathological" does not mean abnormal or unhealthy but—in conformity with the etymology of the word—whatever is a product of passion (*pathos*) or, in general, of sensitive impulses (see *Critique of Pure Reason*).

5. Thomas Aquinas, *Summa Theologica*, IIa–IIae, quest. 123, art. 2, p. 197.

6. Ibid.; Aristotle, *Nicomachean Ethics*, II, 3, 1105a32; Cicero, *Rhetoric, De Inventione*, II, 54.

7. Alain, *Les Propos d'Alain*, NRF, 1920, p. 131 (these are marvelous remarks that I couldn't find in the La Pléiade collection, but perhaps I didn't look hard enough).

8. See Plato, the entire *Laches*, the *Protagoras*, 349d–350d and 358d–360e, *The Republic*, IV, 429a–430d, and the *Laws*, XII, 963a–964d. On courage in Plato (and in the history of philosophy in general), see also Jankélévitch, *Les vertus et l'amour*, ch. 2, as well as the articles by E. Smoes and Sylvain Matton in no. 6 of the series "Morales" of the journal *Autrement* ("Le courage," Paris, 1992).

9. Jankélévitch, *Les vertus et l'amour*, ch. 2, esp. pp. 90–103, in the Champs-Flammarion edition (1986). Aristotle had already said: "Nor indeed was Socrates right in asserting that courage was knowledge" (Aristotle, *Magna Moralia*, I, 20, 1190b26–32, in *The Complete Works of Aristotle*, vol. 2, ed. Jonathan Barnes, Princeton University Press, 1985, p. 1883).

10. Jankélévitch, *Les vertus et l'amour*, vol. 1, p. 110.

11. See my essay "Jean Cavaillès ou l'heroïsme de la raison," in *Une éducation philosophique*, PUF, 1989, esp. pp. 302–08.

12. Epicurus, *Letter to Menoeceus*, 135; Benedict de Spinoza, *The Ethics*, V, in *A Spinoza Reader: The Ethics and Other Works*, ed. and trans. Edwin Curley, Princeton University Press, 1994. This does not mean (pace Jankélévitch, *Les vertus et l'amour*, pp. 98–99) that there is no place for courage in Epicurus and Spinoza or for no other form of courage than the sage's pure *aphobia* (absence of fear). It means, rather, that all the space that wisdom fails to occupy within us is available to courage.

13. Spinoza, *The Ethics*, III, P58, schol., pp. 186–87. See also IV, P63 and dem.

14. Ibid., III, P9 and schol., as well as V, P10, schol., and P41.

15. Jankélévitch, *Les vertus et l'amour*, p. 89. He later qualifies this statement, however.

16. Ibid., p. 96.

17. Alain, "Lettres au Docteur H. Mondor sur le sujet du coeur et de l'esprit," in *Les arts et les dieux*, Bibliothèque de la Pléiade, p. 733.

18. Spinoza, *The Ethics*, IV, P73, schol., p. 238.

19. Aristotle, *Magna Moralia*, I, 20, 1191a33–36, p. 1884. See also *Nicomachean Ethics*, III, 9, 115a33–35, and *Rhetoric*, II, 5, 1382a25–30. La Fontaine devotes a fable, "The Lion and the Hunter," to this kind of person: "The sign and seal of valor / Is how one behaves when cause for fright is near. / Some who took risks at first and sang bass, sing tenor / The moment disparaged foes appear" (La Fontaine, *The Fables of La Fontaine*, trans. Marianne Moore, Viking, 1954, p. 119).

20. Jankélévitch, *Les vertus et l'amour*, p. 107.

21. Ibid., p. 108.

22. See Epictetus and Marcus Aurelius, of course, but also Vladimir Jankélévitch, *La volonté de vouloir*, vol. 3 of *Le Je-ne-sais-quoi et le Presque-rien*, Points-Seuil, 1980 (esp. ch. 2), as well as the *Traité des vertus*, II, 1, p. 125.

23. René Descartes, *The Philosophical Writings of Descartes*, trans. J. Cottingham, R. Stoothof, and D. Murdoch, Cambridge University Press, 1985–91, vol. 1, p. 1913; *Treatise on Passions*, III, art. 173, p. 391. See also, in the *Principles of Philosophy*, the dedicatory letter to Princess Elisabeth: "Thus goodness often results from simplicity, piety from fear, and fortitude from desperation."

24. Aristotle, *Nicomachean Ethics*, III, 11, 1116a1–4.

25. These are three translations for *"to kaolin partisan"* (Aristotle, *Nicomachean Ethics*, III, 8, 1116b30; III, 7, 1115b12–13 and 23).

26. See Aristotle's *Ethics*, III, 7, 1116–17a, and passim.

27. R. A. Gauthier and J. Y. Jolif, trans., *L'Ethique à Nicomaque*, Louvain, 1970, II, 1, pp. 233–34.

28. Matton, pp. 34–35 (see n. 8, above).

29. I am unable to go into greater detail here on problems of interpretation and particularly on the difficulty in reconciling two passages in Aristotle's *Nicomachean Ethics*, namely 1115b33–1116a3, on the one hand, and 1117b10–27, on the other. What transpires is that the coward "is a despairing sort of person; for he fears everything"; but "nor are sanguine people brave . . . yet they closely resemble brave men." In brief,

optimism resembles courage (in its confidence) while being different (in its fragility). I do not for that matter see that courage is "antinomy of hope" (as Sylvain Matton says in his fine article), and in fact, everyone knows that this is not the case; optimists can *also* be courageous. But this is what transpires from these texts, and this is what matters to me, that courage and hope are not only two different things but also independent of each other—in prerogatives and in fact (see Gauthier and Jolif's pertinent remarks in their commentary to the *Nicomachean Ethics*, pp. 232–34). The person who hopes can certainly also be courageous; but he is only truly so when his daring and valor do not stem from hope alone. This is very well explained in *Magna Moralia*, p. 1883 (I, 20, 1191a11–21): "For he whose courage does not endure on the deprivation of something cannot properly be considered brave." He who appears brave "through hope and anticipation of good" is not really brave since his apparent courage would not outlast his hope. Aristotle is here closest to common experience, as he often is; the truly courageous person, for him as for us, is the one who is able to be courageous in defeat, even inescapable defeat, as well as in victory, even assured. Not *all* courage, therefore, is a courage of despair, but it is a touchstone whereby courage can be distinguished from simple confidence.

30. François Rabelais, *Gargantua*, ch. 43, in *The Complete Works of François Rabelais*, trans. Donald M. Frame, University of California Press, 1991, p. 100.

31. Alain, *Souvenirs de guerre*, in *Les passions et la sagesse*, Bibliothèque de la Pléiade, p. 441.

32. Alain, *Souvenirs concernant Jules Lagneau*, in *Les passions et la sagesse*, Bibliothèque de la Pléiade, pp. 751 and 758. See also pp. 738, 741, and 748.

33. Aristotle, *Nicomachean Ethics*, II, 7, 1107a33–1107b4, and III, 9–10, 1115a–1116a15; *Eudemian Ethics*, III, 1, 1228a23–1229b26.

34. Spinoza, *The Ethics*, IV, P69 and schol., p. 236 (the free man, according to Spinoza, is the one who lives under the sole guidance of reason).

6. JUSTICE

1. Alain, Propos du 2 décembre 1912, in *Propos*, Bibliothèque de la Pléiade, vol. 2, p. 280. See also Alain, *Quatre-vingt-un chapitres sur l'esprit et les passions*, IV, 7, and VI, 4, in *Les passions et la sagesse*, Bibliothèque de la Pléiade, pp. 1184 and 1228.

2. Immanuel Kant, *Groundwork of the Metaphysics of Morals*, trans. H. J. Paton, Harper Torchbooks/Academy Library, 1964, p. 61.

3. Ibid., p. 62.

4. See, for example, Immanuel Kant, *The Metaphysical Elements of Justice*, trans. John Ladd, Library of Liberal Arts, Bobbs-Merrill, 1965, Introduction, III and IV.

5. Aristotle, *Nicomachean Ethics*, V, 1, 1129b25–31, in *The Basic Works of Aristotle*, ed. Richard McKeon, Random House, 1941, p. 1003.

6. Kant, *The Metaphysical Elements of Justice*, p. 100.

7. Epicurus, *Principal Doctrines*, 31–38, in *The Essential Epicurus*, trans. Eugene O'Connor, Prometheus Books, 1993, pp. 74–75.

8. Jeremy Bentham, *An Introduction to the Principles of Morals and Legislation*, University of London, 1970; John Stuart Mill, *Utilitarianism*; David Hume, *An Enquiry concerning the Principles of Morals*, in *Enquiries concerning Human Understanding and concerning the Principles of Morals*, Clarendon Press, 1975, sect. 3, as well as *A Treatise of Human Nature*, book 3, part 2.

9. John Rawls, *A Theory of Justice*, Belknap Press of Harvard University Press, 1971.

10. See Aristotle, *Nicomachean Ethics*, V, 2, and V, 9.

11. Ibid., V, 2, 1129a34.

12. Ibid., V, 1, 1129b12.

13. Blaise Pascal, *Pensées*, trans. A. J. Krailsheimer, Penguin, 1966, no. 312, p. 106. See also my preface to Pascal, *Pensées sur la politique*, Rivages Poches, 1992.

14. Thomas Hobbes, *Leviathan*, Penguin Classics, 1976, book 2, ch. 26.

15. As shown by Hobbes (*Leviathan*, book 2, ch. 26), Benedict de Spinoza (*Political Treatise*, in *The Chief Works of Benedict de Spinoza*, vol. 1, trans. R. H. M. Elwes, Dover Publications, 1951, chs. 3 and 4), and later Jean-Jacques Rousseau (*The Social Contract*, book 2, ch. 6). This is where positivism and voluntarism converge: see H. Batiffoll, "Que sais-je?" *La philosophie du droit*, PUF, 1981, pp. 11–15 and 22–24.

16. Pascal, *Pensées*, no. 299, p. 103.

17. Plato, *The Republic*, IV. For a general introduction to the different theories of justice from Plato to Rawls, see also the highly instructive small book by Gérard Potdevin, *La justice*, Quintette, 1993.

18. Pascal, *Pensées*, no. 298, p. 103.

19. Ibid., no. 877, p. 310.

20. Plato, *Crito*, esp. 48–54.

21. Kant, *The Metaphysical Elements of Justice*, II, 1, remark E, p. 104.

22. Pascal, *Pensées*, no. 534.

23. Alain, *Quatre-vingt-un chapitres*, IV, 4, pp. 1229–30.

24. Ibid., VI, 5, pp. 1230–31. The same idea can be found in Simone Weil (who was Alain's student): the virtue of justice "consists of behaving exactly as though there

were equality when one is the stronger in an unequal relationship" (Simone Weil, *Waiting for God*, trans. Emma Craufurd, G. P. Putnam's Sons, 1951, p. 143).

25. Alain, *Quatre-vingt-un chapitres*, VI, 4, p. 1230.

26. Kant, *The Metaphysical Elements of Justice*, Introduction to the Elements of Justice, C, p. 35. See also Immanuel Kant, *On the Old Saw: That May Be Right in Theory but It Won't Work in Practice*, trans. E. B. Ashton, University of Pennsylvania Press, 1974, p. 58: "*Law* is the limitation of each man's freedom to the condition of its consistency with everyone's freedom to the extent possible in accordance with a universal law."

27. Alain, *Quatre-vingt-un chapitres*, p. 1228.

28. Kant, *On the Old Saw*, p. 65. See also Kant, *The Metaphysical Elements of Justice*, general remark A, p. 84 and § 52. Kant remains faithful here to Rousseau, for whom the idea of a social contract is meant not to explain a fact but to found a legitimacy (Rousseau, *The Social Contract*, book 1, ch. 1). Spinoza, for whom the problematic is different, will also increasingly erase any reference to an original historical social contract. On this point, see Alexander Matheron, *Individu et communauté chez Spinoza*, Editions de Minuit, 1969, pp. 307–30.

29. See Kant, *Education*.

30. Ibid.

31. See Rawls, *A Theory of Justice*, esp. sects. 3–4 and 20–30. Rawls's analysis is "highly Kantian in nature," as he says in the preface and as can be seen in his (sometimes debatable but always suggestive) interpretation of Kant in sect. 40.

32. Ibid., sect. 24, p. 137.

33. As Pascal saw: *Pensées*, no. 455, p. 151, and no. 100, p. 38.

34. Rawls, *A Theory of Justice*, sect. 24, p. 139.

35. This is what calls mutual disinterestedness (see Rawls, *A Theory of Justice*, sects. 3, pp. 13–14, and 22, pp. 127–28), and it suffices to clearly distinguish justice from charity.

36. See Rousseau, *The Social Contract*, book 1, ch. 6 (on the original contract) and ch. 2, book 6 (on the general nature of the law).

37. Pascal, *Pensées*, no. 455, p. 152.

38. Fyodor Dostoevsky, *The Brothers Karamazov*, part 2, book 5, ch. 4 ("Rebellion") trans. Constance Garnett, Modern Library, Random House, 1950, p. 281.

39. Aristotle, *Nicomachean Ethics*, V, 7, 1131b1620, and 10, 1134a–b.

40. Spinoza, *A Theologico-Political Treatise*, in *The Chief Works*, vol. 1, trans. R. H. M. Elwes, Dover Publications, 1951, ch. 16, p. 208.

NOTES

41. Spinoza, *A Political Treatise*, in *The Chief Works*, vol. 1, p. 299.

42. See the article "Justice" in the *Encyclopédie philosophique universelle*, II, *Les notions philosophiques*, PUF, 1990, vol. 1, pp. 1406–07. See also Thomas Aquinas, *The "Summa Theologica" of St. Thomas Aquinas*, trans. Fathers of the English Dominican Province, R. & T. Washbourne, 1915, IIa–IIae, quest. 58, art. 1: "Justice is the habit whereby a person with a lasting and constant will renders to each his due," a definition that is "fitting if understood aright."

43. Benedict de Spinoza, *The Ethics*, IV, P37, schol. 2, in *A Spinoza Reader: The Ethics and Other Works*, ed. and trans. Edwin Curley, Princeton University Press, 1994, p. 220; see also Spinoza, *A Political Treatise*, book 2, ch. 23.

44. Spinoza, *The Ethics*.

45. Hobbes, *Leviathan*, book 1, ch. 13, p. 188.

46. "From this it follows that men who are governed by reason—that is, men who, from the guidance of reason, seek their own advantage—want nothing for themselves which they do not desire for other men. Hence they are just, honest, and honorable" (Spinoza, *The Ethics*, IV, P18, schol., p. 210).

47. Traditionally, since Aristotle, a distinction is made between justice "which is manifested in distributions of honor or money" and "justice which plays a rectifying part in transactions between man and man." Distributive justice allocates wealth or honor between the members of a community: it is not subject to equality but to proportion (it can be legitimate for a particular individual to have more than another if, for example, he contributes more to the common good). Rectificatory justice, on the other hand, governs transactions: it must respect the equality of the things exchanged, regardless of the differences between the individuals involved (see Aristotle, *Nicomachean Ethics*, V, 2–4, 1130b–1132b). The same idea can be found in Thomas Aquinas: rectificatory justice, he explains, has as its object "the mutual exchange between two individuals," while distributive justice is "called upon to distribute society's common wealth proportionately" (Aristotle, *Summa Theologica*, IIa–IIae, quest. 61).

48. David Hume, *An Enquiry concerning the Principles of Morals*, sect. 3, part 2, p. 203.

49. Ibid., sect. 3, part 1, pp. 183–84. I am following the argument of the *Enquiry* because it is tighter and more elegant, but essentially the same theses can be found in the Hume, *Treatise of Human Nature*, book 3, part 2.

50. Hume, *Enquiry concerning the Principles of Morals*, sect. 3, part 1, pp. 183–92.

51. Aristotle, *Nicomachean Ethics*, VIII, 1, 1155a26–27.

52. Hume, *Enquiry concerning the Principles of Morals*, sect. 3, part 1, p. 184.

53. Ibid., sect. 3, part 2, p. 201 ("property, which is the object of justice . . .").

54. Rawls, *A Theory of Justice*, sect. 22, pp. 127–28.

55. Hume, *Enquiry concerning the Principles of Morals*, sect. 3, part 1, p. 186. Here, too, Rawls seems to agree with Hume (Rawls, *A Theory of Justice*, sect. 22, pp. 127–28).

56. Tzvetan Todorov, *Facing the Extreme*, trans. Arthur Denner and Abigail Pollak, Metropolitan Books, 1995, pp. 231 and 295.

57. See, for example, Robert Antelme's beautiful book *The Human Race*, in which he draws from his experience as a deportee (trans. Jeffrey Haight and Annie Mahler, Marlboro Press, 1992, p. 88): In the camps, he writes, "we'll have known both the greatest esteem and the most definitive contempt, both love for mankind and loathing for it, with a more total certainty than anywhere else, ever. The SS officers who view us all as one and the same cannot induce us to see ourselves that way. They cannot prevent us from choosing. . . . The inhabitant of the camps is not the abolition of those differences; on the contrary, he is their effective realization."

58. Antelme, *The Human Race*, pp. 88–89. See also Primo Levi's account of his friend Alberto in *If This Is a Man*.

59. Antelme, *The Human Race*, p. 88.

60. Hume, *Enquiry concerning the Principles of Morals*, sect. 4, pp. 210–11: "To carry the matter farther, we may observe that it is impossible for men so much as to murder each other without statutes, and maxims, and an idea of justice and honour. War has its laws as well as peace. . . . Common interest and utility beget infallibly a standard of right and wrong among the parties concerned."

61. Ibid., sect. 3, part 1, pp. 190–91 (italics are in the original).

62. Ibid.

63. Which does not mean that animals have no rights. See my article "Sur les droits des animaux," *Esprit*, no. 217 (Dec. 1995), pp. 140–48.

64. Hume, *Enquiry concerning the Principals of Morals*, sect. 3, part 1, p. 191.

65. Michel de Montaigne, *The Essays of Montaigne*, trans. George B. Ives, Harvard University Press, 1925, vol. 4, book 3, ch. 6 ("On Coaches") and passim. For both Montaigne and Pascal (*Pensées*, nos. 931 and 985), values are determined negatively. We may not know perfect or ideal justice, but we can clearly recognize injustice when we see it: "Although we cannot define what is exactly right we can easily see what is not" (Pascal, *Pensées*, no. 729, p. 224).

66. *The Essays of Montaigne*, vol. 2, book 2, ch. 12, pp. 262–63.

67. Ibid.

68. Hume, *Enquiry concerning the Principals of Morals*, sect. 3, part 1, p. 191.

69. Lucretius, *De Rerum Natura*, V, 1011–23, trans. W. H. D. Rouse, Loeb Classical Library, Harvard University Press, 1982, p. 457. It is possible that, by stressing the emotional life and the protection of the weak in the emergence of justice, Lucretius sets himself apart from the stricter utilitarianism of Epicurus. See Léon Robin (in collaboration with A. Ernout), *Commentaire du De rerum natura*, Les Belles Lettres, 1962, vol. 3, pp. 138–40.

70. Pascal, *Pensées*, no. 298, p. 103. On what I mean by cynicism, in the philosophical sense of the term, see my book *Valeur et vérité (Etudes cyniques)*, PUF, 1994. On Pascal's political thought, see my preface to his *Pensées sur la politique*, Rivages-Poche, 1992.

71. Pascal, *Pensées*, no. 298, p. 103.

72. Aristotle, *Nicomachean Ethics*, V, 10, 1137a31–1138a3, p. 1020.

73. Aristotle, *Rhetoric*, I, 13, 1374a26–27, in *The Basic Works of Aristotle*, p. 1372.

74. Aristotle, *Nicomachean Ethics*, V, 10, 1137b34–1138a3, p. 1020.

75. Cited by Vladimir Jankélévitch, *Traité des vertus*, vol. 2, Champs-Flammarion, 1986, p. 79. Jankélévitch's footnote refers the reader to Aristotle, *Magna Moralia*, II, 2. I am unable to find this remark in my edition, though I found a similar one in Aristotle, *Rhetoric*, I, 13, 17, 1347b: "Equity must be applied to forgivable actions."

76. Aristotle, *Nicomachean Ethics*, V, 1–2, 1129a–1131a, pp. 1002–06; V, 1, 1129b11–1130a13, pp. 1003–04; V, 1, 1129b27–29, p. 1003. The words in italics are from Euripides.

7. GENEROSITY

1. B. Chamfort, *Products of the Perfected Civilization: Selected Writings of Chamfort*, trans. W. S. Merwin, Macmillan, 1969, p. 135.

2. *Dictionnaire historique de la langue française*, ed. A. Rey, Dictionnaires Le Robert, 1992, s.v. "solidaire."

3. Ibid.

4. Blaise Pascal, *Pensées*, trans. W. F. Trotter, Modern Library, Random House, 1941, no. 143, p. 121.

5. Vladimir Jankélévitch, *Traité des vertus*, vol. 2, Champs-Flammarion, 1986, p. 314.

6. Ibid., p. 327.

7. See Aristotle's *Nicomachean Ethics*, IV, 1–3, 1119b22–1122a16 (on liberality) and 7–9, 1123a34–1125a33 (on magnanimity). See also Aristotle, *Eudemian Ethics*, III, 4 and 5, as well as Aristotle, *Magna Moralia*, I, 23–25.

8. René Descartes, *The Philosophical Writings of Descartes*, trans. J. Cottingham, R. Stoothoff, and D. Murdoch, Cambridge University Press, 1985–91, vol. 1, art. 153, p. 384 ("What generosity consists in"). On generosity's double nature, as both passion and virtue, see art. 161, pp. 387–88.

9. Ibid., art. 156, p. 385. See also art. 187, p. 395: "For it is part of generosity to have good will towards everyone."

10. Ibid., art. 161, p. 388.

11. René Descartes, Letter to Queen Christina of Sweden, 20 Nov. 1647, in *The Philosophical Writings of Descartes*, vol. 3, pp. 324–25.

12. Ibid., p. 325.

13. See my *Traité du désespoir et de la béatitude*, PUF, 1988, vol. 2, ch. 4, esp. pp. 67–93 and pp. 142–49.

14. See Immanuel Kant, "Of the Motives of Pure Practical Reason," in *Kant's Critique of Practical Reason and Other Works on the Theory of Ethics*, trans. Thomas Kingsmill, Abbott, Longmans, Green, 1948, p. 176. On the motives of pure practical reason, see ch. 18.

15. Michel de Montaigne, *The Essays of Montaigne*, trans. George B. Ives, Harvard University Press, 1925, vol. 1, book 1, ch. 28 ("On Friendship"), pp. 254–55.

16. Ibid.

17. On this conception of morality, see my essay "Morale ou éthique?" in *Valeur et vérité (Etudes cyniques)*, PUF, 1994, pp. 183–205.

18. Spinoza uses the term in another sense; see Benedict de Spinoza, *The Ethics*, III, P27, dem., cor., and schol., in *A Spinoza Reader: The Ethics and Other Works*, ed. and trans. Edwin Curley, Princeton University Press, 1994.

19. Augustine, *Confessions*, trans. William Watts, Loeb Classical Library, Harvard University Press, 1989, vol. 1, book 3, ch. 1, p. 99.

20. Spinoza, *The Ethics*, IV, P18, schol., p. 209.

21. Spinoza, *The Ethics*, III and IV, passim. See also the first pages of Spinoza, *On the Improvement of the Understanding* and Spinoza, *Short Treatise*, II, 5.

22. Spinoza, *The Ethics*, III, P59, schol., p. 187; italics in original.

23. Ibid. On strength of character, or tenacity, in Spinoza, see above, ch. 5, p. 52.

24. Ibid., IV, P21, p. 211. See also P20 and schol., pp. 210–11.

25. Ibid., IV, P20 and P25 and passim.

26. See Benedict de Spinoza, *Theologico-Political Treatise*, in *The Chief Works of Benedict de Spinoza*, vol. 1, trans. R. H. M. Elwes, Dover Publications, 1951, ch. 1, and Benedict de Spinoza, Letters to Oldenburg, nos. 73, 75, and 78. See also Sylvain Zac, *Spinoza et l'interprétation de l'Ecriture*, PUF, 1965, pp. 190–99, and esp. Alexandre Matheron, *Le Christ et le salut des ignorants chez Spinoza*, Aubier-Montaigne, 1971. Let us recall in passing, in order to avoid any misunderstanding, that Spinoza did not believe in Christ's divinity or his resurrection (see, for example, letters 73 and 78).

27. Spinoza, *The Ethics*, III, P19, P21, P25, P28, P39, and their dems.

28. See Spinoza, *The Ethics*, III, schol. of P22 and P27, schol. and cor. (particularly cor. 3) as well as def. 35 of the affects. See also my ch. 8, below.

29. Spinoza, *The Ethics*, IV, P18, schol., pp. 209–10.

30. Ibid., IV, P41 and P45, p. 224. See also III, schol. of P11, P13, P39, as well as defs. 3 and 7 of the affects.

31. Ibid., IV, P18, schol., p. 210; also P37 and P73, schol.

32. Ibid., IV, P46, dem. and schol. See also P45, cor.

33. Here it is: *"He, who lives according to the guidance of reason strives, as far as he can, to repay the other's hate, anger, and disdain toward him, with love, or nobility"* (ibid., IV, P46, p. 225; see also V, P10, schol.).

34. Ibid., IV, P73, schol., p. 238 (which refers to P47 and P46).

35. Ibid., III, def. 6 of the affects, p. 189. This cause can also be internal, defining self-love or self-esteem (*acquiescentia in se ipso*): Spinoza, *The Ethics*, III, schol. of P30 and P55 (see also P53) and def. 25 of the affects.

36. Since "man is affected with the same affect of joy or sadness from the image of a past or future thing as from the image of a present thing" (Spinoza, *The Ethics*, III, P18, p. 164). This is clarified in the demonstration: "So long as a man is affected by the image of a thing, he will regard the thing as present, even if [*tametsi*] it does not exist."

37. Since "one who loves necessarily strives to have present and preserve the thing he loves" (Spinoza, *The Ethics*, III, P13, schol., p. 162).

38. Ibid., III, P59, schol., and V, schol. of P10 and P42.

39. Ibid., V, P41, p. 263.

40. Ibid., V, P10, schol., p. 251.

41. Ibid., IV, P37, schol. 1, and V, P41. The translation of *pietas* as *morality*, on which most translators agree, is faithful to Spinoza's definition of the word, which does not refer in any way to religion or any feeling of piety ("The desire to do good generated in us by our living according to the guidance of reason, I call morality," IV, P37, schol. 1, p. 218), but also to its Latin meaning, which concerns the accomplishment of duties, not just toward the gods (if that were the case it could legitimately be translated as *piety*) but also toward men (in which case it does indeed correspond rather well to *morality*).

42. Spinoza, *The Ethics*, IV, preface, and schol. of P50 and P58; see also V, P10, schol., as well as P41, dem. and schol. On the relation between Spinoza and Nietzsche, see my essay "Nietzsche et Spinoza," in *De Sils-Maria à Jerusalem: Les intellectuels juifs et Nietzsche*, ed. D. Bourel and J. Le Rider, Cerf, 1991, as well as the pertinent remarks of Sylvain Zac in *La morale de Spinoza*, PUF, 1972, pp. 45ff.

43. Spinoza, *The Ethics*, III, preface, and IV, P18 and schol.

44. To use A. Negri's expression in *L'anomalie sauvage: Puissance et pouvoir chez Spinoza*, PUF, 1982, p. 262.

45. Spinoza, *The Ethics*, IV, schol. of P50 and P73, pp. 226 and 239.

46. David Hume, *An Enquiry concerning the Principles of Morals*, in *Enquiries concerning Human Understanding and concerning the Principles of Morals*, Clarendon Press, 1975, sect. 3, part 1, pp. 184–85. See also, above, my ch. 6, p. 76.

47. Hume, *An Enquiry concerning the Principles of Morals*, V, 2; Spinoza, *The Ethics*, III, P27 and schol. On this mimetic function in Spinoza, see also my *Traité du désespoir et de la béatitude*, vol. 2, ch. 4, pp. 102–09); Sigmund Freud, *Civilization and Its Discontents*.

8. COMPASSION

1. Max Scheler, *The Nature of Sympathy*, trans. Peter Heath, Archon Books, 1970, I, I, p. 5.

2. Ibid.

3. Ibid., I, IX, pp. 135ff.

4. Ibid., I, I, p. 5.

5. See the entry for *karuna* (compassion) in the *Encyclopédie philosophique universelle*, PUF, 1990, vol. 2, 2, p. 2848. As an introduction, see also W. Rahula, *L'enseignement du Bouddha*, Seuil, 1978, pp. 69–70 and 104, as well as L. Silburn, *Le bouddhisme*, Fayard, 1977 (there are many references to karuna in the index).

6. See, for example, Diogenes Laertius, *The Lives and Opinions of the Philosophers*, VII, 123, and Cicero, *Tusculan Disputations*, trans. J. E. King, Harvard University Press, 1965, III, x, 2. This condemnation of pity, which is a constant in Stoicism, does not prevent Epictetus or Marcus Aurelius from using the word in a positive sense; but pity, as they understand it (as an absence of hatred and anger toward the wicked and ignorant), is closer to what I would call *mercy* (see ch. 9, below).

7. Cicero, *Tusculan Disputations*, IV, xxvi, 56, p. 391. We find the same idea in Epicurus: "Let us show our feeling for our lost friends not by lamentation but by meditation" (*Epicurus: The Extant Remains*, trans. Cyril Bailey, Clarendon Press, 1926, LXVI, p. 142).

8. Benedict de Spinoza, *The Ethics*, IV, P50, in *A Spinoza Reader: The Ethics and Other Works*, ed. and trans. Edwin Curley, Princeton University Press, 1994, p. 226.

9. Ibid., IV, P50, cor.

10. Ibid., III, schol. of P22 and P27.

11. Ibid., IV, P37, P46, and passim.

12. Ibid., IV, P50, schol., p. 226. See also Alexandre Matheron, as always remarkably precise and clear, *Individu et communauté chez Spinoza*, Editions de Minuit, 1969, pp. 145–48 and esp. pp. 156–59.

NOTES

13. Spinoza, *The Ethics*, IV, P58, schol., p. 230 (where he writes that "like pity, shame, though not a virtue, is still good").

14. Ibid. See also Sylvain Zac, *La morale de Spinoza*, PUF, 1972, pp. 76–77, as well as Alexandre Matheron on repentance, *Le Christ et le salut des ignorants chez Spinoza*, Aubier-Montaigne, 1971, pp. 111–13.

15. Spinoza, *The Ethics*, III, defs. 35 and 43 of the affects, pp. 194–95.

16. Contrary to what Nietzsche repeatedly advocates. See, for example, Friedrich Nietzche, *The Genealogy of Morals*, I, 11, as well as my contribution to *Pourquoi nous ne sommes pas nietzschéens*, ed. L. Ferry and A. Renaut, Grasset, 1991, esp. pp. 66–68. On the relation between Nietzsche and Spinoza (whom Nietzsche always regarded as a predecessor but also as an opponent, dominated by fear and resentment), see my contribution "Nietzsche et Spinoza" in *De Sils-Maria à Jérusalem: Les intellectuels juifs et Nietzsche*, ed. D. Bourel and J. Le Rider, Cerf, 1991, pp. 47–66.

17. Alain, Propos du 5 octobre 1909, in *Propos*, Bibliothèque de la Pléiade, vol. 1, p. 60 (unless otherwise noted, all references to *Propos* are to the four-volume La Pléiade edition). For the relationship between Alain and Spinoza, see my contribution "Le dieu et l'idole (Alain et Simone Weil face à Spinoza)," in *Spinoza au XXe siècle*, ed. O. Bloch, PUF, 1993, pp. 13–39.

18. Alain, Propos du 13 février 1910, in *Propos*, vol. 2, p. 161.

19. Alain, Propos du 5 novembre 1927, in *Propos*, vol. 1, p. 750.

20. To borrow the distinction made by Sylvain Zac in *La morale de Spinoza*, ch. 5. See also pp. 116–17, where Zac rightly notes that as far as everyone's morality is concerned (particularly its Judeo-Christian form), "Spinoza never challenges its value."

21. Benedict de Spinoza, *A Theologico-Political Treatise*, in *The Chief Works of Benedict de Spinoza*, vol. 1, trans. R. H. M. Elwes, Dover Publications, 1951, ch. 4, pp. 65 and 67.

22. Ibid., ch. 14. See also Matheron, *Le Christ et le salut des ignorants*, chs. 2 and 3, and Zac, *La morale de Spinoza*, Final Remarks.

23. Spinoza, *The Ethics*, III, def. 24 of the affects, p. 192. Here is the Latin text: "*Misericordia est Amor, quatenus hominem ita afficit, ut ex bono alterius gaudeat, et contra ut ex alterius malo contristetur.*"

24. Ibid., III, exp. of def. 18 of the affects, p. 191.

25. Ibid., III, defs. 6, 18, and 24 of the affects.

26. Ibid., III, P21 and P22, schol.

27. Ibid., III, def. 6 of the affects.

28. Ibid., III, P27, cor. 2, p. 168.

29. Ibid., cor. 3: "As far as we can, we strive to free a thing we pity from its suffering." In this, Spinoza is not too far from Descartes; see René Descartes, *Treatise on Passions*, III, arts. 185–89.

30. Vladimir Jankélévitch, *Traité des vertus*, vol. 2, Champs-Flammarion, 1986, pp. 168–69.

31. See, for example, Friedrich Nietzsche, *The Antichrist*, trans. Anthony M. Ludovici, § 7, pp. 131–32, in *The Complete Works of Friedrich Nietzsche*, vol. 16, ed. Oscar Levy, Russell & Russell, 1964: "Christianity is called the religion of *pity*. Pity is opposed to the tonic passions which enhance the energy of the feeling of life: its action is depressing. . . . It preserves that which is ripe for death, it fights in favour of the disinherited and the condemned of life; thanks to the multitude of abortions of all kinds which it maintains in life, it lends life itself a sombre and questionable aspect. People have dared to call pity a virtue (—in every *noble* culture it is considered as a weakness—)." See also Friedrich Nietzsche, *Beyond Good and Evil*, § 260, and *The Will to Power*, III, 227.

32. Vauvenargues, *Réflexions et maximes*, 82, in *Introduction à la connaissance de l'esprit humain*, Garnier-Flammarion, 1981, p. 189.

33. Arthur Schopenhauer, *On the Basis of Morality*, chs. 3 and 4, esp. §§ 16–19 and 22. See also Arthur Schopenhauer, *The World as Will and Representation*, IV, 67.

34. See my essay "Sur les droits des animaux," *Esprit*, no. 217 (Dec. 1995), pp. 140–48.

35. Claude Lévi-Strauss, *Anthropologie structurale deux*, Plon, 1973, ch. 22, esp. pp. 50–56.

36. See, for example, Montaigne's essay "On Cruelty": "I have a wonderful propensity toward mercy and mildness" (*The Essays of Montaigne*, trans. George B. Ives, Harvard University Press, 1925, vol. 1, book 1, ch. 1, p. 7). On the relationship between Lévi-Strauss and Buddhism, see Claude Levi-Strauss, *Tristes tropiques*, Plon, 1995, pp. 471–80; for his relationship to Montaigne, see his *Histoire de lynx*, Plon, 1991, ch. 18, pp. 277ff.

37. Schopenhauer, *On the Basis of Morality*, III, 19 (the citations are of *Discourse on the Origin and the Foundations of Inequality among Men* and *Emile*); Lévi-Strauss, *Anthropologie structurale deux*, pp. 45–56. See also *Tristes tropiques*, ch. 38.

38. Jean-Jacques Rousseau, *Discourse on the Origin and the Foundations of Inequality among Men*, in *The First and Second Discourses and Essay on the Origin of Languages*, ed. and trans. Victor Gourevitch, Harper & Row, 1985, pp. 160–63.

39. Ibid., p. 160. On pity in Rousseau, I recommend the excellent analyses by Jacques Derrida in *De la grammatologie*, Editions de Minuit, 1967, II, ch. 3.

40. Rousseau, *Discourse on the Origin*, p. 163.

41. Ibid., pp. 161–62. Bernard Mandeville, who was born in Holland but lived in England (1670–1733), is the author of *The Fable of the Bees;* the book caused a scandal

because of its subversive vision of moral values, all of which he reduced to pride and self-love. See Paulette Carrive, *Bernard Mandeville*, Vrin, 1980.

42. Aristotle, *Rhetoric*, II, 8, 1385b14–16, in *The Basic Works of Aristotle*, ed. Richard McKeon, Random House, 1941, p. 2207. This is why pity (along with fear) is one of the moving forces of tragedy: see Aristotle's *Poetics*, 1449b27–28, 1452a, 1453b.

43. Ibid., II, 8, 1386a28. La Rochefoucauld: "Pity is often feeling our own sufferings in those of others, a precaution against misfortunes that may befall us" (maxim 264). "If it be true that in showing pity and compassion we think of ourselves, because we fear to be one day or another in the same circumstances as those unfortunate people for whom we feel, why are the latter so sparingly relieved by us in their wretchedness?" (Jean de la Bruyère, "Of the Affections," in *The Characters of Jean de la Bruyère*, trans. Henri van Laun, Brentano's, 1929, p. 92).

44. Hannah Arendt, *On Revolution*, Viking, 1965, p. 85.

45. Ibid., p. 80.

46. Ibid. (Arendt contrasts "the mute compassion of Jesus" with "the eloquent pity of the Inquisitor" in Dostoevsky's "The Grand Inquisitor").

47. Lucretius, *De Rerum Natura*, II, 1–19, trans. W. H. D. Rouse, Loeb Classical Library, Harvard University Press, 1982, p. 95: "Pleasant it is, when on the great sea the winds trouble the waters, to gaze from shore upon another's tribulation: not because any man's troubles are a delectable joy, but because to perceive what ills you are free from yourself is pleasant."

48. This is the case, for example, in Descartes—and with what superiority! See art. 187 of Descartes, *Treatise on Passions*.

49. Alain, Propos du 22 juillet 1922, in *Propos*, II, p. 496.

50. Ibid.

51. Spinoza, *The Ethics*, IV, app. 17, p. 239. See also Matheron's *Individu et communauté*, p. 157.

52. Spinoza, *The Ethics*, III, def. 35 of the affects, p. 194: "Benevolence is a desire to benefit one whom we pity."

53. Immanuel Kant, *The Metaphysical Principles of Virtue*, trans. James W. Ellington, Library of Liberal Arts, Bobbs-Merrill, 1964, § 34 and § 35, pp. 121–22.

54. Ibid., § 35, p. 122: "But though it is not in itself a duty to feel pity and so likewise to rejoice with others, active sympathizing with their lot is a duty. To this end it accordingly is an indirect duty to cultivate our natural (sensitive) feelings for others. . . . Thus it is a duty not to avoid places where the poor, who lack the most necessary things, are to be found; instead, it is a duty to seek them out. It is a duty not to shun sickrooms or prisons and so on in order to avoid the pain of compassion,

which one may not be able to resist. For this feeling, though painful, nevertheless is one of the impulses placed in us by nature for effecting what the representation of duty might not accomplish by itself."

55. The latter interconnection is not contradictory, even for Spinoza; see Spinoza, *The Ethics*, III, P37 and dem., pp. 173–74 ("the greater the sadness, the greater the power of acting with which the man will strive to remove the sadness"). See also Laurent Bove's fine article, "Spinoza et la question de la résistance," *L'enseignement philosophique*, no. 5 (May-June 1993), pp. 3ff.

56. I quote Augustine's excellent summary of the spirit of the Gospels (Augustine, *Commentary on St. John's First Epistle*, treatise 7, ch. 8).

9. MERCY

1. René Descartes, *Letter to More*, 5 Feb. 1649, in *The Philosophical Writings of Descartes*, trans. J. Cottingham, R. Stoothoff, and D. Murdoch, Cambridge University Press, 1985–91, vol. 3, p. 363.

2. J. Colerus, *Vie de Spinoza*, Bibliothèque de la Pléiade, p. 1510.

3. François La Rochefoucauld, *Maxims and Reflections*, trans. Leonard Tancock, Penguin, 1959, maxim 330, p. 80.

4. Oscar Wilde, *The Portrait of Dorian Gray*, Modern Library, Random House, 1992, p. 75.

5. Words pronounced before a Nazi execution squad by one of a group of twenty-three French resisters executed in February 1944, at least according to Aragon's poetic re-creation (based, however, on the victims' letters) in "Strophes pour se souvenir," a poem of fidelity—written in 1955—and of mercy (Aragon, *Le roman inachevé*, Gallimard, 1975, pp. 227–28).

6. Epictetus, *The Discourses as Reported by Arrian, the Manual, and Fragments*, trans. W. A. Oldfather, Loeb Classical Library, 1926, vol. 1, book 1, 18, 9, p. 123.

7. Marcus Aurelius Antonius, *The Meditations*, trans. G. M. A. Grube, Bobbs-Merrill, 1963, book 8, 59, p. 85.

8. Vladimir Jankélévitch, *Le pardon*, Aubier, 1967, pp. 98–99.

9. See, for example, Plato's *Protagoras*, 358c–d, *Meno*, 77b–78b, *Timaeus*, 86d–e, *Laws*, V, 731c and 734b, IX, 860d. This famous thesis, which is a commonplace of Greek wisdom, is later taken up by the Stoics.

10. Vladimir Jankélévitch, *L'innocence et la méchanceté*, vol. 3 of *Traité des vertus*, Champs-Flammarion, 1986, p. 167. See also *Le pardon*, ch. 2.

11. Spinoza, *The Ethics*, in *A Spinoza Reader: The Ethics and Other Works*, ed. and trans. Edwin Curley, Princeton University Press, 1994, III, def. 7 of the affects: "Hate is a sadness, accompanied by the idea of an external cause." See also René Descartes, *Treatise on Passions*, II, art. 140.

12. On this distinction see Kant's *Religion within the Limits of Reason Alone*, in *The Philosophy of Kant*, ed. Carl J. Friedrich, Modern Library, Random House, 1993, pp. 418–27.

13. Jankélévitch, *Le pardon*, p. 209.

14. See my *Vivre*, PUF, 1988, ch. 4, esp. pp. 67–89 and 142–49. See also my essay "L'âme machine, ou ce que peut le corps," in *Valeur et vérité*, PUF, 1994, esp. pp. 124–27.

15. See, for example, Spinoza, *The Ethics*, III, P49, dem. and schol., and IV, schol. of P50 and P73.

16. Benedict de Spinoza, *A Political Treatise*, in *The Chief Works of Benedict de Spinoza*, vol. 1, trans. R. H. M. Elwes, Dover Publications, 1951, ch. 4, p. 288.

17. In my meaning of the word *mercy*, which, let me repeat, is not the one that Spinoza ordinarily gives to it, which corresponds more to our *compassion* (see ch. 8, above, esp. p. 109). Let us note, however, that Spinoza sometimes uses *mercy* (*misericordia*) in the sense I give it: see, for example, Benedict de Spinoza, *A Theologico-Political Treatise*, in *The Chief Works of Benedict de Spinoza*, vol. 1, trans. R. H. M. Elwes, Dover Publications, 1951, ch. 14. At other times, *misericordia* is mainly the opposite of revenge: Spinoza, *A Political Treatise*, I, 5, and Spinoza, *The Ethics*, IV, ch. 13.

18. As Spinoza would say, that is, when he uses the somewhat anthropomorphic language of the *Theologico-Political Treatise*, ch. 14.

19. Spinoza, *The Ethics*, I, app., and IV, P64, dem. and cor. See also B. Rousset, "La possibilité philosophique du pardon (Spinoza, Kant, Hegel)," in the proceedings of a colloquium on *Le pardon* (*Le point théologique*, no. 45 [1987], pp. 188–89).

20. Benedict de Spinoza, Letter 23 to Blyenbergh, in *The Chief Works of Benedict de Spinoza*, vol. 2, p. 348.

21. I have discussed these elsewhere: see *Vivre*, ch. 4, esp. pp. 84–93.

22. Spinoza, *The Ethics*, IV, P45 and cor. 1; *A Theologico-Political Treatise*, ch. 7.

23. Jankélévitch, *Le pardon*, p. 92, which refers in a footnote to R. Misrahi, in *La conscience juive face à l'histoire: Le Pardon*, Congrès juif mondial, 1965, p. 286, and to Spinoza's *A Political Treatise*, I, 4, where the Latin quotation appears. It can be translated as "not to mock, lament, or execrate but to understand human actions" (*The Chief Works of Benedict de Spinoza*, vol. 1, p. 288).

24. Jankélévitch, *Le pardon*, p. 203.

25. See Jankélévitch, *Le pardon*, p. 204, as well as *L'imprescriptible*, Seuil, 1986.

26. See Jankélévitch, *L'imprescriptible*, pp. 14–15.

27. Jankélévitch, *Le pardon*, pp. 204–05. (Of course, the context for these comments is a discussion of Nazi criminals.) See also Jankélévitch, *L'imprescriptible*, pp. 50ff., as well as Jankélévitch, *Traité des vertus*, vol. 3, p. 172.

28. "He who wishes to avenge wrongs by hating in return surely lives miserably. On the other hand, one who is eager to overcome hate by love, strives joyously and confidently" (Spinoza, *The Ethics*, IV, P46, schol., p. 225); IV, P46, dem. and schol.; XIII and XIV, app.

29. Luke 23:34; Acts 7:60. See also the inspiring figure of Msgr. Bienvenu in *Les Misérables*.

30. From this point of view, compare Matthew 5:39 and 10:34.

10. GRATITUDE

1. Benedict de Spinoza, *The Ethics,* in *A Spinoza Reader: The Ethics and Other Works,* ed. Edwin Curley, Princeton University Press, 1994, III, def. 6 of the affects, p. 189 ("Love is a joy, accompanied by the idea of an external cause").

2. Spinoza's term means self-esteem or, literally, peace with oneself, which he defines as "a joy born of the fact that a man considers himself and his own power of acting" (Spinoza, *The Ethics*, III, def. 25 of the affects, p. 192).

3. Spinoza, *The Ethics*, V, P24.

4. See, for example, Friedrich Nietzsche's *Will to Power*, IV, nos. 462, 463, and 464.

5. Jean-Jacques Rousseau, *Discourse on Inequality*, in *The First and Second Discourses and the Foundations of Inequality among Men*, ed. and trans. Victor Gourevitch, Harper & Row, 1985, p. 188: "Gratitude is indeed a duty that ought to be performed, but it is not a right that can be exacted."

6. Spinoza, *The Ethics*, IV, P71, schol.

7. Ibid., III, def. 34 of the affects, p. 194; see also III, P39 and 41, as well as P41, schol. (for the expression "reciprocal love").

8. Immanuel Kant, "Concerning the Duty of Gratitude," in *The Metaphysical Principles of Virtue*, trans. James W. Ellington, Library of Liberal Arts, Bobbs-Merrill, 1964, p. 119.

9. Spinoza, *The Ethics*, III, P41, schol.

10. Ibid., IV, P71, schol.

11. Ibid., V, P42, schol., p. 265.

12. Ibid., III, P41, schol. This is why "men are far more ready for vengeance than for returning benefits" (p. 176).

13. François La Rochefoucauld, *Maxims and Reflections*, trans. Leonard Tancock, Penguin, 1959, maxim 228, p. 67.

14. Claude Bruaire, *L'être et l'esprit*, PUF, 1983, p. 60. See also p. 198.

15. Cited by Seneca, *Ad Lucilium Epistulae Morales (The Epistles of Seneca)*, trans. Richard M. Gummere, William Heinemann, 1925, XV, 9, p. 101. Epicurus also says: "The ungrateful greed of the soul makes the creature everlastingly desire varieties of dainty food" (*Epicurus: The Extant Remains*, trans. Cyril Bailey, Clarendon Press, 1926, LXIX, p. 117). See Marcel Conche's enlightening remarks in his edition of Epicurus, *Lettres et maximes*, PUF, 1987, pp. 52–53.

16. *Epicurus: The Extant Remains*, XLV, 13, p. 299 (*"non vivunt, sed victuri sunt"*).

17. Blaise Pascal, *Pensées*, trans. W. F. Trotter, Modern Library, Random House, 1941, no. 172, pp. 60–61.

18. Epicurus, *Letter to Menoeceus*, 122, in *Epicurus: The Extant Remains*, p. 183. Epicurus's expression seems to indicate (for otherwise it would be pleonastic) that, for him as for us, gratitude can apply to the present—even if, in the writings of Epicurus that have come down to us, it seems primarily linked to memory. But what is conscience, if not memory in and of the present?

19. Epicurus, *Letter to Menoeceus*, 135.

20. *Epicurus: The Extant Remains*, LV, p. 115. On mourning, see also my essay "Vivre, c'est perdre," in the journal *Autrement*, no. 128.

21. Rousseau, *Discourse on Inequality*, II, p. 188; Kant, *The Metaphysical Principles of Virtue*, § 32, p. 119.

22. Kant, *The Metaphysical Principles of Virtue*, § 36, p. 124.

23. At least as far as "most men" are concerned, for whom it is "but a covert desire to receive greater gifts" (maxim 298, *Maxims*, p. 76). See also maxims 223–26.

24. B. Chamfort, *Products of the Perfected Civilization: Selected Writings of Chamfort*, trans. W. S. Merwin, Macmillan, 1969, p. 203.

25. Spinoza, *The Ethics*, IV, P71, schol. See also P70, dem. and schol.

26. Vladimir Jankélévitch, *Traité des vertus*, Champs-Flammarion, 1986, vol. 2, p. 250. See also vol. 1, pp. 112ff.

27. Epicurus, *Sentences vaticanes*, 52, in *Epicurus: The Extant Remains*, p. 115.

11. HUMILITY

1. Michel de Montaigne, *The Essays of Montaigne*, trans. George B. Ives, Harvard University Press, 1925, vol. 2, book 2, ch. 2 , p. 59.

2. Ibid., book 2, ch. 12, p. 403; see also book 3, ch. 13. (These are the concluding remarks of, respectively, Montaigne's longest essay and last essay. Montaigne's last words are of an appeased and joyful humility.)

3. Benedict de Spinoza, *The Ethics*, in *A Spinoza Reader: The Ethics and Other Works*, ed. and trans. Edwin Curley, Princeton University Press, 1994, III, def. 26 of the affects, p. 192.

4. Ibid., III, P55 and schol., p. 182.

5. Ibid., IV, P53, p. 227.

6. Ibid., IV, P54, schol., p. 228.

7. Ibid.

8. Ibid., IV, P53, dem., p. 228. On the difference between "humility as a virtue" and "humility as a vice," see Descartes as well: René Descartes, *The Passions of the Soul*, III, arts. 155 and 159, in *The Philosophical Writings of Descartes*, trans. J. Cottingham, R. Stoothoff, and D. Murdoch, Cambridge University Press, 1985–91.

9. Aristotle, *Nicomachean Ethics*, IV, 9.

10. Spinoza, *The Ethics*, III, def. 29 of the affects, p. 193.

11. Ibid., exp. of def. 28 of the affects.

12. We might say about humility, *mutatis mutandis*, what Alexandre Matheron writes about repentance: "This true knowledge of evil makes us sensitive to liberating truth" (Alexandre Matheron, *Le Christ et le salut des ignorants chez Spinoza*, Aubier-Montaigne, 1971, p. 113). Humility, even as a sadness, can help a person lose his fondness for himself; it is an antidote to narcissism. In fact, it is at least as much a part of the prophetic (Spinoza, *The Ethics*, IV, P54, schol.) and evangelical (Christ's "gentle and humble of heart," Matthew 11:29) message as repentance; and, as we know, Spinoza sees himself as the express heir to this message.

13. "The greater the sadness, the greater is the part of the man's power of acting to which it is necessarily opposed. Therefore, the greater the sadness, the greater the power of acting with which the man will strive to remove the sadness" (Spinoza, *The Ethics*, III, P37, schol., p. 173). There is material here for a "dynamic of resistance"; see Laurent Bove, "Spinoza et la question de la résistance," *L'enseignement philosophique*, no. 5 (May-June 1993).

14. Spinoza, *The Ethics*, IV, P52, schol., p. 227.

15. Immanuel Kant, *The Metaphysical Principles of Virtue*, trans. James W. Ellington, Library of Liberal Arts, Bobbs-Merrill, 1964, Introduction to the First Part of the Elements of Ethics, p. 81.

16. Ibid., ch. 2, § 11, pp. 97–98.

17. Ibid., § 12, p. 99.

18. Ibid.

19. Ibid., Casuistical Questions, p. 99.

20. Ibid., § 11, p. 97.

21. And no longer with the law: ibid., § 11, p. 98.

22. Ibid., Casuistical Questions, p. 100.

23. Spinoza, *The Ethics*, III, def. 29 of the affects, exp., p. 193. See also IV, XXII (as well as Descartes's *The Passions of the Soul*, art. 159).

24. Friedrich Nietzsche, *The Twilight of the Idols*, trans. Anthony M. Ludovici, Maxims and Missiles, aph. 31, in *The Complete Works of Friedrich Nietzsche*, ed. Oscar Levy, Russell & Russell, 1964, vol. 16, pp. 5–6.

25. René Descartes, *Passions of the Soul*, III, art. 155, vol. 1, p. 385; see also the condemnation of pride in art. 157. On humility in the Christian tradition, see Jean-Louis Chrétien's essay *L'humilité* in the journal *Autrement*, no. 8 (1992), pp. 37–52.

26. Spinoza, *The Ethics*, IV, P58, schol., p. 230.

27. Friedrich Nietzsche, *Beyond Good and Evil*, trans. Helen Zimmern, aph. 260, *Complete Works of Friedrich Nietzsche*, vol. 12, p. 229.

28. Ibid., p. 228.

29. Vladimir Jankélévitch, *Traité des vertus*, Champs-Flammarion, 1986, vol. 2, ch. 4 ("L'humilité et la modestie"), p. 286.

30. Ibid., p. 285.

31. Cited in *Vocabulaire de théologie biblique*, Editions du Cerf, 1971, s.v. "Humilité."

32. Jankélévitch, *Traité des vertus*, vol. 2, pp. 287 and 401, for example.

33. Ibid., p. 289.

34. Ibid., pp. 308–09.

12. SIMPLICITY

1. Angelus Silesius, *The Cherubic Pilgrim*, 289.

2. *Proverbs in Prose.*

3. Clément Rosset, *Le philosophe et les sortilèges*, Editions de Minuit, 1985, p. 52. See also *Le réel et son double*, Gallimard, 1984.

4. As Michel Dupuy points out in his article "Simplicité" in the *Dictionnaire de spiritualité ascétique et mystique*, ed. M. Viller, Beauchesne, 1990, vol. 14, p. 92.

5. Christian Bobin, *L'éloignement du monde*, Lettres Vives, 1993, p. 12.

6. Michel de Montaigne, *The Essays of Montaigne*, trans. George B. Ives, Harvard University Press, 1925, vol. 1, book 26, p. 226. This applies to ways of expressing oneself as well, indeed even more: "The way of speaking that I like is a simple and natural speech, the same on paper as on the lips; a style pithy, sinewy, brief, and concise, not so refined and smooth as vehement and quick" (p. 229).

7. Ibid., p. 230.

8. René Descartes, *Discourse on Method*, in *The Philosophical Writings of Descartes*, trans. J. Cottingham, R. Stoothoff, and D. Murdoch, Cambridge University Press, 1985–91, vol. 1, p. 147.

9. Fénelon, "Sur la simplicité," *Lettres et opuscules spirituels*, Bibliothèque de la Pléiade, 1983, vol. 1, p. 677.

10. Ibid., p. 683.

11. Ibid., p. 677.

12. Ibid., pp. 677 and 679.

13. Ibid., p. 686.

14. Vladimir Jankélévitch, *L'innocence et la méchanceté*, vol. 3 of *Traité des vertus*, Champs-Flammarion, 1986, pp. 404ff.

15. François La Rochefoucauld, *Maxims and Reflections*, trans. Leonard Tancock, Penguin, 1959, maxim 289, p. 75.

16. Matthew 6:26–28. See also Luke 12:22–27.

17. Bobin, *L'éloignement du monde*, p. 37.

18. Matthew 7:34.

19. Christian Bobin, *Eloge du rien*, Fata Morgana, 1990, p. 15.

13. TOLERANCE

1. Which doesn't mean it is true but simply that if it is false it must be possible to demonstrate that it is false (see Karl Popper's *The Logic of Scientific Discovery*); nor does it mean that it is only or entirely scientific (see Popper's *Unended Quest*, ch. 37) but simply that part of it eludes opinion—and tolerance as well.

2. François La Rochefoucauld, *Maxims and Reflections*, trans. Leonard Tancock, Penguin, 1959, maxim 19, p. 39.

3. Vladimir Jankélévitch, *Traité des vertus*, Champs-Flammarion, 1986, vol. 2, p. 92.

4. Karl Popper, *The Open Society and Its Enemies*, Routledge & Kegan Paul, 1966, vol. 1, p. 265.

5. John Rawls, *A Theory of Justice*, Belknap Press of Harvard University Press, 1971, p. 220.

6. Jankélévitch, *Traité des vertus*, vol. 2, p. 93.

7. Popper, *Open Society*, vol. 1, p. 265.

8. See Jankélévitch, *Traité des vertus*, vol. 2, p. 93.

9. Montesquieu, *The Spirit of Laws*, III, 1–9; Hannah Arendt, *The Origins of Totalitarianism*, Harcourt Brace Jovanovich, 1979, pp. 461ff. On Stalinism, see also my *Le mythe d'Icare*, PUF, 1994, ch. 2.

10. Alain, *Définitions*, in *Les arts et les dieux*, Bibliothèque de la Pléiade, p. 1095 (definition of tolerance).

11. Arendt, *Origins of Totalitarianism*, p. 474.

12. On these issues, which I can only outline here, see my *Valeur et vérité (Études cyniques)*, PUF, 1994.

13. Michel de Montaigne, *The Essays of Montaigne*, trans. George B. Ives, Harvard University Press, 1925, vol. 4, p. 248; Pierre Bayle, *De la tolérance (Commentaire philosophique sur ces paroles de Jésus-Christ "Contrains-les d'entrer")*, Presses Pocket, 1992, p. 189; Voltaire, *Philosophical Dictionary*, Penguin, 1988, p. 387. See also Voltaire's *Traité sur la tolérance*, esp. chs. 21, 22, 25. Of course, this idea remains completely topical: see Karl Popper, *Conjectures and Refutations*.

14. Voltaire, *Philosophical Dictionary*, p. 393. For the idea of tolerance in the eighteenth century, see Ernst Cassirer, *The Philosophy of the Enlightenment*, IV, 2.

15. Benedict de Spinoza, *A Theologico-Political Treatise*, in *The Chief Works of Benedict de Spinoza*, vol. 1, trans. R. H. M. Elwes, Dover Publications, 1995, esp. ch. 20; John Locke, *Letter on Toleration*.

16. Spinoza, *Theologico-Political Treatise*, p. 261.

17. Ibid., p. 263.

18. *Veritatis splendor (The Splendor of Truth)*, Encyclical Letter Addressed by the Supreme Pontiff Pope John Paul II, St. Paul Books & Media, 1993, pp. 77–78, 10, 118 (the italics are in the original).

19. Ibid., pp. 117, 35–37 (against autonomy), and 53 (against cultural and historical relativism).

20. Ibid., p. 135.

21. Ibid., p. 140 (italics in the original).

22. Ibid., p. 123.

23. Ibid., p. 142.

24. Condorcet, *Esquisse d'un tableau historique des progrès de l'esprit humain*, Vrin, 1970, p. 129.

25. André Lalande, *Vocabulaire technique et critique de la philosophie* of Lalande, 16th ed., PUF, 1968, pp. 1133–36, s.v. "Tolérance." The same kinds of reservations can also be found in Jankélévitch, *Traité des vertus*, pp. 89ff.

26. Jankélévitch, *Traité des vertus*, pp. 86 and 94.

27. F. Abauzit, in Lalande's *Vocabulaire*, p. 1134. Jankélévitch expresses much the same idea (*Traité des vertus*, p. 87).

28. Jankélévitch, *Traité des vertus*, pp. 101–02.

29. The expression *small virtue*, which I have used in reference to politeness, Jankélévitch uses in reference to tolerance (*Traité des vertus*, p. xx).

14. PURITY

1. Augustine, *The Confessions*, XI, 14.

2. Lucretius, *De Rerum Natura*, IV, 1075–81, Loeb Classical Library, Harvard University Press, 1982, p. 360.

3. Simone Weil, *Gravity and Grace*, trans. Emma Craufurd, Routledge & Kegan Paul, 1987, p. 56.

4. Friedrich Nietzsche, *Thus Spoke Zarathustra*, trans. Walter Kaufmann, Penguin, 1966, book 1, ch. 4.

5. Weil, *Gravity and Grace*, p. 58.

6. Ibid.

7. Immanuel Kant, *Religion within the Limits of Reason Alone*, trans. Theodore M. Greene and Hoyt H. Hudson, Open Court, 1934, p. 41.

8. Ibid. See also Immanuel Kant, *The Fundamental Principles of the Metaphysics of Morals*.

9. See Benedict de Spinoza, *The Ethics*, in *A Spinoza Reader: The Ethics and Other Works*, ed. and trans. Edwin Curley, Princeton University Press, 1994, III, def. 6 of the affects, p. 189: "Love is a joy, accompanied by the idea of an external cause." The person, therefore, who gets pleasure only from possessing another person does not love him: he only loves *possessing* another (he takes pleasure not in the idea that the other person exists but in the person's belonging to him), he loves only the pleasure that it affords him, and hence only loves himself. We are of course not to draw from this any condemnation of sexuality as such: see Alexandre Matheron's fine clarification, "Spinoza et la sexualité," *Anthropologie et politique au XVIIᵉ siècle (Etudes sur Spinoza)*, Vrin, 1986, pp. 201–30.

10. See ch. 18 on *erōs, philia*, and *agapē*. Let us recall that these three words signify *love* in Greek, but with three different meanings: *erōs* is lust or passionate love, *philia* is friendship, and *agapē* is selfless love of one's fellowman (translated in Latin as *caritas* and in French as *charité*).

11. Fénelon, "Sur le pur amour," *Lettres et opuscules spirituels*, XXIII, in *Oeuvres*, Bibliothèque de la Pléiade, 1983, vol. 1, pp. 656–71.

12. *De Diligendo Deo*, ch. 14, no. 28, cited in Vladimir Jankélévitch, *Traité des vertus*, Champs-Flammarion, 1986, vol. 2, p. 230.

13. *De Rerum Natura*, IV, 1058, p. 374. According to the Epicureans, pleasure is pure when it is not mixed with suffering, frustration, or anguish—which excludes passion.

14. Ibid., 1071 (*volgivaga Venere*).

15. As Montaigne puts it (Michel de Montaigne, *The Essays of Montaigne*, trans. John Florio, Modern Library, Random House, 1933, p. 764), but it is an expression that Lucretius would accept. See, for example, Lucretius, *De Rerum Natura*, IV, 1278. Similarly we find in Montaigne (Michel de Montaigne, *The Essays of Montaigne*, trans. George B. Ives, Harvard University Press, 1925, vol. 4, p. 175) the expression "conjugal friendship," which would make a disciple of Epicurus happy.

16. Spinoza, *The Ethics*, III, P35, dem. and schol.

17. Plato, *Phaedrus*, 237a–241d (Socrates' first speech).

18. Weil, *Gravity and Grace*, p. 58.

19. Ibid., pp. 58–59.

20. Ibid., p. 111.

21. Romans 14:14; Titus 1:15.

22. Weil, *Gravity and Grace*, p. 111.

23. Fénelon, *Lettres et opuscules*, pp. 672, 662.

24. Ibid., p. 663.

25. Again, this is an idea that can be found in Simone Weil and that sums up all the others; see Aimé Forest, "Simone Weil et l'idée de purification," and Georges Charot, "Simone Weil ou la rencontre de la pureté et de l'amour," in *Cahiers Simone Weil* (Sept. 1983). See also Weil, *Waiting for God*, trans. Emma Craufurd, G. P. Putnam's Sons, 1951.

26. Spinoza, *The Ethics*, V, P42, p. 264 (italics in original).

15. GENTLENESS

1. Denis Diderot, *Letter to Falconnet*, July 1767, cited in Charles Guyot, *Diderot par lui-même*, Seuil, 1957, p. 37.

2. As Tzvetan Todorov notes, in discussing morality and the experience of concentration camps, in Tzvetan Todorov, *Facing the Extreme*, trans. Arthur Denner and Abigail Pollak, Metropolitan Books, 1996, pp. 293–94.

3. Ibid., p. 294.

4. Etty Hillesum, *An Interrupted Life: The Diaries of Etty Hillesum*, trans. Arnold J. Pomerans, Pantheon, 1983, p. 165.

5. Todorov, *Facing the Extreme*, p. 294. "Needless to say," Todorov adds, "when I speak of the couple I am not speaking of the heterosexual paradigm only or of a relationship that is necessarily stable or permanent." Humanity is sexual, and bisexual; but this difference affects each of us, as we know, and of course imposes no particular sexual behavior.

6. Claude Lévi-Strauss, *Tristes tropiques*, Plon, 1973, p. 473.

7. On Swami Prajnanpad (1891–1974), one of the spiritual masters of our time, see S. Prakash, *L'expérience de l'unité*, L'originel, 1986.

8. See, for example, Simone Weil's *Waiting for God* (trans. Emma Craufurd, G. P. Putnam's Sons, 1951), as well as *Gravity and Grace* (trans. Emma Craufurd, Routledge & Kegan Paul, 1987).

9. Benedict de Spinoza, *The Ethics*, IV, P37, schol. 1, in *A Spinoza Reader: The Ethics and Other Works*, ed. and trans. Edwin Curley, Princeton University Press, 1994, p. 218.

10. Michel de Montaigne, *The Essays of Montaigne*, II, 11.

11. Jean-Jacques Rousseau, *Discourse on Inequality*, in *The First and Second Discourses and the Foundations of Inequality among Men*, ed. and trans. Victor Gourevitch, Harper & Row, 1985, p. 163. Jean Starobinski notes quite rightly that this is an implicit reference to Matthew 7:12 and Luke 6:31.

12. Rousseau, *Discourse on Inequality*, p. 163. According to Rousseau, this maxim is inspired by pity, which might be possible, but pity cannot be confused with gentleness: pity presupposes another person's suffering while gentleness, if it anticipates someone's suffering, strives to avoid it. It is like an objectless compassion and thereby freed of suffering (a nonreactive compassion).

13. Jacqueline de Romilly, *La douceur dans la pensée grecque*, Les Belles Lettres, 1979, p. 38.

14. Ibid., p. 1.

15. Plato prefers justice and knowledge. See de Romilly's fruitful and subtle analyses, pp. 176ff. Epicurus, as usual, sides with Aristotle; on Epicurus's "legendary gentleness," see André-Jean Voelke, *Les rapports avec autrui dans la philosophie grecque d'Aristote à Panétius*, Vrin, 1961, pp. 98–101, as well as Epicurus, *Sentence Vaticane* 36 (attributed to Hermarque).

16. Aristotle, *Eudemian Ethics*, II, 3, 1220b35ff. and III, 3, 1231b5–27. See also, of course, Aristotle, *Nicomachean Ethics*, IV, 5, 1125b26–1126b9, in *The Basic Works of Aristotle*, ed. Richard McKeon, Random House, 1941, pp. 995–96, as well as de Romilly's commentary, *La douceur*, pp. 189–96.

17. de Romilly, *La douceur*, p. 195, and as Aristotle also acknowledges (Aristotle, *Nicomachean Ethics*, IV, 5, 1126a2, p. 996).

18. Aristotle, *Nicomachean Ethics*, IV, 5, 1125b32–34, p. 996.

19. Ibid., 1126a7–8, p. 996.

20. As opposed to the teachings of the Gospels, whose extreme radicalism we often tend to forget: "You have heard it was said 'An eye for an eye and a tooth for a tooth.' But I say unto you, Do not resist one who is evil. But if any one strikes you on the right cheek, turn to him the other also; and if any one would sue you and take your coat, let him have your cloak as well" (Matthew 5:38–40).

21. Weil, *Gravity and Grace*, p. 77.

22. Ibid.

23. Marcel Conche, *Le fondement de la morale*, PUF, 1993, pp. 124–30. The quotation is on p. 130, n. 1.

24. Weil, *Gravity and Grace*, p. 78.

25. The third beatitude: Matthew 5:5.

16. GOOD FAITH

1. Compare a *theological* virtue, which has as its object God and which is faith in the Christian tradition.

2. This is indeed the first sentence of the first paragraph of the *Essays* (the marvelous foreword), usually translated as "Loe here a well-meaning Booke . . ."

3. François La Rochefoucauld, *Maximes et réflexions*, Le Livre de poche, 1965, p. 141.

4. François La Rochefoucauld, *Maxims*, trans. Leonard Tancock, Penguin, 1959, maxim 62, p. 53: "Sincerity is openness of heart. It is found in very few, and what is usually seen is subtle dissimulation designed to draw the confidence of others."

5. Michel de Montaigne, *The Essays of Montaigne*, trans. George B. Ives, Harvard University Press, 1925, vol. 3, p. 57.

6. Ibid.

7. Ibid.

8. Ibid., p. 58.

9. Aristotle, *Nicomachean Ethics*, IV, 7, 1127a13–1127b32, in *The Basic Works of Aristotle*, ed. Richard McKeon, Random House, 1941, pp. 998–99.

10. Ibid.; see also II, 7, 1108a19–22, and Aristotle, *Eudemian Ethics*, III, 7, 1233b38–1234a4.

11. Aristotle, *Nicomachean Ethics*, IV, 7, 1127a23–25, p. 998.

12. Ibid., IV, 1127a29–30, p. 999.

13. Ibid., esp. IV, 1127b22–32, pp. 999–1000.

14. Regarding the self-love of the virtuous man (as opposed to the egoism of the wicked), see Aristotle, *Nicomachean Ethics*, IX, 4, 1166a–1166b, pp. 1081–82 and IX, 7–8, 1168a–1169b, pp. 1086–87.

15. Aristotle, *Nicomachean Ethics*, IV, 3, 1124b27–30, p. 994. This kind of pride, which is really a form of magnanimity or nobility of soul, has almost disappeared from the contemporary vocabulary of ethics. Beyond what can be learned from Aristotle, a relatively recent literary example can be found in *The Three Musketeers*, where pride is the virtue that characterizes Athos (this is even clearer in *Twenty Years After* and *The Viscount of Bragelonne*), just as prudence characterizes d'Artagnan, politeness Aramis, and courage—though common, of course, to all of them—Porthos.

16. See Aristotle, *Nicomachean Ethics*, IV, 3, 1123b15–1124a19, p. 992.

17. Benedict de Spinoza, *The Ethics*, in *A Spinoza Reader: The Ethics and Other Works*, ed. and trans. Edwin Curley, Princeton University Press, 1994, IV, P72, p. 237.

18. Ibid., dem.

19. Ibid., IV, P72, schol., p. 238.

20. Ibid., p. 211.

21. Ibid., III, def. 1 of the affects, and passim.

22. Ibid., IV, P2–P4, esp. the cor. of P4, p. 203.

23. Ibid., IV, P72, p. 237.

24. Benedict de Spinoza, *A Political Treatise*, in *The Chief Works of Benedict de Spinoza*, vol. 1, trans. R. H. M. Elwes, Dover Publications, 1951, p. 296.

25. Benedict de Spinoza, *The Ethics*, III, P9, schol. and passim.

26. Ibid., III, def. 1 of the affects, p. 188.

27. The term I prefer for Spinoza's *misericordia*, though Curley translates it as pity; see *The Ethics*, III, def. 24 of the affects, and ch. 8, pp. 108–10.

28. Benedict de Spinoza, *A Theologico-Political Treatise*, in *The Chief Works of Benedict de Spinoza*, vol. 1, trans. R. H. M. Elwes, Dover Publications, 1995, ch. 14.

29. Spinoza, *The Ethics*, IV, P20, dem. and schol., pp. 210–11.

30. Ibid., IV, P66, dem., schol., and cor., p. 235.

31. Immanuel Kant, *The Metaphysical Principles of Virtue*, trans. James W. Ellington, Library of Liberal Arts, Bobbs-Merrill, 1964, § 9, pp. 90–91; Immanuel Kant, *On a Supposed Right to Tell Lies from Benevolent Motives*, in *Kant's Critique of Practical Reason and Other Works on the Theory of Ethics*, trans. Thomas Kingsmill Abbott, Longmans, Green, 1948, pp. 361–66.

32. Kant, *On a Supposed Right to Tell Lies from Benevolent Motives*, pp. 364–65.

33. Cited by Kant in *On a Supposed Right*, p. 361.

34. Ibid., p. 363. See also Kant, *The Metaphysical Principles of Virtue*, § 9, pp. 91–92.

35. Kant, *The Metaphysical Principles of Virtue*, § 9, p. 91.

36. Vladimir Jankélévitch, *Traité des vertus*, Champs-Flammarion, 1986, vol. 2, p. 283.

37. Ibid., pp. 249–50.

38. Ibid.

39. Ibid., p. 249.

40. Ibid., p. 251.

41. Jean-Paul Sartre, *Being and Nothingness*, trans. Hazel E. Barnes, Philosophical Library, 1956, pp. 47–60. See also Marc Wetzel's fine presentation of this difficult text, *Sartre, La mauvaise foi*, Hatier, 1985.

42. Sartre, *Being and Nothingness*, p. 70.

43. Ibid., p. 70 n. 9.

44. Blaise Pascal, *Pensées*, trans. A. J. Krailsheimer, Penguin, 1966, no. 926, p. 295.

45. Spinoza, *The Ethics*, V, P32 and cor., p. 259; P24, p. 257.

46. Sigmund Freud, Letter to James J. Putnam, Mar. 30, 1914; *Analysis Terminable and Interminable*, in *The Standard Edition of the Complete Psychological Works of Sigmund Freud*, trans. and ed. James Strachey, Hogarth Press, 1971, vol. 23, p. 248.

47. Alain, *Définitions,* in *Les arts et les dieux*, Bibliothèque de la Pléiade, p. 1056 (definition of spirit).

48. Spinoza, *The Ethics*, III, nn. of prop. 9 and 39.

17. HUMOR

1. Vladimir Jankélévitch, *Traité des vertus*, Champs-Flammarion, 1986, vol. 2, p. 338.

2. See ch. 16, p. 209 and n. 47.

3. Michel de Montaigne, *The Essays of Montaigne*, trans. George B. Ives, Harvard University Press, 1925, vol. 2, p. 7 (Montaigne derives this opposition from Juvenal).

4. Ibid.

5. Ibid.

6. Ibid.

7. Benedict de Spinoza, *A Political Treatise*, in *The Chief Works of Benedict de Spinoza*, vol. 1, trans. R. H. M. Elwes, Dover Publications, 1951, p. 288: "I have laboured care-

fully, not to mock, lament, or execrate, but to understand human actions." In *The Ethics*, on the other hand, laughter and joking are hailed as "pure joy," but because they are expressly distinguished from mockery (Benedict de Spinoza, *The Ethics*, IV, P45, schol., in *A Spinoza Reader: The Ethics and Other Works*, ed. and trans. Edwin Curley, Princeton University Press, 1994, p. 224). See also Benedict de Spinoza, *The Short Treatise*, II, ch. 1, § 1 and § 2.

8. Søren Kierkegaard, *Concluding Unscientific Postscript to Philosophical Fragments*, trans. D. F. Swenson, Princeton University Press, 1974, p. 449.

9. Rainer Maria Rilke, *Letters to a Young Poet*, trans. M. D. Herter Norton, W. W. Norton.

10. Søren Kierkegaard, *Concluding Unscientific Postscript to Philosophical Fragments*, trans. H. V. Hong and E. H. Hong, Princeton University Press, 1992, vol. 1, p. 553.

11. As noted by Theodor Lipps and cited by Luigi Pirandello in *On Humor*.

12. Cf. Pirandello: "As a rhetorical figure irony presupposes a sham that is completely contrary to the nature of real humor. This rhetorical figure implies a contradiction, a fictitious contradiction, between what we say and what we want to imply. In humor the contradiction is never fictitious but essential."

13. "L'illusion, la vérité, et la moquette de Woody Allen," *Valeur et vérité*, PUF, 1994, p. 16.

14. Spinoza, *A Political Treatise*, p. 288.

15. Sigmund Freud, *Humour*, in *The Standard Edition of the Complete Psychological Works of Sigmund Freud*, trans. and ed. James Strachey, Hogarth Press, 1964, vol. 21, p. 162.

16. Ibid., pp. 164 and 166.

17. Ibid., p. 162.

18. Ibid., p. 163.

19. Ibid., p. 166.

20. Ibid., p. 163.

21. Ibid., p. 161.

22. Ibid., p. 162.

23. Ibid.

24. Christian Bobin, *L'éloignement du monde*, Lettres vives, 1993, pp. 50–51.

25. The quotation is from Noguez's excellent article on the structure of humorous language, *Revue d'esthétique*, vol. 22 (1969), pp. 51–52. See also R. Escarpit, *L'humour*, PUF, 1972, pp. 114–17, as well as Vladimir Jankélévitch, *L'ironie*, Champs-Flammarion, 1991, pp. 171–72. Usage, Jankélévitch notes, "gives to the word *humor* a

nuance of kindness and affectionate good nature that it sometimes does not give to the ironist. Scathing irony has a certain malevolence and something resembling a bitter nastiness that excludes indulgence; irony is sometimes spiteful, scornful, and aggressive. Humor, on the other hand, is not without sympathy. It is really the 'smile of reason' and not the reproach of hard sarcasm. While misanthropic irony maintains a polemical attitude with regard to men, humor commiserates with the thing it makes fun of; it is secretly an accomplice of ridiculousness and feels in league with it." The same individual, let me say again, can of course mix humor and irony, but they nevertheless remain different. This is what Pirandello stresses in *On Humor:* "Even when used to beneficial ends, one cannot disassociate from irony the idea of something *mocking* and *caustic.* Certainly humorous writers can be mocking and caustic, but their humor does not consist of this caustic mockery."

26. Kierkegaard, *Concluding Unscientific Postscript,* trans. Hong and Hong, vol. 1, p. 553.

27. Woody Allen, *Without Feathers,* Warner Books, 1975, p. 109.

28. Ibid., p. 10.

29. Woody Allen, *Getting Even,* Vintage, 1971, p. 25.

30. Ernest Jones, *The Life and Work of Sigmund Freud,* Basic Books, 1957, vol. 3, p. 465.

31. Kierkegaard, *Concluding Unscientific Postscript,* p. 259.

32. Ibid., p. 440.

33. Ibid., pp. 259, 438.

34. Allen, *Without Feathers,* p. 8.

18. LOVE

1. See Immanuel Kant's "Of the Motives of Pure Practical Reason," in *Critique of Practical Reason,* and esp. "Concerning the Love of Mankind," *The Metaphysical Principles of Virtue,* trans. James W. Ellington, Library of Liberal Arts, Bobbs-Merrill, 1964: "Love is a matter of sensation, not of willing; and I cannot love because I would, still less because I should (being obligated to love). Hence a duty to love is nonexistent" (p. 60).

2. In *The Metaphysical Principles of Virtue,* Kant shows the moral law takes the form of *duty* only for "men as rational natural beings": "The latter are unholy enough to be influenced by pleasure to transgress the moral law, although they recognize its authority. And even when they do obey it, they do so without gladness (in conflict with their inclinations); the constraint really consists in this" (p. 36). Also: "A duty is a constraint to an end that is not gladly adopted" (p. 43).

3. Friedrich Nietzsche, *Beyond Good and Evil,* trans. Helen Zimmern, aph. 153, in *The Complete Works of Friedrich Nietzsche,* vol. 12, ed. Oscar Levy, Russell & Russell, 1964, p. 98.

4. Immanuel Kant, "Of the Motives of Pure Practical Reason," in *Kant's Critique of Practical Reason and Other Works on the Theory of Ethics*, trans. Thomas Kingsmill Abbott, Longmans, Green, 1948, p. 178.

5. Kant, *The Metaphysical Principles of Virtue*, p. 60.

6. Kant, "Of the Motives of Pure Practical Reason," p. 176.

7. Ibid.

8. As Augustine puts it felicitously in a phrase that has nothing to do with laxness but, on the contrary, is the most demanding, as well as the most liberating, advice possible (Commentary on 1 John).

9. Matthew 5:17.

10. Benedict de Spinoza, *A Theologico-Political Treatise*, in *The Chief Works of Benedict de Spinoza*, vol. 1, trans. R. H. M. Elwes, Dover, 1951, ch. 4, p. 65 ("He doubtless taught His doctrines as eternal truths, and did not lay them down as laws, thus freeing the minds of His hearers from the bondage of that law which He further confirmed and established"). On the difference between Nietzsche and Spinoza on this point, see my contribution to *Pourquoi nous ne sommes pas nietzschéens*, ed. L. Ferry and A. Renaut, Grasset, 1991, esp. pp. 65–68, as well as my "Nietzsche et Spinoza," in *De Sils-Maria à Jérusalem: Les intellectuels juifs et Nietzsche*, ed. D. Bourel and J. Le Rider, Cerf, 1991, pp. 47–66.

11. On the difference between morality and ethics (and on morality as a *semblance of love*), see my essay "Morale ou éthique?" in *Valeur et vérité*, PUF, 1994, pp. 183–205.

12. Blaise Pascal, *Pensées*; David Hume, *Treatise of Human Nature*, book 3, part one, sects. 1 and 2, and *An Enquiry concerning the Principles of Morals*, in *Enquiries concerning Human Understanding and concerning the Principles of Morals*, Clarendon Press, 1975, esp. app. 1; Henri-Louis Bergson, *The Two Sources of Morality and Religion*. Aristotle, before them, already noted: "That which moves therefore is a single faculty and the faculty of appetite," and "mind is never found producing movement without appetite" (Aristotle, *De Anima*, III, ch. 10, 433a21–24, in *The Basic Works of Aristotle*, ed. Richard McKeon, Random House, 1941, p. 598). This is one of the many points on which Epicurus and Lucretius would agree with Aristotle.

13. Plato, *The Symposium*, 198c–199b, pp. 550–51.

14. See, for example, Plato, *Symposium*, 177d, p. 532 ("I claim that love is the one thing in the world I understand"), 198d, p. 550 ("to claim a special knowledge of the subject"), 212b ("I cultivate and worship all the elements of Love myself"). See also Plato, *Lysis*, 204c, p. 146.

15. Plato, *Symposium*, 178a–197e, pp. 532–50. For a wordy but suggestive discussion of *The Symposium*, see Jacques Lacan's *Le transfert* (*Séminaire, VIII*), Seuil, 1991, esp. pp. 29–195. On the cosmological role of love in Hesiod, Parmenides, and Empedocles, see Aristotle's *Metaphysics*, A, 4, 884b23–985a10 (*Basic Works*, pp. 695–97). See also the surprising "remake" of *The Symposium* (based, in part, on the theses

of Francesco Alberoni, Boris Cyrulnik, Eric Fuchs, and Jacques Lacan), Hubert Aupetit and Catherine Tobin's unclassifiable and stimulating *L'amour déboussolé*, Editions François Bourin, 1993.

16. Plato, *Symposium*, 189a–193e, pp. 542–46.

17. Léon Robin, *Le banquet*, Les Belles Lettres, 1992, pp. lix–lxiii.

18. Hume, *An Enquiry concerning Human Understanding*, sect. X.

19. Lucretius, *De Rerum Natura*, 4, 1105–12, trans. W. H. D. Rouse, Loeb Classical Library, Harvard University Press, 1982, p. 363.

20. Ibid., 4, 1133–34, p. 365.

21. Plato, *Symposium*, 199b, p. 551.

22. Ibid., 199d–200b, pp. 551–52. According to Plato, this is also true of friendship (*philia*): *Lysis*, 221d–e.

23. Ibid., 201b, p. 553.

24. Ibid., 200e, p. 553.

25. Ibid.

26. Plotinus, *The Enneads*, III, 5, trans. Stephen MacKenna, Faber and Faber, 1956, p. 197. For Plotinus's theory of love and its relation to Plato's, see P. Hadot's introduction to his translation of treatise 50 (Cerf, 1990) and his *Plotin ou la simplicité du regard*, Etudes augustiniennes, 1989, ch. 4, as well as Jean-Louis Chrétien's meditation on "l'amour du neutre" in *La voix nue*, Editions de Minuit, 1990, pp. 329ff.

27. Plato, *Symposium*, 206e, p. 558.

28. Plato, *Phaedrus*, 251d, p. 498.

29. Plato, *Symposium*, 200a–201c and 204a–206a.

30. Lacan, *Le transfert*, pp. 29–195.

31. Plato, *Symposium*, 206b–207a, pp. 558–59.

32. Ibid., 207a–d, p. 559.

33. Ibid., 207d–208e, p. 559–60.

34. Ibid., 208e–209e, pp. 560–61.

35. Ibid., 210a.

36. On love as a longing for death, see Léon Robin, *La théorie platonicienne de l'amour*, PUF, 1964, p. 182. On the beautiful as a manifestation of the good, see p. 188.

37. See Socrates' first speech in Plato, *Phaedrus* (237–41). His second speech (244–57) reaches the same religious or idealist inspiration as the *Symposium* does but by other means (through nostalgia rather than hope). For a comparison of the two dialogues (along with the *Lysis*), see Robin's *La théorie platonicienne de l'amour*, ch. 1.

38. Plato, *Phaedrus*, 241d, p. 488.

39. Transference, in the Freudian sense, might point to the meaning, specifically, of Alcibiades' speech (212–22), or rather Socrates' "interpretation" of it, which is in turn interpreted by Lacan, *Le transfert*, pp. 179–213; see also p. 460.

40. Plato, *Symposium*, 200e, p. 552.

41. Denis de Rougemont, *Love in the Western World*, trans. Montgomery Belgion, Pantheon, 1956, I, 9, p. 45.

42. René Allendy, *L'amour*, Denoël, 1962, p. 144.

43. *Stendhal: On Love*, trans. H. B. V. under the direction of C. K. Scott-Moncrieff, Doubleday-Anchor, 1957 (esp. chs. 2–12 and note to ch. 15); André Breton, *L'amour fou*, Gallimard, 1971.

44. de Rougement, *Love in the Western World*, I, 11, pp. 51–52: "European romanticism may be compared to a man for whom sufferings, and especially the sufferings of love, are a privileged mode of understanding."

45. Ibid., p. 45.

46. Richard Wagner, *Tristan and Isolde*, cited by de Rougemont, p. 50.

47. Plato, *Phaedrus*, 64, pp. 46–47. On the absence of being and the love of death in Plato, see my *Vivre*, PUF, 1988, ch. 4, pp. 21–29.

48. Marcel Proust, *Remembrance of Things Past*, trans. C. K. Scott-Moncrieff, Random, 1981, p. 425.

49. Ibid., p. 516. See also Stendhal, *Stendhal: On Love*, p. 16: "If you are deserted, crystallization starts again."

50. de Rougement, *Love in the Western World*, I, 8, pp. 41–42.

51. Ibid., I, 11, p. 53.

52. Ibid., I, 9, p. 46. Similarly in Plato, "love is a kind of death" or tends to be confused with "the desire for death" (Robin, *La théorie platonicienne de l'amour*, p. 182).

53. *The Romance of Tristan and Iseult*, as retold by Joseph Bédier, trans. Hilaire Belloc and completed by Paul Rosenfeld, Pantheon, 1945.

54. Clément Rosset, *Le principe de cruauté*, Editions de Minuit, 1988, p. 54.

55. Spinoza, *The Ethics*, in *A Spinoza Reader: The Ethics and Other Works*, ed. and trans. Edwin Curley, Princeton University Press, 1994, IV, P21.

56. Being happy, for Plato as for anyone else, is having what we desire (Plato, *Symposium*, 204e–205a).

57. Ibid., 200e.

58. Ibid., 200b–e.

59. Jean-Paul Sartre, *Being and Nothingness*, trans. Hazel E. Barnes, Philosophical Library, 1956, p. 575.

60. Ibid., p. 397.

61. See my *Une éducation philosophique*, PUF, 1989, pp. 350–53.

62. Spinoza, *The Ethics*, defs. of the affects, XII (with the exp. for XIII), and esp. IV, P47, with dem. and schol.

63. Plato, *Symposium*, 199d–e.

64. Ibid., 200d.

65. Ibid., 200d–e.

66. See Aristotle, *Nicomachean Ethics*, VIII and IX. The quotes are taken from VIII, 8, 1159a25–34, in *Basic Works*, p. 1067. See also the *Eudemian Ethics*, VII, and *Magna Moralia*, II, 11–16. On friendship in antiquity, see Jean-Claude Fraisse's *Philia: La notion d'amitié dans la philosophie antique*, Vrin, 1984 (containing a long chapter on Aristotle, pp. 189–286) as well as André-Jean Voelke's *Les rapports avec autrui dans la philosophie grecque d'Aristote à Panétius*, Vrin, 1961. Finally, let us also point out the suggestive pages, unfortunately few in number, that Pierre Aubenque devotes to friendship in Aristotle, in the appendix to *La prudence chez Aristote*, PUF, 1963 (recently reprinted in the Quadrige series).

67. Spinoza, *The Ethics*, III, schol. of P9 and defs. of the affects, I.

68. Ibid., III, P6–P13, with dem. and schol., and the general def. of the affects, with exp. I will not reiterate what I discuss in "Spinoza contre les herméneutes," *Une éducation philosophique*, pp. 245ff.

69. Spinoza, *The Ethics*, III, P6–P3, and defs. of the affects, VI, with exp.

70. Ibid., III, general def. of the affects, pp. 196–97.

71. Ibid., III, P59, schol.

72. Especially, according to Denis de Rougemont, with European languages; see *Les mythes de l'amour*, NRF, 1978, pp. 15–16. While we are on the subject of linguistic considerations, let us note in passing, for purists, that the plural of the French word *amour* can be either masculine or feminine ("the usage is not set," notes Grevisse; "the masculine is always allowed," we are reminded by Hanse) and ordinarily remains "masculine in the singular as in the plural, in general usage" (V. Thomas, *Dictionnaire des difficultés de la langue française*, Larousse, 1976). The feminine plural, which always seems studied and often emphatic, is hardly used anymore except to designate romantic relationships.

73. *Stendhal: On Love*, p. 6.

74. Spinoza, *The Ethics*, III, defs. of the affects, VI, p. 189.

75. Plato, *Symposium*, 204d–e.

76. Spinoza, *The Ethics*, III, P41 and schol.

77. Ibid., III, P58 and P59, with dem. and schol. See also V, P40.

78. Ibid., III, defs. of the affects, VI, exp., pp. 189–90; the comments in brackets are mine. Compare with Descartes's *Treatise on the Passions*, II, arts. 79 and 80.

79. See Spinoza, *The Ethics*, III, P19 and dem. See also P21.

80. Ibid., I, A3 and P28.

81. Ibid., I, A4.

82. Aristotle, *Nicomachean Ethics*, VIII, 8, 1159a27–33, p. 1067. See also VIII, 12, 1161b26 and especially IX, 4, 1166a7–9: we define a friend "as one who wishes his friend to exist and live, for his sake; which mothers do to their children . . . or one who grieves and rejoices with his friend; and this too is found in mothers most of all."

83. Ibid., VIII, 12, 1162a15–33, p. 1073.

84. Ibid., VIII, 12, 1161b16–1162a15. See also Aristotle, *Eudemian Ethics*, VII, 10, 1242a23–b (in *The Complete Works of Aristotle*, vol. 2, ed. Jonathan Barnes, Bollingen Series 71, Princeton University Press, p. 1969), where Aristotle shows that "household is a kind of friendship" and even that "in the household first we have the sources and springs of friendship, of political organization, and of justice."

85. Aristotle, *Nicomachean Ethics*, VIII, 5, 1157a6–15 and IX, 1, 1164a2–13.

86. Ibid., VIII, 4, 1156b6–35, p. 1061.

87. Ibid., VIII, 2, 1155b27–31, pp. 1059–60: "of the love of lifeless objects we do not use the word 'friendship'; for it is not mutual love, nor is there a wishing of good to the other (for it would surely be ridiculous to wish wine well; if one wishes anything for it, it is that it may keep, so that one may have it oneself); but to a friend we say we ought to wish what is good for his sake." According to Aristotle, there can be no friendship toward an animal (ibid., VIII, 11, 1161b2–3) or toward the gods (ibid., VIII, 9). See also Aristotle, *Magna Moralia*, II, 11, 1208b28–32 (in *Complete Works*, vol. 2, p. 1913): "For there is, people think, a friendship toward god and toward things without life, but here they are wrong. For friendship, we maintain, exists only where there can be a return of affection, but friendship toward god does not admit of love being returned, nor at all of loving. For it would be strange if one were to say that he loved Zeus." This is a point on which Thomas Aquinas does not agree with Aristotle: "Charity," he writes in *Summa Theologica*, "is the friendship of man for God" (*The "Summa Theologica" of St. Thomas Aquinas*, trans. Fathers of the English Dominican Province, R. & T. Washbourne, 1915, 2nd number, IIa–IIae, quest. 23, art. 1, p. 264). The reason, of course, is that a "reciprocity of love," as Aquinas puts it, is possible with his kind of God but was not with Zeus. Let us note, however, that even in Aristotle the requirement of reciprocity is not always an absolute precondition to friendship, as is clear from the example of mothers, who love their newborn children without being loved in return and who continue to love them even when they are

obliged to abandon them to the permanent care of nurses or adopted mothers and the children do not know them or love them in return. Which proves, for Aristotle, that friendship lies in "loving rather than in being loved" (Aristotle, *Nicomachean Ethics*, VIII, 8, 1159a28–32, p. 1067; see also Aristotle, *Eudemian Ethics*, VII, 5, 1239a34–40).

88. See, for example, Aristotle, *Nicomachean Ethics*, VIII, 8, 1159a25–28.

89. Ibid., VIII, 2, 1155b–1156a5. Yet goodwill can be unrequited without ceasing to be a *philia* (for example, a mother's love for her newborn): see Aristotle, *Nicomachean Ethics*, VIII, 7, 1159a27–33.

90. Ibid., IX, 12, 1171b29–1172a8. See also Aristotle, *Politics*, III, 9, 1280b39, in *Basic Works*, p. 1189: "the will to live together is friendship."

91. See, for example, Aristotle, *Eudemian Ethics*, VII, 2, 1237a30–b27, in *Complete Works*, p. 1960: "active loving is mutual choice with pleasure in each other's acquaintance. . . . For friendship seems something stable. . . . There is no stable friendship without confidence, but confidence needs time."

92. I am borrowing this expression from Denis de Rougemont (who, of course, contrasts it, as I do, with passion, in *Love in the Western World*, VII), but without betraying Aristotle's meaning: "it is better to love than to be loved. For to love is a pleasurable activity and a good, whereas from being loved there results no activity to the object of the love" (Aristotle, *Magna Moralia* II, 11, 1210b6–8, p. 1916). On love as an activity in Aristotle, see also Voelke, *Les rapports avec autrui*, p. 33.

93. Aristotle, *Nicomachean Ethics*, VIII, 12, 1162a16–33, p. 1073. As R. Flacelière notes, Aristotle, "who married twice, and quite happily," has thereby "rehabilitated conjugal love in the eyes of philosophers by explicitly placing it in the *philia* category, the road to virtue (*aretē*)" (*L'amour en Grèce*, Hachette, 1961, pp. 198–99) (Etienne Gilson, *Le thomisme*, Vrin, 1979, p. 347).

94. Aristotle, *Eudemian Ethics*, VII, 2, 1237a37–38, p. 1960.

95. Friedrich Nietzsche, *Thus Spoke Zarathustra*, trans. Walter Kaufmann, Penguin, 1966, pp. 70–71.

96. "Paroles d'amour," organized by Family Planning of Isère in Grenoble, 16–17, 1990. The concluding lecture, which I had been requested to deliver, contains an outline of some of the theses developed here (*Paroles d'amour*, Syros, 1991).

97. de Rougemont, *Love in the Western World*, VII, 4, p. 310.

98. Michel de Montaigne, *The Essays of Montaigne*, trans. George B. Ives, Harvard University Press, 1925, vol. 4, book 3, ch. 9, p. 173. On love and friendship, see his famous "On Friendship," book 1, ch. 28.

99. de Rougemont, *Love in the Western World*, I, 11, p. 50. The Latin is from Augustine's *Confessions*, III, 1 (*"Nondum amabam et amare amabam"*: "I did not love yet, and I loved to love").

100. de Rougemont, *Love in the Western World*, p. 51.

101. André Gide, *The Fruits of the Earth*, trans. Dorothy Bussy, Knopf, 1949, in *The André Gide Reader*, ed. David Littlejohn, Knopf, 1971, p. 173 ("Families, I hate you! closed circles round the hearth; doors fast shut; jealous guardians of happiness").

102. Alain, *Les sentiments familiaux*, in *Les passions et la sagesse*, Bibliothèque de la Pléiade, p. 335.

103. See Claude Lévi-Strauss, "Family," in *The View from Afar*, trans. Joachim Neugroschel and Phoebe Hoss, University of Chicago Press, 1992, p. 61: "But, in every case, the word of the Scripture, 'You will leave your father and your mother,' provides the golden rule (or, possibly, the iron rule) for the establishment of any society." Indeed, it is known that the prohibition of incest, because it obliges families to "intermingle, rather than each family, for its own benefit and with itself," is, according to Lévi-Strauss, the universal rule where we "can place the passage from nature to culture, from the animal condition to the human condition" (p. 53). See also Lévi-Strauss, *The Elementary Structures of Kinship*, particularly the introduction and chs. 1 and 2.

104. Aquinas, *Summa Theologica*, Ia–IIae, quest. 26, art. 4, pp. 316–17. See also Gilson, *Le thomisme*, pp. 335–44 (*The Christian Philosophy of St. Thomas Aquinas*, trans. L. K. Shook, Random House, 1956).

105. Gilson, *Le thomisme*, p. 340.

106. Aquinas, *Summa Theologica*, vol. 2, p. 317. See Aristotle's *Rhetoric*, II, 4, 1380b34–1381b2: "We may describe friendly feeling towards any one as wishing for him what you believe to be good things, not for your own sake but for his, and being inclined, so far as you can, to bring these things about (*Basic Works*, p. 1386). See also Aristotle, *Nicomachean Ethics*, IX, 4, 1166a2–3, p. 1081: "We define a friend as one who wishes and does what is good, or seems so, for the sake of his friend."

107. Aquinas, *Summa theologica*, Solutions, 1, p. 317. The same distinction can be found in the seventeenth century, in Francis of Sales: "We divide love into two kinds."

108. Ibid., Solutions, 3, p. 317.

109. Aristotle, *Nicomachean Ethic*, VIII, 7, 1159a27–33, p. 1067.

110. Ibid., VIII, 13, 1162b36–37, p. 1074.

111. On this *philautia* (self-love, in the sense not of egoism but of the wise person being a friend to himself), see Aristotle, *Nicomachean Ethics*, IX, 4 and 8.

112. Bernard of Clairvaux, *Traité de l'amour de Dieu*, ch. 7 (*Oeuvres mystiques de saint Bernard*, trans. A. Béguin, Seuil, 1992, p. 60). For a discussion of the degrees of love in Saint Bernard, see also Etienne Gilson, *La théologie mystique de saint Bernard*, Vrin, 1986, esp. pp. 53–61 and 108–12.

113. Bernard of Clairvaux, *Traité de l'amour de Dieu*, chs. 9 and 10. See also ch. 12.

NOTES

114. Aristotle, *Nicomachean Ethics*, chs. 1, 4, 7, and 10. See also Fraisse, *Philia*, pp. 257ff., as well as Voelke, *Les rapports avec autrui*, pp. 59–61, which shows that "friendship is not a virtue among others but the crowning virtue" (Aquinas, *Summa Theologica*, Ia–IIae, quest. 26, arts. 2–4, vol. 2, and IIa–IIae, quest. 23, vol. 3, pp. 159–167). See also Gilson, *Le thomisme*, pp. 335ff. (esp. p. 338 n. 5: "Friendship is not a passion but a virtue").

115. Emile Chartier [Alain, pseud.], *The Gods*, trans. Richard Pevear, New Directions, 1974, p. 181.

116. Aristotle, *Nicomachean Ethics*, VIII, 1, 1115a29–30.

117. Epicurus, *Epicurus: The Extant Remains*, trans. Cyril Bailey, Clarendon Press, 1926, XXIII, p. 351. G. Rodis Lewis is probably right to preserve the lesson of the manuscript (as is Jean Bollack); see *Epicure et son école*, Gallimard, 1975, p. 364, as well the *Actes du VIIIᵉ Congrès de l'Association Guillaume Budé*, Les Belles Lettres, 1969, pp. 223–26. On the relation between morality and friendship in Epicurus, see my *Vivre*, pp. 124–31.

118. See p. 4, above.

119. Aristotle, *Nicomachean Ethics*, IX, chs. 4 and 8; Bernard of Clairvaux, *Traité de l'amour de Dieu*, ch. 8. On the limits of this *philautie*, see also Vladimir Jankélévitch, *Traité des vertus*, Champs-Flammarion, 1986, vol. 2, pp. 179–206.

120. See, for example, letters 43 (to J. Osten) and 76 (to Albert Burgh). See also Spinoza, *A Theologico-Political Treatise*, ch. 14. On Spinoza's attitude toward Christ (for him he is neither God nor the son of God but the greatest of spiritual masters), see Sylvain Zac, *Spinoza et l'interprétation de l'Ecriture*, PUF, 1965, esp. pp. 190–99, and Alexandre Matheron, *Le Christ et le salut des ignorants chez Spinoza*, Aubier-Montaigne, 1971.

121. Matthew 5:43–44. See also Luke 6:27.

122. Paul is referring to Christ crucified, which is the very image of that love (1 Corinthians 1:23).

123. 1 John 4:8 and 4:16.

124. René Descartes, *Metaphysical Meditations*, III and V; Gottfried Wilhelm Leibniz, *Discourse on Metaphysics*, § 1, *Monadology* § 41. A good presentation of the problem can be found in Bernard Sève's *La question philosophique de l'existence de Dieu*, PUF, 1994, esp. ch. 1 for Descartes and Liebniz.

125. Aristotle, *Metaphysics*, XII, 7, esp. 1072b3, in *Basic Works*, p. 879.

126. Ibid., 7–9, pp. 879–85. See also Anders Nygren, *Agape and Eros*, trans. A. G. Hebert, Society for Promoting Christian Knowledge, 1937, pp. 140–58.

127. Plotinus, *The Enneads*, III, 5, p. 197.

128. Aristotle, *Magna Moralia* II, 11, 1208b30–32.

129. Aristotle, *Nicomachean Ethics*, IX, 4–9.

130. Spinoza, *The Ethics*, III, schol. of P11 and D2 of the affects. See also II, D2.

131. Ibid., III, P6ff. See also the first part of schol. of P11.

132. Ibid., V, P17, dem. and cor., p. 253.

133. Ibid., I, D6, P11 (with dem. and schol.) and cor. 2 of P20.

134. Ibid., I, P15 and P18, and V, P35.

135. Simone Weil, *Gravity and Grace*, trans. Emma Craufurd, Routledge & Kegan Paul, 1987, pp. 99–137.

136. Simone Weil, *Waiting for God*, trans. Emma Craufurd, G. P. Putman's Sons, 1951, p. 217.

137. Ibid., p. 216.

138. Chartier [Alain], *The Gods*, p. 149. On the relationship between Simone Weil and Alain and on their common rejection of pantheism and God as power, see my essay "Le Dieu et l'idole (Alain et Simone Weil face à Spinoza)" in *Spinoza au XXe siècle*, ed. O. Bloch, PUF, 1993, pp. 13–39 (the essay also appeared in *Cahiers Simone Weil*, vol. 14, no. 3 (Sept. 1991), pp. 213ff.

139. Weil, *Gravity and Grace*, p. 99.

140. Ibid., p. 62.

141. Weil, *Waiting for God*, p. 123.

142. Ibid.

143. Ibid., p. 146. This theme of creation-withdrawal, hence of the world as the absence of God, already existed, it seems, in the Jewish mystical tradition. On this subject, see Richard A. Freund's "La tradition mystique juive et Simone Weil," *Cahiers Simon Weil*, vol. 10, no. 3 (Sept. 1987). Apparently, this is a coincidence rather than an influence; it is known that Simone Weil, whose parents were secular and agnostic Jews, was harsh with regard to Judaism.

144. Weil, *Gravity and Grace*, p. 10, and *Waiting for God*, p. 141 ("It is a general and necessary law of nature to rule whatever one can"). The quotation from Thucydides comes from the *History of the Peloponnesian War*, V, 105.

145. Weil, *Waiting for God*, p. 144.

146. Weil, *Gravity and Grace*, p. 30. There is here an implicit reference to 1 Philippians 2:7 ("he was in the form of God . . . but emptied himself").

147. Weil, *Waiting for God*, p. 144.

148. Simone Weil, *La connaissance surnaturelle*, Gallimard, 1950, p. 267.

149. Weil, *Gravity and Grace*, p. 101.

150. Alain, *Cahiers de Lorient*, vol. 2, Gallimard, 1964, p. 313. See also my essay "Alain et Simone Weil face à Spinoza," as well as "L'existence et l'esprit selon Alain," *Bulletin de l'Association des Amis d'Alain*, no. 77 (June 1994).

151. Alain, *Entretiens au bord de la mer*, in *Les passions et la sagesse*, Bibliothèque de la Pléiade, pp. 1369–70.

152. One of the chapter titles of *Gravity and Grace*.

153. Alain, *Préliminaires à la mythologie*, in *Les arts et les dieux*, Bibliothèque de la Pléiade, pp. 1178–79.

154. See Alain, *Entretiens au bord de la mer*, p. 1368, and Chartier [Alain, pseud.], *The Gods*, p. 181.

155. See, for example, Fénelon, *Lettres et opuscules spirituels*, Bibliothèque de la Pléiade, vol. 1, 1983, pp. 656ff., as well as ch. 14, above.

156. Nygren, *Agape and Eros*, part 1, pp. 52ff., for example. See also, for the contrast to *erōs*, the chart on p. 171.

157. Montaigne, *Essays*, vol. 1, p. 251.

158. Nygren, *Agape and Eros*, part 1, p. 52.

159. Ibid., p. 53.

160. Ibid., p. 54.

161. de Rougement, *Love in the Western World*, VII, 4–5.

162. For Nygren's critique of these three (from a Lutheran perspective), see *Agape and Eros*, part 2, vol. 2, ch. 2 (on Augustine) and ch. 4 (on Aquinas and Bernard de Clairvaux), as well as the conclusion, where Nygren contrasts the Catholic *caritas* (which seems to contain "more Hellenistic Eros-love than primitive Christian Agape-love") with the Lutheran conception of love, which is "throughout determined by the Christian Agape motif" and where we look in vain "for any single feature of Eros" (pp. 521ff.). For a more positive presentation of the three Church fathers, see the three books by Etienne Gilson devoted to them: *Introduction à l'étude de saint Augustin*, Vrin, 1982; *La théologie mystique de saint Bernard*, Vrin, 1986; *Le thomisme* (*The Christian Philosophy of St. Thomas Aquinas*, trans. Shook).

163. 1 Corinthians 8:5.

164. "The love we exercise in hope certainly goes toward God, but it returns to us ... and as it goes this love is really love, but covetous and selfish love" (Francis of Sales, *Traité de l'amour de Dieu*, Bibliothèque de la Pléiade, II, 17, pp. 459–62).

165. See, for example, Francis of Sales, *Traité de l'amour de Dieu*, II, 22, p. 246: Charity "is a form of friendship and not a selfish love, for through charity we love God for the love of God himself" (and not, as with hope, for the goods we expect from it; see pp. 459–60). Or, as Francis of Sales also says, "sovereign love only exists in

charity; for in hope love is imperfect" (p. 462). Yet it is possible, according to Francis of Sales as well as to Bernard of Clairvaux to go from one to the other: "God, by a progress of ineffable ease, leads the soul out of the Egypt of sin, from love to love, as from one accommodation to another, until he has made him enter the Promised Land, I mean holy charity" (p. 476).

166. Aquinas, *Summa Theologica*, IIa–IIae, quest. 23, art. 1, p. 264.

167. Pseudo-Plato, *Définitions*, 412e, trans. Léon Robin, Bibliothèque de la Pléiade, vol. 2, p. 1395. See also Marcel Conche, *Vivre et philosopher*, pp. 199–201.

168. Indeed, it seems (though the writings that have been preserved do not contain any absolute evidence) that Epicurus wished to universalize friendship, which would have changed its nature and brought it closer to *philanthropia*. See G. Rodis-Lewis, *Epicure et son école*, Gallimard, 1975, pp. 362ff., and J. Salem, *Tel un dieu parmi les hommes: L'éthique d'Epicure*, Vrin, 1989, pp. 152–59.

169. Epicurus, *Sentences Vaticanes* 52.

170. Spinoza, *The Ethics*, III, schol. of P9.

171. Nietzsche, *Thus Spoke Zarathustra*, pp. 58–60.

172. Weil, *Gravity and Grace*, p. 29.

173. Ibid., p. 30. See also Gaston Kempfner's splendid little book (probably the best introduction to Simone Weil's thought) *La philosophie mystique de Simone Weil*, Editions du Vieux Colombier, 1960, or, in a more scholarly vein, Miklos Vetö's *La métaphysique religieuse de Simone Weil*, Vrin, 1971.

174. As Freud explains in what is certainly his greatest text, *Beyond the Pleasure Principle*.

175. Weil, *Waiting for God*, p. 217.

176. Weil, *Gravity and Grace*, p. 57.

177. Ibid., p. 56.

178. See Weil, *Gravity and Grace*, pp. 18–19, where Simone Weil comes very close to what I call despair. See also Weil, *Waiting for God* and Simone Weil, *Pensées sans ordre concernant l'amour de Dieu*, Gallimard, 1962, pp. 13–14.

179. Weil, *Waiting for God*, p. 217.

180. Weil, *Gravity and Grace*, p. 27.

181. Ibid., p. 101.

182. Ibid., p. 99.

183. Ibid., p. 30.

184. Weil, *Waiting for God*, p. 139.

185. *Diligere* is the Latin equivalent of *agapan*, just as *amare* is the equivalent of *philein*. Hence the old word *dilection*, now obsolete (but frequently used until the seventeenth century in religious or mystical texts), modeled on the Latin *dilectio*, which is sometimes used in the Vulgate to translate *agapē* (yet not as often as *caritas*, which is used ninety times as opposed to twenty-four times for *dilectio*). See *Dictionnaire de spiritualité,* vol. 2, Beauchesne, 1953, s.v. "Charité."

186. See Weil's *Waiting for God*, p. 200: "Preference for some human being is necessarily a different thing from charity. Charity does not discriminate." Compare with Alain, *Quatre-vingt-un chapitres sur l'esprit et les passions*, IV, 8, in *Les passions et la sagesse*, Bibliothèque de la Pléiade, p. 1187.

187. *Dictionnaire de la spiritualité*, s.v. "Charité," p. 509, quoting the famous Gospel statement that translates into English as "Love your enemies" (Matthew 5:44 and Luke 6:27).

188. As Jean Prat notes in the same entry, p. 510.

189. Aristotle, *Nicomachean Ethics*, IX, 10, 1171a15–20.

190. Jankélévitch, *Traité des vertus*, vol. 2, p. 171.

191. Ibid.

192. Blaise Pascal, *Pensées*, trans. W. F. Trotter, Modern Library, Random House, 1941, no. 468, p. 154.

193. Weil, *Gravity and Grace*, p. 55. See also Alain Vinson, "L'ordre de la charité chez Pascal, chez Péguy et chez Simone Weil," *Cahiers Simone Weil*, vol. 14, no. 3 (Sept. 1991), pp. 234–54.

194. Pascal, *Pensées*, no. 455, p. 151.

195. To use, in another context, Jean-Louis Chrétien's elegant formulation in *La voix nue*, p. 329.

196. Galatians 5:14: "For the whole law is fulfilled in one word, 'You shall love your neighbor as yourself.'" The same idea is found in Romans 13:8–10: "Owe no one anything, except to love one another; for he who loves his neighbor has fulfilled the law.... Love does not wrong to a neighbor; therefore love is fulfilling of the law." For a study of Paul, see Stanislas Breton, *Saint Paul*, PUF, 1988. On Pauline *agapē*, see Nygren, *Agape and Eros*, part 1, pp. 76–108. Finally, let us recall in passing that Spinoza, who was faithful to the spirit of Christ, felt an affinity for Paul's message (which he interprets in his own way, as immanence and the road to it); see Sylvain Zac's *Spinoza et l'interprétation de l'Ecriture*, pp. 170–71.

197. 1 Corinthians 13, called the "hymn to charity." The Greek word *agapē* is translated as *love* in some translations and *charity* in others. We are tempted to use the word *love* in order to avoid the somewhat negative implications of almsgiving or condescension associated with charity in the modern sense. But the word *love* gives rise to other wrong meanings that are less obvious and hence more dangerous. Stanislas

Breton, a Catholic priest, points out that this hymn is often used at weddings (Breton, *Saint Paul*, p. 115), where I imagine *agapē* is translated as love, suggesting (in the matrimonial context!) that being in love suffices in order to live in harmony with the highest ethics, which, to say the least, experience hardly confirms; being in love does not suffice in order to live as a Christian, any more than being a Christian suffices to stay in love. To use the word *charity* is also misleading, as I have just pointed out, but more obviously and therefore less dangerously misleading. No one will confuse such selfless love with what Paul turns into a mockery (as Stanislas Breton observes) or at least sees as futile, namely "the gesture of merciful almsgiving which hands out to those who have nothing crumbs from the table of the powerful" (Breton, *Saint Paul*, p. 115). This is what is called "charitable giving." But in my youth it was said that "charitable giving is to charity what lovemaking is to love"—occasionally an expression thereof, occasionally a caricature.

198. See n. 196, above.

199. Augustine, *Soliloquies*, I, 7, and *Sermons*, 158, 9; Aquinas, *Summa Theologica*, IIa–IIae, quest. 18, art. 2.

200. *Summa Theologica*, Ia–IIae, quest. 65, art. 5, p. 184. Conversely, Francis of Sales notes that all love connected with hope is always imperfect (Francis of Sales, *Traité de l'amour de Dieu*, II, 17, pp. 459–62).

201. See, for example, the beginning of the second section of Immanuel Kant, *Groundwork for a Metaphysics of Mores*, and Immanuel Kant, *Religion within the Limits of Simple Reason*, I, 3 (where Kant cites Saint Paul). On love as an ideal, see also "Of the Motives of Pure Practical Reason," in *The Critique of Practical Reason*.

202. Christian Bobin, *La part manquante*, Gallimard, 1989, p. 24.

203. Alain, *Quatre-vingt-un chapitres*, V, 4, p. 1199.

204. On the two kinds of laughter, see pp. 213–14, and n. 7 on p. 324.

205. See the end of ch. 8.

206. Jankélévitch, *Traité des vertus*, II, 2, p. 168.

207. As opposed to Epicurean friendship; *Sentences Vaticanes* 23 and 39; see also Diogenes Laertius, X, 120.

208. To paraphrase Spinoza from another point of view, inspired by Romans 3:28 and 7:6 (Spinoza, *A Theologico-Political Treatise*, ch. 4, pp. 65 and 67).

209. Augustine, *City of God against the Pagans*, vol. 4, trans. Philip Levine, Loeb Classical Library, Harvard University Press, XV, xxii, p. 345.

Acknowledgments

I wish to thank the editors of the journal *Autrement*, in which chapters 1, 2, 11, and 14 of this book first appeared in a somewhat different form. In particular, my thanks to Nicole Czechowski for allowing me to use these essays here. I would also like to thank my colleagues and friends Laurent Bove, Monique Canto-Sperber, and Marcel Conche, who were kind enough to read the manuscript and share their critical remarks with me. Needless to say, they are not responsible for any of the opinions expressed here or for any of the book's flaws, for which I alone am responsible.

Index

beauty, 44, 57; love of, 236–37
Bedos, Guy, 213–14
Beethoven, Ludwig van, 136
benevolence, 102, 112, 116
benevolent love, 262, 280
bénignité, 188
Bentham, Jeremy, 62
Bergson, Henri-Louis, 16; on justice, 62; love and, 225; on morality, 25
Bernard de Clairvaux, Saint, 179, 264, 279
Bible, belief in, 159
Bobin, Christian: on humor vs. irony, 217–18; on love, 183, 288; on simplicity, 151, 156
body: desire for, 180–81, 182; oneness of love and, 231–32
Bon usage, le (Grevisse), 13
Brahms, Johannes, 136
Brassens, George, 255
Breton, 240
Bruaire, Claude, 136
Bruno, Giordano, 169
Buddha, 206; compassion and, 22, 106, 111, 116, 117, 289; gentleness and, 186; humility and, 144

Calas, Jean, 169
Camus, Albert, 62
capacity, 242–43, 248–49
capital punishment, 66, 192–93
caritas, 270
casuistry, 65, 198–99
Catholic Church, 168–69. *See also* Christianity
Cavaillès, Jean, 25, 52, 54, 145
Chamfort, Sebastien, 86, 138–39
Char, René, 257
charity, 74, 99; *agape* as, 269–70, 276, 281, 284–90; compassion and, 110, 116–17; as "good works," 115; gentleness vs., 189; gratitude and, 139; humility and, 147; nonviolence and, 191; path to, 279–80; wisdom vs. pity and, 108
child(ren): abuse of, 125; exchange of goods and, 68; forgiving parents, 121; generosity and, 92–93, 96, 98; justice and, 62–63, 81, 83; love for, 121, 178,

180, 182, 236, 246–47, 261–63, 265–66; murderers of, 192; politeness and, 9, 11–15; prudence and, 35, 36–37; simplicity and, 155
Christ, 206; abolishes law by fulfilling, 225; compassion and, 106, 114, 117; forgiveness and, 123, 130; gentleness and, 186, 190; love and, 267, 269; virtue and, 100
Christianity: charity and, 22; God's love and, 278; forgiveness and, 118, 128; generosity and, 93; humility and, 144, 148; tolerance and, 168–69, 170
Cicero: on courage, 50; on generosity, 93; on pity, 107; on prudence, 34
Claudel, Paul, 170
clemency, 112, 119
Clouds, The (Aristophanes), 215
commiseratio, 107–8, 109
compassion, 102, 103–17; absolute morality and, 31; charity and, 115–17, 289; gentleness and, 186, 187; humility and, 147; justice and, 81, 83; mercy vs., 119–20, 121, 122; truthfulness and, 205, 206–7
conatus (effort of living), 54, 100, 274; love as opposite of, 281–82
concentration camps: justice and, 78–79; memory and, 22; mercy and, 128; tolerance and, 159
Conche, Marcel, 23, 193
concupiscent love, 238, 262–63
Condorcet, Marquis de, 170–71
Constant, Benjamin, 203
contempt, 101; humility vs., 146; irony and, 218; pity and, 114–15; tolerance and, 170–71
Corneille, Pierre, 93
"correct principle of living," 101
couple (lovers); *agape* and, 275–76; *eros* and, 237–39; *eros, philia,* and *agape* and, 279; *eros* and *philia* combined in, 245–46, 250–51, 254–56, 263–64; falling out of love, 256–57; fidelity and, 27–29; generosity and, 96; humanity found in, 187; *philia* and, 257–61. *See also* marriage
courage, 5, 44–59, 102, 136; despair and, 56–57, 142–43; fear and, 101; fidelity

André Comte-Sponville is one of the most important of the new wave of young French philosophers. He teaches at the Sorbonne and is the author of five highly acclaimed scholarly books of classical philosophy as well as the hugely popular *A Small Treatise on the Great Virtues*, which is being translated into nineteen languages. Comte-Sponville lives in Paris.